DICTIONARY *OF* CHEMISTRY

DICTIONARY *OF* CHEMISTRY

Edited by:

Dr. N. Pardeep Sharma

GYAN PUBLISHING HOUSE

NEW DELHI-110002

DICTIONARY OF CHEMISTRY
(*Chemistry*)

ISBN: 81-212-0579-4

Published in India in 1998 by
Gyan Publishing House
5, Ansari Road, Darya Ganj
New Delhi-110 002

Laser Typesetting at A.S. Printers, Delhi.

Printed at Mehra Offset Press, New Delhi.

PREFACE

With the adoption of the National Policy on Education in 1986 emphasising on science at all stages of education, there has been considerable change in curriculum of chemistry at all levels. This transition coupled with the sincere and consistent efforts on the part of teachers and planners of chemical education at worldwide level to improve the standards of chemistry has led to a more scientific approach towards the curriculum.

The editor of this dictionary who has himself been associated with the reforms in chemistry has consistently tried to improve the quality of this work in all possible ways. The present form is totally recast and minutely checked.

It is editor's firm conviction that for a clear understanding of the fundamental points, the treatment must be lucid and well explained and that all attempts at brevity will be at the cost of exactness and clarity. An attempt has been made to avoid over simplification which often leads to misunderstanding about various terms of chemistry.

The editor sincerely hopes that the methods of presentation of this dictionary will enable the reader to read the subject with pleasure and thorough understanding, if it does that the editor will feel amply rewarded for the pains taken.

The editor is grateful to all the authors and publishers whose works have directly or indirectly captured his attention.

Comments, criticism and suggestions would be gratefully accepted by the editor because no man is complete in this world.

Dr. N. Pardeep Sharma

A

A_r The symbol for *relative atomic mass.* The relative atomic mass value for an *element* is a measure of the *mass* of an average atom of the element compared to the mass of an atom of the *isotope* carbon-12.

abrasive A hard material used to wear away or break up softer materials. Examples are *diamond,* silicon carbide (SiC), boron nitride (BN), and aluminium oxide (Al_2O_3).

absolute configuration A way of denoting the absolute structure of an optical isomer. Two conventions are in use: The D-L convention relates the structure of the molecule to some reference molecule. In the case of sugars and similar com-pounds, the dextrorotatory form of glyceraldehyde ($HOCH_2CH(OH)CHO$), 2, 3-dihydroxypropanal) was used. The rule is as follows: Writing the structure of this molecule down with the asymmetric carbon in the centre, the –CHO group at the top, the –OH on the right, the $-CH_2OH$ at the bottom, and the –H on the left. Now imagine that the central carbon atom is at the centre of a tetrahedron with the four groups at the corners and that the –H and –OH come out of the paper and the –CHO and $-CH_2OH$ groups go into the paper. The resulting three dimensional structure was taken to be that of *d*-glyceraldehyde and called D-glyceraldehyde. Any compound that contains an asymmetric carbon atom having this configuration belongs to the D-series. One having the opposite configuration belongs to the L-series. It is important to note that the prefixes D- and L- do not stand for dextrorotatory and laevorotatory (i.e. they are not the same as *d*- and *l*-). In fact the arbitrary configuration assigned to D-glyceraldehyde is now known to be the correct one for the dextrorotatory form, although this was not known at the time. However, all D-compounds are not dextrorotatory. For instance, the acid obtained by oxidizing the –CHO group of glyceraldehyde is glyceric acid (1,2-dihydroxypropanoic acid). By convention, this belongs to the D-series, but it is in fact laevorotatory; i.e. its name can be written as D-glyceric acid or *l*-glyceric acid. To avoid confusion it is better to use + (for dextrorotatory) and - (for laevorotatory), as in D-(+)-glyceraldehyde and D(-) glyceric acid.

absolute temperature A temperature on the 'absolute'or Kelvin scale usually denoted by T; the Zero of this scale is the temperature at which a perfect gas would occupy zero volume if it could be cooled indefinitely without liquefaction or solidification. The absolute zero (0K) is –273.16°C, and one degree absolute is equivalent to one degree Centigrade.

T(K) = temperature (°C) + 273.16.

absorption It is a uniform process which take up of a gas by a solid or liquid, or the take up of a liquid by a solid. Absorption differs from adsorption in that the absorbed substance permeates the bulk of the absorbing substance. Alternatively, the conversion of the energy of electromagnetic radiation, sound, streams of particles, etc., into other forms of energy on passing through a medium. A beam of light, for instance, passing through a medium, may lose intensity because of two effects: scattering of light out of the beam, and absorption of photons by atoms or molecules in the medium. When a photon is absorbed, there is a transition to an excited state.

absorption indicator A type of indicator used in reactions that involve precipitation. The yellow dye fluorescein is a common example, used for the reaction

$$NaCl(aq) + AgNO_3(aq) \rightarrow AgCl(s) + NaNO_3(aq)$$

acid 1. A type of compound that contains hydrogen and dissociates in water to produce positive hydrogen ions. The reaction, for an acid HX, is commonly written :

$$HX \rightleftharpoons H^+ + X^-$$

In fact, the hydrogen ion (the proton) is solvated, and the complete reaction is :

$$HX + H_2O \rightleftharpoons H_3O^+ + X^-$$

The ion H_3O^+ is the *oxonium ion* (or *hydroxonium ion* or *hydronium ion*). This definition of acids comes from the *Arrhenius theory*. Such acids tend to be corrosive substances with a sharp taste, which turn litmus red and give colour changes with other indicators. They are referred to as *protonic acids* and are classified into *strong acids*, which are almost completely dissociated in water (e.g. sulphuric acid and hydrochloric acid), and *weak acids*, which are only partially dissociated (e.g. ethanoic acid and hydrogen sulphide). The strength of an acid depends on the extent to which it dissociates, and is measured by its dissociation constant. *See also* base.

2. In the *Lowry—Bronsted theory* of acids and bases (1923), the definition was extended to one in which an acid is a proton donor, and a base is a proton acceptor. For example, in

$$HCN + H_2O \rightleftharpoons H_3O^+ + CN^-$$

the HCN is an acid, in that it donates a proton to H_2O. The H_2O is acting as a base in accepting a proton. Similarly, in the reverse reaction H_3O^+ is an acid and CN^- a base. In such reaction, two species related by loss or gain of a proton are said to be *conjugate.* Thus, in the reaction above HCN is the *conjugate acid* of the base CN^- and CN^- is the *conjugate base* of the acid HCN. Similarly, H_3O^+ is the conjugate acid of the base H_2O. An equilibrium, such as that above, is a competition for protons between an acid and its conjugate base. A strong acid has a weak conjugate base, and vice versa. Under this definition water can act as both acid and base. Thus in

$$NH_3 + H_2O \rightleftharpoons NH_4^+ + OH^-$$

the H_2O is the conjugate acid of OH^-. The definition also extends the idea of acid-base reaction to solvents other than water. For instance, liquid ammonia, like water, has a high dielectric constant and is a good ionizing solvent. Equilibria of the type

$$NH_3 + Na^+Cl^- \rightleftharpoons Na^+ NH_2^- + HCl$$

can be studied, in which NH_3 and HCl are acids and NH_2^- and Cl^- are their conjugate bases.

3. A further extension of the idea of acids and bases was made in the *Lewis theory* (G.N. Lewis, 1923). In this, a *Lewis acid* is a compound or atom that can accept a pair of electrons and a *Lewis base* is one that can donate an electron pair. This definition encompasses 'traditional' acid-base reactions. In

$$HCl + NaOH \rightarrow NaCl + H_2O$$

the reaction is essentially

$$H^+ + :OH^- \rightarrow H:OH$$

i.e. donation of an electron pair by OH^-. But it also includes reactions that do not involve ions, e.g.

$$H_3N: + BCl_3 \rightarrow H_3NBCl_3$$

in which NH_3 is the base (donor) and BCl_3 the acid (acceptor). The Lewis theory establishes a relationship between acid—base reactions and oxidation-reduction reactions.

$$HX \rightleftharpoons H^+ + X^-$$

acidic **1.** Describing a compound that is an acid. **2.** Describing a solution that has an excess of hydrogen ions. **3.** Describing a compound that forms an acid when dissolved in water. Carbon dioxide, for example, is an acidic oxide. pH of these solution is less than 7.

acidic hydrogen (acid hydrogen) A hydrogen atom in an acid that forms a positive ion when the acid dissociates. For instance, in methanoic acid

$$HCOOH \rightleftharpoons H^+ + HCOO^-$$

the hydrogen atom on the carboxylate ion group is the acidic hydrogen (the one bond directly to the carbon atom does not dissociate).

acidimetry Volumetric analysis using standard solutions of acids to determine the amount of base present.

acid salt A salt of a polybasic acid (i.e. an acid having two or more acidic hydrogens) in which not all the hydrogen atoms have been replaced by positive ions. For example, the dibasic acid carbonic acid (H_2CO_3) forms acid salts (hydrogencarbonates) containing the bicarbonate ion HCO_3^-. Some salts of monobasic acids are also known as acid salts. For instance, the compound potassium hydrogendifluoride, KHF_2, contains the ion $[F...H–F]^-$, in which there is hydrogen bonding between the fluoride ion F^- and a hydrogen fluoride molecule.

acid value A measure of the amount of free acid present in a fat, equal to the number of milligrams of potassium hydroxide needed to neutralize this acid. Fresh fats contain glycerides of fatty acids and very little free acid, but the glycerides decompose slowly with time and the acid value increases.

actinides The 14 elements (from atomic number 90 to 103 in the periodic table) following actinium in the modern periodic table are known as actinides. Their properties are quite similar and they are placed in one box only. They are placed in *f*-block of the periodic table.

actinium

see radioactive series

active site 1. A site on the surface of a catalyst at which activity occurs. **2.** The site on the surface of an enzyme molecule that binds the substrate molecule. The properties of an active site are determined by the three-dimensional arrangement of the polypeptide chains of the enzyme and their constituent amino acids. These govern the nature of the interaction that takes place and hence the degree of substrate specificity and susceptibility to inhibition.

activation energy The minimum amount of energy required for a chemical reaction to take place. In a reaction, the reactant molecules come together and chemical bonds are stretched, broken, and formed in producing the products. During this process the energy of the system increases to a maximum, then decreases to the energy of the products. The activation energy is the difference between the maximum energy and the energy of the reactants; i.e. it is the energy barrier that has to be overcome for the reaction to proceed. The activation energy determines the way in which the rate of the reaction varies with temperature. It is usual to express activation energies in joules per mole of reactants.

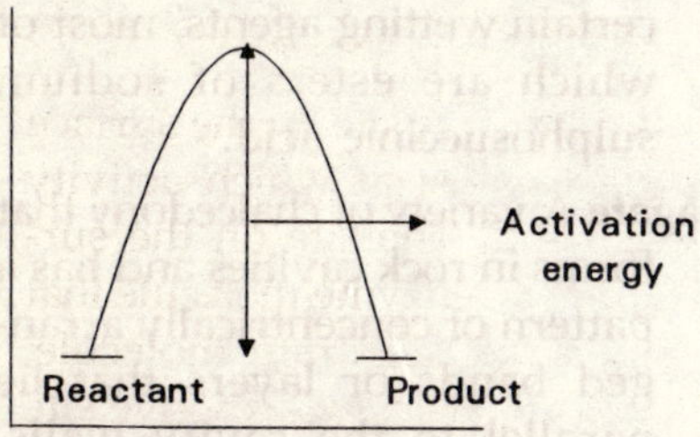

acylation The process of introducing an acyl group (RCO–) into a compound. The most common method is to react an alcohol with an acyl halide or a carboxylic acid anhydride; e.g.

$RCOCl + R'OH \rightarrow RCOOR' + HCl$

The introduction of an acetyl group (CH_3CO—) is *acetylation*, a process used for protecting –OH group in organic synthesis.

additive A small amount of substance added to a material to give it particular properties. They are widely used today. Examples are:

(a) Anti-foaming agents in washing powders.

(b) Colouring materials in food and soft drinks.

(c) *Emulsifiers* in margarines.

adduct A compound formed by an addition reaction. The term is used specifically for compounds formed by coordination between a Lewis acid (acceptor) and a Lewis base (donar).

adhesive A substance used to stick one material to another. Examples are glues, plant resins and *epoxy resins.* Adhesives are *polymers* (repeated units). Some are dissolved in a solvent which, when used, evaporates and leaves the adhesive behind to hold materials together. Others come as two components, the *monomer* and an *initiator,* which have to be mixed when needed. Mixing produces the polymer which forms a strong *bond.*

adiabatic system is one in which the reaction is carried out at constant enthalpy or heat. i.e. DH = 0, temperature may increase or decrease.

adrenaline A hormone, produced by the medulla of the adrenal glands, that increases heart activity, improves the power and prolongs the action of muscles, and increases the rate and depth of breathing to prepare the body for 'fright, flight, or fight'. At the same time it inhibits digestion and excretion. Also known as epinephrine.

Adsorption The formation of a layer of gas on the surface of a solid or liquid, depending upon the nature of forces of attraction involved. They are categorised as *chemisorption* where the attachment to surface is by chemical bonds, and *Physisorption* (Physical adsorption) where the attachment to surface is by weak Vander Waals forces *also see application of adsorption.*

adsorption Isobar It is a graph between the amount of substance adsorbed per gram

and temperature 't' at constant pressure.

The adsorption isobars for physical and chemical adsorption are shown in figure. $\left(\frac{x}{m}\right)$

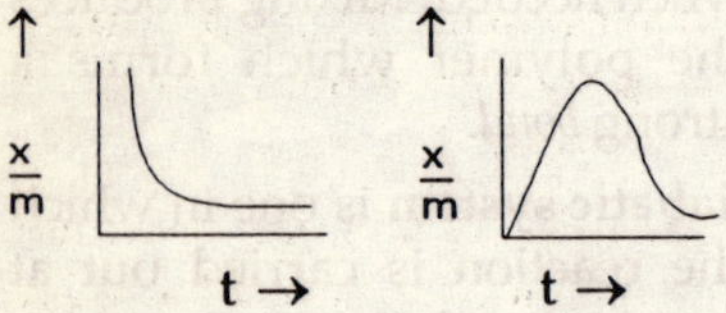

(a) Physical adsorption (b) Chemisorption

aerosol, aerogel A dispersion in which a finely divided solid is suspended in air and the particles are of colloidal dimensions, e.g. smoke. Aerosols can often be formed by the rapid condensation of a vapour such as that of a metal oxide.

Aerosol sprays consist of a material dissolved or suspended in a liquid which when pressure is released volatilizes to produce a fine spray. The spray carries the active material. Used in hair lacquers, paints, etc.; the propellant should be inert and non-inflammable. Chlorofluirocarbons have been used extensively but are now being replaced.

Aerosol is also a trade name for certain wetting agents, most of which are esters of sodium sulphosuccinic acid.

agate A variety of chalcedony that forms in rock cavities and has a pattern of concentrically arranged bands or layers that lie parallel to the cavity walls. There is a perfect lattice in it. These layers are frequently alternating tones of brownish-red. *Moss agate* does not show the same banding and is a milky chalcedony containing moss-like or dendritic patterns formed by inclusions of manganese and iron oxides. Agates are used in jewellery and for ornamental purposes.

albumin (albumen) One of a group of globular proteins that are soluble in water but form insoluble coagulates when heated. Albumins occur in egg white, blood, milk, and plants. Serum albumins, which constitute about 55% of blood plasma protein. It helps in regulating the osmotic pressure and hence plasma volume. They also bind and transport fatty acids. a-lactalbumin is one of the proteins in milk.

alcohols Alcohols are important organic compounds. They possess the arrangement of atoms:

$$-\overset{|}{\underset{|}{C}}-OH$$

The —OH group is the functional group of the alcohols and is attached to the aliphatic system. In IUPAC nomenclature the alcohol names end in the suffix —ol. Ethanol is the most important alcohol but see also methanol, glycol (Dihydric alcohol) and glycerol (Trihydric alcohol).

Alcohols with low molecular-mass are flammable liquids which dissolve in water. Some of the important properties of alcohols are that they can be oxidized easily, they form *esters* and react with *sodium* to produce *hydrogen.*

aldol condensation Two molecules of aldehydes or ketones having at least one a-hydrogen atom condense to yield Aldol in presence of a dilute base. The product on treatment with dilute acid loses water molecule to produce a, b-unsaturated carbonyl compounds.

aliphatic compounds Organic compounds that are alkanes, alkenes, or alkynes (having single, double and triple bond respectively) or their derivatives. The term is used to denote compounds that do not have the special stability of aromatic compounds. All noncyclic organic compounds are aliphatic. Cyclic aliphatic compounds are said to be *alicyclic, e.g., cyclohexane.*

alkane (paraffin)

Saturated hydrocarbons with general formula CnH_{2n+2}. These hydrocarbons contain single bonds. Lower members are gases and higher members are waxy solids. e.g. CH_4 methane, C_2H_6 ethane etc.

alkenes (olefines; olefins) Unsaturated hydrocarbons that contain one or more double carbon—carbon bonds in their molecules (C = C). In systematic chemical nomenclature alkene names end in the suffix *-ene.* Alkenes that have only one double bond form a homologous series (the *alkene series*) starting ethene (ethylene). CH_2=CH_2 propene, CH_3CH:CH_2, etc. The general formula is C_nH_{2n}. Higher members of the series show isomerism depending on position of the double bond; for example, butene (C_4H_8) has two isomers, which are (1) but- 1-ene (C_2H_5CH:CH_2) and (2) but-2-ene.

(CH_3CH:$CHCH_3$)

Alkenes can be made by dehydration of alcohols (passing the vapour over hot pumice):

$RCH_2CH_2OH \rightarrow RCH = CH_2 + H_2O$

An alternative method is the removal of a hydrogen atom and halogen atom from a haloalkane by potassium hydroxide in hot alcoholic solution:

$RCH_2CH_2Cl + KOH_{(alc)} \rightarrow KCl + H_2O + RCH = CH_2$

Alkenes typically undergo addition reactions to the double bond. (hydrogenation; oxo reaction; ozonolysis; Ziegler process.)

alkali metals The elements of group 1 (i.e. Na, K, Rb, Cs and Fr) are known as alkali metals. Their general electronic configuration is ns^1, i.e., they have one electron in their outer most 's' orbit.

Reactions

$2 M + 2H_2O \rightarrow 2 MOH + H_2$

$2 M+2HC \equiv CH \rightarrow 2 M–C \equiv CH+H_2$

$2 M + X_2 \rightarrow 2 M X$ (X = H, Cl)

$2 M + O_2 \rightarrow M_2O_2$ (M = Na)

$4 M + O_2 \rightarrow 2M_2O$ (M = Na, K, Rb)

Alkynes Unsaturated hydrocarbons containing triple carbon-carbon bond (s) with general formula C_nH_{2n-2} e.g. HC≡CH (acetylene or ethyne).

$H_3C–C \equiv C–CH_3$ But 2-yne

alloy A material consisting of two or more metals (e.g. brass is an alloy of copper and zinc) or a metal and a non-metal (e.g. steel) is an alloy of iron and carbon, sometimes with other metals included). Alloys may be compounds, solid solutions, or mixtures of the components.

allyl group Previously it was known as the organic group $CH_2 = CHCH_2–$. It was used in names such as *allyl alcohol* ($CH_2 = CHCH_2 OH$, prop-2-en-1-ol).

alnico A trade name for a series of alloys (mixture of two or more metals) containing iron, aluminium, nickel, cobalt, and copper, used to make permanent magnets.

alpha particle (a-particle) A helium nucleus emitted by a larger nucleus during the course of the type of radioactive decay known as *alpha decay.* As a helium nucleus consists of two protons and two neutrons bound together as a stable entity the loss of an alpha particle involves a decrease in nucleon number of 4 and decrease of 2 in the atomic number, e.g. the decay of a uranium-238 nucleus into a thorium-234 nucleus. A stream of alpha particles is known as an *alpha-ray or alpha-radiation.*

aluminate A salt formed when aluminium hydroxide [Al $(OH)_3$] or g-alumina is dissolved in solutions of strong bases, such as sodium hydroxide. Aluminates exist in solutions containing the aluminate ion, commonly written as $[Al(OH)_4]^-$. In fact the ion probably is a complex hydrated ion and can be regarded as formed from a hydrated Al^{3+} ion by removal of four hydrogen ions:

$$[Al(H_2O)_6]^{3+} + 4OH^- \rightarrow 4H_2O + [Al(OH)_4(H_2O)_2]^-$$

Other aluminates and polyaluminates, such as $[Al(OH)_6]^{3-}$ and $[(HO)_3AlOAl(OH)_3]^{2-}$, are also present, e.g. aluminium hydroxide.

aluminium Symbol Al. A silvery-white lustrous metallic element belonging to group III of the periodic table; a.n. 13; r.a.m. 26.98; r.d. 2.7; m.p. 660°C; b.p. 2467°C. The metal itself is highly reactive but is protected by a thin transparent layer of the oxide, which forms quickly in air. Aluminium and its oxide are amphoteric. The metal is extracted from purified bauxite (Al_2O_3) by electrolysis; the main process uses a Hall-Heroult cell but other electrolytic methods are under development, including conversion of bauxite with chlorine and electrolysis of the molten chloride. Pure aluminium is soft and ductile but its strength can be increased by work-hardening. A large number of alloys are manufactured; alloying elements include copper, manganese, silicon, zinc, and magnesium. Its lightness, strength (when alloyed), corrosion resistance, and electrical conductivity (62% of that of copper) make it suitable for a variety of uses, including vehicle and aircraft construction, building (window and door frames), and overhead power cables. Although it is the third most abundant element in the earth's crust (8.1% by weight) it was not isolated until 1825 by H.C. Oersted (1777-1851).

americium Symbol Am. A radioactive metallic transuranic element belonging to the actinoids; a.n. 95: mass number of most stable isotope 243 (half-life 7.95 ´10^3 years); r.d. 13.67 (20°C); m.p. 994 ± 4°C; b.p. 2607°. Ten isotopes are known. The element was discovered by G.T. Seaborg and associates in 1945, who obtained it by bombarding uranium–238 with alpha particles.

amides General formula

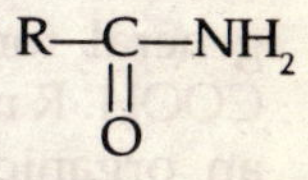

Amides are formed when a molecule of carboxylic acid (or its derivatives like acid chlorides, anhydrides or esters) condense with ammonia (or its derivatives like amines). In IUPAC their systematic name is given by replacing "oic acid" by the suffix—"amide". e.g.

CH_3CONH_2 (ethanamide); $CH_3CONHCH_3$ (N-methylethanamide).

amines These are the organic compounds derived by replacing one or more of the hydrogen atoms in ammonia by organic groups. *Primary amines* have one hydrogen replaced, e.g. methylamine, CH_3NH_2. They contain the functional group $-NH_2$ (the *amino group*). *Secondary amines* have two hydrogens replaced, e.g. methylethylamine, $CH_3(C_2H_5)NH$. The group $>C=NH$ is the *imino group*. *Tertiary amines* have all three hydrogens replaced, e.g. trimethylamine $(CH_3)_3N$. Amines are produced by the decomposition of organic matter. They can be synthesized by reducing nitro compounds or amides.

amino acid Any of a group of water-soluble organic compounds that possess both a carboxyl (–COOH) and an amino ($-NH_2$) group attached to the a-carbon atom. Amino acid can be represented by the general formula R—$CH(NH_2)$COOH. R may be hydrogen or an organic group and determines the properties of any particular amino acid. Through the formation of peptide bonds, amino acids join together to form short chains (peptides) or much longer chains (polypeptides). Proteins are composed of various proportions of about 20 commonly occurring amino acids (see table). The sequence of these amino acids in the protein polypeptides determines the shape, properties, and hence biological role of the protein. Some amino acids that never occur in proteins are nevertheless important, e.g. ornithine and citrulline, which are intermediates in the urea cycle.

Plants and many microorganisms can synthesize amino acids from simple inorganic compounds, but animals rely on adequate supplies in their diet. The essential amino acids must be present in the diet whereas others can be manufactured from them.

amphiprotic The ability of a substance to react with itself to produce both a conjugate acid and base. Water is amphiprotic, producing H_3O^+ and OH^-.

amphoteric A compound that can act as both an acid and a base (in the traditional sense of the term). For instance, aluminium hydroxide is amphoteric as a base Al $(OH)_3$ it reacts with acids to form aluminium salts; as an acid H_3AlO_3 it reacts with alkalis to gave aluminates. H_2O can also behave as an acid or a base. Oxides of metals are typically basic and oxides of nonmetals tend to be acidic. The existence of amphoteric oxides is sometimes regarded as evidence that an element is a metalloid.

TABLE

amino acid	*abbreviation*	*formula*
alanine	ala	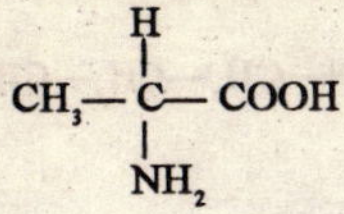
arginine	arg	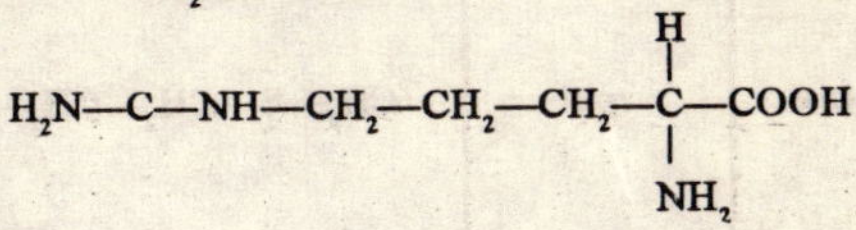
asparagine	asn	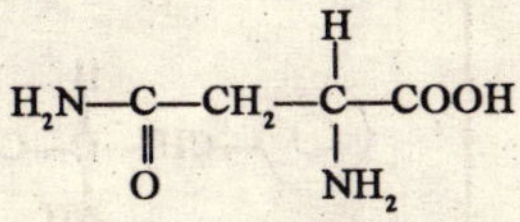
aspartic acid	asp	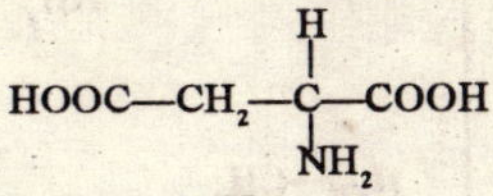
cysteine	cys	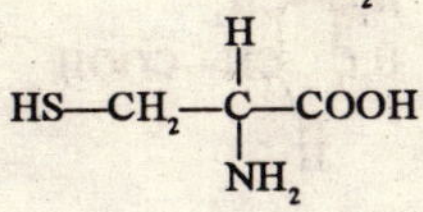
glutamic acid	glu	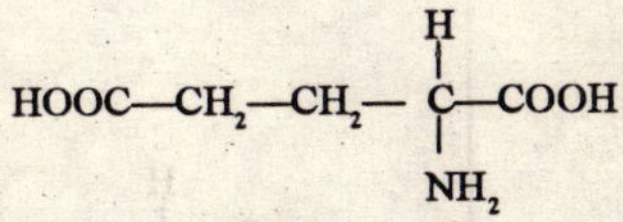
glutamine	gln	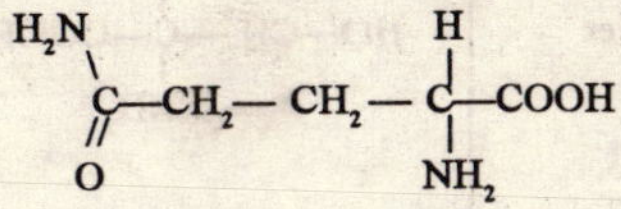
glycine	gly	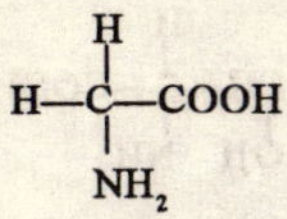
*histidine	his	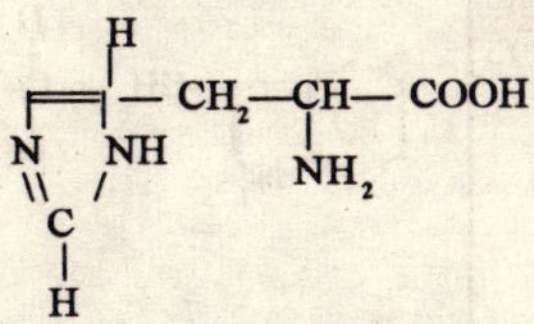
*isoleucine	ile	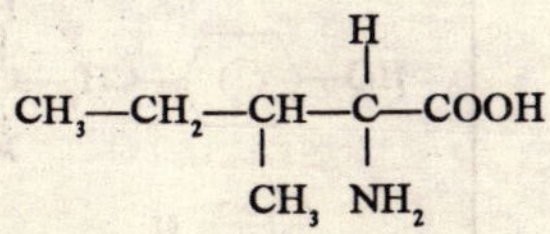
*isoleucine	ile	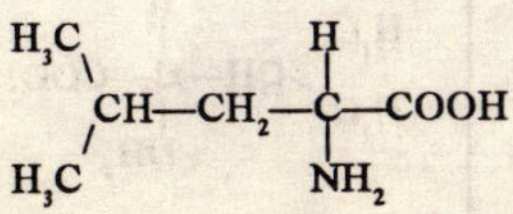

Contd.

TABLE

amino acid	*abbreviation*	*formula*
*lysine	lys	$H_3N{-}CH_2{-}CH_2{-}CH_2{-}CH_2{-}C(H)(NH_2){-}COOH$
*methionine	met	$CH_3{-}S{-}CH_2{-}CH_2{-}C(H)(NH_2){-}COOH$
*phenylalanine	phe	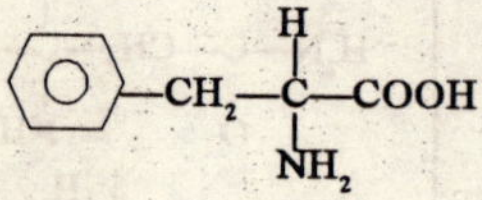
proline	pro	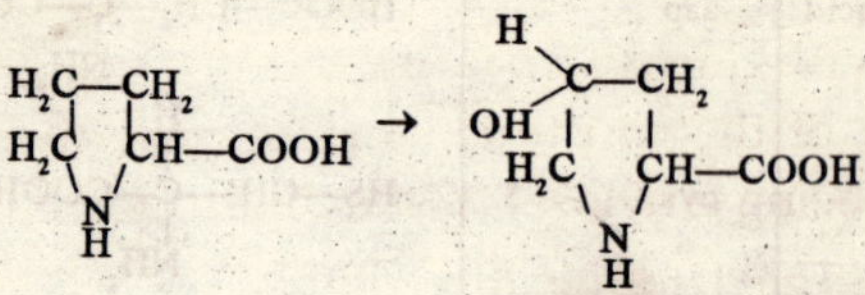 4-hydroxyproline
serine	ser	$HO{-}CH_2{-}C(H)(NH_2){-}COOH$
*threonine	thr	$CH_3{-}CH(OH){-}C(H)(NH_2){-}COOH$
*tryptophan	trp	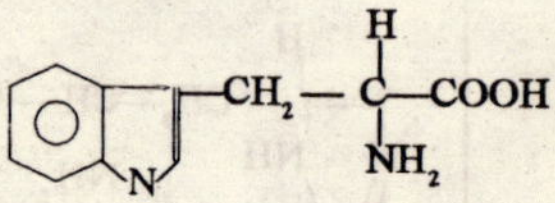
tyrosine	tyr	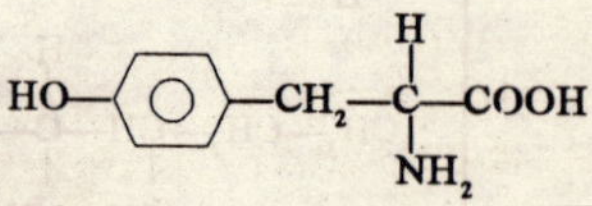
*valine	val	$(H_3C)_2CH{-}C(H)(NH_2){-}COOH$

amylose It is a polymer of polysaccharide consisting of linear chains of between 100 and 1000 linked glucose molecules. Amylose is a constituent of starch. In water, amylose reacts with iodine to give a characteristic blue colour.

amyl group Formerly, any of several isomeric groups with the formula C_5H_{11}—.

amylopectin A polysaccharide comprising highly branched chains of glucose molecules. It is one of the constituents (the other being amylose) of starch.

analysis The determination of the components in a chemical sample. Mainly they are two types, *Qualitative analysis* involves determining the nature of a pure unknown compound or the compounds present in a mixture. Various chemical tests exist for different elements or types of compound, and systematic analytical procedures can be used for mixtures. *Quantitative analysis* involves measuring the proportions of known components in a mixture. Chemical techniques for this fall into two main classes: volumetric analysis and gravimetric analysis. In addition, there are numerous physical methods of qualitative and quantitative analysis, including spectroscopic techniques, mass spectrometry, polarography, chromatography, activation analysis, etc.

anhydrides These are the substances which react with *water* to produce *acids.* All *acidic oxides* are anhydrides, but some will give rise to one acid only whilst others will produce two. For example:

(a) SO_3 gives rise to H_2SO_4.

(b) NO_2 gives rise to HNO_3 and HNO_2.

anhydrite It is an important rock-forming anhydrous mineral form of calcium sulphate, $CaSO_4$. It is chemically similar to gypsum but is harder and heavier and crystallizes in the rhombic form (gypsum is monoclinic). Under natural conditions anhydrite slowly hydrates to form gypsum. It occurs chiefly in white and greyish granular masses and is often found in the caprock of certain salt domes. It is used as a raw material in the chemical industry and in the manufacture of cement and fertilizers.

antimony Symbol Sb. An element belonging to group VA of the periodic table; a.n. 51; r.a.m. 121.75; r.d. 6.73; m.p. 630.5°C; b.p. 1380°C. Antimony has several allotropes. The stable form is a bluish white metal. Yellow antimony and black antimony are unstable monmetallic allotropes made at low temperatures. The main source is stibnite (Sb_2S_3), from which antimony is extracted by reduction with iron metal or by roasting (to give the oxide) followed by reduction with carbon and sodium carbonate. The main use of the metal is as an alloying agent in lead-accumulator plates, type metals, bearing alloys, solders, Britannia metal, and pewter. It is also an agent for producing pearlitic cast iron. Its compounds are used in flame-proofing, paints, ceramics, enamels, glass dyestuffs, and rubber technology. The element will burn in air but is unaffected by water or dilute acids. It is attacked by oxidizing acids and by halogens. It was first reported by Tholden in 1450.

applications of adsorption (A surface phenomenon)

(i) In gas masks to remove poisonous gases such as CO, CH_4 etc. (activated charcoal).

(ii) In decolourisation of sugar. (animal charcoal)

(iii) For removing moisture and controlling humidity. (silica)

(iv) In creating a high vacuum. (charcoal cooled in liquid air)

(v) In chromatographic purification of compounds. (silica gel)

(vi) In volumetric analysis as adsorption indicator. (fluorescein)

(vii) For removal of hardness of water, in ion-exchange resins.

aqua regia (HNO_3 and HCl in 1:3 ratio) A mixture of concentrated nitric acid and concentrated hydrochloric acid in the ratio 1:3 respectively. It is a very powerful oxidizing mixture and will dissolve all metals (except silver, which forms an insoluble chloride) including such noble metals as gold and platinum, hence its name 'royal water'. Nitrosyl chloride (NOCl) is believed to be one of the active constituents.

aquation It is the process that involves the replacement of some other ligand by water and then water behaves as a ligand.

aqueous Describing a solution in water, e.g. aqueous KCl means solution of KCl in water.

argentic compounds Compounds of silver in its higher (+2) oxidation state; e.g. argentic oxide is silver (II) oxide (AgO).

argon Symbol : Ar; a.n. 18; r.a.m. 39°95; m.p.—189.2°C; b.p. —185.7°C; d. 1.78 kgm^{-3} It is an inert colourless and odourless monatomic element of the rare-gas group having atomic number 18. It forms 0.93% by volume of air. Argon is used to provide an inert atmosphere in electric and fluorescent lights and in welding.

aromaticity The characteristic properties of compounds having a cyclic, planar structure, with (4n+2) number of delocalized p-electrons (Hückel's Rule, where 'n' is an integer having values 0, 1, 2, 3...). e.g. Benzene C_6H_6, (n=1 i.e. 6p electrons)

The aromatic compounds exhibit extra stability.

Arrhenius equation An equation of the form

$$k = A\exp(-E_A/RT)$$

where k is the rate constant of a given reaction and E_A the activation energy. A is a constant for a given reaction, called the *pre-exponential factor*. Often the equation is written in logarithmic form

$$\ln K = \ln A - E_A/RT$$

A group of ln$k$ against $1/T$ is a straight line with a gradient $-E_A/R$ and an intercept on the ln K axis of ln A.

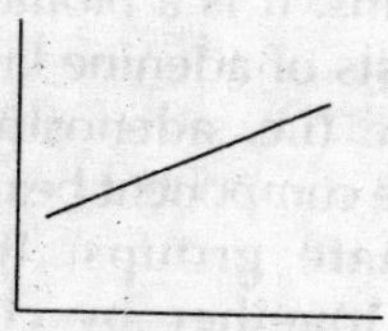

arsenic Symbol: As; m.p. 817°C (grey) at 3 MPa pressure; sublimes at 613°C (grey); r.d. 5.73 (grey); p.n. 33; r.a.m. 74.92.

It is a poisonous metalloid element existing in several allotropic forms; the most stable is a brittle grey metal. It belongs to group V of the periodic table. Arsenic is found native and in several ores including mispickel having formula (FeSAs), realgar (AsS), and orpiment (As_2S_3). It is used in semiconductor devices, alloys, and gun shot. Various compounds are used in medicines and agricultural insecticides and poisons.

arseneous sulphide, As_2S_3 It is used as a yellow pigment for oil paints.

asbestos Any one of a group of fibrous amphibole minerals [amosite, crocidolite (blue asbestos), tremolite, anthophyllite, and actinolite] or the fibrous serpentine mineral chrysotile. Asbestos has widespread commercial uses because of its resistance to heat, chemical inertness, and high electrical resistance. The fibres may be spun and woven into fire-proof cloth for use in protective clothing, curtains, brake linings, etc., or moulded into blocks. Exposure to large amounts of asbestos can cause the respiratory disease asbestosis. Canada and Russia are the largest producers of asbestos; others include South Africa, Zimbabwe, China and to some extent even India.

astatine Symbol At. A radioactive halogen element; having a.n. 85; r.a.m. 211; m.p. 302°C; b.p.

377°C. It occurs naturally by radioactive decay from uranium and thorium isotopes. Astatine forms at least 20 isotopes, the most stable astatine-210 has a half-life of 8.3 hours. It can also be produced by alpha bombardment of bismuth-200. Astatine is stated to be more metallic than iodine; at least 5 oxidation states are known in aqueous solutions. It will form interhalogen compounds, such as AtI and AtCl. The existence of At_2 has not yet been established. The element was synthesized by nuclear bombardment in 1940 by D.R. Corson, K.R. MacKenzie, and E. Segre at the University of California.

atmolysis Gases are diffused and then they are separated by using their different rates of diffusion.

atmosphere (atm.) A unit of pressure equal to 101325 pascals. This is equal to 760.0 mm of mercury. The actual atmospheric pressure fluctuates around this value. The unit is usually used for expressing pressures well in excess of standard atmospheric pressure, e.g. in high-pressure chemical processes.

atomic bomb It is a bomb based on the principle of nuclear fission. (Nucleus breaking)

atomicity It is the number of atoms in a given molecule. For example, oxygen (O_2) has an atomicity of 2, ozone (O_3) an atomicity of 3, benzene (C_6H_6) an atomicity of 12, hydrogen (H_2) an atomicity of 2 etc.

atomic mass unit (amu) Symbol μ. A unit of mass used for atoms and molecules, equal to 1/12 of the mass of an atom of carbon-12. It is equal to 1.660 33 × 10^{-27} kg.

atomic number (proton number) Symbol Z. The number of protons in the nucleus of an atom. The atomic number is equal to the number of electrons orbiting the nucleus in a neutral atom. Electronic configuration is based on it.

atomic volume The relative atomic mass of an element divided by its density (r).

ATP (adenosine triphosphate) A nucleotide that is of fundamental importance as a carrier of chemical energy in all living organisms. It is a biomolecule. It consists of adenine linked to D-ribose (i.e. adenosine); the D-ribose component bears three phosphate groups, linearly linked together by covalent bonds. These bonds can undergo hydrolysis to yield either a molecule of *ADP (adenosine diphosphate)* and inorganic phosphate or a molecule of *AMP (adenosine monophosphate)* and pyrophosphate. Both these reactions yield a large amount of energy (about 30.6 kJ mol^{-1}) that is used to bring about such biological processes as muscle contraction, the active transport of ions and molecules across cell membranes, and the synthesis of biomolecules. The reactions bringing about these processes often involve the enzyme-catalysed transfer of the phosphate group to intermediate substrates. Most ATP-mediated reactions require Mg^{2+} ions as co-factors.

ATP is regenerated by the rephosphorylation of AMP and ADP using the chemical energy obtained from the oxidation of food. This takes place during glycolysis and the Krebs cycle but, most significantly, is also a result of the reduction—oxidation (gain or loss of electron) reactions of the electron transport chain, which ultimately reduces molecular oxygen to water (oxidative phosphorylation).

atropine A very toxic crystalline alkaloid, $C_{17}H_{23}NO_3$; m.p. 114—16°C. It can be extracted from deadly nightshade and other solanaceous plants and is used in medicine to treat colic, to reduce secretions, and to dilate the pupil of the eye.

atto Symbol : a. A prefix denoting 10^{-18}. For example, 1 attometre (am) = 10^{-18} metre (m).

Aufbau principle (building up) A principle that gives the order in which orbitals are filled in successive elements in the periodic table. The order of filling is 1*s*, 2*s*, 2*p*, 3*s*, 3*p*, 4*s*, 3*d*, 4*p*, 5*s*, 4*d*, 5*p*, 6*s*, 4*f*, 5*d*, 6*p*, 7*s*, 5*f*, 6*d*. (lower to higher energy level)

Avogadro constant Symbol: N_A. The number of particles in one mole of a substance. Its value is 6.023 × 10^{23} mol^{-1}.

Avogadro's law Equal volumes of all gases under similar conditions of temperature and pressure contain equal number of molecules. The law, often called *Avogadro's hypothesis,* is true only for ideal gases. It was first proposed in 1811 by Count Amadeo Avogadro (1776-1856).

azeotropic distillation If two substances have similar boiling points or form an azeotrope, separation by fractional distillation is either very difficult or impossible. The method of azeotropic distillation consists of adding a third substance which forms azeotropic mixture with the other two; there azeotropes are then further treated to obtain pure compounds. Used in separating ethanol and water using benzene.

azeotropic mixtures Mixtures of liquids when distilled may reach a stage at which the composition of the liquid is the same as that of the vapour.

Many liquid mixtures exhibit a minimum boiling point (e.g. methanol and chloroform; *n*-propanol and water) whilst others show a maximum b.p. (e.g. hydrochloric acid and water) when vapour pressures are plotted as a function of change in composition (A+B) where a minimum is seen is shown in the figure. The upper curve represents the composition of the vapour phase whilst the lower that of the liquid. When the liquid of composition x boils at temperature *t* it is seen that the composition of the vapour (*v*) differs in that it is richer in constituent A than the liquid, and an increase in the b.p. would eventually give pure B.

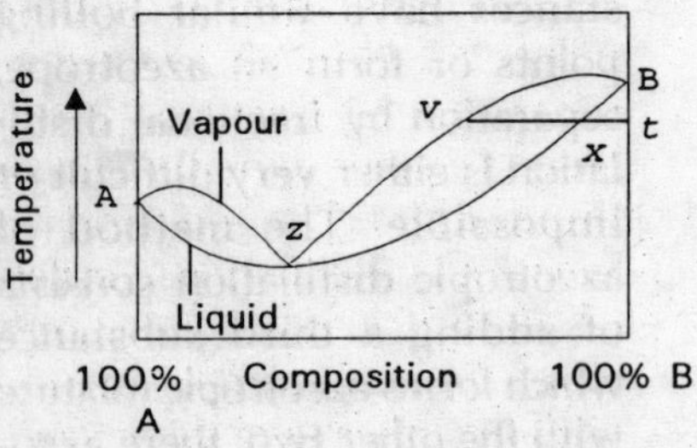

At z in the curve, however (the minimum of vapour pressure), the solution and vapour are in equilibrium and the liquid at this point will distil without any change in composition. The mixture at *z* is said to be azeotropic or a constant boiling mixture. The composition of the azeotropic mixture does vary with pressure.

azine An organic heterocyclic compound containing a six-membered ring formed from carbon and nitrogen atoms. Pyridine is an example containing one nitrogen atom (C_5H_5N). The structure of Pyridine is N

Diazines have two nitrogen atoms in the ring (e.g. $C_4H_4N_2$), and isomers exist depending on the relative positions of the nitrogen atoms. *Triazines* contain three nitrogen atoms.

azo compounds An organic compound containing the group –N = N– linking two other groups. They can be formed by reaction of a diazonium ion with a benzene ring.

azo dye A type of dye used in acid dyes for wool and cotton. The dyes are azo compounds; usually sodium salts of sulphonic acids.

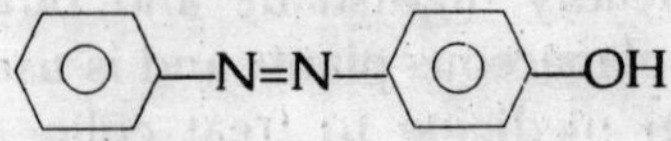

B

Babbit metal If any of a group of related alloys used for making bearings. They consist of tin containing antimony (about 10%) and copper (1-2%) and often lead. The original alloy was invented by the US inventor Isaac Babbit (1799-1862) in 1839.

Babo's law If a non-volatile solid is added to a liquid in which it is soluble, there occurs a lowering of vapour pressure of the solvent. The lowering of vapour pressure is proportional to the amount of substance dissolved and is one of the colligatine properties.

back donation A type of chemical bonding in which a ligand forms a sigma bond to an atom or ion by donating a pair of electrons, and the central atom donates electrons back by overlap of its *d*-orbitals with empty *p*- or *d*-orbitals on the ligand. Here a coordinate bond is formed.

back e.m.f. An electromotive force that opposes the main current flow in a circuit, e.g. in an electric cell, polarization causes a back e.m.f. to be set up by chemical means.

Bakelite It is a thermosetting plastic. It is a phenol formaldehyde resin, prepared by action of phenol and formaldehyde in the presence of some base. The reaction involves the formation of methylene bridges in ortho- and para-positions. *(See Diagram on Next Page)*

Soft bakelites are obtained with low degree of polymerisation while hard bakelites are obtained with high degree of polymerisation. Hard bakelites are used in manufacture of frame, bucket, toys, combs, fountain pen, etc. Soft bakelites are used as bonding glue for wooden planks. They are also used in the manufacture of varnishes and lacquers. Sulphonated bakelites are used as ion exchangers for softening of hard water.

baking powder It is a mixture of a *carbonate* (CO_3^-) and a weak *acid* which is used in cooking. When *water* is added to the *solid* mixture or the *mixture* is heated, *carbon dioxide* is produced. This produces bubbles in the dough or cake mixture and it rises, producing a product with an open texture. The mixture usually contains *sodium*

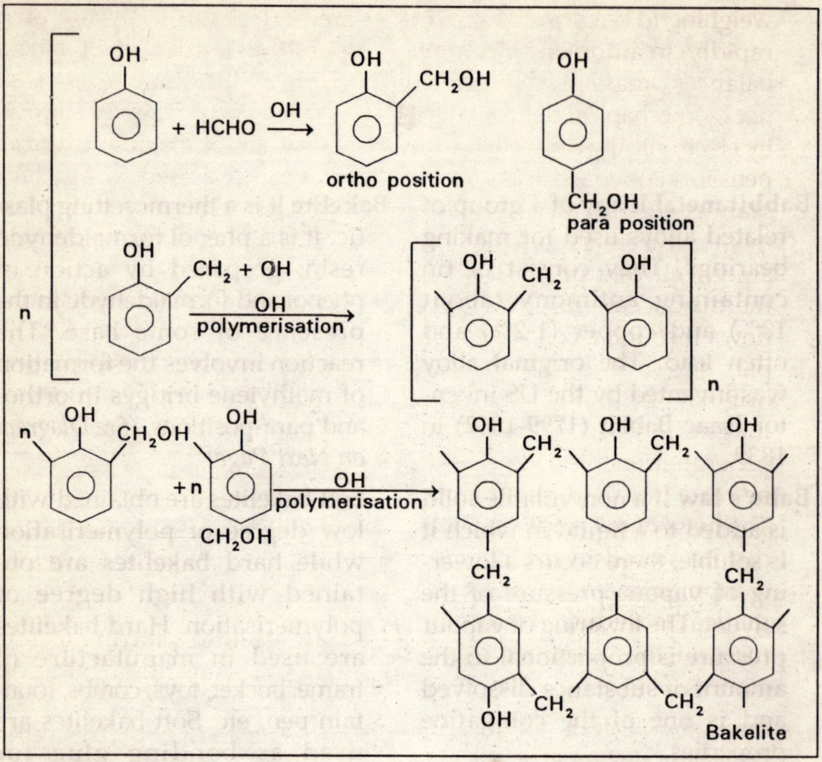

hydrogencarbonate or *sodium bicarbonate* ($NaHCO_3$) and tartaric.

The powder can be made up in the kitchen by mixing cream of tartar (the *potassium* salt of tartaric acid) and baking soda (sodium hydrogencarbonate). This prevents the *reaction* from occurring before it is required.

balance It is an accurate weighing device. The simple *beam balance* consists of two pans suspended from a centrally pivoted beam. Known masses are placed on one pan and the substance or body to be weighed is placed on the other. When the beam is exactly horizontal the two masses are equal. An accurate laboratory balance weighs to the nearest hundredth of a milligram. Specially designed balances can be accurate to a millionth of a milligram. More modern *substitution balances* use the substitution principle. In this calibrated weights are removed from the single lever arm to bring the single pan suspended from it into equilibrium with a fixed counter weight. The substitution balance is more accurate than the two-pan device and enables weighing to be carried out more rapidly. In automatic electronic balances, mass is determined not by mechanical deflection but by electronically controlled compensation of an electric force. A scanner monitors the displacement of the pan support generating a current proportional to the displacement. This current flows through a coil forcing the pan support to return to its original position by means of a magnetic force. The signal generated enables the mass to be read from a digital display. The mass of the empty container can be stored in the balance's computer memory and automatically deducted from the mass of the container plus its contents.

banana bond It is an informal name for the type of electron-deficient bond holding the B–H–B bridges in boranes and similar compounds.

Barbitone, having formula $C_8H_{12}N_2O_3$. It is diethylmalonylurea. It is a white crystalline solid and its sodium salt is used as a sedative.

barium Symbol Ba. A silvery-white reactive element belonging to group II of the periodic table; a.n. 54; r.a.m. 137.33; r.d. 3.51; m.p. 725°C; b.p. 1640°C having electronic configuration $[Xe]6S^2$. It occurs as the minerals barytes ($BaSO_4$) and witherite. Extraction is by high-temperature reduction of barium oxide with aluminium or silicon in a vacuum, or by electrolysis of fused barium chloride. The metal is used as a getter in vacuum systems. It oxidizes readily in air and reacts with ethanol and water. Soluble barium compounds are extremely poisonous. It was first identified in 1774 by Karl Scheele, and was extracted by Humphry Davy in 1808.

barium carbonate A white insoluble compound, having formula $BaCO_3$; r.d. 4.43. It decomposes on heating to give barium oxide and carbon dioxide.

barium chloride, having formula $BaCl_2$ A white non-hygroscopic solid (which does not absorb moisture from air) which crystallises as $BaCl_2 . 2H_2O$. It is used as a laboratory reagent.

barrel 1. A cask for holding beer. It has a *volume* of exactly 32 imperial gallons.

2. A unit volume in the *petroleum* industry. One barrel = approximately 35 imperial gallons (159 litres).

barytes (barite) An orthorhombic (lattice) mineral form of barium sulphate, $BaSO_4$; the chief ore of barium. It is usually white but may also be yellow, grey, or brown. Large deposits occur in Andalusia, Spain, and in the USA.

basalt A fine-grained basic igneous rock. It is composed mainly of calcium-rich plagioclase feldspar and pyroxene; other minerals present may be olivine, magnetite, and apatite. Basalt is the commonest type of lava.

base A compound that reacts with a protonic acid to give water (and a salt). The definition comes from the Arrhenius theory of acids and bases. Typically, bases are metal oxides, hydroxides, or compounds (such as ammonia) that give hydroxide ions in aqueous solution. Thus, a base may be either: (1) An insoluble oxide or hydroxide that reacts with an acid, e.g.

$$CuO(s) + 2HCl(aq) \rightarrow CuCl_2(aq) + H_2O(l)$$

Here the reaction involves hydrogen ions from the acid

$$CuO(s) + 2H^+(aq) \rightarrow H_2O(l) + Cu^{2+}(aq)$$

(2) A soluble hydroxide, in which case the solution contains hydroxide ions. The reaction with acids is a reaction between hydrogen ions and hydroxide ions :

$$H^+ + OH^- \rightarrow H_2O$$

(3) A compound that dissolves in water to produce hydroxide ions. For example, ammonia reacts as follows:

$$NH_3(g) + H_2O(l) = NH_4^+(aq) + {}^-OH$$

A base that dissolves in water to give hydroxide ions is called an *alkali.* Ammonia and sodium hydroxide are common examples.

The original Arrhenius definition of a base has been extended by the Lowry—Bronsted theory and by the Lewis theory. *See* acid.

basic 1. Describing a compound that is a base. **2.** Describing a solution containing an excess of hydroxide ions; alkaline.

basic equation for electrolysis

$$E_{app} = E_{cell} + E_{ov} + iR$$

E_{app} → potential applied to the electrodes;

E_{cell} → potential of the cell when current is not flowing;

E_{ov} → over potential at the electrodes;

i → current;

R → total resistance of the circuit.

bastnaesite A mineral having formula $CeFCO_3$. It is used as a source of lighter lanthanides.

battery A number of electric cells joined together. The common car battery, or accumulator, usually consists of six secondary cells connected in series to give a total e.m.f. of 12 volts. A torch battery is usually a dry version of the Leclanche named after the scientist) primary cell, two of which are often connected in series. Batteries may also have cells connected in parallel, in which case they have the same e.m.f. as a single cell, but their capacity is increased, i.e. they will provide more total charge. The capacity of a battery is usually specified in ampere-hours, the ability to supply 1 A for 1 hr, or the equivalent.

bauxite It is the chief ore of aluminium, consisting of hydrous aluminium oxides and aluminous laterite. It is a clay like amorphous material formed by the weathering of silicate rocks under tropical conditions. The chief producers are Australia, Guinea, Jamaica, USSR, Brazil, and Surinam.

becquerel Symbol Bq. The SI unit of activity (radiation units). The unit is named after the discoverer of radioactivity A. H. Becquerel (1852-1908).

bell metal It is an alloy of Copper with composition of Copper 80%, Tin 20%. It is used for bells, gongs, etc.

Benedict's test It is a biochemical test to detect reducing sugars in solution, it is devised by the US chemist S.R. Benedict (1884-1936). *Benedict's reagent*—a mixture of copper (II) sulphate ($CuSO_4$) and a filtered mixture of hydrated sodium citrate and hydrated sodium carbonate (Na_2CO_3)—is added to the test solution and boiled. A high concentration of reducing sugars induces the formation of a red precipitate; a lower concentration produces a yellow precipitate. Benedict's test is a more sensitive alternative to Fehling's test.

Benedict's solution A *solution* which can be used as a test for a *reducing agent* (agents which reduce other's and get themselves oxidised). It consists of a mixture of copper (II) sulphate, sodium carbonate and sodium citrate dissolved in water. A brown/red/yellow colour is formed when a *reducing agent* is warmed with the solution. It is most often used to test for reducing *sugars*, such as *glucose.*

bendrofluzide A white crystalline powder. It is a diuretic used against oedema and hypertension. (high blood pressure)

beneficiation (ore dressing) The separation of an ore into the valuable components and the waste material (gangue). This may be achieved by a number of processes, including crushing, grinding, magnetic separation, froth flotation, etc. The dressed ore, consisting of a high proportion of valuable components, is then ready for smelting or some other refining process by which they can be refined.

benzene (C_6H_6) The simplest

aromatic compound. It is a toxic liquid *hydrocarhon* which can cause cancer. Its widespread use in schools has been replaced by that of *methylbenzene*. It is produced from *naphtha*, and is an important source of *organic* compounds which are used to produce *poly (phenylethene), phenol, detergents* and *nylon*. It has a resonating structure *See* aromaticity.

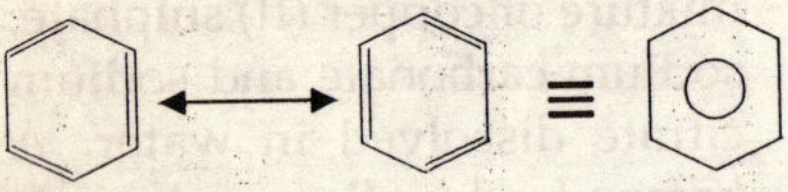

benzene

benzenecarbaldehyde (benzaldehyde) A yellowish volatile oily liquid, C_6H_5CHO; r.d. 1.04; m.p. –26°C; b.p. 178.1°C. The compound occurs in almond kernels and has an almond-like smell. It is made from methylbenzene (by conversion to dichloromethyl benzene, $C_6H_5CHCl_2$, followed by hydrolysis). Benzenecarbaldehyde is used in flavourings, perfumery, and the dyestuffs industry. Structure of benzaldehyde is

benzenecarbonyl chloride (benzoyl chloride) A colourless liquid, C_6H_5COCl; r.d. 1.21; m.p. 0°C; b.p. 197.2°C. It is an acyl halide, used to introduce benzenecarbonyl groups into molecules. The structure of benzoyl chloride is

benzenecarboxylic acid (benzoic acid) A white crystalline compound, C_6H_5COOH; r.d. 1.27; m.p. 122.4°C; b.p. 249°C. It occurs naturally in some plants and is used as a food preservative. Benzenecarboxylic acid has a carboxyl group bound directly to a benzene ring. It is a weak carboxylic acid ($K_a = 6.4 \times 10^{-5}$ at 25°C) which is slightly soluble in water. It also undergoes substitution reactions on the benzene ring. The structure of benzoic acid is

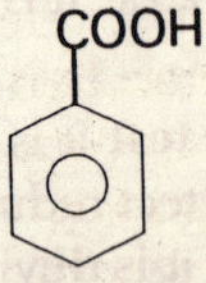

benzene hexachloride (BHC) A crystalline substance, $C_6H_6Cl_6$, made by adding chlorine to benzene in UV light. It is used as a pesticide and exist in several isomeric forms, the most active is gamma-BHC, known as *lindane*. Like DDT, concern has been expressed at its environmental effects.

benzenediazonium chloride, $C_6H_5N_2$ **Cl** A colourless solid which turns brown on exposure to air. It is used to prepare aryl fluorides and iodides and many other organic compounds. Structure of benzenediazonium chloride is

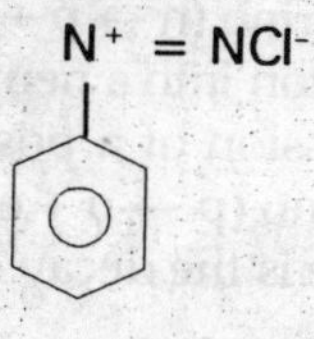

also see diazolization

benzoylation A chemical reaction in which a benzoyl group (benzenecarbonyl group, C_6H_5CO) is introduced into a molecule.

Bergius process A process for making hydrocarbon mixtures (for fuels) from coal by heating powdered coal mixed with tar and iron(III) oxide catalyst at 450°C under hydrogen at a pressure of about 200 atmospheres. In later developments of the process, the coal was suspended in liquid hydrocarbons and other catalysts were used. The process was developed by the German chemist Friederich Bergius (1884-1949) during World War I, as a source of motor fuel.

Berkelium Symbol Bk. A radioactive metallic transuranic element belonging to the actinoids; a.n. 97; mass number of the most stable isotope 247 (half life 1.4×10^3 years); r.d. (calculated) 14. There are eight known isotopes. It was first produced by G.T. Seborg and associates in 1949 by bombarding americium-241 with alpha particles.

Berkley and Hartley's method It is a method for the measurement of osmotic pressure. (π)

$$\pi V = nRT$$

beryl A hexagonal mineral form of beryllium aluminium silicate, $Be_3Al_2Si_6O_{18}$; the chief ore of beryllium. It may be green, blue, yellow, or white and has long been used as a gemstone. Beryl is present throughout the world in granite and pegmatites. Emerald, the green gem variety, occurs more rarely and is of great value. Important sources of beryl are found in Brazil, Madagascar, and the USA.

beryllate A compound formed in solution when beryllium metal (Be, gp II) or the oxide or hydroxide, dissolves in strong alkali. The reaction (for the metal) is often written

$$Be + 2OH^-(aq) \rightarrow BeO_2^{2-}(aq) + H_2(g)$$

The ion BeO_2^{2-} is the beryllate ion. In fact, as with the aluminates, the ions present are probably hydroxy ions of the type

$Be(OH)_4^{2-}$ [the *tetrahydroxoberyllate (II)* ion] together with polymeric ions.

beryllium Symbol Be. A grey metallic element of group II of the periodic table. a.n. 4; r.a.m. 9.012; r.d. 1.85; m.p. 1285°C; b.p. 2970°C. Beryllium occurs as beryl ($3BeO.Al_2O_3.6SiO_2$) and chrysoberyl ($BeO.Al_2O_3$). The metal is extracted from a fused mixture of BeF_2/NaF by electrolysis or by magnesium reduction of BeF_2. It is used to manufacture Be-Cu alloys, which are used in nuclear reactors as reflectors and moderators because of their low absorption cross section. Beryllium oxide is used in ceramics and in nuclear reactors. Beryllium and its compounds are toxic and can cause serious lung diseases and dermatitis. The metal is resistant to oxidation by air because of the formation of an oxide layer, but will react with dilute hydrochloric and sulphuric acids. Beryllium compounds show high covalent character. The element was isolated independently by F.Wohler and A.A. Bussy in 1828.

beryllium hydroxide A white crystalline compound, $Be(OH)_2$, precipitated from solutions of beryllium salts by adding alkali. Like the oxide, it is amphoteric (both act as acid as well as base) and dissolves in excess alkali to give beryllates.

Bessemer process This process is used to make steel from pig iron or cast iron.

beta decay (β-decay) A type of radioactive decay in which an unstable atomic nucleus changes into a nucleus of the same mass number but different proton number. The change involves the conversion of a neutron into a proton with the emission of an electron and an antineutrino ($n \rightarrow p + e^- + \bar{v}$) or of a proton into a neutron with the emission of a positron and a neutrino ($p \rightarrow n + e^+ + v$). An example is the decay of carbon-14:

$$^{14}_{6}C \rightarrow {}^{14}_{7}N + e^- + \bar{v}$$

The electrons or positrons emitted are called *beta particles* and streams of beta particles are known as *beta radiation*.

beta particles These are *electrons* (e^-) which are produced in the following *nuclear reaction:*

$$^{1}_{0}n \rightarrow {}^{1}_{1}p + {}^{0}_{-1}e$$

neutron proton electron

For example,

$$^{31}_{15}P + {}^{1}_{0}n \rightarrow {}^{32}_{15}P \rightarrow {}^{32}_{16}S + {}^{0}_{1}e$$

In this *radioactive* decay the electrons are expelled from the *nucleus* of the *atom*. They travel at high speeds (up to 98% of the speed of light) and have a greater penetrating power than *alpha particles* (a-particles). When this reaction occurs, the atom concerned changes its *atomic number* because it gains a *proton*.

beta-iron A nonmagnetic allotrope of iron that exists between 768°C and 900°C.

bidentate ligand Any ligand that is capable of coordinating through two different sites from different parts of the molecule or anion, e.g. cyanide ion.

$$\begin{array}{ll} CH_2\ddot{N}H_2, & COO^- \\ | & | \\ CH_2\ddot{N}H_2 & COO^- \text{ etc.} \end{array}$$

bimolecular reaction (A reaction of two molecules) or a step in a chemical reaction that involves two molecules.

binary (Formed by two) Describing a compound or alloy formed from two elements.

binary acid An acid in which the acidic hydrogen atom(s) are bound directly to an atom other than oxygen. Examples are hydrogen chloride (HCl), and hydrogen sulphide (H_2S). Such compounds are sometimes called *hydracids. Compare* oxo acid.

biochemistry It is the study of the chemistry of living organisms, especially the structure and function of their chemical components (principally proteins, carbohydrates, lipids, and nucleic acids). Biochemistry has advanced rapidly with the development, from the mid-20th century, of such techniques as chromatography, X-ray diffraction, radioisotopic labelling, and electron microscopy. Using these techniques to separate and analyse biologically important molecules, the steps of the metabolic pathways in which they are involved (e.g. glycolysis) have been determined. This has provided some knowledge of how organisms obtain and store energy, how they manufacture and degrade their biomolecules, and how they sense and respond to their environment.

biomolecules These are the complex organic molecules which are basic constituent of life i.e. which build up living organism and are required for their growth and maintenance e.g. carbohydrates, proteins, amino acids, etc.

biotin It is a part of vitamin B-complex . It is the coenzyme for various enzymes that catalyse the incorporation of carbon dioxide into various compounds. Adequate amounts are normally produced by the intestinal bacteria; other sources include cereals, vegetables, milk, and liver.

biotite An important rock-forming silicate mineral, a member of the mica group of minerals, in common with which it has a sheet-like crystal structure. It is usually black, dark brown, or green in colour.

Birkland-Eyde process It is a process used for the manufacture of nitric acid (HNO_3). Atmospheric oxygen and nitrogen are made to combine under the influence of an electric arc (3000-3500°C) to form nitric oxide (NO) which is then oxidised to NO_2 and absorbed in water to get HNO_3.

bismuth Symbol Bi. A white crystalline metal with a pinkish tinge belonging to group V of the periodic table; a.n. 83; r.a.m. 208.98; r.d. 9.78; m.p. 271.3°C; b.p. 1560°C. The most important ores are bismuthinite (Bi_2S_3) and bismite (Bi_2O_3). Peru, Japan, Mexico, Bolivia and Canada are major producers. The metal is extracted by carbon reduction of its oxide. Bismuth is the most diamagnetic of all metals and its thermal conductivity is lower than any metal except mercury. The metal has a high electrical resistance and a high Hall effect when placed in magnetic fields. It is used to make low-melting point casting alloys with tin and cadmiun. These alloys expand on solidification to give clear replication of intricate features. It is also used to make thermally activated safety devices for fire detection and sprinkler systems. More recent applications include its use as a catalyst for making acrylic fibres, as a constituent of malleable iron, as a carrier of uranium-235 fuel in nuclear reactors and as a specilized thermocouple material. Bismuth compounds (when lead free) are used for cosmetics and medical preparations. It is attacked by oxidizing acids, steam (at high temperatures). and by moist halogens. It burns in air with a blue flame to produce yellow oxide fumes. C.G. Junine first demonstrated that it was different from lead in 1753.

biuret test A test to detect proteins in solution, named after the substance *biuret* ($H_2NCONHCONH_2$), which is formed when urea is heated.

$$NH_2\,CONH_2 \xrightarrow{\Delta} \text{biuret}$$

Sodium hydroxide is mixed with the test solution and drops of 1% copper (II) sulphate solution are then added slowly. A positive result is indicated by a violet ring, caused by the reaction of peptide bonds in the proteins or peptides. Such a result will not occur in the presence of free amino acids.

bivalent (or divalent) Having a valency of two.

blackdamp (choke damp) Air left depleted in oxygen following the explosion of fire-damp in a mine.

blast furnace A furnace which allows the continuous production of iron. It is used for smelting of iron. It is charged with a mixture of coke, iron ore and lime stone. At the bottom of the furnace, coke and lime stone react to produce carbon dioxide.

$$C(s) + O_2(g) \rightarrow CO_2(g)$$

It is exothermic reaction and temperature is increased to about 1800°C.

More coke (C) then reacts with CO_2 to produce CO.

$$C(s) + CO_2(g) \rightarrow 2\,CO(g)$$

The carbon monoxide (CO) reduces the oxides of iron to iron.

$$Fe_2O_3(s) + 3CO(g) \rightarrow 3CO_2(g) + Fe(l)\ \text{(ore)}$$

The molten iron flows to the bottom of the furnace from where it is tapped off.

blasting gelatin A high explosive gelatine made from nitroglycerine and gun cotton (cellulose nitrate).

bleach A substance used to decolourize materials, e.g. *fabrics* and *paper*. Sunlight and *oxygen* act as bleaches but the most commonly found bleach is sodium chlorate(I) *solution* (NaClO). This is produced when *chlorine* is reacted with *sodium hydroxide* solution:

$$Cl_2(g) + 2NaOH(aq) \rightarrow NaCl(aq) + NaClO(aq) + H_2O(l)$$

Domestic bleaches such as 'Domestos' contain sodium chlorate(I) solution. The chlorate(I) decomposes to give oxygen which acts as an *oxidizing agent* which oxidises others and get itself reduced.

$$NaClO + \underset{\text{material}}{\text{coloured}} \rightarrow NaCl + \underset{\text{material}}{\text{oxidized (decolourized)}}$$

bleaching powder, $CaOCl_2$ (calcium oxy chloride) A white solid. It is manufactured by passing chlorine over slaked lime in a Hasenclever plant. It is a source of chlorine.

$$Ca(OH)_2 + Cl_2 \rightarrow CaOCl_2 + H_2O$$

blende A naturally occurring metal sulphide, e.g. zinc blende (ZnS).

blockboard Material made from two sheets of veneer which are separated by a core made up of lengths of softwood. Blockboard is cheap but strong and is often used for doors.

boehmite It is a mineral form of a mixed aluminium oxide and hydroxide, (AlO.OH). It is named after the German scientist J. Böhm

Bohr theory The theory was published in 1913 by the Danish physicist Niels Bohr (1885-1962) to explain the line spectrum of hydrogen. This theory also explains the drawbacks in Rutherford theory. He assumed that a single electron of mass *m* travelled in a circular orbit of radius *r*, at a velocity *v*, around a positively charged nucleus. The angular momentum of the electron would then be *mvr*. Bohr proposed that electrons could only occupy orbits in which this angular momentum had certain fixed values, $\eta/2\pi$, $2\eta/2\pi$, $3\eta/2\pi$,...$n\eta/2\pi$, where η is the Planck constant. This means that the angular momentum is quantized, i.e. can only have certain discrete values, each of which is a multiple of *n*. Each permitted value of *n* is associated with an orbit of different radius and Bohr assumed that when the atom emitted or absorbed radiation of frequency Υ, the electron jumped from one orbit to another; the energy emitted or absorbed by each jump is equal to $\eta\Upsilon$. This theory gave good results in predicting the series of lines observed in the hydrogen spectrum but not with any other spectrum. The idea of quantized values of angular momentum was later explained by the wave nature of the electron. Each orbit has to have a whole number of wavelengths around it; i.e. $n\lambda = 2\pi r$, where l is the wavelength and *n* a whole number. The wavelength of a particle is given by h/mv, so $nh/mv = 2\pi r$, which leads to $mvr = nh/2\pi$. Modern atomic theory does not allow subatomic particles to be treated in the same way as large objects, and Bohr's reasoning is somewhat discredited. However, the idea of quantized angular momentum has been retained.

boiling The change from the *liquid* state to the *gas* state at a fixed *temperature:* the *boiling point*. Boiling takes place when the *vapour* pressure of the liquid equals the *pressure* of the *atmosphere* above the liquid. Boiling point of a liquid is different at different heights because of difference in pressure.

boiling point (b.p.) The temperature at which the saturated vapour pressure of a liquid equals the external atmospheric pressure. As a consequence, bubbles form in the liquid and the temperature remains constant until all the liquid has evaporated. As the boiling point of a liquid depends on the external atmospheric pressure, boiling points are usually quoted for standard atmospheric pressure (760 mmHg = 101 325 Pa).

boiling-point-composition diagram A graph showing how the boiling point and vapour composition of a mixture of two liquids depends on the composition of the mixture. The abscissa shows the range of compositions from 100% A at one end to 100% B at the other. The diagram has two curves: the lower one gives the boiling points (at a fixed pressure) for the different compositions. The upper one is plotted by taking the composition of vapour at each temperature on the boiling-point curve. The two curves would coincide for an ideal mixture, but generally they are different because of deviations from Raoult's law. In some cases, they may show a maximum or minimum and coincide at some intermediate composition, explaining the formation of azeotropes.

Boltzmann constant Symbol *k*. The ratio of the universal gas constant (*R*) to the Avogadro constant (N_A). It may be thought of therefore as the gas constant per molecule. The value of gas constant is 8.314 J/mol/k and that of Avagadro's number is 6.023 ´ 10^{23}

$$k = R/N_A = 1.380\ 622 \times 10^{-23}\ J\ K^{-1}$$

It is named after Austrian physicist Ludwig Boltzmann (1844-1906).

bomb calorimeter It is an apparatus used for measuring heats of combustion (e.g. calorific values of fuels and foods). It consists of a strong container in which the sample is sealed with excess oxygen and ignited electrically. The heat of combustion at constant volume can be calculated from the resulting rise in temperature. (Temperature may be varied)

bond It refers to the attractive force that keeps atoms or group of atoms bound together.

e.g. C-C, N≡N, O=O, etc.

bond energy An amount of energy associated with a bond in a chemical compound. It is obtained from the heat of atomization. For instance, in methane the bond energy of the C–H bond is one quarter of the enthalpy of the process

$$CH_4(g) \rightarrow C(g) + 4H(g)$$

Bond energies can be calculated from the standard ethalpy of formation of the compound and from the enthalpies of atomization of the elements. Energies calculated in this way are called *average bond energies or bond-energy terms*. They depend to some extent on the molecule chosen; the C–H bond energy in methane will differ slightly from that in ethane. The *bond dissociation energy* i.e. energy required to break the bond is a different measurement, being the energy required to break a particular bond; e.g. the energy for the process:

$$CH_4(g) \rightarrow CH_3.\ (g) + H.\ (g)$$

bond angle It is the angle between two bonds. It depends upon the type of hybridisation i.e. mixing of orbitals, involved in the formation of a molecule and the dipole moment in the molecule.

bond length It is the distance between the nuclei of bonded atoms. Bond length r of different molecules is as follows:

H – Cl = 136 pm
H – H = 74 pm

borane (boron hydride) Any of a group of compounds of boron and hydrogen, many of which can be prepared by the action of acid on magnesium boride (MgB_2). Hydrogen has negative valency in it. Others are made by pyrolysis of the products of this reaction in the presence of hydrogen and other reagents. They are all volatile, reactive, and oxidize readily in air, some explosively so. The boranes are a remarkable group of compounds and their structures cannot be described using the conventional two-electron covalent bond model (electron-deficient compound). The simplest example is *diborane* (B_2H_6). Other boranes include B_4H_{10}, B_5H_9, B_5H_{11}, B_6H_{10}, and $B_{10}H_4$. The larger borane molecules have open or closed polyhedra of boron atoms. In addition, there is a wide range of borane derivatives containing atoms of other elements, such as carbon and phosphorus.

boric acid, H_3BO_3 It is a white crystalline powder and is a weak acid used in the manufacture of enamels, glazes for pottery. Its weak solution is used as an eye wash under the trade name *boric lotion*. It is a mild antiseptic.

boride A compound of boron with a metal. Most metals form at least one boride of the type MB, MB_2, MB_4, MB_6, or MB_{12}. The compounds have a variety of structures; in particular, the hexaborides contain clusters of B_6 atoms. The borides are all hard high-melting materials with metal-like conductivity. They can be made by direct combination of the elements at high temperature (over 2000°C) or, more usually, by high-temperature reduction of a mixture of the metal oxide and boron oxide using carbon or aluminium. Chemically, they are stable to non-oxidizing acids but are attacked by strong oxidizing agents which will oxidise others and get themselves reduced by strong alkalis. Magnesium boride (MgB_2) is unusual it can be hydrolysed to boranes. Industrially, metal borides are used as refractory materials. The most important are CrB, CrB_2, TiB_2, and ZnB_2. Generally, they are fabricated using high-temperature powder metallurgy, in which the article is produced in a graphite die at over 2000°C and at very high pressure. Items are pressed as near to final shape as possible as machining requires diamond cutters and is extremely expensive.

Born-Haber cycle This cycle shows how a reaction or a physical process can be considered to be made up of a number of steps. It is used for calculation of lattice energy of a crystal e.g. For NaCl crystal, we know enthalpy change for formation ΔH_f for it is –98 kcal/mole.

$Na(s)+\frac{1}{2}Cl_2(g)\rightarrow NaCl(s)$; DH_f =–98 kcal.

It can be considered to be passing through following steps.

$Na(s) \rightarrow Na\ (g)$, ΔH_{vap} = +26 kcal

$\frac{1}{2}\ Cl_2\ (g) \rightarrow Cl\ (g)$, ΔH_{diss} = +29 kcal

$Na\ (g) \rightarrow Na^+\ (g) + e^-$ $\Delta H_{ionisation\ energy}$ = 118 kcal

$Cl\ (g) + e^- \rightarrow Cl^-\ (g)$ $\Delta H_{electron\ affinity}$ =–83 kcal

$Na^+\ (g) + Cl^-\ (g) \rightarrow NaCl\ (s)$ $\Delta H_{crystal\ lattice}$ = ?

From the above we can find out (by using Hess's law that DH crystal lattice = –188 kcal.

bornite It is an important ore of copper composed of a mixed copper-iron sulphide, Cu_5FeS_4. Freshly exposed surfaces of the mineral are a metallic reddish-brown but a purplish iridescent tarnish soon develops—hence it is popularly known as *peacock ore.* Bornite is mined in Chile, Peru, Bolivia, Mexico, and the USA.

boron Symbol B, a.n. 5, r.a.m. 10.81, m.p. 2300°C, r.d. 2.34-2.37

A non-metallic *element (non-metal)* in *group* III of the *periodic table.* It is a 'p'-block element. Its *oxide* is used to make *glass (e.g. borosilicate glass).* It is a component of *alloys* and is a moderator in nuclear reactors.

boron nitride It is a solid and is represented by BN. It is insoluble in cold water and slowly decomposed by hot water; r.d. 2.25 (hexagonal); sublimes above 3000°C. Boron nitride is manufactured by heating boron oxide to 800°C on an acid-soluble carrier, such as calcium phosphate, in the presence of nitrogen or ammonia. It is isoelectronic with carbon and, like carbon, it has a very hard cubic form *(borazon)* and a softer hexagonal form; unlike graphite this is a nonconductor. It is used in the electrical industries where its high thermal conductivity and high resistance are of especial value.

boron hydrides They are collectively known as boranes. Hydrogen has a negative valency. Their general formula is B_nH_{n+4} and B_nH_{n+6}. They catch fire spontaneously in air. They react with ammonia to form different compounds depending upon the conditions.

borosilicate Any of a large number of substances in which BO_3 and SiO_4 units are linked to form networks with a wide range of structures. Borosilicate glasses are particularly important; the addition of boron to the silicate network enables the glass to be fused at lower temperature than pure silica and also extends the plastic range of the glass. Thus, such glasses as Pyrex have a wider range of applications than soda glasses (narrow plastic range, higher thermal expansion) or silica (much higher melting point). Borosilicates are also used in glazes and enamels and in the production of glass wools.

borosilicate glass The glass made by the addition of *boron oxide* (B_2O_3) during its manufacture. This results in a material which does not expand very much. Consequently, the glass can be heated or cooled rapidly without cracking. 'Pyrex' glassware is like this.

Boyle's law The volume *(V)* of a given mass of gas is inversely proportional to its pressure *(P)* at constant temperature $V \propto \frac{1}{P}$ i.e. PV = constant. This is true only for an ideal gas. This law was discovered in 1662 by the Irish physicist Robert Boyle (1627-91). On the continent of Europe it is known as *Mariotte's law* after E. Mariotte (1620-84), who discovered it independently in 1676.

Bragg equation A beam of monochromatic X-rays of wavelength λ impinges on a crystal, strong scattering occurs in certain directions only. For diffraction the path difference between waves scattered from successive planes of atoms in the crystal must equal an integral number of wavelengths, n (n=1,2,3,...), which is expressed by the equation $n\lambda = 2d \sin \theta$.

where 'd' is the distance separating successive planes in the crystal and q is the angle which is incident beam of X-rays makes with the same planes.

brass A group of alloys consisting of copper and zinc. A typical yellow brass might contain about 67% copper and 33% zinc.

brewing A process which involves the *fermentation* of *sugars* to the *alcohol, ethanol*. Beers, wines and spirits are produced by the brewing industry.

bridge An atom joining two other atoms in a molecule. For example, aluminium chloride; borane.

Brin process It is a process formerly used for making oxygen by heating barium oxide in air to form the peroxide and then heating the peroxide at higher temperature (>800°C) to produce oxygen

$$2BaO_2 \xrightarrow{\Delta} 2BaO + O_2$$

brine It is a concentrated aqueous solution of sodium chloride.

Britannia metal A silvery alloy consisting of 80-90% tin, 5-15% antimony, and sometimes small percentages of copper, lead, and zinc. It is used in bearings and some domestic articles.

British thermal unit (Btu) The Imperial unit of heat, being originally the heat required to raise the temperature of one pound (1 lb) of water by 1°F. 1 Btu is now defined as 1055.06 joules or 1.05506 KJ.

bromate A salt or ester of a bromic acid ($HBrO_3$).

bromic (I) acid, HBrO It is hypobromous acid which is a pale yellow liquid. It is a good bleaching and oxidising agent, i.e. it oxidises others and get itself reduced.

bromic (V) acid It is a colourless liquid, $HBrO_3$, made by adding sulphuric acid to barium bromate. It is a strong acid.

bromide A *compound* of *bromine* and another *element*. *Metal* bromides are usually *ionic* solids, e.g. sodium bromide NaBr. *Non-metal* bromides are usually *covalent* compounds, e.g. hydrogen bromide HBr.

bromide paper It is a photographic paper. It has silver bromide (AgBr) coating.

bromination A chemical reaction in which a bromine atom is introduced into a molecule.

bromine Symbol : Br,

a.n. 35; r.a.m. 79.9; rd. 3.13; m.p. –7.2°C; b.p. 58.78°C;

A member of the *halogen* group of *elements*. It is a volatile red *liquid* at room *temperature*. The liquid is very corrosive and the vapour is both irritating and toxic.

Although it is less reactive than *chlorine*, bromine will react vigorously with metals forming *bromides*. It can be represented by following reaction:

$$Mg(s) + Br_2(l) \rightarrow MgBr_2(s)$$

bromoethane (ethyl bromide) A colourless flammable liquid, C_2H_5Br; r.d. 1.43; m.p. –119°C; b.p. 38.4°C. It is a typical haloalkane, which can be prepared from ethene and hydrogen bromide. Bromoethane is used as a refrigerant.

$$H_2C = CH_2 + HBr \rightarrow C_2H_5Br$$

bromomethane (methyl bromide) A colourless volatile nonflammable liquid, CH_3Br; r.d. 1.73; m.p. –93°C; b.p. 4.5°C. It is a typical haloalkane.

bromothyl blue It is an indicator pH range 6.0 (yellow) to 7.6 (blue).

Brownian motion It is a zig-zag motion of particles suspended in a *liquid* or *gas*, such as pollen in *water* or smoke in *air*, are seen to move in a random way. The explanation is that the microscopic particles which make up the liquid or gas, e.g. water and air *molecules*, are moving randomly and are hitting against the larger particles of pollen or smoke, causing them to move. Brownian motion is put forward as evidence for the *kinetic theory of gases*.

Named after the Scottish botanist Robert Brown, 1773-1858, who was the first to observe the phenomenon.

brucite A mineral form of magnesium hydroxide, $Mg(OH)_2$.

Buchner funnel A type of funnel with an internal perforated tray on which a flat circular filter paper can be placed, used for filtering by suction. It is named after the German chemist Eduard Buchner (1860-1917).

buffer solution A solution that contains a weak acid and its conjugate, base or a weak base and its conjugate acid is known as a buffer solution. They may be prepared by combining a solution of a weak acid or weak base with one of its soluble salts. It is used to maintain the pH of a solution during reaction. For example,

CH_3COOH (aq) + CH_3COONa (aq) and NH_4OH (aq) + NH_4Cl (aq) are buffer solutions.

bumping It is a violent boiling of a liquid caused by superheating so that bubbles form at a pressure above atmospheric pressure. It can be prevented by putting pieces of porous pot in the liquid to enable bubbles of vapour to form at the normal boiling point.

bunsen burner It is a type of gas burner that is commonly used in chemistry laboratory. It consists of a metal tube (brass) having an adjustable air valve. So we get an oxidised flame.

bunsen cell A primary cell which cannot be recharged and consisting of a zinc cathode immersed in dilute sulphuric acid and a carbon anode immersed in concentrated nitric acid. The electrolytes are separated by a porous pot. The cell gives an e.m.f. of about 1.9 volts.

burette A graduated glass tube with a tap at one end leading to a fine outlet tube, used for delivering known volumes of a liquid. It is used in titrations.

butanal, $CH_3CH_2CH_2CHO$ An aldehyde which is commonly called *butyraldehyde*. It is used in rubber industries and plastics. It is a colourless inflammable liquid.

butane It is an aliphatic . gaseous hydrocarbon, C_4H_{10}; r.d. 0.58 g cm^{-3}; m.p. –135°C; b.p. 0°C. Butane is obtained from petroleum (from refinery gas or by cracking higher hydrocarbons). The fourth member of the alkane series, it has a straight chain of carbon atoms and is isomeric with 2-methyl-propane [$CH_3CH(CH_3)CH_3$, formerly called *isobutane*]. It can easily be liquefied under pressure and is supplied in cylinders for use as a fuel gas. It is also a raw material for making buta-1, 3-diene (for synthetic rubber).

butanedioic acid (succinic acid) A colourless crystalline fatty acid, $(CH_2)_2\ (COOH)_2$; r.d. 1.5; m.p. 185°C; b.p. 235°C. A weak carboxylic acid which is present in some plants, it is produced by fermentation of sugar or ammonium tartrate and used as a sequestrant and in making dyes.

butanoic acid, C_3H_7COOH Its common name is butyric acid. It is a colourless liquid with an unpleasant smell and is a weak carboxylic acid.

butanol Either of two aliphatic alcohols with the formula C_4H_9OH. *Butan-1-ol,* $CH_3\ (CH_2)_3\ OH$, is a primary alcohol; r.d. 0.81; m.p. –89.5°C; b.p. 117.3°C. *Butan-2-ol,* $CH_3CH(OH)C_2H_5$, is a secondary alcohol; r.d. 0.81; m.p. –114.7°C; b.p. 100°C. Both are colourless volatile liquids obtained from butane and used as solvents in laboratories.

butanone, $CH_3COC_2H_5$ It is a colourless liquid which is used as a solvent for vinyl resins and synthetic rubber.

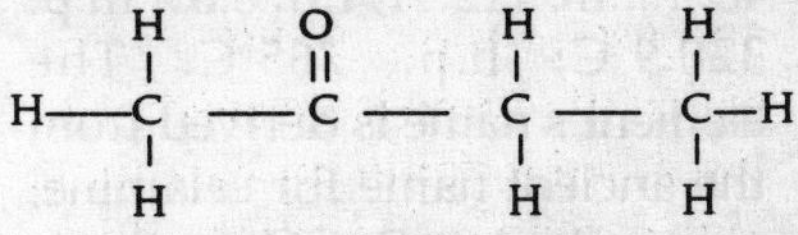

butyl group The alkyl group $CH_3(CH_2)_3$.

2-butyne-1, 4-diol,

$$OHCH_2C \equiv CCH_2.OH$$

It is a white solid and is used in electroplating and in paint.

by-product Something which is produced in a reaction in addition to the product which is required. For example, *slag* is a by-product when making *iron* in the *blast furnace* and *carbon dioxide* is a by-product of the *fermentation* process. It is important, if processes are to be economic, that by-products are sold, e.g. slag is sold as road-making material.

C

cadmium Symbol Cd. A soft bluish metal belonging to group IIB of the periodic table having a.n. 48; r.a.m. 112.41; r.d. 8.65; m.p. 320.9°C; b.p. 765°C. The element's name is derived from the ancient name for calamine, zinc carbonate $ZnCO_3$, and it is usually found associated with zinc ores, such as sphalerite (ZnS), but does occur as the mineral greenockite (CdS). Cadmium is usually produced as an associate product when zinc, copper, and lead ores are reduced. Cadmium is used in low-melting-point alloys to make solders, in Ni–Cd batteries, in bearing alloys, and in electroplating (over 50%). Cadmium compounds are used as phosphorescent coatings in TV tubes. Cadmium and its compounds are extremely toxic at low concentra-tions; great care is essential where solders are used or where fumes are emitted. It has similar chemical properties to zinc but shows a greater tendency towards complex formation. The element was discovered in 1817 by F. Stromeyer.

caesium Symbol Cs. It is an alkali metal having a.n. 55 and is 's' block element. A soft silvery-white metallic element belonging to group I of the periodic table; r.a.m. 132.905; r.d. 1.88; m.p. 28.4°C; b.p. 678°C. It occurs in small amounts in a number of minerals, the main source being carnallite ($KCl.MgCl_2.6H_2O$). It is obtained by electrolysis of molten caesium cyanide. The natural isotope is caesium-133. There are 15 other radioactive isotopes. Caesium-137 (half-life 33 years) is used as a gamma source. As the heaviest alkali metal, caesium has the lowest ionization potential of all elements, hence its use in photoelectric cells, etc.

calamine A zinc mineral ($ZnCO_3$ or zinc silicate). It is used in medicines as a lotion or powder for sun burn.

calcite A *mineral* form of *calcium carbonate* ($CaCO_3$) which is found in *limestone* and *chalk*.

calcium It is an alkaline earth metal which belongs to 's' block element. Symbol Ca. A soft grey metallic element belonging to group II of the periodic table; a.n. 20; r.a.m. 40.08; r.d. 1.55; m.p. 840°C; b.p. 1484°C. Calcium compounds are common in the earth's crust; e.g. limestone and marble ($CaCO_3$), gypsum ($CaSO_4.2H_2O$), and fluorite (CaF_2). The element is extracted by electrolysis of fused calcium chloride and is used as a getter in vacuum systems and a deoxidizer in producing nonferrous alloys. It is also used as a reducing agent in the extraction of such metals as thorium, zirconium, and uranium.

Calcium is an essential element for living organisms, being required for normal growth and development.

calcium carbonate A white solid, $CaCO_3$, which is only sparingly soluble in water. Calcium carbonate decomposes on heating to give calcium oxide (quicklime) and carbon dioxide. $CaCO_3 \rightleftharpoons CaO + CO_2$. It occurs naturally as the minerals calcite (rhombohedral; r.d. 2.71) and aragonite (rhombic, r.d. 2.93). Rocks containing calcium carbonate dissolve slowly in acidified rainwater (containing dissolved CO_2) to cause temporary hardness. In the laboratory, calcium carbonate is precipitated from limewater by carbon dioxide. Calcium carbonate is used in making lime (calcium oxide) and is the main raw material for the Solvay process.

calcium chloride A white deliquescent compound, $CaCl_2$, which is soluble in water; r.d. 2.15; m.p. 772°C; b.p. 7600°C. There are a number of hydrated forms, including the monohydrate, $CaCl_2.H_2O$, the dihydrate, $CaCl_2.2H_2O$ (r.d. 0.84), and the hexahydrate, $CaCl_2.6H_2O$ (trigonal; r.d. 1.71; the hexahydrate loses $4H_2O$ at 30°C and the remaining $2H_2O$ at 200°C). Large quantities of it are formed as a by-product of the Solvay process and it can be prepared by dissolving calcium carbonate or calcium oxide in hydrochloric acid. $CaO+HCl \rightarrow CaCl_2 + H_2O$. Crystals of the anhydrous salt can only be obtained if the hydrated salt is heated in a stream of hydrogen chloride. Solid calcium chloride is used in mines and on roads to reduce dust problems, whilst the molten salt is the electrolyte in the extraction of calcium. An aqueous solution of calcium chloride is used in refrigeration plants.

calcium carbide, CaC_2 Pure CaC_2 is white powder but commercial CaC_2 is grey coloured. It is used for preparation of acetylene. Carbon has a negative valency in it.

$$CaC_2 + 2H_2O \rightarrow Ca(OH)_2 + \underset{\text{acetylene}}{C_2H_2}$$

A mixture of CaC_2 and CO is used as a fertilizer under the name nitroleum. Nitroleum is obtained when lime and coke are heated in an electric furnace to about 3000°C

$$CaO + 3C \xrightarrow{3000°C} \underbrace{CaC_2 + CO}_{\text{Nitroleum}}$$

calcium cyanamide It is a poisonous colourless solid, $CaCN_2$, which sublimes at 1150°C. It is prepared by heating calcium dicarbide at 800°C in a stream of nitrogen:

$$CaC_2(s) + N_2(g) \rightarrow CaCN_2(s) + C(s)$$

The reaction has been used as a method of fixing nitrogen in countries in which cheap electricity is available to make the calcium dicarbide (the *cyanamide process*). Calcium cyanamide can be used as a fertilizer because it reacts with water to give ammonia and calcium carbonate:

$$CaCN_2(s) + 3H_2O(l) \rightarrow CaCO_3(s) + 2NH_3(g)$$

It is also used in the production of melamine, urea, and certain cyanide salts.

calcium fluoride A white crystalline solid, CaF_2; r.d. 3.2; m.p. 1360°C; b.p. 2500°C. It occurs naturally as the mineral fluorite (or fluorspar) and is the main source of fluorine. The *calcium fluoride* is of crystal structure and its lattice explains that it has the calcium ions and each surrounded by eight fluoride ions arranged at the corners of a cube. Each fluoride ion is surrounded by four calcium ions at the corners of a tetrahedron.

calcium hydrogencarbonate (calcium bicarbonate) A compound having formula $Ca(HCO_3)_2$, that is stable only in solution and is formed when water containing carbon dioxide dissolves calcium carbonate:

$$CaCO_3(s) + H_2O(l) + CO_2(g) \rightarrow Ca(HCO_3)_2(aq)$$

It is the cause of temporary hardness in water, because the calcium ions react with soap to give scum. Calcium hydrogencarbonate is unstable when heated and decomposes to give solid calcium carbonate. This explains why temporary hardness is removed by boiling and the formation of 'scale' in kettles and boilers.

calcium nitrate It is a white deliquescent compound, $Ca(NO_3)_2$, that is very soluble in water; cubic; r.d. 2.50; m.p. 561°C. It can be prepared by neutralizing HNO_3 with calcium carbonate and crystallizing it from solution as the tetrahydrate $Ca(NO_3)_2.4H_2O$, which exists in two monoclinic crystalline forms (α, r.d. 1.9; β, r.d. 1.82). There is also a trihydrate, $Ca(NO_3)_2.3H_2O$. The anhydrous salt can be obtained from the hydrate by heating but it decomposes on strong heating to give the oxide, nitrogen dioxide, and oxygen. Calcium nitrate is sometimes used as a nitrogenous fertilizer.

calcium phosphate, $Ca_3(PO_4)_2$ It is commonly found in bones and mineral phosphorite. It is used in the manufacture of phosphorus, phosphoric acid and calcium super phosphate.

calcium sulphate It is a white solid compound, $CaSO_4$; r.d. 2.96; 1450°C. It occurs naturally as the mineral anhydrite, which has a rhombic structure, transforming to a monoclinic form at 200°C. More commonly, it is found as the dihydrate, gypsum, $CaSO_4.2H_2O$ (monoclinic; r.d. 2.32). When heated, gypsum loses water at 128°C to give the hemihydrate, $2CaSO_4.H_2O$, better known as Plaster of Paris. Calcium sulphate is sparingly soluble in water and is a cause of permanent hardness of water due to impurities. It is used in the manufacture of certain paints, ceramics, and paper. The naturally occurring forms are used in the manufacture of sulphuric acid.

calgon It is a trade name for a water-softening agent. (hardness of water.)

caliche It is an impure form of $NaNO_3$.

californium Symbol Cf. It is a 'f' block element, radioactive metallic transuranic element belonging to the actinoids; having a.n. 98; mass number of the most stable isotope 251 (half-life about 700 years). Nine isotopes are known; californium-252 is an intense neutron source, which makes it useful in neutron activation analysis and potentially useful as a radiation source in medicine. The element was first produced by G.T. Seaborg and associates in 1950.

calomel half cell (calomel electrode) It is a type of half cell in which the electrode is mercury coated with calomel (HgCl) and the electrolyte is a solution of potassium chloride (which is a strong electrolyte) and saturated calomel. The standard electrode potential is –0.2415 volt (25°C). In the calomel half cell the reactions are

$$HgCl(s) \rightleftharpoons Hg^+(aq) + Cl^-(aq)$$
$$Hg^+(aq) + e \rightleftharpoons Hg(s)$$

The overall reaction is

$$HgCl(s) + e \rightleftharpoons Hg(s) + Cl^-(aq)$$

This is equivalent to a $Cl_2(g)/Cl^-(aq)$ half cell in which the pressure is the dissociation pressure of HgCl.

calor gas It is a mixture of *hydrocarbon* compounds which is used as a portable supply of *gas.* It is made up of mainly *propane* (C_3H_8) and *butane* (C_4H_{10}) and these *compounds* are stored in metallic bottles under *pressure.*

calorie The quantity of heat required to raise the temperature of 1 gram of water by 1°C (1 K). It is a C.G.S. unit and is now largely replaced by the joule, an SI unit. 1 calorie = 4.1868 joules.

calorific value It is the heat per unit mass produced by complete combustion of a given substance. Calorific values are used to express the energy values of fuels. Its units are megajoules per kilogram (MJ kg^{-1}). They are also used to measure the energy content of foodstuffs; i.e. the energy produced when the food is oxidized in the body. The units here are kilojoules per gram (kJ g^{-1}), although Calories (kilocalories) are often still used in nontechnical contexts. Calorific values are measured using a bomb calorimeter.

canada balsam A yellow-tinted resin used for mounting specimens in optical microscopy. Its optical properties are similar to that of glass.

Cannizzaro's reaction Two molecules of aldehyde or ketone having no α-hydrogen, in presence of base, undergo self oxidation-reduction reaction to yield one molecule of alcohol (reduced product) and one molecule of acid salt (oxidised product).

caproic acid, $C_6H_{12}O_2$ It is n-hexanoic acid. It is found in glycerides, in the milk of cows and goats, in palm oil and coconut oil.

carbohydrate They are the *organic* compounds which contain the *elements, carbon, hydrogen* and *oxygen* only. Their formulae are always of the form: $C_x(H_2O)_y$, e.g. *sugars* such as *glucose* ($C_6H_{12}O_6$), *sucrose* ($C_{12}H_{22}O_{11}$) and ribose ($C_5H_{10}O_5$) and *polymers* such as *starch* $(C_6H_{10}O_5)_n$ and *cellulose* $(C_6H_{10}O_5)_n$.

carbon Symbol C. A nonmetallic element belonging to group IV of the periodic table, a.n. 6; r.a.m. 12.011; m.p.~ 3550°C; b.p.~4289°C. Carbon has two main allotropic forms (*See* allotropy).

Diamond is a precious stone and (r.d. 3.52) occurs naturally and small amounts can be produced synthetically. It is extremely hard and has highly refractive crystals. The hardness of diamond results from the covalent crystal structure, in which each carbon atom is linked by covalent bonds to four others situated at the corners of a tetrahedron. The C—C bond length is 0.154 nm and the bond angle is 109.5°.

Graphite (r.d. 2.25) the other allotrope, is a soft black slippery substance (sometimes called *black lead or plumbago).* It occurs naturally and can also be made by the Acheson process. In graphite the carbon atoms are arranged in layers, in which each carbon atom is surrounded by three others to which it is bound by single or double bonds. The layers are held together by very weak forces of attraction, van der Waals' forces. The carbon-carbon bond length in the layers is 0.142 nm and the layers are 0.34 nm apart. Graphite is a good conductor of heat and electricity. It has a variety of uses including electrical contacts, high-temperature equipment, and as a solid lubricant. Graphite mixed with clay is the 'lead' in pencils (hence its alternative name). There are also several amorphous forms of carbon, such as carbon black and charcoal.

There are two stable isotopes of carbon (proton numbers 12 and 13) and four radioactive ones (10, 11, 14, 15). Carbon-14 is used in carbon dating. Chemically, carbon is unique in its ability to form many compounds containing chains and rings of carbon atoms.

carbonate These are the salt of carbonic acid containing the carbonate ion, CO_3^{2-}. The free ion has a plane triangular structure. Metal carbonates (M_2CO_3) may be ionic or may contain covalent metal-carbonate bonds (complex carbonates) via one or two oxygen atoms. The carbonates of the alkali metals are all soluble but other carbonates are insoluble; they all react with mineral acids to release carbon dioxide.

carbon cycle The circulation of element carbon and its compounds in nature is known as carbon cycle. Most of this cycle is the result of the metabolic processes of living organisms.

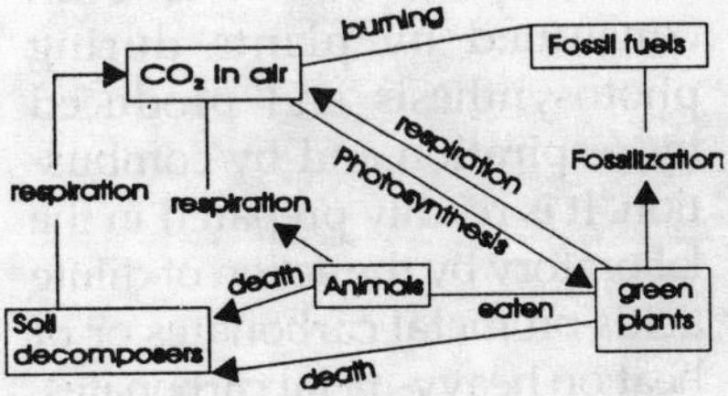

carbon dating The method of telling the age of once-living material is called carbon dating. *Carbon* has a *radioactive* isotope ($^{14}_{6}C$) and the atmospheric *carbon dioxide* contains a small constant proportion of this *isotope.* All carbon *compounds* in living tissue contain this carbon-14 isotope in the same constant proportion. When an animal or plant dies, however, the proportion falls at a known rate. It falls because plants no longer take in the isotope through *photosynthesis* and animals no longer take in the isotope by eating plants. All the time the isotope is decaying. The *half-life* of $^{14}_{6}C$ is 5730 years. By measuring the amount of radioactivity in a dead material it is possible to estimate the age of the material. The technique is used by archaeologists.

carbon dioxide It is a colourless, odourless gas, CO_2, soluble in water, ethanol, and acetone; d. 1.977 g dm^{-3} (0°C); m.p.–56.6°C; b.p. –78.5°C. It occurs in the atmosphere (0.03% by volume) but has a short residence time in this phase as it is both consumed by plants during photosynthesis and produced by respiration and by combustion. It is readily prepared in the laboratory by the action of dilute acids on metal carbonates or of heat on heavy-metal carbonates. Carbon dioxide is a by-product from the manufacture of lime and from fermentation processes. It turns lime water milky.

Carbon dioxide has a small liquid range and liquid carbon dioxide is produced only at high pressures. The molecule CO_2 is linear with each oxygen making a double bond to the carbon. Chemically, it is unreactive and will not support combustion. It dissolves in water to give carbonic acid.

Large quantities of solid carbon dioxide (*dry ice*) are used in processes requiring large-scale refrigeration. It is also used in fire extinguishers as a desirable alternative to water for most fires, and as a constituent of medical gases as it promotes exhalation. It is also used in carbonated drinks.

The level of carbon dioxide in the atmosphere has been the subject of much environmental controversy as it is argued that extensive burning of fossil fuels will increase the overall CO_2 concentration and then, by the greenhouse effect, increase atmospheric temperatures and cause climatic modification. The full significance of all the factors remains to be established.

carbon disulphide It is also known as carbon disulphide. A colourless highly refractive liquid, CS_2, slightly soluble in water and soluble in ethanol and ether; r.d. 1.261; m.p. –110°C; b.p. 46.3°C. Pure carbon disulphide has an ethereal odour but the commercial product is contaminated with a variety of other sulphur compounds and has a most unpleasant smell. It was previously manufactured by heating a mixture of wood, sulphur, and charcoal; modern processes use natural gas and sulphur. Carbon disulphide is an excellent solvent for oils, waxes, rubber, sulphur, and phosphorus, but its use is decreasing because of its high toxicity and its flammability. It is used for the preparation of xanthates in the manufacture of viscose yarns.

carbon fibres They are the fibres of carbon in which the carbon has an oriented crystal structure. Carbon fibres are made by heating textile fibres and are used in strong composite materials for use at high temperatures.

carbonic anhydrase It is an enzyme which catalyses the reaction between carbon dioxide and water.

carbonium ion It is an organic ion with a positive charge on a carbon atom; i.e. an ion of the type R_3C^+. Carbonium ions are intermediates in certain type of organic reaction (e.g. Williamson's synthesis).

carbonize (carburize) It is a process of changing an organic compound into carbon by heating, or to coat something with carbon in this way.

C=O	carbon monoxide
O=C=O	carbon dioxide
O=C=C=C=O	tricarbon dioxide (carbon suboxide)

Oxides of carbon

carbon monoxide A colourless, odourless gas having molecular formula CO and is sparingly soluble in water and soluble in ethanol and benzene; d. 1.25 g dm.$^{-3}$ (0°C); m.p. –199°C; b.p. –191.5°C. It is flammable and highly toxic. In the laboratory it can be made by the dehydration of methanoic acid (formic acid) using concentrated sulphuric acid. Industrially it is produced by the oxidation of natural gas (methane) or (formerly) by the water-gas reaction. It is formed by the incomplete combustion of carbon and is present in car-exhaust gases.

It is a neutral oxide, which burns in air to give carbon dioxide, and is a good reducing agent, used in a number of metallurgical processes. It has the interesting chemical property of forming a range of transition metal carbonyls, e.g. $Ni(CO)_4$. Carbon monoxide is able to use vacant *p*=orbitals in bonding with metals; the stabilization of low oxidation states, including the zero state, is a consequence of this. This also accounts for its toxicity, which is due to the binding of the CO to the iron in haemoglobin, thereby blocking the uptake of oxygen.

carbonyl chloride (phosgene) A highly poisonous, colourless gas, $COCl_2$ 'with an odour of freshly cut hay. It is used in organic chemistry as a chlorinating agent, and was formerly used as a war gas.

carbonyl compound A compound

containing the carbonyl group >C = O. Aldehydes, ketones, and carboxylic acids are examples of organic carbonyl compounds. Inorganic carbonyls are complexes in which carbon monoxide has coordinated to a metal atom or ion, as in nickel carbonyl, $Ni(CO)_4$., where they act as ligands.

carboxylic acid An *organic acid* with the *formula* R—COOH, where 'R' is an aryl or alkyl group.

carboxy haemoglobin CO is poisonous because it combines with the haemoglobin in the blood to form carboxy haemoglobin. It is a complex molecule.

carcinogen It is an agent that produces cancer, e.g. tobacco smoke, certain industrial chemicals, and ionizing radiation (such as X-rays and ultraviolet rays).

carius method It is a method of determining the amount of sulphur and halogens in an organic compound, by heating the compound in a sealed tube with silver nitrate in concentrated nitric acid. The compound is decomposed and silver sulphide and halides are precipitated, separated, and weighed.

carnallite It is a mineral KC1. $MgC1_2.6H_2O$.

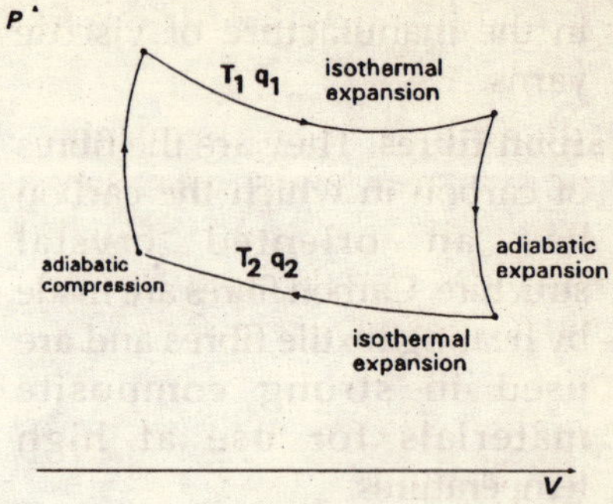

Carnot cycle

Carnot cycle The most efficient cycle of operations for a reversible heat engine is known as Carnot cycle. Published in 1824 by the French physicist N.L.S. Carnot (1746—1832), it consists of four operations on the working substance in the engine:

(i) Isothermal expansion at thermodynamic temperature T_1 with heat Q_1 taken in.

(ii) Adiabatic expansion with a fall of temperature to T_2.

(iii) Isothermal compression at temperature T_2 with heat Q_2 given out.

(iv) Adiabatic compression with a rise of temperature back to T_1.

According to the *Carnot principle*, the efficiency of any reversible heat engine depends only on the temperature range through which it works, rather than the properties of the working substances. In any reversible engine, the efficiency (η) is the ratio of the work done *(w)* to the heat input (Q_1). i.e. $\eta = W/Q_1$. As, according to the first law of thermodynamics (also known as law of conservation of energy) $W=Q_1-Q_2$, it follows that $\eta=(Q_1-Q_2)/Q_1$. As the system is reversible, $Q_1/Q_2=T_1/T_2$, therefore $\eta=(T_1-T_2)/T_1$. For maximum efficiency T_1 should be as high as possible and T_2 as low as possible.

carnotite A radioactive mineral consisting of hydrated uranium potassium vanadate, $K_2(UO_2)_2(VO_4)_2 \cdot nH_2O$. Its colour varies from bright yellow to lemon or greenish-yellow. It is a source of uranium, radium, and vanadium. The chief occurrences are in the Colorado Plateau, USA; Radium Hill, Australia; and Katanga, Zaire.

carotene It is member of a class of carotenoid pigments. Examples are β-carotene and lycopene, which colour carrot roots and ripe tomato fruits respectively. α- and β-carotene yield vitamin A when they are broken down during animal digestion.

carotenoid Any of a group of yellow, orange, red, or brown plant pigments chemically related to terpenes. Carotenoids are responsible for the characteristic colour of many plant organs, such as ripe tomatoes, carrots, and autumn leaves. They also function in the light reactions of photosynthesis.

carron oil It is a mixture of vegetable oil (cotton seed or olive) with lime water. It is useful in treatment of burns.

cascade process Any process that takes place in a number of steps, usually because the single step is too inefficient to produce the desired result is called cascade process. For example, in various uranium-enrichment processes the separation of the desired isotope is only poorly achieved in a single stage; to achieve better separation the process has to be repeated a number of times, in a series, with the enriched fraction of one stage being fed to the succeeding stage for further enrichment. Another example of cascade process is that operating in a cascade liquefier.

cast iron It is an impure form of iron containing about 2.5% carbon as impurity. It is used in making stoves, pipes, radiators, toys, gutter pipes and lamp posts.

catalysis The process of changing the rate of a chemical reaction by the use of a catalyst is called catalysis.

catalyst It is a substance which may increase or decrease the rate of a reaction without being consumed in it. (i.e. they do not go for any permanent chemical change). Catalysts that have the same phase as the reactants are *homogeneous catalysts* (e.g. enzymes in biochemical reactions). Those that have a different phase are *heterogeneous catalysts* (e.g. metals or oxides used in many industrial gas reactions). The catalyst provides an alternative pathway by which the reaction can proceed, in which the activation energy is lower. It thus increases the rate at which the reaction comes to equilibrium, although it does not alter the position of the equilibrium. The catalyst itself takes part in the reaction and consequently may undergo physical change (e.g. conversion into powder). In certain circumstances, very small quantities of catalyst can speed up very large reactions. Some catalysts are also highly specific in the type of reaction they catalyse, particularly in biochemical reactions.

catalyser It is a part of the exhaust system of modern *petrol* engines. A *platinum/rhodium catalyst* in a honeycomb structure converts carbon monoxide (CO), nitric oxide (NO) and unburnt *hydrocarbon* compounds from the *petrol* into *carbon dioxide* (CO_2), *nitrogen* (N_2) and nitrous oxide (N_2O). This is one way of reducing the amount of air *pollution* caused by the internal combustion engine.

catechol *See* 1,2-dihydroxybenzene.

catenation The formation of chains of atoms in chemical compounds is known as catenation.

cathetometer It is a telescope or microscope fitted with cross-wires in the eyepiece and mounted so that it can slide along a graduated scale. Cathetometers are used for accurate measurement of lengths without mechanical contact. The microscope type is often called a *travelling microscope* which is used to see very small objects.

cathode The negatively charged pole in a *battery* or *electrolysis cell* is called cathode. Positively charged *ions (cations)* are attracted to the cathode during *electrolysis*. They gain electrons at the cathode.

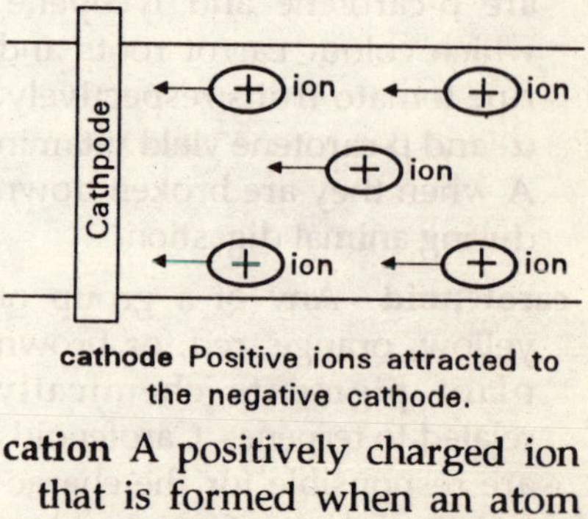

cathode Positive ions attracted to the negative cathode.

cation A positively charged ion that is formed when an atom loses one or more electrons e.g. Na^+, K^+, NH_4^+, Mg^{2+}.

caustic Describing a substance that is strongly alkaline. For example, Caustic Soda.

celestine A mineral form of strontium sulphate, $SrSO_4$.

cell 1. A device for obtaining electrical *energy* from chemical *reactions*. It is also called a *battery*.

celluloid A transparent highly flammable substance made from cellulose nitrate with a camphor plasticizer. It was formerly widely used as a thermoplastic material, especially for film. However, this use is now discontinued owing to the inflammability of celluloid.

cellulose A *carbohydrate* which is also a *polymer*. It is made up of *glucose monomers*. The *formula* is $(C_6H_{10}O_5)_n$ and is the material from which cell walls of plants are made. Cellulose is useful to us in several ways. It is used in manufacture of *paper* and *rayon*.

cellulose ethanoate (cellulose acetate) A compound prepared by treating cellulose (cotton linters or wood pulp) with a mixture of ethanoic anhydride, ethanoic acid, and concentrated sulphuric acid. Cellulose in the cotton is ethanoylated and when the resulting solution is treated with water, cellulose ethanoate forms as a flocculent white mass. It is used in manufacture of lacquers, nonshatterable glass, varnishes, and as a fibre.

celsius scale It is a temperature scale in which the fixed points are the temperatures at standard pressure of ice in equilibrium with water (0°C) and water in equilibrium with steam (100°C) $H_2O(l) \rightleftharpoons H_2O(g)$. The scale, between these two temperatures, is divided in 100 degrees. The degree Celsius (°C) is equal in magnitude to the kelvin (°C + 273). This scale was formerly known as the *centigrade scale;* the name was officially changed in 1948 to avoid confusion with a hundredth part of a grade. It is named after the Swedish astronomer Anders Celsius (1701-44), who devised the inverted form of this scale (ice point 100°, steam point 0°) in 1742.

cement It is a substance made by heating *chalk* or *limestone* together and then powdering the product.

The result is a mixture of *calcium* silicate and calcium aluminate, which is usually of grey colour. When *water* is added a corrosive *mixture* is produced which is *alkaline*. Cement is very important *adhesive* material in the building industry:

cement + sand + water → *mortar* (which is very hard substance)

cement + sand + gravel + water → *concrete*

cementation Any metallurgical process in which the surface of a metal is impregnated by some other substance, especially an obsolete process for making steel by heating bars of wrought iron to red heat for several days in a bed of charcoal is known as cementation. It results in hardening.

centi- Symbol c. A prefix used in the metric system to denote one hundredth. For example, 0.01 metre = 1 centimetre (cm).

centrifuge It is a device in which solid or liquid particles of different densities are separated by rotating them in a tube in a horizontal circle. The denser particles tend to move along the length of the tube to a greater radius of rotation, displacing the lighter particles to the other end.

ceramic It is an *inorganic* material having following properties:

(a) Great hardness and resistance to water;

(b) Very high *melting* point; because of strong force of attraction between various atoms;

(c) Chemically *inert*.

Ceramic materials include, *glass, enamel,* pottery, *clay* products, *abrasive* and *refractory* material.

ceresin It is a hard, brittle paraffin wax. It is used as a substitute for bees wax in paints and polishes.

cerium Symbol Ce. It belongs to '*f*'' block (lanthanides). A silvery metallic element; a.n. 58; r.a.m. 140.12; r.d. 6.77 (20°C); m.p. 798°C; b.p. 3433°C. It occurs in allanite, bastnasite, cerite, and monazite. Four isotopes occur naturally: cerium –136, –138, –140 and –142; fifteen radioisotopes have been identified. Cerium is used in mischmetal, a rare-earth metal containing 25% cerium, for use in lighter flints. The oxide is used in the glass industry. It was discovered by M.H. Klaproth in 1803.

cermet A composite material consisting of a ceramic in combination with a sintered metal, it is used when a high resistance to temperature, corrosion, and abrasion is needed.

cerussite An ore of lead consisting of lead carbonate, $PbCO_3$. It is usually of secondary origin, formed by the weathering of galena. Pure cerussite is white but the mineral may be grey due to the presence of impurities. It forms well-shaped orthorhombic crystals. It is found in the USA, Spain, and SW Africa.

cetane number It is a number that provides a measure of the ignition characteristics of a Diesel fuel when it is burnt in a standard Diesel engine. It is the percentage of cetane (hexadecane) in a mixture of cetane and 1-methylnaphthalene that has the same ignition characteristics as the fuel being tested. *Compare* octane number.

c.g.s. units A system of units based on the centimetre, gram and second. Derived from the metric system, it was badly adapted to use with thermal quantities (based on the inconsistently defined calorie) and with electrical quantities (in which two systems, based respectively on unit permittivity and unit permeability of free space, were used). c.g.s. units have now been replaced by SI units for scientific purposes.

chain A line of atoms of the same type in a molecule. In a *straight chain* the atoms are attached only to single atoms, not to groups. Propane, for example, is a straight-chain alkane, $CH_3CH_2CH_3$, with a chain of three carbon atoms. A *branched chain* is one in which there are side groups attached to the chain. Thus, 3-ethyloctane, $CH_3CH_2CH(C_2H_5)\ C_5H_{11}$, is a branched-chain alkane in which there is a *side chain* (C_2H_5) attached to the third carbon atom. A *closed chain* is a ring of atoms in a molecule; otherwise the molecule has an *open chain*.

chalk It is a rock which has been formed from the shells of marine animals. It is mainly *calcium carbonate* ($CaCO_3$). It is a softer rock than *limestone* thus its uses are limited.

change of phase (change of state) A change of matter in one physical state (solid, liquid, or gas) into another. The change is invariably accompanied by the evolution or absorption of energy, even if it takes place at constant temperature.

charcoal It is an allotropic form of carbon. It is an amorphous form and is a good adsorbent. It is used in removing colouring matter from syrups of sugar etc.

Charles Law At constant pressure, the volume of given mass of a gas is directly proportional to the absolute temperature.

$$V \propto T, \text{ where } T = 273 + t^\circ C$$

cheddite Any of a group of high explosives made from nitro compounds mixed with sodium or potassium chlorate.

chelates Such ligands which have two or more donor sites in the molecule can coordinate to form a ring complex which is called a *chelate* and such ligands are called *chelating ligands*. The process is called *Chelation*. They form the coordinate bonds which are shown by → (donor to acceptor) e.g. two molecules of ethylene diamine (en), $NH_2\ CH_2—CH_2\ NH_2$ forms a chelate ring with cupric ion (Cu^{2+}).

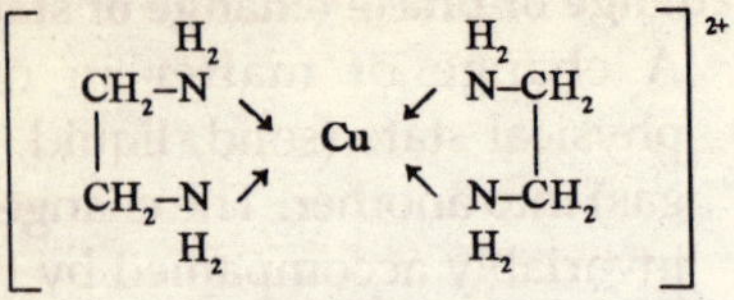

chemical combination The combination of elements to give compounds is known as chemical combination. There are three laws of chemical combination.

(a) The *law of constant composition* states that the proportions of the elements in a compound are always the same, no matter how the compound is made. It is also called the *law of constant proportions* or *definite proportions.*

(b) The *law of multiple proportions:* The law states that "when two elements A and B combine to form more than one compound, then the masses of B that combine with a fixed mass of A are in simple ratio to one another." For example, carbon forms two oxides. In one, 12 grams of carbon is combined with 16 grams of oxygen (CO); in the other 12g of carbon is combined with 32 grams of oxygen (CO_2). The oxygen masses combining with a fixed mass of carbon are in the ratio 16:32, i.e. 1:2.

(c) The *law of equivalent proportions:* According to this law, when two elements A and B each form a compound with a third element C, then a compound of A and B will contain A and B in the relative proportions in which they react with C. For example, sulphur and carbon both form compounds with hydrogen. In methane 12 g of carbon react with 4 g of hydrogen. In hydrogen sulphide, 32 g of sulphur react with 2 g of hydrogen (i.e. 64 g of S for 4 g of hydrogen). Sulphur and carbon form a compound in which the C:S ratio is 12:64 (i.e. CS_2). The law is sometimes called the law of *reciprocal proportions.*

chemical dating It is an absolute dating technique that depends on measuring the chemical composition of a specimen. Chemical dating can be used when the specimen is known to undergo slow chemical change at a known rate. For instance, phosphate in buried bones is slowly replaced by fluoride ions from the ground water. Measurement of the proportion of fluorine present gives a rough estimate of the time that the bones have been in the ground. Another, more accurate, method depends on the fact that amino acids in living organisms are L-optical isomers. After death, these racemize and the age of bones can be estimated by measuring the relative amounts of D-and L-amino acids present.

chemical energy It is the energy stored in an atom/molecule.

Chemical energy can be released by chemical reaction.

chemical equation It refers to a way of denoting a chemical reaction using the symbols for the participating particles (atoms, molecules, ions, etc.); for example,

$$xA + yB \rightarrow zC + wD$$

The single arrow is used for an irreversible reaction; double arrows ($\rightleftharpoons$) are used for reversible reactions, i.e. the reaction can occur in both the directions. When reactions involve different phases it is usual to put the phase in brackets after the symbol (s = solid; l = liquid; g = gas; aq = aqueous). The numbers *x, y, z,* and *w,* showing the relative numbers of molecules reacting, are called the *stoichiometric coefficients.* The sum of the coefficients of the reactants minus the sum of the coefficients of the products ($x + y - z - w$ in the example) is the *stoichiometric sum.* If this is zero the equation is balanced. Sometimes a generalized chemical equation is considered

$$v_i A$$

In this case the reaction can be written $\Sigma v_i \; A_i = 0$, where the convention is that stoichiometric coefficients are positive for reactants and negative for products. The stoichiometric sum is Σv_i.

chemical equilibrium A reversible chemical reaction in which the concentrations of reactants and products do not change with time because the system is in thermodynamic equilibrium. For example, the reversible reaction

$$3H_2 + N_2 \rightleftharpoons 2NH_3$$

is in chemical equilibrium when the rate of the *forward reaction*

$$3H_2 + N_2 \rightarrow 2NH_3$$

is equal to the rate of the *back reaction*

$$2NH_3 \rightarrow 3H_2 + N_2$$

chemical fossil Any of various organic compounds found in ancient geological strata which appear to be biological in origin and are assumed to indicate that life existed when the rocks were formed. The presence of chemical fossils in Precambrian strata indicates that life existed over 3000 million years ago.

chemical kinetics It is the branch of chemistry that deals with the speed or rate of reaction.

chemical potential Symbol μ. For a given component in a mixture, the coefficient $\delta G/\delta n$, where *G* is the Gibbs free energy and *n* the amount of substance of the component. The chemical potential is the change in Gibbs free energy with respect to change in amount of the component, with pressure, temperature, and amounts of other components being constant. Components are in equilibrium if their chemical potentials are equal.

chemical reaction It is a change in which one or more chemical elements or compounds (the *reactants*) form new compounds (the *products*). All reactions are to some extent *reversible;* i.e. the products can also react to give the original reactants. However, in many cases the extent of this back reaction is negligibly small, and the reaction is regarded as *irreversible*. It also refers to number of effective collision between the atoms of reactants.

chemical reactivity It is the tendency of an element to lose or gain electrons in a chemical reaction.

chemistry The study of the elements and the compounds they form. It is mainly concerned with effects that depend on the outer electrons in atoms. *See* biochemistry; geochemistry; inorganic chemistry; organic chemistry; physical chemistry.

chirality The property of existing in optically active forms. Carbon has all different groups attached to it.

chloric acid Any of the oxoacids of chlorine: chloric(I) acid, chloric(III) acid, chloric(V) acid, and chloric(VII) acid. The term is commonly used without specification of the oxidation state of chlorine to mean chloric(V) acid, $HClO_3$.

chloric(III) acid It is also known as chlorous acid, a pale-yellow acid known only in solution, $HClO_2$. It is formed by the reaction of chlorine dioxide and water and is a weak acid and an oxidizing agent.

chloric(VII) acid, $HClO_4$ It is called perchloric acid. It is hygroscopic in nature and a strong oxidising agent.

chlorination Treatment with chlorine; for instance, the use of chlorine to disinfect water.

chlorine Symbol Cl. It belongs to '*p*' block. A halogen element; a.n. 17; r.a.m. 35.453; d. 3.214 g dm^{-3}; m.p. −100.98°C; b.p. −34.6°C. It is a poisonous greenish-yellow gas and occurs widely in nature as sodium chloride in seawater and as halite (NaCl), carnallite ($KCl.MgCl_2.6H_2O$), and sylvite (KCl). It is manufactured by the electrolysis of brine and also obtained in the Downs process which is used for making sodium. It has many applications, including the chlorination of drinking water, bleaching, and the manufacture of a large number of organic chemicals.

It reacts directly with many elements and compounds and is a strong oxidizing agent.

Chlorine compounds contain the element in the 1, 3, 5, and 7 oxidation states. It was discovered by Karl Seele in 1774 and Humphry Davy confirmed it as an element in 1810.

chlorine dioxide A yellowish-red explosive gas, ClO_2; d. 3.09 gdm^{-3}; m.p. –59.5°C; b.p. 9.9°C. It is soluble in cold water but decomposed by hot water to give chloric (VII) acid, chlorine, and oxygen. Because of its high reactivity, chlorine dioxide is best prepared by the reaction of sodium chlorate and moist oxalic acid at 90°C-100°C, as the product is then diluted by liberated carbon dioxide. Commercially the gas is produced by the reaction of sulphuric acid containing chloride ions (Cl^-) with sulphur dioxide (SO_2). Chlorine dioxide is widely used as a bleach in flour milling and in wood pulping and also used for purifying water.

chlorite A chlorate(III) salt; i.e. a salt of chloric(III) acid (chlorous acid).

chlorobenzene, C_6H_5Cl

$$C_6H_6 + Cl_2 \xrightarrow[\text{Dark}]{FeCl_3} \underset{\text{(Chlorobenzene)}}{C_6H_5Cl} + HCl.$$

It is used in the manufacture of DDT, phenol and aniline.

2-chlorobuta-1, 3-diene (chloroprene) A colourless liquid chlorinated diene, $CH_2{:}CClCH{:}CH_2$; r.d. 0.96; b.p. 59°C. It is polymerized to make synthetic rubbers (e.g. neoprene).

chloroethene (or vinyl chloride) $CH_2 = CHCl$

$$CH \equiv CH + HCl \xrightarrow[Hg^{2+}]{340K} CH_2 = CHCl$$

The *monomer* from which *poly(chloroethene)* or polyvinylchloride (PVC) *is made.*

chloromethane (methyl chloride) A colourless flammable gas, CH_3Cl; r.d. 0.916; m.p. –97°C; b.p. –24°C. A haloalkane, made by direct chlorination of methane and used as a local anaesthetic and refrigerant.

chlorophyll It is a green colour pigment in plants which helps in the process of photosynthesis. The chlorophyll molecule is the principal site of light absorption in the light reactions of photosynthesis. It is a magnesium-containing porophyrin, chemically related to cytochrome and haemoglobin.

chloroplatinic acid (platinic chloride, H_2PtCl_6) A reddish compound prepared by dissolving platinum in aqua regia. When crystallized from the resulting solution, crystals of the hexahydrate ($H_2PtCl_6.6H_2O$) are obtained. The crystals are needle-shaped and deliquesce on exposure to moist air. Chloroplatinic acid is a relatively strong acid, which gives rise to the family of chloroplatinates.

cholesterol A sterol found in animal tissues and also in some higher plants and algae. It can exist as a free sterol or esterified with a long-chain fatty acid. Cholesterol is absorbed through the intestine or manufactured in the liver. It serves principally as a constituent of blood plasma lipoproteins and of the lipid-protein complexes that form cell membranes. It is also important as a precursor of various steroids, especially the bile acids, sex hormones, and adrenocorticoid hormones. The derivative 7-dehydrocho-lesterol is converted to vitamin D_3 by the action of sunlight on skin. Increased levels of dietary and blood cholesterol have been associated with *atherosclerosis,* a condition in which lipids accumulate on the inner walls of arteries and eventually obstruct blood flow. The increase in its percentage may be fatal to life.

chromatography It is a technique used to separate or analyse complex mixtures. That is why it is regarded as one of the method of separation. A number of related techniques exist; the most important are *column chromatography, paper chromatography, thinlayer chromatography, gas chromatography,* and *ion exchange*. These chromatographic techniques require a sample to be placed at one end of a column of a solid or a liquid, which is held on an inert packing material. These columns are known as the stationary phase. A liquid or a gas, known as the mobile phase, is passed through the column. The components of the sample will dissolve in, and be carried along by, the mobile phase. Some of the components, however, will tend to cling to the stationary phase more than others and their progress through the column will be slower. The mixture will separate as the solvent moves through the stationary phase. In chromatography used for purification, separated components are collected as they emerge from the end of the column. For analysis purposes, however, the different components can often be identified simply by comparing their rate of progress through the column with that of known standards.

Components of the mixture are held back by the stationary phase either by adsorption (e.g. on the surface of alumina) or because they dissolve in it (e.g. in the moisture within chromatography paper).

chromatogram It is a volume/ speed curve which illustrates a chromatographic separation.

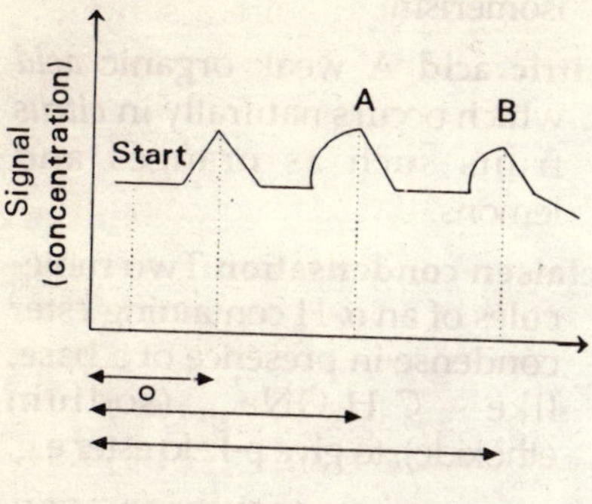

Typical chromatogram

chrome iron ore A mixed iron-chromium oxide, having formula $FeO.Cr_2O_3$. It is used to make ferrochromium for chromium steels.

chrome red A basic lead chromate, $PbO.PbCrO_4$. It is used as a red pigment.

chromium Symbol Cr. a.n. 24. It belongs to *'d'* block and has a very high melting point. A transition metal that occurs naturally as chromite ($FeO.Cr_2O_3$), large deposits of which are found in Zimbabwe. The ore is converted into sodium dichromate(VI) and then reduced with carbon to chromium(III) oxide and finally to metallic chromium with aluminium. Chromium is used in strong alloy steels and stainless steel and for plating articles. It is a hard silvery metal that resists corrosion at normal temperatures. It reacts slowly with dilute hydrochloric and sulphuric acids to give hydrogen and blue chromium(II) compounds, which quickly oxidize in air to green chromium(III) ions. The oxidation states are +6 in chromates (CrO_4^{2-}) and dichromates ($Cr_2O_7^{2-}$), +3 (the most stable), and +2. In acidic solutions the yellow chromate(VI) ion changes to the orange dichromate (VI) ion. Dichromates are used as oxidizing agents in the laboratory; for example as a test for sulphur dioxide and to oxidize alcohols. Symbol: Cr; m.p. 1900°C; b.p. 2640°C; r.d. 7.19; r.a.m. 52.00.

chromium(II) oxide A black insoluble powder, CrO. Chromium(II) oxide is prepared by oxidizing chromium amalgam with air. At high temperatures it is reduced to the metal by hydrogen.

chromium(VI) oxide, CrO_3 It is chromic anhydride and is used as an oxidising agent in volumetric analysis. It is also used as disinfectant with glacial acetic acid.

chromium potassium sulphate A red crystalline solid, having molecular formula $K_2SO_4.Cr_2(SO_4)_3.24H_2O$; r.d. 1.91. It is used as a mordant. *See also* alums.

chromophore It is a group causing colouration in a dye. Chromophores are generally groups of atoms having delocalized electrons.

chromyl chloride (CrO_2Cl_2) A dark red covalent liquid prepared either by distilling a dry mixture of potassium dichromate and sodium chloride with concentrated sulphuric acid or by the action of concentrated sulphuric acid on chromium (coordination number VI) oxide dissolved in concentrated hydrochloric acid. Chromyl chloride is hydrolysed by water and with solutions of alkalis it undergoes immediate hydrolysis to produce chromate ions. It is used as an oxidizing agent in organic chemistry. Chromyl chloride oxidizes methyl groups at the ends of aromatic side chains to aldehyde groupings (Etard's reaction).

cinchonine, $C_{19}H_{22}ON$ It is an optically active solid having a structure similar to quinine. (The only difference being absence of methoxy group.)

cinnabar A bright red mineral form of mercury(II) sulphide, HgS, crystallizing in the hexagonal system; the principal ore of mercury. It is deposited in veins and impregnations near recent volcanic rocks and hot springs. It is chiefly found in Spain, Italy, and Yugoslavia.

cis Designating an isomer with groups that are adjacent i.e. on same side *see.* geometrical isomerism.

citric acid A weak organic *acid* which occurs naturally in *citrus* fruits such as oranges and lemons.

claisen condensation Two molecules of an α-H containing ester condense in presence of a base, like C_2H_5ONa (sodium ethoxide), to give p-keto ester e.g.

$$2CH_3COOR \rightarrow CH_3COCH_2COOR + ROH$$

Clapeyron-Clausius equation It is a thermodynamic equation that is applicable to a two-phase equilibrium for a pure substance. It is

$$\frac{dP}{dT} = \frac{\Delta H_v}{T\Delta V}$$

where P = pressure
T = absolute temperature
ΔH_v = molar latent heat of vapourisation
ΔV = change in volume.

If one of the phase is vapour then the above equation can be written as $l_n.P.=C-\frac{\Delta H_v}{RT}$

where C = constant for a particular substance
and R = gas constant. (8.314 J/mol/K)

cleavage The splitting of a crystal along planes of atoms, to form smooth surfaces.

close packing It is the packing of spheres so as to occupy the minimum amount of space. In a single plane, each sphere is surrounded by six close neighbours in a hexagonal arrangement. The spheres in the second plane fit into depressions in the first layer, and so on. Each sphere has 12 other touching spheres. There are two types of close packing. In *hexagonal close packing* the spheres in the third layer are directly over those in the first, etc., and the arrangement of planes is ABAB....In *cubic close packing* the spheres in the third layer occupy a different set of depressions than those in the first. The arrangement is AB-CABC as in cubic crystals.

closed system In such a system only energy can be exchanged between the system and the surroundings. There is no exchange of mass between system and surroundings.

coagulation The process in which colloidal particles come together to form larger masses. Coagulation can be brought about by adding ions to neutralize the charges stabilizing the colloid. Ions with a high charge are particularly effective (e.g. alum, containing Al^{3+}, is used in styptics to coagulate blood). Another example of ionic coagulation is in the formation of river deltas, which occurs when colloidal silt particles in rivers are coagulated by ions in sea water. Heating is another way of coagulating certain colloids. e.g. coagulation of albumin due to boiling of an egg.

coal Its main component is carbon. The carbon content of various varieties of coal is as Anthracite 90%.

coal gas It is a fuel gas produced by the destructive distillation of coal. In the late-19th and early-20th centuries coal gas was a major source of energy and was made by heating coal in the absence of air in local gas works. Typically, it contained hydrogen (50%), methane (35%), and carbon monoxide (8%). By-products of the process were coal tar and coke. The use of this type of gas declined with the increasing availability of natural gas, although since the early 1970s interest has developed in using coal in making SNG.

cobalt Symbol Co, a.n. 27 r.a.m. 58.93; r.d. 8.9; m.p 1495°C; b.p. 2870

A *transition metal* belongs to '*d*' block and its atomic number is 27. It is a magnetic element and is used alloyed with *iron* in the manufacture of magnets. The radioactive *isotope* ${}_{27}^{60}Co$ emits *gamma rays* and it is used in the treatment of cancer. Cobalt(II) chloride is blue when *anhydrous* and pink when *hydrated*, and so the *compound* is used as a test for the presence of *water*.

cobalt(II) oxide A pink solid, having molecular formula CoO; cubic; r.d. 6.45; m.p. 1795°C. The addition of potassium hydroxide to a solution of cobalt(II) nitrate gives a bluish-violet precipitate, which on boiling is converted to pink impure cobalt(II) hydroxide. On heating this in the absence of air, cobalt(II) oxide is formed. The compound is readily oxidized in air to form tricobalt tetroxide, Co_3O_4. It is readily reduced by hydrogen to the metal.

cobalt(III) oxide (cobalt sesquioxide) A black grey insoluble solid, having molecular formula Co_2O_3; hexagonal or rhombic; r.d. 5.18; decomposes at 895°C. It is produced by the ignition of cobalt nitrate; the product, however, never has the composition corresponding exactly to cobalt(III) oxide. On heating it readily forms Co_3O_4, which contains both Co(II) and Co(III), and is easily reduced to the metal by hydrogen. Cobalt(III) oxide dissolves in strong acid to give unstable brown solutions of trivalent cobalt salts. Cobalt(II) salts are formed by reaction of cobalt(III) oxide with dilute acids.

coenzyme It is also known as cofactor, it refers to a substance that is needed along with the enzyme for an enzyme catalysed reaction to occur.

coherent units A system or subset of units (e.g. SI units) in which the derived units are obtained by multiplying or dividing together base units, with no numerical factor involved.

coke It is the material left behind when the *volatile* compounds have been removed from *coal.* It contains over 80% *carbon.* It was made during the production of coal gas but now is made in *coke ovens* from special *coking coal.* Coke is used to make *carbon monoxide* in the *blast furnace* and is an important (smokeless) *fuel.*

colchicine An alkaloid, derived from the autumn crocus. *Colchicum autumnale.* It inhibits cell division. Colchicine is used in genetics, cytology, and plant-breeding research, and also in cancer therapy to inhibit cell division.

collagen An insoluble fibrous protein occurring in the connective tissue of skin, tendons, and bone. The polypeptide chains of collagen (containing the amino acids glycine and proline predominantly) form triple-stranded helical coils that are bound together to form fibrils, which have great strength and limited elasticity. Collagen accounts for over 30% of the total body protein of mammals.

colligative properties These are the properties which depend only on the number of particles of solute present in solution and do not depend on the nature of solute present in solution e.g.

(i) Relative lowering of vapour pressure, $\frac{\Delta P}{P_A^{\circ}}$.

(ii) Elevation of boiling point, ΔT_b.

(iii) Depression of freezing point, ΔT_f

(iv) Osmotic pressure, π.

collimator An arrangement for producing a parallel beam of radiation for use in a spectrometer or other instrument. A system of lenses and slits is utilized.

collodion A thin film of cellulose nitrate made by dissolving the cellulose nitrate in ethanol or ethoxyethane, coating the surface, and evaporating the solvent.

colloids These are the substances which do not pass through membrane in their dissolved state e.g. starch, glue, gelatin etc.

colorimetric analysis It is the quantitative analysis of solutions by estimating their colour, e.g. by comparing it with the colours of standard solutions.

combustion It is the process in which substances undergo a chemical reaction with oxygen. Heat and light are generally produced during combustion.

complex ion A *cation* (e.g. *metal* ions or *hydrogen* ions) which is bonded to one or more small *molecules* by a *coordinate bond*, *ammonium ion* and the *oxonium ion*, are the examples of complex ions, where the *lone pair of electrons* on the *nitrogen* and *oxygen* atoms forms the bond.

Transition metal ions form a large number of complex ions because they can easily accept the donated *electron* pairs.

complexometric analysis A type of volumetric analysis in which the reaction involves the formation of an inorganic complex is called complexometric analysis.

compound It is a substance formed by the combination of elements in fixed proportions. The formation of a compound involves a chemical reaction; i.e. there is a change in the configuration of the valence electrons of the atoms. Compounds, unlike mixtures, cannot be separated by physical means.

concentrated It is a solution having a relatively high concentration of solute.

concentration It is the amount of substance per unit volume in a solution. The unit is the mol dm^{-3}. *Mass concentration* is mass of solute per unit volume. *Molal concentration* is amount of substance per kilogram of solute.

condensation The change of a vapour or gas into a liquid. The change of phase is accompanied by the evolution of heat (sometimes referred as latent heat).

condensation polymers Polymers which are formed because of condensation reaction between monomer units are called condensation polymers, e.g. polyesters, polyamides etc.

condensation reaction A chemical reaction in which two molecules combine to form a larger molecule with elimination of a small molecule e.g. H_2O.

conductor It is a substance which allows heat or electricity to flow through it is known as good conductor of heat and electricity. An *electrical* conductor is a substance which will allow an electric *current* to flow through it. *Metals, solutions* which contain *ions,* and molten *ionic* compounds are conductors; all other substances are *insulators. Graphite* (a form of *carbon*) is a notable exception. Certain *metalloids* are *semiconductors.*

The term 'conductor' is also applied to substances which allow *heat energy* to flow through them. Metals are also good conductors of heat.

conductiometric titration A type of titration in which the electrical conductivity of the reaction mixture is continuously monitored as one reactant is added. The equivalence point is the point at which this undergoes a sudden change. This method is used for titrating coloured solutions, which cannot be used with normal indicators.

condy's fluid A mixture of calcium and potassium permanganates (manganate (VII)). It is used as an antiseptic.

configuration 1. The arrangement of electrons around the nucleus of an atom. *see* electronic configuration.

2. The arrangement of atoms or groups in a molecule in space.

conformations These are the different spatial arrangements that arise because of the rotation about a carbon-carbon single bond. Eclipsed and staggered forms are the two extreme forms of ethane.

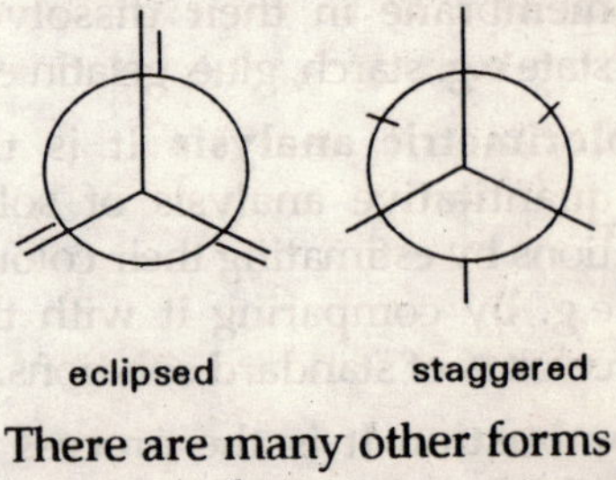

eclipsed staggered

There are many other forms in between these two extremes which are known as skew forms.

In eclipsed form the similar hydrogen atoms attached to the carbon atoms eclipse each other and repulsion between them is maximum.

In staggered conformation the similar, hydrogen atoms attached to two carbon atoms are at maximum distance apart and the force of repulsion between them is minimum.

congeners Elements that belong to the same group in the periodic table.

congo red It is a dark red bisazo dye which is used for dyeing cotton. It has N-N linkage.

conjugated Describing double or triple bonds in a molecule that are separated by one single bond. For example, the organic compound buta-1, 3-diene, $H_2C= CH–CH = CH_2$, has conjugated double bonds. In such molecules, there is some delocalization of electrons in the pi orbitals between the carbon atoms linked by the single bond.

conjugated acid-base According to Bronsted-Lowry concept of acids and bases, acid is a proton donor and base is a proton acceptor e.g. $NH_3 + HCl \rightarrow NH_4^+ + Cl^-$. In this reaction Cl^- is the conjugate base of acid HCl and NH_4^+ is the conjugate acid of base NH_3.

conservation of energy Law was enunciated by Helmholtz in 1847, this law states that in all processes occurring in an isolated system the energy of the system remains constant. The law does of course permit energy to be converted from one form to another. This may also be called as 1st law of thermodynamics.

consolute temperature The temperature at which two partially miscible liquids become fully miscible as the temperature is increased is known as consolute temperature.

constantan (*Trademark*) A copper-nickle (cupronickel) alloy containing 45% nickel. Due to high electrical resistivity and very low temperature coefficient of resistance it is used in thermocouples and resistors.

constant current electrolysis Electrolysis is carried out by continuously regulating E_{app} so as to keep the current constant and measuring the time needed for electrolysis to be completed. The process is quantified by Faraday's law

$$M = \frac{(M.M.)\ i.t}{n\ F}$$

where

M = Mass in grams of the ion given off at the electrode

M.M. = Molecular mass of ion

i = current in amperes

t = time in seconds

n = number of moles of electrons involved in the reaction

F = Faraday's constant having a fixed value of (96500 coulombs)

constant proportions Law was formulated by Proust in 1779 after the analysis of a large number of compounds, the principle that the proportion of each element in a compound is fixed or constant. It follows that the composition of a pure chemical compound is not dependent on the method of preparation. It is also called the *law of definite proportions* and the *law of constant composition.*

contact process A process for making sulphuric acid from sulphur dioxide (SO_2), which is made by burning sulphur or by roasting sulphide ores. A mixture of sulphur dioxide and air is passed over a hot catalyst

$$2SO_2 + O_2 \rightarrow 2SO_3$$

The reaction is exothermic i.e. heat is evolved (ΔH = –ve) and the conditions are controlled to keep the temperature at an optimum 450°C. Formerly, platinum catalysts were used but vanadium-vanadium oxide catalysts are now mainly employed (although less efficient, they are less susceptible to poisoning). The sulphur trioxide is dissolved in sulphuric acid and the oleum is then diluted.

$$H_2SO_4 + SO_3 \rightarrow H_2S_2O_7$$

continuous spectrum In a spectrum if one colour merges into another without a gap then the spectrum is known as continuous spectrum. Such a spectrum is obtained from incandescent substances.

coordinate bond It is a *covalent bond* in which *both* the *electrons* in the bonds have come from the *same atom*. Electrons have been *donated* by one atom rather than one donated from each atom. The bond is also known as a dative bond. In coordinate bonding, the donor atom uses a *lone pair of electrons*. It is donated by → (donor to acceptor).

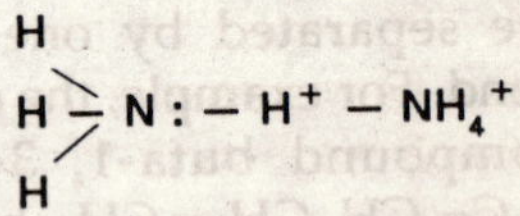

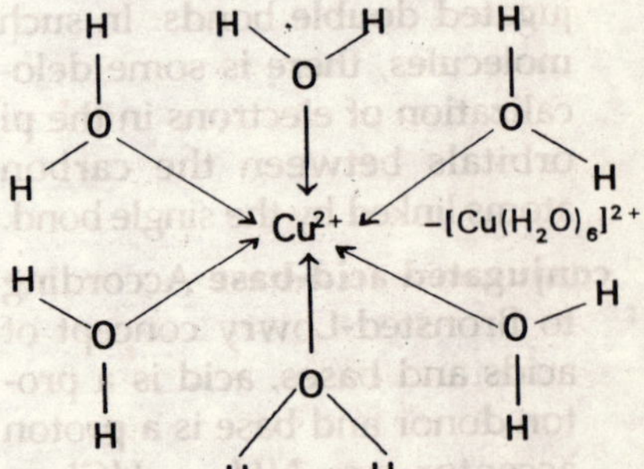

coordinate bonds

coordination number The number of coordinate bonds formed to a metal atom or ion in a complex.

coordination sphere In coordination complexes the central metal is always attached to some non-ionisable ligands. This part of the complex is written in a square bracket which is known as coordination sphere, e.g. in $[Ag(NH_3)_2]Cl$ $[Ag(NH_3)_2]$ is the coordination sphere.

copper Symbol Cu; a.n. 29; r.a.m. 63.5; r.d. 8.93; m.p. 1083°C; b.p. 2582°C

Its 'd' block element. A *transient element* which plays an important part in our lives. It is a vital trace element in our bodies—we need between one and two milligrammes per day.

Copper is an unreactive metal, coming low down in the *electrochemical series*. It will not liberate *hydrogen* from dilute *acids*.

It can be purified by using the impure metal as the *anode* with copper(II) sulphate as the *electrolyte* and a small pure copper cathode in an *electrolysis cell*.

Copper metal is used in plumbing, for electrical wiring and for coinage. (Copper is a good conductor of heat and electricity.) It is extracted commercially from its *sulphide* ores:

Chalcopyrite	($CuFeS_2$)
Bornite	(Cu_5FeS_4)

and its carbonate ores:

Malachite	($CuCO_3.Cu(OH)_2$)
Azurite	($2CuCO_3.\ Cu(OH)_2$)

Copper is also found as the free element, an indication of its lack of *reactivity*.

copper(I) chloride A white solid compound, having molecular formula CuCl; cubic; r.d. 4.14; m.p. 430°C; b.p. 1490°C. It is obtained by boiling a solution containing copper(II) chloride, excess copper turnings, and hydrochloric acid. Copper(I) is present as the $[CuCl_2]^-$ complex ion. On pouring the solution into air-free distilled water copper(I) chloride precipitates. It must be kept free of air and moisture since it oxidizes to copper(II) chloride under those conditions.

Copper(I) chloride is essentially covalent and its structure is similar to that of diamond; i.e. each copper atom is surrounded tetrahedrally by four chlorine atoms and vice versa. In the vapour phase, dimeric and trimeric species are present. Copper(I) chloride is used in conjunction with ammonium chloride as a catalyst in the dimerization of ethyne to but-1-ene-3-yne (vinyl acetylene), which is used in the production of synthetic rubber. In the laboratory a mixture of copper(I) chloride and hydrochloric acid is used for converting benzene diazonium chloride to chlorobenzene. This reaction is known as the Sandmeyer reaction.

copper(II) chloride $CuCl_2$ Anhydrous $CuCl_2$ is a dark brown solid but hydrated ($Cu\ Cl_2.2H_2O$) is blue solid. It is used to give green colour to fire works and for removal of sulphur from petroleum.

copper glance A mineral form of copper (I) sulphide, Cu_2S.

copper(II) nitrate (cupric nitrate, $Cu(NO_3)_2$) A compound prepared by dissolving either excess copper(II) oxide or copper(II) carbonate in dilute nitric acid. On crystallization, deep blue crystals of the trihydrate ($Cu(NO_3)_2.3H_2O$) are obtained. The crystals are prismatic in shape and are extremely deliquescent. On heating, copper(II) nitrate decomposes to give copper(II) oxide, nitrogen(IV) oxide, and oxygen. By adding a solution of dinitrogen pentoxide in nitric acid to crystals of the trihydrate the white anhydrous salt is produced.

copper(I) oxide It is a red insoluble solid, having molecular formula Cu_2O; r.d. 6.0; m.p. 1235°C. It is obtained by reduction of an alkaline solution of copper(II) sulphate. Since the addition of alkalis to a solution of copper(II) salt results in the precipitation of copper(II) hydroxide the copper(II) ions are complexed with tartrate ions; under such conditions the concentration of copper(II) ions is so low that the solubility product of copper(II) hydroxide is not exceeded.

copper(II) oxide It is a black insoluble solid, CuO; monoclinic; r.d. 6.3; having a very high melting point m.p. 1326°C. It is obtained by heating either copper(II) carbonate or copper(II) nitrate. It decomposes on heating above 800°C to copper(I) oxide and oxygen. Copper(II) oxide reacts readily with mineral acids on warming, with the formation of copper(II) salts; it is also readily reduced to copper on heating in a stream of hydrogen. Copper(II) oxide is soluble in dilute acids forming blue solutions of cupric salts.

copper sulphate, $CuSO_4$ $5H_2O$ It is called blue vitriol *(Neela Thotha)*. It is used as a germicide in agriculture, for electroplating, in refining of metals and as a mordant in dyeing and calico printing.

cordite An explosive mixture of cellulose nitrate and nitroglycerin, with added plasticizers and stabilizers. It is used as a propellant for guns.

corrosion It is the process of the slow and continuous deterioration of metals and alloys by chemical or electrochemical actions of environments e.g. rusting of iron (unwanted decay).

corundum A mineral form of aluminium oxide, Al_2O_3. It crystallizes in the trigonal system and occurs as well-developed hexagonal crystals. It is colourless and transparent when pure but the presence of other elements gives rise to a variety of colours. Ruby is a red variety containing chromium; sapphire is a blue variety containing iron and titanium. Corundum occurs as a rock-forming mineral in both metamorphic and igneous rocks. It is chemically resistant to weathering processes and so also occurs in alluvial (placer) deposits. The second hardest mineral after diamond (it has a hardness of 9 on the Mohs' scale), it is used as an abrasive.

cotton It is a natural *cellulose fibre* which forms strong and hard-wearing fabrics. Cotton is good to wear next to the skin in hot climates because of its ability to absorb *water*.

cottrel smoke precipitator It is a device used for controlling the pollution. The outgoing smoke from a chimney when allowed to pass through it, can be made free of collodial particles of carbon.

It consists of two metal discs charged to a very high potential.

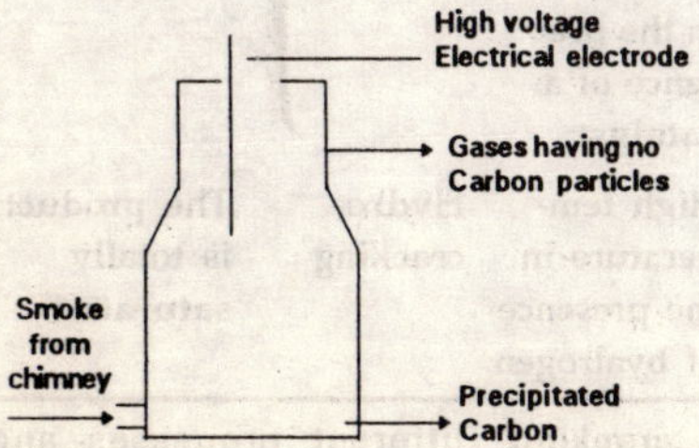

coulomb It is the S.I. unit of electric charge. It is equal to the charge carried by an electric current of one ampere flowing for one second.

coupling A chemical reaction in which two groups or molecules join together. An example is the formation of azo compounds which takes place between benzene diazonium chloride and aniline.

covalent crystal A crystal in which the atoms are held together by covalent bonds. Covalent crystals are sometimes called *macromolecular* or *giant-molecular crystals*. They are hard high-melting substances. Diamond and boron nitride are the examples of covalent crystal.

covalent radius It is an effective radius assigned to an atom in a covalent compound. In the case of a simple diatomic molecule, the covalent radius is half the distance between the nuclei. Thus, in Cl_2 the internuclear distance is 0.198 nm so the covalent radius is taken to be 0.099 nm. Covalent radii can also be calculated for multiple bonds; for instance, in the case of carbon the values are 0.077 nm for single bonds, 0.0665 nm for double bonds, and 0.0605 nm for triple bonds. The values of different covalent radii can sometimes be added to give internuclear distances. For example, the length of the bond in interhalogens (e.g. ClBr) is nearly equal to the sum of the covalent radii of the halogens involved. This, however, is not always true because of other effects (e.g. ionic contributions to the bonding).

cracking It is a process of decomposing, higher hydrocarbons of the petroleum fraction into lower hydrocarbons with low boiling points, by strong heating, e.g.

$$\underset{\text{decane}}{CH_3(CH_2)_8CH_3} \xrightarrow{770K} \underset{\text{octane}}{C_8H_{16}} + \underset{\text{ethene}}{C_2H_4}$$

Various types of cracking are:

(i) Vapour phase cracking.

(ii) Liquid phase cracking.

(iii) Catalytic cracking.

(iv) Steam cracking.

cristobalite A mineral form of silicon(IV) oxide, SiO_2.

critical point The conditions of temperature and pressure under which a liquid being heated in a closed vessel becomes indistinguishable from the gas or vapour phase is called its critical point. At temperatures below the critical temperature (T_c) the substance can be liquefied by applying pressure; at temperatures above T_c this is not possible. For each substance there is one critical point; for example, for carbon dioxide it is at 31.1°C and 73.0 atmospheres.

critical pressure It is the pressure of a fluid in its critical state; i.e. when it is at its critical temperature and critical volume.

critical temperature It is that temperature above which it is impossible to liquify a gas by application of pressure alone, no matter how great is the pressure.

critical volume The volume of one mole of a substance at its critical point.

cross linkage A short side chain of atoms linking two longer chains in a polymeric material.

cross linking Chemical *bonds* formed beween *polymer* molecules lying side by side.

Conditions	*Process name*	*Products*
High temperature	Thermal cracking	*Unsaturated* & *saturated* molecules are produced
High temperature in the presence of *steam*	Steam cracking	
High tempreature in the presence of a catalyst	Catalytic cracking	
High temperature in the presence of byalrogen	Hydrocracking	The product is totally saturated

cracking Different processes and their products.

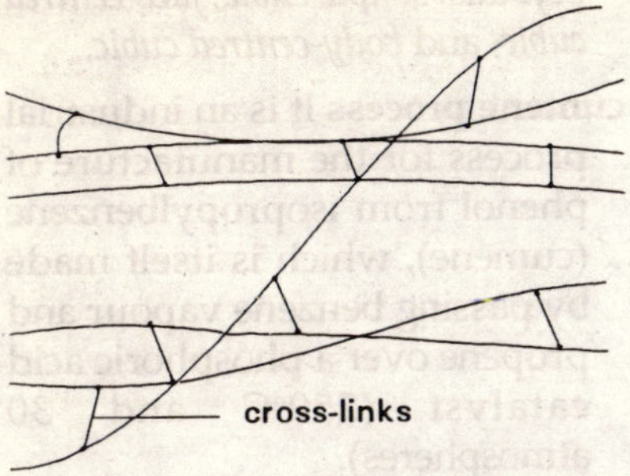

cryogenic pump It is a vacuum pump in which pressure is reduced by condensing gases on surfaces maintained at about 20 K by means of liquid hydrogen or at 4 K by means of liquid helium. Pressures down to 10^{-8} mm Hg (10^{-6} Pa) can be maintained; if they are used in conjunction with a diffusion pump, pressures as low as 10^{-15} mmHg (10^{-13} Pa) can be reached.

cryohydrate A eutectic mixture of ice and some other substance (e.g. an ionic salt) obtained by freezing a solution.

cryolite It is a *mineral.* In the extraction of *aluminium, bauxite* (Al_2O_3) is dissolved in molten cryolite (3 $NaF.AlF_3$) at 900°C and the *mixture* is then electrolysed. Aluminium is produced at the *cathode.* Cryolite is only found naturally in Greenland. The amounts needed in the extraction of aluminium have to be produced by the reaction between aluminium oxide (Al_2O_3) and hydrogen fluoride (HF).

crystal A solid with a regular polyhedral shape. All crystals of the same substance grow so that they have the same angles between their faces. However, they may have different external appearance because different faces can grow at different rates, depending on the conditions. The external form of the crystal is referred to as the *crystal habit.* The atoms, ions, or molecules forming the crystal have a regular arrangement and this is the *crystal structure.*

crystal field theory In this theory it is assumed that the bonds between the central atom and the ligands are purely electrostatic. It helps to explain the magnetic and spectroscopic properties of the complexes.

crystalline It denotes a substance that forms crystals. Crystalline substances have a regular internal arrangement of atoms, even though they may not exist as geometrically regular crystals. For instance, lead (and other metals) are crystalline. Such substances are composed of accumulations of tiny crystals. *Compare* amorphous.

crystallite A small crystal, e.g. one of the small crystals forming part of a microcrystalline substance.

crystallization The process of forming crystals from a liquid or gas.

crystallography It is the branch of science that deals with the geometry, properties and structures of crystals and crystalline substances.

crystal system It is a system or method of classifying crystalline substances on the basis of their unit cell. There are seven crystal systems. If the cell is a parallelopiped with sides *a*, *b*, and *c* and if α is the angle between *b* and *c*, β the angle between *a* and *c*, and γ the angle between *a* and *b*, the systems are:

(1) *cubic* $a = b = c$
and $\alpha = \beta = \gamma = 90°$
(2) *tetragonal* $a = b = c$
and $\alpha = \beta = \gamma = 90°$
(3) *rhombic* (or *orthorhombic*)
$a = b = c$ and $\alpha = \beta = \gamma = 90°$
(4) *hexagonal* $a = b = c$
and $\alpha = \beta = \gamma = 90°$
(5) trigonal $a = b = c$
and $\alpha = \beta = \gamma = 90°$
(6) monoclinic $a = b = c$
and $\alpha = \gamma = 90° = \beta$
(7) triclinic $a = b = c$
and $\alpha = \beta = \gamma$

cubic It denotes a crystal in which the unit cell is a cube. In a *simple cubic* crystal the particles are arranged at the corners of a cube. *See also* body-centred cubic crystal, face-centred cubic crystal, crystal system.

cubic crystal A crystal in which the unit cell is a cube (*see* crystal system). There are three possible packings for cubic crystals: *simple cubic*, *face-centred cubic*, and *body-centred cubic*.

cumene process It is an industrial process for the manufacture of phenol from isopropylbenzene (cumene), which is itself made by passing benzene vapour and propene over a phosphoric acid catalyst (250°C and 30 atmospheres).

$$C_6H_6 + CH_2{:}CH(CH_3) \rightarrow C_6H_5CH(CH_3)_2$$

The isopropylbenzene is oxidized by air to a 'hydroperoxide':

$$C_6H_5C(CH_3)_2\text{-O-O-H}$$

This is hydrolysed by dilute acid to phenol (C_6H_5OH) and propanone (CH_3COCH_3), which is a valuable by- product.

cupellation A method of separating noble metals (e.g. gold or silver) from base metals (e.g. lead) by melting the mixture with a blast of hot air in a shallow porous dish is called cupellation (the *cupel*). The base metals are oxidized, the oxide being carried away by the blast of air or absorbed by the porous container.

cuprammonium ion The tetraamminecopper(II) ion $[Cu(NH_3)_4]^{2+}$.

cupric compounds Compounds containing copper in its higher (+2) oxidation state; e.g. cupric chloride is copper(II) chloride ($CuCl_2$).

cuprite A red mineral cubic form of copper(I) oxide, Cu_2O; an important ore of copper. It occurs where deposits of copper have been subjected to oxidation. The mineral has been mined as a copper ore in Chile, Zaïre, Bolivia, Australia, the USSR, and the USA.

cupronickel A series of strong coppernickel alloys containing up to 45% nickel. Those containing 20% and 30% nickel are very malleable, can be worked cold or hot, and are very corrosion-resistant. They are used, for example, in condenser tubes in power stations. Cupronickel with 25% nickel is widely used in coinage.

curie It is the unit of activity i.e. rate of disintegration.

1 curie = amount of radioactive element which gives 3.7×10^{10} disintegrations per second.

curium It belongs to '*f*' block (Actinides) and has a.n. 96. A highly toxic radioactive silvery element of the actinoid series of metals. A transuranic element, it is not found naturally on Earth but is synthesized from plutonium. Curium-244 and Curium-242 have been used in thermoelectric power generators.

Symbol: Cm; m.p. 1340°C; r.d. 13.5 (calc.); stablest isotope ^{247}Cm (half-life 1.6×10^7 years).

cyanamide, H_2NCN A colourless, crystalline, unstable compound which is weakly acidic. It polymerises to melamine.

cyanamide process It is an industrial process for fixing nitrogen by heating calcium dicarbide in air. The reaction takes place as follows:

$$CaC_2 + N_2 \rightarrow CaCN_2$$

The product, calcium cyanamide, hydrolyses to ammonia and can be used as a fertilizer. The process is expensive due to the high cost of calcium dicarbide.

cyanides A range of compounds which contain the –CN group of atoms. The best known examples are potassium cyanide (K^+CN^-) and hydrogen cyanide ($H–C \equiv N$). They are very poisonous. Cyanides prevent the flow of *energy* within the body and so are effective very quickly.

cyanic acid Also known as fulminic acid, an unstable explosive acid, HOCN. The compound has the structure $H–O–C \equiv N$. Its salts and esters are *cyanates* (or *fulminates*). The compound is a volatile liquid, which readily polymerizes. In water it hydrolyses to ammonia and carbon dioxide. It is isomeric with another acid, $H–N = C = O$, which is known as *isocyanic acid*. Its salts and esters are *isocyanates*.

cyanine dyes A class of dyes that

contain a –CH = group linking two nitrogen-containing heterocyclic rings. They are used as sensitizers in photography.

cyanogen, C_2N_2 A colourless, poisonous gas. It is combustible and burns with a violet flame and the reaction may be represented as

$$C_2N_2 + 2O_2 \rightarrow 2CO_2 + N_2$$

cyanohydrins They are organic compounds formed by the addition of hydrogen cyanide to aldehydes or ketones (in the presence of a base). The first step is attack by a CN^- ion on the carbonyl carbon atom. The final product is a compound in which a –CN and –OH group are attached to the same carbon atom. For example, ethanal reacts as follows:

$$CH_3CHO + HCN \rightarrow CH_3CH(OH)(CN)$$

The product is 2-hydroxypropanonitrile. Cyanohydrins of this type can be oxidized to α-hydroxy carboxylic acids.

cyanuric acid A white crystalline water-soluble trimer of cyanic acid, $(HNCO)_3$. It is a cyclic compound having a six-membered ring made of alternating imide (NH) and carbonyl (CO) groups.

cyclic compound A compound having a ring of atoms.

cyclic AMP It is a derivative of ATP that is widespread in animal cells as an intermediate messenger in many biochemical reactions induced by hormones. Upon reaching their target cells, the hormones activate the enzyme that catalyses cyclic AMP production. Cyclic AMP ultimately activates the enzymes of the reaction induced by the hormone concerned. Cyclic AMP is also involved in controlling gene expression and cell division, in immune responses, and in nervous transmission.

cyclization A reaction in which a straight-chain compound is converted into a cyclic compound, i.e. they are converted into cyclic compounds.

cycloalkanes They are cyclic saturated hydrocarbons containing a ring of carbon atoms joined by single bonds. They have the general formula C_nH_{2n}, for example cyclohexane, C_6H_{12}, etc. In general they behave like the alkanes but are rather less reactive.

cyclohexane It is a colourless liquid alkane, having molecular formula C_6H_{12} and is commonly used as a solvent and in the production of hexanedioic acid (adipic acid) for the manufacture of nylon. Cyclohexane, itself, is manufactured by the reformation of longer chain hydrocarbons present in crude-oil fractions. It is also interesting from a structural point of view, existing as a 'puckered' six-membered ring, having all bonds between carbon atoms at 109.9° (the tetrahedral angle). The molecule undergoes rapid interconversion between two 'chair-like' conformations,

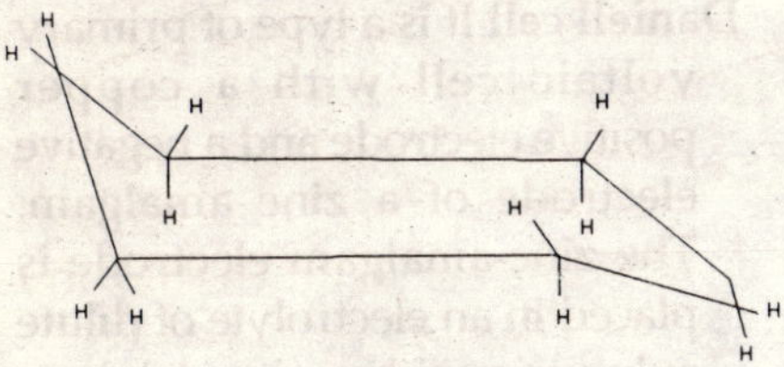

chair form

which are energetically equivalent, passing through a 'boat-like' structure of higher energy. It is commonly represented by a hexagon.

cyclonite (RDX) A highly explosive nitro compound, $(CH_2N.NO_2)_3$. It has a cyclic structure with a six-membered ring of alternating CH_2 groups and nitrogen atoms, with each nitrogen being attached to a NO_2 group. It is made by nitrating hexamine, $C_6H_{12}N_4$, which is obtained from ammonia and methanal. Cyclonite is a very powerful explosive and hence mainly for military purposes.

cyclopropane, 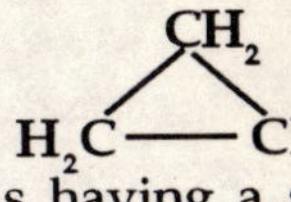 A colourless gas having a sweet odour. It is used as an anaesthetic.

cystine A molecule resulting from the oxidation reaction between the sulphydryl (–SH) groups of two cysteine molecules (*see* amino acid). This often occurs between adjacent cysteine residues in polypeptides. The resultant *disulphide bonds* (–S–S–) are important in stabilizing the structure of protein molecules.

cytochrome Any of a group of proteins, each with an iron-containing haem group, that form part of the electron transport chain in mitochondria and chloroplasts is known as a cytochrome. Electrons are transferred by reversible changes in the iron atom between the reduced Fe(II) and oxidized Fe(III) states.

cytosine A pyrimidine derivative. It is one of the principal component bases of nucleotides and the nucleic acids DNA and RNA.

D

Dalton's atomic theory A theory explaining the formation of compounds by elements. It was first published by John Dalton in 1803. It was the first modern attempt to describe chemical behaviour in terms of atoms. The theory was based on certain postulates:

(1) All elements are composed of small particles, which Dalton called atoms.

(2) All atoms of the same element are identical.

(3) Atoms can neither be created nor destroyed.

(4) Atoms combine to form 'compound atoms' (i.e. molecules) in simple ratios.

Dalton also suggested symbols for the elements. The theory was used to explain the law of conservation of mass and the laws of chemical combination.

Dalton's law It states that the total pressure of a mixture of gases or vapours is equal to the sum of the partial pressures of its components, i.e. the sum of the pressures that each component would exert if it were present alone and occupied the same volume as the mixture of gases. Strictly speaking, the principle is true only for ideal gases.

Daniell cell It is a type of primary voltaic cell with a copper positive electrode and a negative electrode of a zinc amalgam. The zinc-amalgam electrode is placed in an electrolyte of dilute sulphuric acid or zinc sulphate solution in a porous pot, which stands in a solution of copper sulphate in which the copper electrode is immersed. While the reaction takes place ions move through the porous pot, but when it is not in use the cell should be dismantled to prevent the diffusion of one electrolyte into the other. The e.m.f. of the cell is 1.08 volts with sulphuric acid and 1.10 volts with zinc sulphate. It was invented in 1836 by the British chemist John Daniell (1790-1845).

d-block elements The transition elements of the first, second, and third, long periods, i.e. Sc to Zn, Y to Cd, and La to Hg. They are called d-block elements because in general they have inner d-levels with configurations of the type $(n-1)d^x ns^2$ where $x = 1-10$.

Deacon process A former process for making chlorine by oxidizing hydrogen chloride in air at temperature of 723K using a copper chloride catalyst. It was patented in 1870 by Henry Deacon (1822-76).

deamination It is the process of removal of an amino group ($-NH_2$) from a compound. Enzymatic deamination occurs in the liver and is important in amino-acid metabolism, especially in their degradation and subsequent oxidation. The amino group is removed as ammonia and excreted, either unchanged or as urea or uric acid.

de Broglie wave It is a wave associated with a particle, such as an electron or proton. In 1924, Louis de Broglie suggested that, since electromagnetic waves can be described as particles (photons), particles of matter could also have wave properties. The wavelength (λ) has the same relationship to momentum (p) as in electromagnetic radiation:

$$\lambda = h/p$$

where h is the Planck constant having value 6.624×10^{-34} Js.

Debye-Huckel theory According to this theory, the activity coefficient of an electrolyte depend markedly upon concentration. In dilute solution, because of the forces of coulombic attraction and repulsion, the ions tend to surround themselves within atmosphere of oppositely charged ions. Debye and Huckel could explain the abnormal activity coefficient for very dilute solutions of electrolytes.

deca Symbol **da**. A prefix used in the metric system to denote ten times. For example, 10 coulombs = 1 decacoulomb (daC).

decanoic acid, $C_9H_{19}COOH$ A white crystalline solid with unpleasant odour. Esters of this acid are used in the manufacture of flavouring materials and perfumes.

decomposition Chemical reaction in which a compound breaks down into simpler compounds or into elements is known as decomposition.

decrepitation It refers to the cracking sound produced by certain substances on being heated due to removal of water of crystallisation.

defect It is a discontinuity in a crystal lattice. A *point defect* consists either of a missing atom or ion creating a *vacancy* in the lattice (a vacancy is sometimes called a *Schottky defect*) or an extra atom or ion between two normal lattice points creating an *interstitial*. A *Frenkel defect* consists of a vacancy in which the missing atom or ion has moved to an interstitial position. If more than one adjacent point defect occurs in a crystal there may be a slip along a surface causing a *line defect* (or *dislocation*). Defects are caused by strain or, in some cases, by irradiation. All crystalline solids contain an equilibrium number of point defects above absolute zero; this number increases with temperature. The existence of defects in crystals is important in the conducting properties of semiconductors.

degradation A chemical reaction wherein the decomposition of a molecule into simpler molecules e.g. conversion of amide into amine in the presence of bromine and alcoholic KOH.

$$R\,CONH_2 \xrightarrow{Br_2/KOH} R\,NH_2$$

dehydration It is the process of removal of water molecule from a substance. The substance used is called dehydrating agent, e.g. dehydration of ethyl alcohol in presence of conc. H_2SO_4.

$$CH_3CH_2OH \xrightarrow[-H_2O]{H^+} C_2H_4.$$

dehydrogenase Any enzyme that catalyses the removal of hydrogen atoms in biological reactions. Dehydrogenases occur in many biochemical pathways but are particularly important in driving the electron-transport-chain reactions of cell respiration. They work in conjunction with the hydrogen-accepting coenzymes NAD and FAD.

deliquescence The absorption of water from the atmosphere by a hygroscopic solid to such an extent that a concentrated solution of the solid eventually forms.

delocalization In certain chemical compounds the valence electrons cannot be regarded as restricted to definite bonds between the atoms but are 'spread' over several atoms in the molecule. Such electrons are said to be *delocalized*. Delocalization occurs particularly when the compound contains alternating (conjugated) double or triple bonds, the delocalized electrons being those in the pi (π) orbitals. The molecule is then more stable than it would be if the electrons were localized, an effect accounting for the properties of benzene and other aromatic compounds. Another example is in the ions of carboxylic acids, containing the carboxylate group $-COO^-$. In terms of a simple model of chemical bonding, this group would have the carbon joined to one oxygen by a double bond (i.e. C=O) and the other joined to O^- by a single bond ($C-O^-$). In fact, the two C–O bonds are identical because the extra electron on the O^- and the electrons in the pi bond of C=O are delocalized over the three atoms.

denaturating It refers to the process by which ethyl alcohol is made unfit for drinking. For this some methyl alcohol, pyridine or mineral naphtha is added to ethyl alcohol.

dendritic growth Growth of crystals in a branching habit is called dendritic growth.

dendrochronology It is an absolute dating technique using the growth rings of trees. It depends on the fact that trees in the same locality show a characteristic pattern of growth rings resulting from climatic conditions. Thus it is possible to assign a definite date for each growth ring in living trees, and to use the ring patterns to date fossil trees or specimens of wood (e.g. used for buildings or objects on archaeological sites) with life-spans that overlap those of living trees. The bristlecone pine *(Pinus aristata)*, which lives for up to 5000 years, has been used to date specimens over 8000 years old. Fossil specimens accurately dated by dendrochronology have been used to make corrections to the carbon-dating technique. Dendrochronology is also helpful in studying past climatic conditions. Analysis of trace elements in sections of rings can also provide information on past atmospheric pollution.

depolymerisation It is the process of breaking down of polymers into their original monomers.

depolarization The prevention of polarization in a primary cell. For example, manganese oxide having the coordination number (IV) (the *depolarizer*) is placed around the positive electrode of a Leclanche cell to oxidize the hydrogen released at this electrode.

derivative A compound that is derived from some other compound and usually maintains its general structure, e.g. trichloromethane (chloroform; $CHCl_3$) is a derivative of methane (CH_4).

derived unit A unit defined in terms of base units, and not directly from a standard value of the quantity it measures. For example, the newton is a unit of force defined as a kilogram metre second^{-2} (kg ms^{-2}). *See also* SI units.

desalination It is the process of the removal of salt from sea water for irrigation of the land or to provide drinking water. The process is normally only economic if a cheap source of energy, such as the waste heat from a nuclear power station, can be used. Desalination using solar energy has the greatest economic potential since shortage of fresh water is most acute in hot regions. The methods employed include evaporation, often under reduced pressure (flash evaporation);

freezing (pure ice forms from freezing brine); reverse osmosis; electrodialysis; and ion exchange.

desiccator A device used to store substances which need a dry *atmosphere,* e.g. *deliquescent* or *hygroscopic* (which absorb moisture from atmosphere) substances.

A desiccator is airtight and contains a *dehydrating agent* which makes the air dry.

desorption It is the process of removal of an adsorbed substance from the surface at which it is adsorbed.

detergent It is a cleaning agent also known as a *surfactant.* It does two things when used in washing, e.g. clothes or dishes. It reduces the surface tension of the water and so allows the water to wet things more thoroughly. It also acts to bring together the water and (normally insoluble) *fat, oil* or grease into an *emulsion.* If the presence of a detergent is accompanied by rapid movement, e.g. in a washing machine, then particles of dirt and grit are removed and the article is cleaned.

Mostly the detergents are alkyl sulphonates e.g.

$$CH_3(CH_2)_{11}\ C_6H_4\ SO_2\ Na^+$$

Detergents form an emulsion because one part of their molecule is *ionic* and is attracted to water and because the other part (the *hydrocarbon* chain) is attracted to the oil molecules. Detergents, thus, hold the two together.

deuterated compound A compound in which some or all of the hydrogen atoms have been replaced by deuterium atoms.

dewar flask It is also known as vacuum flask, a double-walled container of thin glass with the space between the walls evacuated and sealed to stop conduction and convection of energy through it. The glass is often silvered to reduce radiation.

dextrorotatory An optically active compound that rotates the plane-polariged light to the right (clockwise).

diagonal relationship It refers to the similarities in properties shown by the first element of a group to the second element of second period, e.g. Li to Mg, Be to Al, B to Si, C to P etc.

dialysis It is a method by which large molecules (such as starch or protein) and small molecules (such as glucose or amino acids) in solution may be separated by selective diffusion through a semipermeable membrane. For example, if a mixed solution of starch and glucose is placed in a closed container made of a semipermeable substance, for example Cellophane, which is then immersed in a beaker of water, the smaller glucose molecules will pass through the membrane into the water while the starch molecules remain behind. The cell membranes of living organisms are semipermeable, and dialysis takes place naturally in the kidneys for the excretion of nitrogenous waste. An artificial kidney *(dialyser)* utilizes the principle of dialysis by taking over the functions of diseased kidneys.

diamond A valuable *mineral* which is an *allotrope* of *carbon*. It occurs naturally, mainly in South Africa and the Soviet Union. It is the hardest naturally occurring substance known and is used in drill tips and saw blades. Diamond is considered as a precious stone because of its rarity and the sparkle it produces. The carbon *atoms* are arranged in the *crystal lattice* in a *tetrahedral* formation and are *covalently bonded* to each other.

diatomic Describing a molecule that consists of two atoms. Hydrogen (H_2), oxygen (O_2), nitrogen (N_2), and the halogens such as Cl_2, Br_2 etc. are examples of diatomic elements.

diazonium salts Unstable salts containing the ion $C_6H_5N_2^+$ (the *diazonium ion*). They are formed by diazotization reactions.

diazotization The formation of a diazonium salt by reaction of an aromatic amine with nitrous acid at low temperature (below 278 K). The nitrous acid is produced in the reaction mixture from sodium nitrite and hydrochloric acid:

$$ArNH_2 + NaNO_2 + HCl \rightarrow ArN_2^+ + Cl^- + Na^+ + OH^- + H_2O$$

dichlorine oxide Cl_2O An orange gas made by passing chlorine over mercury(II) oxide. It is also known as chloride monoxide. It is a strong oxidizing agent and dissolves in water to give chloric(I) acid.

dichromate(VI) ion ($Cr_2O_7^{2-}$) An *ion* which contains *chromium* and *oxygen* atoms and has a *valency* of 6. Its formula is $Cr_2O_7^{2-}$ and it is usually used as the bright orange *potassium* or *ammonium dichromates*.

$$K_2Cr_2O_7 \quad (NH_4)_2Cr_2O_7$$

Dichromate ion is an *oxidizing agent* which is reduced to *chromium*(III) ions Cr^{3+}.

Diels-Alder reaction A type of chemical reaction in which a compound containing two double bonds separated by a single bond (i.e. a conjugated diene) adds to a suitable compound containing one double bond (known as *dienophile*) to give a ring compound. In the dienophile, the double bond must have a carbonyl group on each side. It is named after the German chemists Otto Diels (1876-1954) and Kurt Alder (1902-58) by whom it was discovered in 1928.

diene An alkene that has two double bonds in its molecule. If the two bonds are separated by one single bond, the compound is a *conjugated diene,* e.g. buta-1, 3 diene (CH_2:CH CH:CH_2)

dienoestrol, $C_{18}H_{18}O_2$ A white powder having oestrogenic properties.

diesel fuel A *fuel/air mixture* is injected into diesel engines where it is compressed. The *temperature* produced in the compression causes the fuel/air mixture to explode. The fuel is produced from *petroleum* and is made up mainly of *alkanes* in the boiling range 200-350°C. It is often sold as 'DERV' fuel: Diesel, Engine, Road, Vehicle.

diffusion The complete mixing of two *gases* that are at first separated and then allowed to mix, e.g. air, nitrogen dioxide. This happens because the molecules in the gases are moving about randomly at high speed because of the *thermal energy* they possess.

Diffusion occurs at a faster rate when the temperature is raised. The *less* dense a gas is, the *greater* is its rate of diffusion (see *density*). Diffusion also occurs in *liquids, solutions* and *solids.*

diffusion pump It is also known as condensation pump, a vacuum pump in which oil or mercury vapour is diffused through a jet, which entrains the gas molecules from the container in which the pressure is to be reduced. The diffused vapour and entrained gas molecules are condensed on the cooled walls of the pump. Pressures down to 10^{-7} Pa can be reached by sophisticated forms of the diffusion pump.

digitoxin, $C_{41}H_{64}O_{13}$ A white crystalline solid used as a heart stimulant.

dihedral (dihedron) An angle formed by the intersection of two planes. The *dihedral angle* is the angle formed by taking a point on the line of intersection and drawing two lines from this point, one in each plane, perpendicular to the line of intersection, e.g. angle formed by two faces of a polyhedron.

dihydrate A crystalline compound with two molecules of water of crystallization per molecule of compound.

dihydrogen Molecular hydrogen, H_2. It is a colourless, odourless gas in liquid form, it is used as a rocket fuel. It is also used in hydrogenation of vegetable oils.

1,2-dihydroxybenzene (catechol) $C_6H_6O_2$ colourless crystals; m.p. 105°C; b.p. 240°C. Strong reducing agent. Obtained by fusing *o*-bentenedisulphonic acid with NaOH. Used as photographic developer, in preparation of dyes and pharmaceuticals, also as an antioxidant.

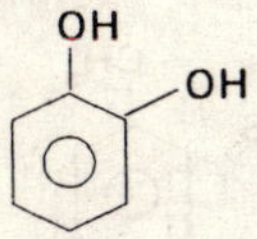

1,3-dihydroxybenzene (Resorcinol) $C_6H_6O_2$ colourless needles; m.p. 110°C, b.p. 276°C, obtained by fusing m-bentenedisulphonic acid with NaOH. Used in the preparation of dyes and for the production of plasticizeers, resins, adhesives.

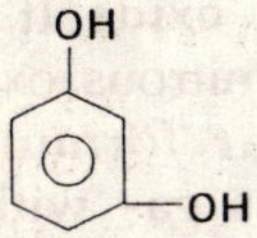

1,4-dihydroxybenzene (Hydroquinone) $C_6H_6O_2$ colourless prisms; m.p. 170°C, b.p. 285°C/730 mm. Obtained by reduction of quinone with sulphur dioxide. Used as a photographic developer and antioxidant.

diiodine hexachloride (iodine trichloride, I_2Cl_6) A yellow crystalline solid made by reacting excess chlorine with iodine. It is a strong oxidizing agent and at 343 K it dissociates into iodine monochloride and chlorine.

dilead(II) lead(IV) oxide A red amorphous powder, Pb_3O_4; r.d. 9.1; decomposes at 500°C to lead(II) oxide. It is prepared by heating lead(II) oxide to 673K and has the unusual property of being black when hot and red-orange when cold. The compound is nonstoichiometric, generally containing less oxygen than implied by the formula. It is largely covalent and has $Pb(IV)O_6$ octahedral groups linked together by Pb(II) atoms, each joined to three oxygen atoms. It is used in glass making but its use in the paint industry has largely been discontinued because of the toxicity of lead. Dilead(II) lead(IV) oxide is commonly called *red lead* or, more accurately, *red lead oxide.*

dilute It denotes a solution in which the amount of solute is low relative to that of the solvent. The term is always relative and includes dilution at trace level as well as the common term 'bench dilute acid', which usually means a 2*M* solution. *Compare* concentrated.

dilute solution A *solution* which contains a relatively low *concentration* of *solute.* If you want to make a solution *more* dilute it is usually to add more solvent to it. Dilute *acids* usually have concentrations of 2 *mol/dm³* or even less.

dilatometer It is an apparatus that is used to measure small changes in volume of a liquid solution or a solid immersed in a liquid.

dimer It is an association of two identical molecules linked together. The molecules may react to form a larger molecule, as in the formation of dinitrogen tetroxide (N_2O_4) from nitrogen dioxide (NO_2), or the formation of an aluminium chloride dimer (Al_2Cl_6) in the vapour. Alternatively, they may be held by hydrogen bonds. For example, carboxylic acids form dimers in organic solvents, in which hydrogen bonds exist between the O of the C = O group and the H of the –O–H group.

dimethylamine $(CH_3)_2NH$ A colourless gas having an ammoniacal odour. It is used in dehairing hides and as a rubber accelerator.

dimethylbenzene $C_6H_4(CH_3)_2$ Also known as xylene, an organic hydrocarbon present in the light-oil fraction of crude oil. It is used extensively as a solvent. There are three isomeric compounds with this name and formula, distinguished as 1,2-,1,3-and 1,4- dimethylbenzene according to the positions of the methyl groups on the benzene ring also setterred as *o*-, m-and *p*-xyleness respectively.

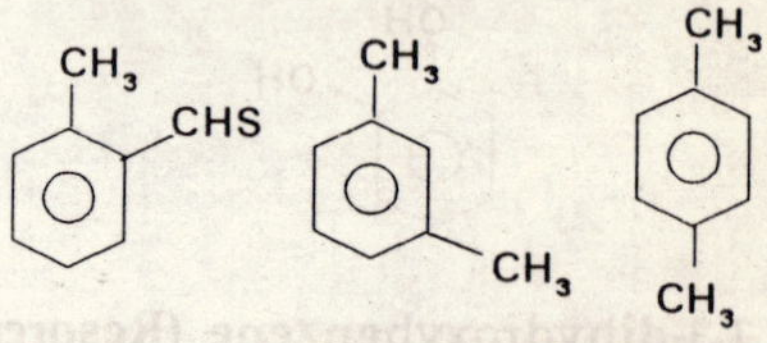

o-xylene m-xylene p-xylene

dimethyl ether, $(CH_3)_2O$ A water soluble gas used as a refrigent and also a low temperature solvent.

$$(CH_3–O–CH_3)$$

dinitrogen oxide It's common name is nitrous oxide having molecular formula N_2O. A colourless gas with a faintly sweet odour and taste. It is appreciably soluble in water (1.3 volumes in 1 volume of water at 0°C) but more soluble in ethanol. It is prepared commercially and in the laboratory by the *careful* heating of ammonium nitrate:

$$NH_4NO_3(s) \rightarrow N_2O(g) + 2H_2O(g)$$

Dinitrogen oxide is fairly easily decomposed on heating to temperatures above 793K giving nitrogen and oxygen. The gas is used as a mild anaesthetic in medicine and dentistry, being marketed in small steel cylinders. It is sometimes called *laughing gas* because it induces a feeling of elation.

dinitrogen tetroxide It is a colourless to pale yellow liquid or a brown gas, N_2O_4; r.d. 1.45 (liquid); m.p. –11.2°C; b.p. 21.2°C. It dissolves in water with reaction to give a mixture of nitric acid and nitrous acid. It may be readily prepared in the laboratory by the reaction of copper with concentrated nitric acid; mixed nitrogen oxides containing dinitrogen oxide may also be produced by heating metal nitrates. The solid compound is wholly N_2O_4 and the liquid is about 99% N_2O_4 at the boiling point; N_2O_4 is diamagnetic. In the gas phase it dissociates to give *nitrogen dioxide*

$$N_2O_4 \rightleftharpoons 2NO_2$$

Because of the unpaired electron this is paramagnetic and brown. Liquid N_2O_4 has been widely studied as a nonaqueous solvent system (self-ionizes to NO^+ and NO_3^-). Dinitrogen tetroxide, along with other nitrogen oxides, is a product of combustion engines and is thought to be involved in the depletion of stratospheric ozone.

diol Any alcohol that has two hydroxyl groups (–OH) per molecule of a compound.

dioxan A colourless toxic liquid, $C_4H_8O_2$; r.d. 1.03; m.p. 11°C; b.p. 101.5°C. The molecule has a six-membered ring containing four CH_2 groups and two oxygen atoms at opposite corners. It can be made from ethane-1, 2-diol and is used as a solvent.

dioxygenyl compounds Compounds containing the positive ion O_2^+, as in dioxygenyl hexafluoroplatinate O_2PtF_6—an orange solid that sublimes in vacuum at 373K. Other ionic compounds of the type $O_2^+[MF_6]^-$ can be prepared, where M is P, As, or Sb.

diphosphane Also known as diphosphine, having molecular formula P_2H_4. A yellow liquid that can be condensed out from phosphine in a freezing mixture. It ignites spontane- ously in air.

disaccharide A sugar consisting of two linked monosaccharide molecules. For example, sucrose comprises one glucose molecule and one fructose molecule bonded together.

dislocation It is used to denote line imperfections which extend along some direction in crystal lattice.

dispersion force A weak type of intermolecular force. Generally the van der Waals forces.

dispersed phase In case of colloidal solution it refers to the component that is present in small quantities and consists of particles of the size 1-100 nm.

dissociation It is the process of breaking up of a *compound* into smaller simpler *molecules* or *ions*. The dissociation is sometimes *reversible*.

$$NH_4Cl(s) \underset{\text{Cool}}{\overset{\text{heat}}{\rightleftharpoons}} NH_3(g) + HCl(g)$$

ammonium chloride ammonia hydrogen chloride

dissociation constant The equilibrium constant of a dissociation reaction. For example, the dissociation constant of a reaction:

$$AB = A + B$$

is given by:

$$K = [A][B]/[AB]$$

Often the degree of dissociation is used – the fraction (α) of the original compound that has dissociated at equilibrium. For an original amount of AB of n moles in a volume V, the dissociation constant is given by:

$$K = \alpha^2 n/(1-\alpha)V$$

Note that this expression is for dissociation into two molecules.

Acid dissociation constants (or *acidity constants*, symbol: K_a) are dissociation constants for the dissociation into ions in solution.

$$HA + H_2O \rightarrow H_3O^+ + A^-$$

The concentration of water can be taken as unity, and the acidity constant is given by:

$$K_a = [H_3O^+][A^-]/[HA]$$

The acidity constant is a measure of the strength of the acid. Base dissociation constants (K_b) are similarly defined.

The expression:

$$K = \alpha^2 n/(1-\alpha)V$$

applied to an acid is known as *Ostwald's dilution law*. In particular if α is small (a weak acid) then $K = \alpha^2 n/V$, or $\alpha = C\sqrt{V}$, where C is a constant. The degree of dissociation is then proportional to the square root of the dilution.

dissociation pressure When a solid compound dissociates to give one or more gaseous products, the dissociation pressure is the pressure of gas in equilibrium with the solid at a given temperature. For example, when calcium carbonate is maintained at a constant high temperature in a closed container, the dissociation pressure at that temperature is the pressure of carbon dioxide from the equilibrium

$$CaCO_3(s) \rightleftharpoons CaO(s) + CO_2(g)$$

calcium carbonate calcium oxide carbon dioxide

dissolve To become mixed with and absorbed in a liquid. When a *solute* dissolves in a *solvent* to form a *solution* it is dispersed throughout the whole *volume* of the solvent. The *structure* of the solute is broken up.

distillate The material (generally liquid) that is vapourised and condensed during distillation.

distillation It is the process of boiling a liquid and condensing and collecting the vapour. The liquid collected is the *distillate.* It is used to purify liquids and to separate liquid mixtures.

disulphur dichloride Also known as sulphur monochloride, having molecular formula S_2Cl_2. A red fuming liquid with a strong smell. It is prepared by passing chlorine over molten sulphur and is used to harden rubber.

disulphuric(VI) acid (pyrosulphuric acid) A colourless hygroscopic crystalline solid, $H_2S_2O_7$; r.d. 1.9; m.p. 308K. It is commonly encountered mixed with sulphuric acid as it is formed by dissolving sulphur trioxide in concentrated sulphuric acid. The resulting fuming liquid, called *oleum* or *Nordhausen sulphuric acid,* is produced during the contact process and is also widely used in the sulphonation of organic compounds.

dithionate A salt of dithionic acid, containing the ion $S_2O_6^{2-}$, usually formed by the oxidation of a sulphite using manganese(IV) oxide. The ion has neither pronounced oxidizing nor reducing properties.

dithionic acid An acid, having molecular formula, $H_2S_2O_6$, known in the form of its salts (dithionates).

d-lines Two close lines in the yellow region of the visible spectrum of sodium, having wavelengths 589.0 and 589.6 nm. They are used as a standard in spectroscopy as they are prominent and easily recognised.

Dobereiner's triads Triads of chemically similar elements in which the central member, when placed in order of increasing atomic weight, has an atomic weight approxima- tely equal to the average of the outer two. Other chemical and physical properties of the central member also lie between those of the first and last members of the triad. Döbereiner noted this relationship in 1817; the triads are now recognized as consecutive members of a group of the periodic table; e.g. Ca, Sr, and Ba and Cl, Br, and I.

dodecene A straight-chain alkene, $CH_3(CH_2)_9CH:CH_2$, obtained from petroleum and used in making dodecylbenzene.

dodecylbenzene A hydrocarbon, $CH_3(CH_2)_{11}C_6H_5$, manufactured by a Friedel-Crafts reaction between dodecene (CH_3 $(CH_2)_9$ $CH:CH_2$) and benzene. It can be sulphonated, and the sodium salt of the sulphonic acid is the basis of common detergents.

dolomite A mineral, $CaCO_3.MgCO_3$, used as an ore of magnesium.

donor an ion or molecule that provides a pair of electrons in forming a coordinate bond.

dopa(dihydroxyphenylalanine) It is a derivative of the amino acid tyrosine. It is found in particularly high levels in the adrenal glands and is a precursor in the synthesis of dopamine, noradrenaline, and adrenaline. The laevorotatory form, *L-dopa,* is administered in the treatment of Parkinson's disease, in which brain levels of dopamine are reduced.

double decomposition (Also known as precipitation reactions) This process occurs when ionic substances react in *solution.* The product is an insoluble *solid.* For example:

$$CaCl_2(aq) + Na_2CO_3(aq) \rightarrow CaCO_3(s) + 2NaCl(aq)$$

OR

$$Ca^{2+}(aq) + CO_3^{2-}(aq) \rightarrow CaCO_3(s)$$

double refraction The property, possessed by certain crystals (especially calcite) of forming two refracted rays from a single incident ray. The *ordinary ray* obeys the normal laws of refraction. The other refracted ray, called the *extraordinary ray,* follows different laws. The light in the ordinary ray is polarized at right angles to the light in the extraordinary ray. Along an optic axis the ordinary and extraordinary rays travel with the same speed. Some crystals, such as calcite, quartz, and tourmaline, have only one optic axis; they are *uniaxial crystals.* Others, such as mica and selenite, have two optic axes; they are *biaxial crystals.* The phenomenon is also known as *birefringence* and the double-refracting crystal as a *birefringent crystal.*

dow's process This process is used for converting haloarenes to aniline. Haloarenes react with aqueous ammonia in the presence of cupric oxide at 202°C and under a pressure of 60 atmospheres to yield aniline.

dry cell A *battery* in which the *electrolyte* is in the form of a paste to avoid it spilling from the battery. The only common *wet* battery used today is the lead-acid *accumulator.*

dry corrosion Refers to corrosion of metals involving direct chemical action between metals and dry gases.

dryers Devices used in chemical processes to remove a liquid from a solid by evaporation. Drying equipment is classified by the method of transferring heat to a wet solid. This can be by direct contact between hot gases and the solid (direct dryers), heat transfer by conduction through a retaining metallic wall (indirect dryers), or infrared rays (infrared dryers).

dry ice Solid *carbon dioxide.* This material *sublimes* and hence the name *dry.* It is used for keeping things cold and in the theatre for producing smoke and cloud effects on stage. Its sublimation point is –40°C.

Dulong and Petit's law For a solid element the product of the relative atomic mass and the specific heat capacity is a constant equal to about 25 J mol^{-1} K^{-1}. Formulated in these terms in 1819 by the French scientists Pierre Dulong (1785-1838) and A.T. Petit (1791-1820), the law in modern terms states: the molar heat capacity of a solid element is approximately equal to 3*R*, where *R* is the gas constant. The law is only approximate but applies with fair accuracy at normal temperatures to elements with a simple crystal structure.

Duma's method This method is used to estimate the amount of nitrogen in an organic compound. In it organic compound is heated with copper oxide and the combustion product is passed over bright copper spiral, carbon dioxide and sulphur dioxide produced are absorbed in caustic soda solution and from the volume of nitrogen collected over caustic soda, the amount of nitrogen present in the given organic compound can be found out.

dynamite An explosive invented by Alfred Nobel, 1833-96. He discovered that if the unstable explosive nitroglycerine was absorbed into a clay called *kieselguhr* the result was a *stick* of explosive which was safe until it was detonated. It results in explosion.

Dysprosium, Dy. At No. 66 At. wt. 162-5, M.f. 1409, D 8.5, A 8.5. A lanthanide, used to measure neutron fluxes. Dry compounds are used in lasers and used phosphors.

E

Earth The planet that revolves around the sun between the planets Venus and Mars. The earth consists of three layers: the gaseous atmosphere, the liquid *hydrosphere,* and the solid *lithosphere.* The solid part of the earth also consists of three layers: the *crust* with a mean thickness of about 32 km under the land and 10 km under the seas; the *mantle,* which extends some 2900 km below the crust; and the *core,* part of which is believed to be liquid. The composition of the crust is: oxygen 47%, silicon 28%, aluminium 8%, iron 4.5%, calcium 3.5%, sodium and potassium 2.5% each, and magnesium 2.2%. Hydrogen, carbon, phosphorus, and sulphur are all present to an extent of less than 1%.

earth's atmosphere It is the gas that surrounds the earth. The composition of dry air at sea level is: nitrogen 78.08%, oxygen 20.95%, argon 0.93%, carbon dioxide 0.03%, neon 0.0018%, helium 0.0005%, krypton 0.0001%, and xenon 0.00001%. In addition to water vapour, air in some localities contains sulphur compounds, hydrogen peroxide, hydrocarbons, and dust particles. Nitrogen is having the maximum percentage.

Earth's structure The Earth is made up of 3 layers: a crust, the mantle and a core. The crust is a relatively thin layer which varies in thickness from about 7 km under the sea to about 40 km under the continents; the top metre or so is soil. The mantle is about 2870 km thick and is made up of a molten layer held between two more rigid layers. The core is about 3500 km thick and is made up mainly of iron and nickel.

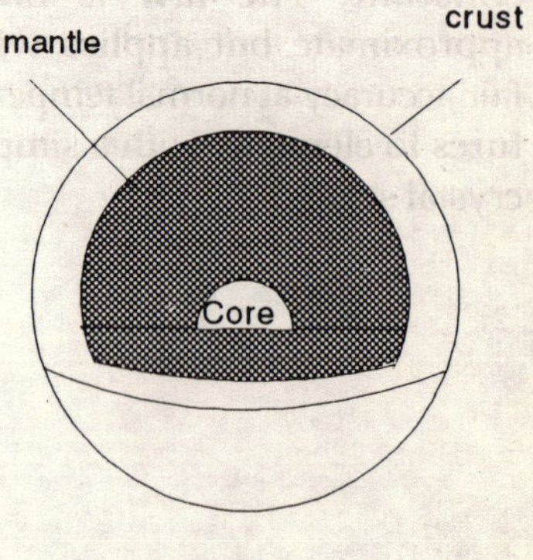

Earth's structure

ebulioscopic constant It is molal elevation constant. It is designated by ΔT_b.

EDTA Ethylenediaminetetracetic acid,

$(HOOCCH_2)_2N(CH_2)_{2-}N(CH_2COOH)_2$

A compound used as a chelating agent in inorganic chemistry.

efferverscene The process in which small gas molecules escape in the form of bubbles from a liquid generally because of some chemical reaction.

eigenfunction An allowed wave function (ψ) of a system in quantum mechanics. The associated energies are *eigenvalues.*

Einstein It is a unit of radiant energy.

Einstein equation 1. Einstein in 1905 gave the mass-energy relationship in the form $E = mc^2$, where E is a quantity of energy, m its mass, and c is the speed of light. It presents the concept that energy possesses mass. 2. The relationship $E_{max} = hf - W$, where E_{max} is the maximum kinetic energy of electrons emitted in the photoemissive effect, h is the Planck constant, f the frequency of the incident radiation, and W the work function of the emitter. This is also written $E_{max} = hf - \phi e$, where e is the electronic charge and ϕ a potential difference, also called the work function. (Sometimes W and ϕ are distinguished as *work function energy* and *work function potential.*) The equation can also be applied to photoemission from gases, when it has the form: $E = hf - I$, where I is the ionization potential of the gas.

einsteinium A member of *'f'* block, a radioactive transuranic element of the actinoid series, not found naturally on Earth. Several short-lived isotopes have been synthesized.

Symbol: Es; p.n. 99; stablest isotope ^{254}Es (half-life 276 days).

elastomer Material (usually a *polymer*) with *elastic properties;* in other words, it has the ability to stretch and return to its original shape. Examples are *synthetic* and natural *rubber.*

electret A permanently electrified substance or body that has opposite charges at its extremities. Electrets show resemblance permanent magnets in many ways. An electret can be made by cooling certain waxes in a strong electric field.

electric-arc furnace A furnace used in melting metals for manufacturing alloys, especially in steel manufacture, in which the heat source is an electric arc. In the direct-arc furnace, such as the Heroult furnace, an arc is formed between the metal and an electrode. In the indirect-arc furnace, such as the Stassano furnace, the arc is formed between two electrodes and the heat is radiated onto the metal.

electrochemical equivalent Symbol z. The mass of an element released from a solution of its ion when a current of one ampere flows for one second during electrolysis.

electrochemical series *Elements* differ in their reactivity. When a *metal* is dipped into a *solution* of one of its salts, e.g. *zinc* in zinc sulphate solution, the following *reaction* occurs:

zinc → zinc ions + 2 electrons

$$Zn(s) \rightarrow Zn^{2+}(aq) + 2e^-$$

The *ions* go into solution and the *electrons* cling to the metal. If the metal and solution are made part of a circuit the electrons will flow round the circuit. The force with which the electrons move is directly proportional to the reactivity of the metal. The more reactive a metal is, the greater the force with which the electrons move.

The series is useful because it allows us to compare reactivities and hence predict *reactions*.

electrochemistry It is the branch of chemistry that is concerned with the study of relationship between electrical energy and chemical energy and conversion of one form into another.

electrode It is a conductor that emits or collects electrons in a cell, thermionic valve, semiconductor device, etc. The *anode* is the positive electrode and the *cathode* is the negative electrode.

electrodeposition The process of depositing a layer of solid (metal) on an electrode by electrolysis. Cations in solution gain electrons at the cathode and are deposited as atoms. Copper, for instance, can be deposited on a metal cathode from copper sulphate solution.

electrode A conductor which dips into an electrolyte and allows current to flow to and from the electrolyte. Copper, carbon and platinum are the examples of electrodes which are commonly used in electrolysis.

During electrolysis the electrode connected to the positive pole of the battery is called *anode* and that connected to negative pole is called *cathode*. Chemical reactions occur at both electrodes.

electrode potential It is denoted by 'E'. The potential difference produced between the electrode and the solution in a half cell. It is not possible to measure this directly since any measurement involves completing the circuit with the electrolyte, thereby introducing another half cell. *Standard electrode potentials* are defined by measuring the potential relative to a standard hydrogen half cell using 1.0 molar solution at 25°C. The convention is to designate the cell so that the oxidized form is written first. For example,

$$Pt(s) \mid H_2(g)H^+(aq) \mid Zn^{2+}(aq) \mid Zn(s)$$

The e.m.f. of this cell is –0.76 volt (i.e. the zinc electrode is negative). Thus the standard electrode potential of the $Zn^{2+} \mid Zn$ half cell is –0.76 V. Electrode potentials are also called *reduction potentials.*

electrolysis A reaction which requires electrical energy from some external source to bring about a chemical change. Electrolysis is used to extract metals and non-metals from compounds.

electrolyte Either a molten ionic compound:

$$NaCl(l) \quad PbI_2(l)$$

or a *solution* which contains *ions:*

$HCl(aq)$, $NaOH(aq)$, $KI(aq)$, $CuSO_4(aq)$

Chemical changes takes place when a direct electric *current* is passed through an electrolyte *(electrolysis).*

With molten *compounds* such as sodium chloride the changes are simple:

$$2Na^+Cl^-(l) \rightarrow 2Na(l) + Cl_2(g)$$

The elements are produced.

The processes are more complex in case of ionic solutions. The products depend on the *concentration* of the solution, the voltage which is applied, the type of *electrode* which is used, and the nature of the ions present in the solution. They are of two types: strong and weak.

electrolytic cell It is a cell in which electrolysis occurs; i.e. one in which current is passed through the electrolyte from an external source through circuit.

electrolytic corrosion Corrosion that occurs due to an electrochemical reaction.

electromagnetic radiation It is a form of energy. Such a radiation possesses a wave character. It propagates through the space with the speed of light.

electromagnetic spectrum It is the range of wavelengths over which electromagnetic radiation extends. The longest waves (10^5–10^{-3} metres) are radio waves, the next longest (10^{-3}–10^{-6} m) are infrared waves, then comes the narrow band (4–7×10^{-7} m) of visible radiation, followed by ultraviolet waves (10^{-7}–10^{-9} m) and X-rays and gamma radiation (10^{-9}–10^{-14} m).

electrometallurgy The uses of electrical processes in the separation of metals from their ores. It is used for refining of metals, or the forming or plating of metals.

electrometric titrations It is an analytical method. In it the progress of titration is followed by measuring e.m.f. of an inert electrode dipped in the solution.

electromotive series (electrochemical series) A series of chemical elements arranged in order of their electrode potentials. The hydrogen electrode ($H^+ + e \rightarrow \frac{1}{2}H_2$) is taken as having zero electrode potential. Elements that have a greater tendency than hydrogen to lose electrons to their solution are taken as *electropositive;* those that gain electrons from their solution, are below hydrogen in the series are called *electronegative.* The series shows the order in which metals replace one another from their salts; electropositive metals (such as Na, K, Ca etc.) will replace hydrogen from acids. The chief metals and hydrogen, placed in order in the series, are: potassium, calcium, sodium, magnesium, aluminium, zinc, cadmium, iron, nickel, tin, lead, hydrogen, copper, mercury, silver, platinum, gold.

electron An elementary particle having charge of –1.602192 C and rest mass 9.109558 kg. Electrons are present in all atoms in shells around the nucleus.

electron affinity It is denoted by 'E_a'. It is the amount of energy released when an electron is added to an isolated neutral atom in the ground state. $M(g) + e^- \rightarrow M^- + E_a$. Since energy is given out so E_a has a negative sign. However in some cases electron affinity values have positive value. In such cases the work must be done to force the atom under consideration to accept an additional electron. It increases as we move along a period and decreases as we go down a group in the periodic table.

electron capture 1. The formation of an anion by an atom or molecule when it acquired an extra free electron. 2. A radioactive transformation in which a nucleus acquires an electron from an inner orbit of the atom, thereby transforming, initially, into a nucleus with the same mass number but an atomic number one less than that of the original nucleus (capture of the electron transforms a proton into a neutron). This type of capture is accompanied by emission of an X-ray photon or Auger electron as the vacancy in the inner orbit is filled by an outer electron.

electron-deficient compounds These are the compounds in

which the number of electrons available for bonding is insufficient for the bonds to consist of conventional two-electron covalent bonds. Diborane or boron hydride B_2H_6, is an example in which each boron atom has two terminal hydrogen atoms bound by conventional electron-pair bonds and in addition the molecule has two hydrogen atoms bridging the boron atoms (B-H-B). In each bridge there are only two electrons for the bonding orbital.

electron diffraction This is a method that is used to find out the structure of substances, mainly the shapes of molecules in gaseous phase. A beam of electrons directed through a gas at low pressure produces a series of concentric ring on the photographic plates.

electronegative Describing elements that tend to gain electrons and form anions (e.g. Cl + 1e → Cl^-). The halogens are typical electronegative elements. For example, in hydrogen chloride, the chlorine atom is more electronegative than the hydrogen and the molecule is polar, with negative charge on the chlorine atom. There are various ways of assigning values for the *electronegativity* of an element. *Mulliken electronegativities* are calculated from $E = (I + A)/2$, where I is ionization potential and A is electron affinity. More commonly, *Pauling electrone- gativities* are used. These are based on bond dissociation energies using a scale in which fluorine, the most electronegative element, has a value 4. Some other values on this scale are B 2, C 2.5, N 3.0, O 3.5, Si 1.8, P 2.1, S 2.5, Cl 3.0, Br 2.8.

electronic configuration A configuration is an *arrangement. Electrons* move around the *nucleus* of an *atom.* The movement takes place in clearly-defined regions (*orbitals*) in the atoms. Electrons are pictured as being arranged in orbits, or what are called *shells,* each of which can contain a *maximum* number of electrons.

Shell number:	①	②	③	④	⑤
Maximum number of electrons:	2	8	18	32	50

As we go across the *periodic table* the number of electrons increases by one per atom as the *atomic number* increases. The shells are filled up in turn— ① first, then ② etc.— so that the electrons go into the region of the atom which has the lowest *energy,* e.g. Electronic configuration of Na having atomic number 11 can be written as follows:

$$1s^2\ 2s^2\ 2p^6\ 3s^1$$

electron microscope It is a form

of microscope that uses a beam of electrons instead of a beam of light (as in the optical microscope) to form a large image of a very small object. In optical microscopes the resolution is limited by the wavelength of the light. High-energy electrons, however, can be associated with a considerably shorter wavelength than light; for example, electrons accelerated to an energy of 105 electronvolts have a wavelength of 0.004 nanometre (*see* de Broglie wavelength) enabling a resolution of 0.2-0.5 nm to be achieved. The *transmission electron microscope* has an electron beam, sharply focused by electron lenses, passing through a very thin metallized specimen (less than 50 nanometres thick) onto a fluorescent screen, where a visual image is formed. This image can be photographed. The *scanning electron microscope* can be used with thicker specimens and forms a perspective image, although. The resolution and magnification are lower. In this type of instrument a beam of primary electrons scans the specimen and those that are reflected, together with any secondary electrons emitted, are collected. This current is used to modulate a separate electron beam in a TV monitor, which scans the screen at the same frequency, consequently building up a picture of the specimen. The resolution is limited to about 10-20 nm.

electron transport chain (respiratory chain) A sequence of biochemical redox reactions that forms the final stage of aerobic respiration. It results in the transfer of electrons or hydrogen atoms derived from the Krebs cycle to molecular oxygen, with the formation of water. At the same time it conserves energy from good or light in the form of ATP. The chain comprises a series of electron carriers that undergo reversible oxidation-reduction reactions, accepting electrons and then donating them to the next carrier in the chain. In the mitochondria, NADH and FADH2, generated by the Krebs cycle, transfer their electrons to a chain comprising flavin mononucleotide (FMN), coenzyme Q, and a series of cytochromes. This process is coupled to the formation of ATP at three sites along the chain. The ATP is then carried across the mitochondrial membrane in exchange for ADP. An electron transport chain also occurs in the light reaction of photosynthesis.

electron spin resonance It is denoted by ESR. A similar technique to nuclear magnetic resonance, but applied to unpaired electrons in a molecule (rather than to the nuclei). It is a powerful technique for studying free radicals and transition-metal complexes.

electrophile An ion or molecule that is electron deficient and can accept electrons. Electrophiles are often reducing agents and Lewis acids. They are either cations (positively changed ions) (e.g. NO_2^+) or molecules that have a positive charge on a particular atom (e.g. SO_3, which has an electron-deficient sulphur atom). In organic reactions they tend to attack negatively charged parts of a molecule.

electrophilic addition An addition reaction in which the first step is attack by an electrophile (e.g. a cation) on an electron-rich part of the molecule. An example is addition to the double bonds in alkenes.

Electrophilic Substitution A reaction in which the substitution takes place by the attack of an electrophile. Most of the reactions in benzene like halogenation, nitration, sulphonation, alkylation etc. are well known electrophilic substitution reactions.

electrophoresis It is the process in which the movement of colloidal particles, towards cathode or anode under the influence of electric field take place.

electroplating It is a method of plating one metal with another by electrodeposition. The articles to be plated are made the cathode of an electrolytic cell and a rod or bar of the plating metal is made the anode. Electroplating is used for covering metal with a decorative, more expensive, or corrosion-resistant layer of another metal.

electropositive Describing elements that tend to lose electrons and form cations. The alkali metals are typical electropositive elements.

element A *pure* substance which cannot be broken down into anything simpler by chemical means. There are 104 elements known to us. Most of these occur naturally on the earth but several have been made in laboratories by *nuclear reactions.* All elements have a unique number of *protons* in their atoms. There are three classes of elements:

(a) *Metals*, e.g. *iron, sodium, copper* etc.;

(b) *Non-metals*, e.g. *oxygen;*

(c) *Metalloids*, e.g. *arsenic.*

elevation of boiling point It refers to the increase in the boiling point of a liquid when a solid is dissolved in it. The elevation is proportional to the number of particles dissolved (molecules or ions) and is given by $\Delta t = K_B C$, where C is the molal concentration of solute. The constant K_B

is the *ebullioscopic constant* of the solvent and if this is known, the molecular weight of the solute can be calculated from the measured value of Δt. The elevation is measured by a Beckmann thermometer.

elimination reaction A reaction involving the removal of a small molecule, often water or hydrogen chloride, from an organic molecule to give an unsaturated compound. An example is the elimination of a water molecule from an alcohol to produce an alkene.

An elimination reaction is often in competition with a substitution reaction and the predominant product will depend on the reaction conditions. The reaction of bromoethane with sodium hydroxide could yield either ethene (by elimination of HBr) or ethanol (by substitution of the Br with OH). The former product predominates if the reaction is carried out in an alcoholic solution and the latter if the solution is aqueous.

$$CH_3CH_2Br + NaOH \xrightarrow{(alc)} H_2C{=}CH_2 + NaBr + H_2O$$

eluent It is the solvent that is used to separate the components of a mixture in column chromatography.

elution The process of the removal of an adsorbed substance in a chromatography column or ion-exchange column using a solvent (*eluent*). The chromatography column can selectively absorb one or more components from the mixture. To ensure efficient recovery of these components graded elution is used. The eluent is changed in a regular manner starting with a non-polar solvent and gradually replacing it by a more polar one. This will wash the strongly polar components from the column.

elutriation It is a method of separating a material into fractions of various sizes by allowing it to settle against.

emerald The green gem variety of beryl, one of the most highly prized gemstones. The finest specimens occur in the Muzo mines, Colombia. Other occurrences include the Ural Mountains, the Transvaal in South Africa, and Kaligunan in India. Emeralds can also be successfully synthesized.

energy Denoted by W. A property of a system; a measure of its capacity to do work. Energy and work have the same unit: the joule (J). It is convenient to divide energy into *kinetic energy* (energy of motion) and *potential energy* ('stored' energy). Different forms of energy are (chemical, electrical, nuclear, etc.); the only real difference lies in the system under discussion. For example, chemical energy is the kinetic and potential energies of electrons in a chemical compound.

energy band It is a range of energies that electrons can have in a solid. In a single atom, electrons exist in discrete energy levels. In a crystal, in which large numbers of atoms are held tightly together in a lattice, electrons are influenced by a number of adjacent nuclei and the sharply defined levels of the atoms become bands of allowed energy; this approach to energy levels in solids is often known as the *band theory*. Each band represents a large number of allowed quantum states. Between the bands are *forbidden bands.* The outermost electrons of the atoms, that is, the ones responsible for chemical bonding) form the *valence band* of the solid. This is the band, of those occupied, that has the highest energy.

The band structure of solids accounts for their electrical properties. In order to move through the solid, the electrons have to change from one quantum state to another. From lower energy level to higher energy level. This can only occur if there are empty quantum states close to the electrons. In general, if the valence band is full, electrons cannot change to new quantum states in the same band. For conduction to occur, the electrons have to be in an unfilled band—the *conduction band.* Metals are good conductors either because the valence band and the conduction band are only half-filled or because the conduction band overlaps with the valence band; in either case vacant states are available. In insulators which are bad conductors the conduction band and valence band are separated by a wide forbidden band and electrons do not have enough energy to 'jump' from one to the other.

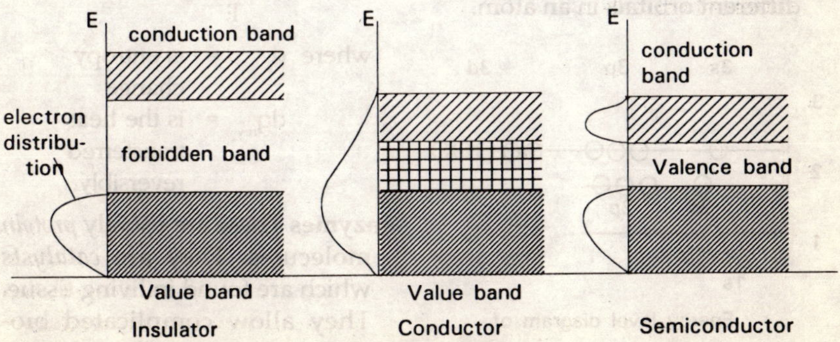

Energy bands

In intrinsic semiconductors the forbidden gap is narrow and, at normal temperatures, electrons at the top of the valence band can move by thermal agitation into the conduction band (at absolute zero, a semiconductor would act as an insulator). Doped semiconductors have extra bands in the forbidden gap.

energy change When chemical reactions occur, *heat energy* can be released from the reactants—they are *exothermic* (ΔH = –ve) or can be taken in by the reactants—they are *endothermic* (ΔH = +ve).

Energy changes are measured in *joules* (J) or *kilojoules* (kJ) and refer to a particular amount of substance, usually a *mole*. So, the energy change for the *Haber process* is –92 kilojoules per *mole* (–92 kJ/mol).

energy level diagram It is in accordance with Aufbau's principle. It is a diagram that depicts the relative energies of different orbitals in an atom.

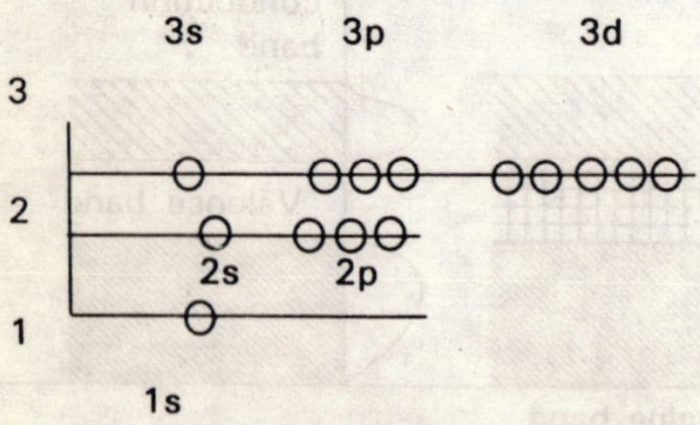

Energy level diagram of hydrogen atom

enrichment The process of increasing the abundance of a specified isotope in a mixture of isotopes. It is usually applied to an increase in the proportion of U-235, or the addition of Pu-239 to natural uranium for use in a nuclear reactor or weapon.

enthalpy It is the amount of *heat energy* possessed by a chemical substance. It is denoted by the symbol *H*. It cannot be measured but, when chemicals react, the difference in the heat energy between the reactants and products can be measured by using a *thermometer*. This difference is the enthalpy change and is given the symbol Δ*H*. Δ*H* is negative for an *exothermic* reaction and positive for an *endothermic* one.

$$H = E + PV$$

entropy (s) It is a measure of degree of disorder or randomness of a system. It is denoted by S.

$$\frac{dq_{rev}}{T}$$

where d_s = is entropy change

dq_{rev} = is the heat transferred reversibly.

enzymes These are usually *protein* molecules. They are *catalysts* which are found in living tissue. They allow complicated biochemical *reactions* take place at low *temperatures* and *pressures* inside the body. It is thought that an enzyme is a particular shape which allows two reacting *molecules* to come close together on the enzyme. This makes the reaction easy to carry out.

epimerism A form of isomerism in which the isomers (*epimers*) differ in the positions of –OH groups. the α- and β- forms of glucose are epimers.

epitaxy (epitaxial growth) Growth of a layer of one substance on a single crystal of another, such that the crystal structure in the layer is the same as that in the substrate. It is used in manufacture of semiconductor devices.

epoxy resins Strong, *inert polymers* which are electrical *insulators.* They have variety of uses as *adhesives,* coatings and *composite* materials. The resins are produced when and where needed by mixing a *poly(ether)* with a chemical reagent.

epsomite A mineral form of magnesium sulphate heptahydrate, having molecular formula $MgSO_4.7H_2O$.

epsomsalt It is $Mg\ SO_4.\ 7H_2O$. It is used in medicines as purgative.

equation of state It is an equation that relates the pressure P, volume V, and thermodynamic temperature T of an amount of substance n. The simplest is the ideal gas law:

$$PV = nRT, \text{(for } n \text{ moles of gas)}$$

and ($PV = RT$ for one mole of gas)

where R is the universal gas constant. Applying only to ideal gases, this equation takes no account of the volume occupied by the gas molecules (according to this law if the pressure is infinitely great the volume becomes zero), nor does it take into account any forces between molecules. A more accurate equation of state would therefore be

$$(p + k)(V - nb) = nRT,$$

where k is a factor that reflects the decreased pressure on the walls of the container as a result of the attractive forces between particles, and nb is the volume occupied by the particles themselves when the pressure is infinitely high. In the *van der Waals equation of state,* proposed by the Dutch physicist J.D. van der Waals (1837-1923),

$$k = n^2a/V^2,$$

where a is a constant. This equation more accurately reflects the behaviour of real gases; several others have done better but are more complicated.

equilibrium A state of balance or rest. In a *reversible reaction* the *reaction* proceeds in both directions, i.e. in forward as well as backward direction.

$$3Fe(s)+4H_2O(g) \rightleftharpoons Fe_3O_4(s)+4H_2(g)$$

The reactants (*iron* and *steam*) produce the *oxide* and *hydrogen*. As soon as the products are made, they begin to react to reform steam and iron. There eventually comes a time when the *rate* of the forward → reaction equals the rate of the reverse ← reaction. At this point the proportion of substances present is constant. There seems to be no reaction taking place. There is an equilibrium between the forward and reverse reactions.

It is important to realize that such an equilibrium is *dynamic*, that is, it produces motion. However, in an equilibrium, the reactions are occurring but, because they are taking place at the same rate, no change can be seen. Many important reactions involve equilibria.

In the *Haber process* (used to prepare ammonia) with the usual operating conditions, less than 20% of the *hydrogen* and *nitrogen* are converted into *ammonia*. This is the equilibrium *yield* of ammonia in the reaction.

equivalent conductance It is denoted by 'λ_m'. It is given by the relation

$$\lambda_m = \frac{K}{C_{eq}}$$

where C_{eq} = concentration of solution in equivalents per litre

K = conductivity (specific conductance) of solution.

It can also be defined as the conducting power of all the ions produced by dissolving 1 g equivalent of electrolyte in solution

$$\lambda_{eq} = \frac{K \times 1000}{C_{eq}}$$

where C_{eq} is the normality of solution.

units—$ohm^{-1}\ cm^2\ equi^{-1}$, $s\ cm^2\ equi^{-1}$

equipartition of energy The principle which states that the total energy of a molecule is, on average, equally distributed among the available degrees of freedom. It is only approximately true in most cases.

equivalence point The point in a titration at which reaction is complete (can be observed by change in colour of the solution).

equivalent weight Denoted by (Eq. Wt). The mass of an element or compound that could combine with or displace one gram of hydrogen (or eight grams of oxygen or 35.5 grams of chlorine) in a chemical reaction. The equivalent weight represents the 'combining power' of the substance. For an element, it is the relative atomic mass divided by the valency. For a compound, it depends on the reaction considered.

erbium It belongs to *'f'* block a soft malleable silvery element of the lanthanoid series of metals. It occurs in association with other lanthanoids. Erbium has uses in the metallurgical, nuclear, and glass industries.

Symbol: Er; m.p. 1520°C; b.p. 2863°C; r.d. 9.07; p.n. 68; r.a.m. 167.26.

ergosterol A sterol occurring in fungi, bacteria, algae, and higher plants. It is converted into vitamin D_2 by the action of ultraviolet light.

essential amino acid It is an amino acid that an organism is unable to synthesize in sufficient quantities. It must therefore be present in the diet. In man the essential amino acids are arginine, histidine, lysine, threonine, methionine, isoleucine, leucine, valine, phenylalanine, and tryptophan. These are required for protein synthesis and deficiency leads to retarded growth and other symptoms. Most of the amino acids required by man are also essential for all other multicellular animals and for most protozoans.

essential element Any of a number of elements required by living organisms to ensure normal growth, development, and maintenance. Apart from the elements found in organic compounds (i.e. carbon, hydrogen, oxygen, and nitrogen), plants, animals, and microorganisms all require a range of elements in inorganic forms in varying amounts, depending on the type of organism. The *major elements*, present in tissues in relatively large amounts (greater than 0.005%), are calcium, phosphorus, potassium, sodium, chlorine, sulphur, and magnesium. The *trace elements* occur at much lower concentrations and thus requirements are much less. The most important are iron, manganese, zinc, copper, iodine, cobalt, selenium, molybdenum, chromium, and silicon. Each element may fulfil one or more of a variety of metabolic roles.

essential fatty acid These are the *fatty acid* which are needed in the human diet because the body does not produce any or enough of it. There are four main essential fatty acids, all of which are found in vegetable oils.

essential oil A natural oil with a distinctive scent secreted by the glands of certain aromatic plants. Terpenes are the main constituents. Essential oils are extracted from plants by steam distillation, extraction with cold neutral fats or solvents (e.g. alcohol), or pressing and used in perfumes, flavourings, and medicine. Examples are citrus oils, flower oils (e.g. rose, jasmine), and oil of cloves.

esters These are the products obtained by the action of an acid and an alcohol. Their functional group is —COOR where 'R' is an alkyl or aryl group.

$$\underset{\text{Alcohol}}{ROH} + HOOCR' \rightarrow \underset{\text{Ester}}{H\,COOR'} + H_2O$$

Lower members of the ester family have a pleasant smell and are used in perfumes.

esterification It is the reaction of an acid with an alcohol to form an ester general formula (RCOOR') and water. The reaction is an equilibrium of the form:

$$CH_3COOH + C_2H_5OH \rightarrow CH_3COO - C_2H_5 + H_2O$$

In the preparation of esters the ester is distilled off or the water is removed to increase the yield. The reverse reaction is hydrolysis.

etard's reaction The oxidation of toluene with chromyl chloride to yield benzaldehyde is referred to as Etard's reaction.

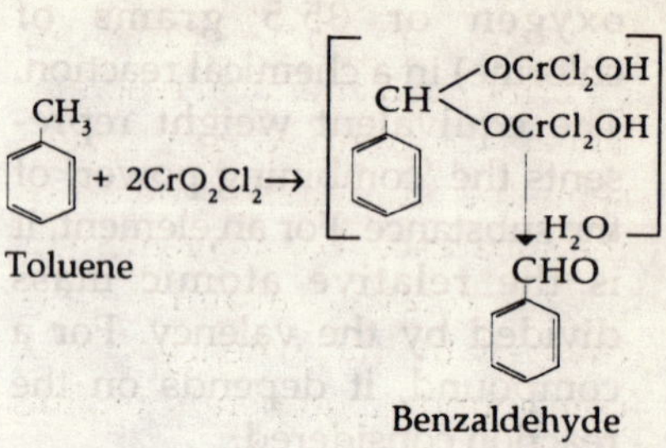

ethanal It is an aldehyde having molecular formula CH_3CHO and commonly known as acetaldehyde. A water-soluble liquid aldehyde used as a starting material in the manufacture of several other compounds. Ethanal can be prepared by the oxidation of ethanol. It is manufactured by the catalytic oxidation of ethyne with oxygen using copper(II) chloride and palladium(II) chloride as catalysts. The mixture of gases is bubbled through an aqueous solution of the catalysts; the reaction involves formation of an intermediate organometallic complex with Pd^{2+} ions. With dilute acids ethanal polymerizes to *ethanal trimer* $(C_3O_3H_3(CH_3)_3$, formerly called *paraldehyde*), which is a sleep-inducing drug. Below 0°C *ethanal tetramer* is formed $(C_4O_4H_4)(CH_3)_4$, formerly called *metaldehyde*), which is used as a slug poison and a fuel in small portable stoves.

ethanamide (acetamide) A colourless solid crystallizing in the form of long white crystals with a characteristic smell of mice, CH_3CONH_2; r.d. 1.159; m.p. 82.3°C; b.p. 221.25°C. It is prepared by the dehydration of ammonium ethanoate or by the action of ammonia on ethanoyl chloride, ethanoic anhydride, or ethyl ethanoate.

ethane (C_2H_6) An *alkane*. It is colourless, flammable gas which is found in all *natural gas* (35% of North Sea gas). *Ethene* ($H_2C = CH_2$) is formed when ethane is subjected to *cracking*.

ethane-1, 2-diol (ethylene glycol; glycol) A colourless viscous hygroscopic liquid, CH_2OHCH_2OH; m.p. –13°C; b.p. 470 K. It is made by hydrolysis of epoxyethane (from ethene) and used as an antifreeze and a raw material for making polyesters (e.g. Terylene).

ethanol It is an alcohol having molecular formula C_2H_5OH and is commonly known as ethyl alcohol. A colourless volatile liquid alcohol. Ethanol occurs in intoxicating drinks, in which it is produced by fermentation of sugar:

$$C_6H_{12}O_6 \rightarrow 2C_2H_5OH + 2CO_2$$

Yeast is used to cause the reaction. At about 15% alcohol concentration (by volume) the reaction stops because the yeast is killed. Higher concentrations of alcohol are produced by distillation.

Ethanol forms an azeotrope with water so its not possible to obtain more than 95.6% alcohol by weight, by distillation of an aquous solution. To manufacture 100% ethanol, known as *absolute alcohol*, azeotropic distillation is employed.

Apart from its use in drinks, alcohol is used as a solvent. Formerly, the main source was by fermentation of molasses, but now catalytic hydration of ethene is used to manufacture industrial ethanol.

ethanoyl chloride Commonly known as acetyl chloride having molecular formula CH_3COCl. A liquid acyl chloride is used as an acetylating agent.

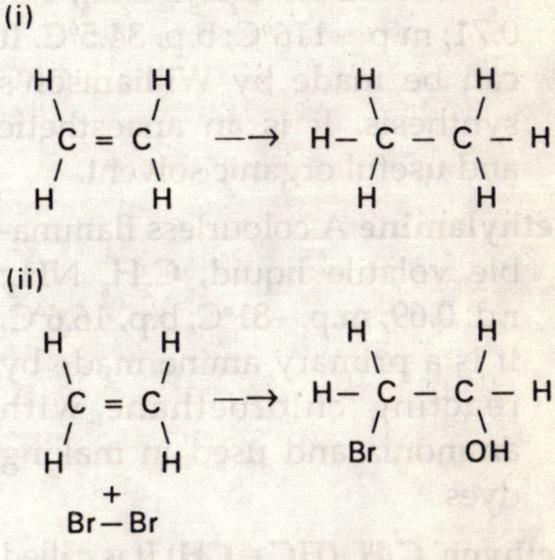

ethene (i) The compound (ii) adding molecules across its double bond to produce ethanol and ethylene dibromide.

ethene (formerly *ethylene*) ($H_2C = CH_2$). A gaseous *alkene* which is produced by *cracking alkanes* (e.g. *ethane* and *naphtha*).

It is carbon-carbon double bond.

Because it is an *unsaturated* compound it is reactive. It is a very important chemical being used to make *plastics* such as *poly (ethene)* and *poly (chloroethene)*. Ethene can add molecules across its *double bond*, e.g. to produce *ethanol*. These are addition reactions.

ethenyl ethanoate (vinyl acetate) An unsaturated organic ester, CH_2:$CHOOCCH_3$; r.d. 0.9; m.p. –100°C; b.p. 346 K. It is made by catalytic reaction of ethanoic acid and ethene and used to make polyvinylacetate.

ethoxyethane (diethyl ether; ether) A colourless flammable volatile ether, $C_2H_5OC_2H_5$; r.d. 0.71; m.p. –116°C; b.p. 34.5°C. It can be made by Williamson's synthesis. It is an anaesthetic and useful organic solvent.

ethylamine A colourless flammable volatile liquid, C_2H_5 NH_2; r.d. 0.69; m.p. –81°C; b.p. 16.6°C. It is a primary amine made by reacting chloroethane with ammonia and used in making dyes.

ethyne, C_2H_2 (HC ≡ CH) It is called acetylene. It is used for artificial ripening of fruits, as an illuminant, in oxy-acetylene flames etc. It is also used in the manufacture of CH_3CHO, CH_3COOH, Westrol, synthetic rubber, synthetic fibre etc.

europium belongs to 'f' block A silvery element of the lanthanoid series of metals. It occurs in association with other lanthanoids. Its main use is in a mixture of europium and yttrium oxides widely employed as the red phosphor in television screens.
Symbol: Eu; m.p. 822°C; b.p. 1597°C; r.d. 5.24; a.n. 63; r.a.m. 151.96.

eutrophic Over-rich in nutrients. Eutrophication is caused by fertilizers and other chemicals such as *phosphates* from sewage works. These get into the *water* and cause the rapid growth of plants such as weed. The weed chokes the water and removes a lot of the *oxygen* and prevents sunlight penetrating down into the water. A lake or river is described as eutrophic if there is not enough oxygen in the water to support animal and plant life.

evaporation The process of change of state of a liquid into a vapour at a temperature below the boiling point of the liquid. (liquid ⇌ vapour.) Evaporation occurs at the surface of a liquid, some of those molecules with the highest kinetic energies escaping into the gas phase. The result is a fall in the average kinetic energy of the molecules of the liquid and consequently a fall in its temperature.

exa-Symbol E. A prefix used in the metric system to denote 10^{18} times. For example, 10^{18} metres= 1 exametre (Em).

excitation energy It is the energy that is required to change an atom, molecule etc. from one quantum state to another state of higher energy.

excited state A state of an atom molecule, or other system, with an energy greater than that of the ground state. *Compare* ground state.

exothermic reaction Refers to those reactions which are accompanied by a release (evolution) of heat energy i.e. enthalpy change (ΔH) is -ive (or ΔH products < ΔH reactants), e.g. $H_2(g) + O_2(g) = H_2O(g)$; $\Delta H = -242.7$ KJ/mole.

explosives Substances that undergo rapid chemical reaction evolving heat (exothermic) and causing a sudden increase in pressure. The volume of gas produced by an explosive is great compared with the volume of the original substance. Examples of explosive substances are gunpowder, cellulose nitrate, TNT, nitroglycerin, and cyclonite.

extensive properties Those properties of a system which depend upon the quantity of matter contained in the system are called extensive properties e.g. mass, volume, energy, entropy etc.

F

Face-centred cubic crystal (f.c.c.) A crystal structure in which the unit cell has atoms, ions, or molecules at each corner and each face centre of a cube (also called *cubic close-packed*). It has a coordination number of 12. The structure is close-packed and made up of layers of atoms in which each atom is surrounded by six others arranged hexagonally. Copper and aluminium have face-centred cubic structures.

The layers are packed one on top of the other, with the second layer fitting into the holes of the first layer. The third layer is in a different set of holes formed by the second layer. If the layers are designated A, B, C, the packing is ABCABC in contrast to hexagonal close packing, in which the layers are arranged ABABAB.

fad (flavin adenine dinucleotide) A coenzyme important in various biochemical reactions. It comprises a phosphorylated vitamine B_2 (riboflavin) molecule linked to the nucleotide adenine monophosphate (AMP). FAD is usually tightly bound to the enzyme forming a *flavoprotein*. It functions as a hydrogen acceptor in dehydrogenation reactions, being reduced to $FADH_2$. This in turn is oxidized to FAD by the electron transport chain, thereby generating ATP (two molecules of ATP per molecule of $FADH_2$).

Fahrenheit scale It is a temperature scale in which (by modern definition) the temperature of boiling water is taken as 212 degrees and the temperature of melting ice as 32 degrees. It was invented in 1714 by the German scientist G.D. Fahrenheit (1686-1736), who set the zero at the lowest temperature he knew how to obtain in the laboratory (by mixing ice and common salt) and took his own body temperature as 96°F. The scale is no longer in scientific use. To convert to the Celsius scale the formula is $C = 5\,(F-32)/9$.

fall-out 1. (or radioactive fall-out) Radioactive particles deposited from the atomsphere either from a nuclear explosion or from a nuclear accident. *Local fall-out*, within 250 km of an explosion, falls within a few hours of the explosion. *Tropospheric fall-out* consists of fine particles deposited all round the earth in the approximate latitude of the explosion within about one week. *Stratospheric fall-out* may fall anywhere on earth over a period of years. The most dangerous radioactive isotopes in fall-out are the fission fragments iodine-131 and strontium-90. Both can be taken up by grazing animals and passed on to human populations in milk, milk products, and meat. Iodine-131 accumulates in the thyroid gland and strontium-90 accumulates in bones. **2. (or chemical fall-out)** Hazardous chemicals discharged into and subsequently released from the atmosphere, especially by factory chimneys.

farad Its symbol is 'F'. The SI unit of capacitance. When the plates of a capacitor are charged by one coulomb and there is a potential difference of one volt between them, then the capacitor has a capacitance of one farad. $1\ F = 1\ C\ V^{-1}$. 1 farad = 1 coloumb volt^{-1} ($C\ V^{-1}$).

faraday (F) The amount of electric charge possessed by a *mole* of *electrons*. The charge is approximately 96500 C. This amount of electricity is needed to liberate one mole of *atoms* of a *univalent element* (e.g. silver) during *electrolysis:*

Ag^+	+	e^-	→	Ag
One mole of silver ions.		One mole of electrons.		One mole of silver atoms.

Named after the English physicist and chemist Michael Faraday, 1791-1867.

Faraday's laws:

First law: It states that the amount of substance decomposed during electrolysis is directly proportional to the quantity of electricity passed.

$$w \propto c \times t$$

or $$w = z.\ c.\ t.$$

where z is a constant known as electrochemical equivalent (ECE).

Second law: It states that the amount of different substances liberated by passing the same quantity of electricity are proportional to their equivalent weights. Mathematically

$$\frac{\text{weight of A deposited}}{\text{eq. wt. of A}} = \frac{\text{wt. of B deposited}}{\text{eq. wt. of B}}$$

fats *Esters* of *fatty acids.* They are common constituents of food and a good source of *energy*, but there are worries that the UK diet contains too much fat. Oils are fats which are *liquid* at 293 K.

***f*-block elements** *f*-block consists of two series of 14 elements each placed at the bottom of the table. They have incomplete *f*-orbitals in their configuration. The elements from z = 58 to z = 71 are known as lanthanides and those with z = 89 onwards (14 elements) are known as actinides, e.g. Ce (z = 58), Nd (z = 60), Ac (z = 89), Np (z = 93) etc.

Fehling's solution It is a mixture of freshly prepared copper sulphate solution with alkaline potassium sodium 2, 3-dihydroxy butanedioate (tartarate). It is used to test for presence of aldehydic group in an organic compound.

feldspars It is a group of silicate minerals, the most abundant minerals in the earth's crust. They have a structure in which (Si, Al)O_4 tetrahedra are linked together with potassium, sodium, and calcium and very occasionally barium ions occupying the large spaces in the framework. The chemical composition of feldspars may be expressed as combinations of the four components:

anorthite (An), $CaAl_2Si_2O_8$;
albite (Ab), $NaAlSi_3O_8$;
orthoclase (Or), $KAlSi_3O_8$; and
celsian (Ce), $BaAl_2Si_2O_8$.

The feldspars are subdivided into two groups: the *alkali feldspars* (including microcline, orthoclase, and sanidine), in which potassium is dominant with a smaller proportion of sodium and negligible calcium; and the *plagioclase feldspars,* which vary in composition in a series that ranges from pure sodium feldspar (albite) through to pure calcium feldspar (anorthite) with negligible potassium. Feldspars form colourless, white, or pink crystals with a hardness of 6 on the Mohs' scale. ($FeSO_4.(NH_4)_2SO_4$)

feldspathoids A group of alkali aluminosilicate minerals that are similar in chemical composition to the feldspars but are relatively deficient in silica and richer in alkalis. The structure consists of a framework of (Si,Al)O_4 tetrahedra with aluminium and silicon atoms at their centres. The feldspathoids occur chiefly with feldspars but do not coexist with free quartz (SiO_2) as they react with silica to yield feldspars. The chief varieties of feldspathoids are:

nepheline, $KNa_3(AlSiO_4)_4$;
leucite, $KAlSi_2O_6$;
analcime, $NaAlSi_2O_6.H_2O$;
cancrinite, $Na_8(AlSiO_4)_6(HCO_3)_2$;
and the sodalite subgroup comprising
sodalite, $3(NaAlSiO_4).NaCl$;
nosean, $3(NaAlSiO_4).Na_2SO_4$;
haüyne, $3(NaAlSiO_4).CaSO_4$;
and lazurite $(Na,Ca)_8(Al,Si)_{12}O_{24}(S,SO_4)$

femto- Symbol f. A prefix denoting 10^{-15}. For example, 1 femtometre (fm) = 10^{-15} metre (m).

fermentation A process whereby *chemical changes* are made to *organic* chemicals by the use of living organisms such as *yeasts* and bacteria. The changes are brought about by *enzymes* which act as *catalysts.*

One important example is the changing of *sugars* to *ethanol* by the action of yeast:

$$C_6H_{12}O_6 \xrightarrow{\text{zymase}} 2C_2H_5OH + 2CO_2$$

glucose → ethanol + carbon dioxide

This reaction is used to make alcoholic drinks:

malted barley → beer
malted barley → whisky (after *fractional distillation*)

fruit, e.g. grapes → wine
fruit, e.g. grapes → sherry and port
fruit, e.g. grapes → brandy (after fractional distillation)

fermi A unit of length which was formerly used in nuclear physics. It is equal to 10^{-15} metre. In SI units this is equal to 1 femtometre (fm). It was named after the Italian-born US physicist Enrico Fermi (1901-54).

Fermi level It is the energy in a solid at which the average number of particles per quantum state is ½; i.e. one half of the quantum states are occupied. The Fermi level in conductors lies in the conduction bond (*see* energy bands), in insulators it lies in the valence band, and in semiconductors it falls in the gap between the conduction band and the valence band. At absolute zero all the electrons would occupy energy levels up to the Fermi level and no higher levels would be occupied.

fermium A member of '*f*' block. A radioactive transuranic element of the actinoid series, not found naturally on Earth. Several short-lived isotopes have been synthesized.

Symbol: Fm; p.n. 100; stablest isotope ^{257}Fm (half-life 80 days).

ferric compounds These are the compounds of iron in its +3 oxidation state; e.g. ferric chloride is iron(III) chloride, $FeCl_3$.

ferricyanide A compound containing the complex ion $[Fe(CN)_6]^{3-}$, that is the hexacyanoferrate(III) ion.

ferrocene, $[Fe(\eta^5-C_5H_5)_2]$ It has a sandwich structure. It is a π - complex.

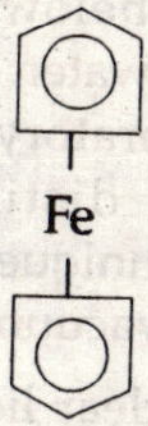

ferrocyanide A compound containing the complexion $[Fe(cN)_6]^4$ hexacyanoferrate(II) ion.

fertilizer A substance which is added to the soil to replace the nutrients which have been removed by plants. Fertilizers are of 2 types: natural, e.g. manure and compost, or artificial, e.g. ammonium nitrate, superphosphate.

fibres These are polyamide polymers. In them the interparticle forces are hydrogen bonds which are considered to be very strong bonds. They have high modulus and high tensile strength e.g. Nylon, dacron, terylene etc.

filter A device for separating solid particles from a liquid or gas. The simplest laboratory filter for liquids is a funnel in which a cone of filter paper is placed. Special containers with a porous base of sintered glass are also used.

filter pump It is a type of vacuum pump in which a jet of water forced through a nozzle carries air molecules out of the system. Filter pumps cannot produce pressures below the vapour pressure of water. They are used in the laboratory for vacuum filtration, distillation, and similar techniques requiring a low-grade vacuum.

filtrate The clear liquid obtained by filtration.

filtration It is the process of removing suspended particles from a fluid by passing or forcing the fluid through a porous material (the *filter*). In laboratory filtration, filter paper or sintered glass is commonly used.

fine chemicals Chemicals produced industrially in relatively small quantities and with a high purity; for example, dyes and drugs.

fine structure These are the closely spaced spectral lines arising from transitions between energy levels that are spilt by the vibrational or rotational motion of a molecule or by electron spin. They are visible only at high resolution. *Hyperfine structure*, visible only at very high resolution, results from the influence of the atomic nucleus on the allowed energy levels of the atom.

firedamp Methane (CH_4) occurring in coal mines. Explosions can occur if quantities of methane accumulate. The air left after an explosion is called *black-damp*. *Afterdamp* is the toxic carbon monoxide formed.

fire extinguisher It is a device that helps in extinguishing the fire. Generally it supplies a fluid that stops combustion. CO_2 gas is also used as an extinguisher.

fire triangle A *symbol* summarizing the three things which have to be present for a fire to burn: *fuel, heat* and *oxygen*.

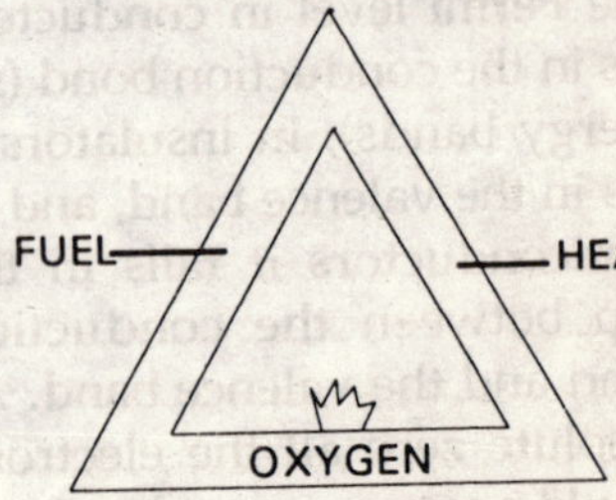

fire triangle

Fischer-Tropsch process An

industrial method of making hydrocarbon fuels from carbon monoxide and hydrogen. The process was invented in 1933 and used by Germany in World War II to produce motor fuel. H_2 and CO are mixed in the ratio 2:1 (water gas was used with added hydrogen) and passed at 473 K over a nickel or cobalt catalyst. The resulting hydrocarbon mixture can be separated into a higher-boiling fraction for Diesel engines and a lower-boiling gasoline fraction. The gasoline fraction contains a high proportion of straight-chain hydrocarbons and has to be reformed for use in motor fuel. Alcohols, aldehydes, and ketones are also present. The process is also used in the manufacture of SNG from coal. It is named after the German chemist Franz Fischer (1852-1932) and the Czech Hans Tropsch (1839-1935).

fission It is the process in which a larger nuclei breaks up to give smaller nuclei. A fission reaction is generally accompanied by release of a large amount of energy. These are the exothermic reactions.

fission-track dating It is a method of estimating the age of glass and other mineral objects by observing the tracks made in them by the fission fragments of the uranium nuclei that they contain. By irradiating the objects with neutrons to induce fission and comparing the density and number of the tracks before and after irradiation it is possible to estimate the time that has elapsed since the object solidified.

fixed point A temperature that can be accurately reproduced to enable it to be used as the basis of a temperature scale.

fixing nitrogen Any process which converts atmospheric *nitrogen* into *compounds* which are useful as *fertilizers.* Fixing occurs in the *Haber process* and is carried out by bacteria found on the roots of certain plants, such as peas and beans.

flame It is a hot luminous mixture of gases undergoing combustion. The chemical reactions in a flame are mainly free-radical chain reactions and the light comes from fluorescence of excited molecules or ions or from incandescence of small solid particles for example, carbon.

flame colouration Some elements when burnt into a Bunsen flame impart a characteristic colour to the flame. For example, sodium—yellow, lithium—red, potassium—violet, barium—green etc.

flame test A test used to identify *metal ions* present in *compounds* is known as flame test.

A clean nichrome or *platinum* wire is dipped into *concentrated hydrochloric acid* and then into a sample of the compound under test. The wire, which now has a small amount of the compound attached to it, is then put into the hottest part of the *flame*. Metals are characterized by specific colours: Following metals give following colours in oxidising flame:

Copper:	green/blue	Potassium:	lilac
Calcium:	brick red	Barium:	apple green
Sodium:	yellow/orange	Lithium:	bright red

flash photolysis This method is used to study very fast reactions, that usually involve atoms or radicals in the gas phase.

flash point It is the temperature at which the vapour above a volatile liquid forms a combustible mixture with air. At the flash point the application of a naked flame gives a momentary flash rather than sustained combustion, for which the temperature is too low.

fluorescence The absorption of energy by atoms, molecules, etc., followed by immediate emission of electromagnetic radiation as the particles make transitions to lower energy states.

fluorination A chemical reaction in which a fluorine atom is introduced into a molecule.

fluorine (F_2) Its a.n. 9. r.a.m, 18.9984, d 1.7 gdm^{-3}, m.p. 219.62°C b.p. A gaseous, nonmetallic *element* in *group* VII of the *periodic table*. It is a *halogen* and the most reactive element known.

Fluorine is a vigorous *oxidizing agent* which will even oxidize *chloride ion* and *water:*

$$2Cl^-(aq) + F_2(g) \rightarrow 2F^-(aq) + Cl_2(aq)$$

$$2H_2O(l) + F_2(g) \rightarrow 4HF(g) + O_2(g)$$

fluorocarbon Any compound derived from a hydrocarbon by replacement of its hydrogen atoms with fluorine, e.g. CCl_2F_2 (freon).

foam A dispersion of bubbles in a liquid. Foams can be stabilized by surfactants. Solid foams (e.g. expanded polystyrene or foam rubber) are made by foaming the liquid and allowing it to set.

folic acid Also known as folacin. A vitamin of the vitamin B complex. In its active form, tetrahydrofolic acid, it is a coenzyme in various reactions involved in the metabolism of amino acids, purines, and pyrimidines. It is synthesized by intestinal bacteria and is widespread in food, especially green leafy vegetables. Deficiency causes poor growth and nutritional anaemia.

food value It refers to the energy released on combustion of a food. It is an exothermic reaction.

fossil fuel Coal, oil, and natural gas, the fuels used by man as a source of energy. They are formed from the remains of living organisms and all have a high carbon or hydrogen content. Their value as fuels relies on the exothermic oxidation of carbon to form carbon dioxide ($C + O_2 \rightarrow CO_2$) and the oxidation of hydrogen to form water $H_2 + ½O_2 \rightarrow H_2O$).

formalin An *aqueous solution* of *methanal (formaldehyde)*. It is used in preservation of biological specimens.

formula It is a way of representing a chemical compound using symbols for the atoms present. Subscripts are used for the numbers of atoms. The *molecular formula* simply gives the types and numbers of atoms present. For example, the molecular formula of ethanoic acid is $C_2H_4O_2$. The *empirical formula* gives the atoms in their simplest ratio; for ethanoic acid it is CH_2O. The *structural formula* gives an indication of the way the atoms are arranged. Commonly, this is done by dividing the formula into groups; ethanoic acid can be written $CH_3.CO.OH$ (or more usually simply CH_3COOH). It is also known as acetic acid. Structural formulae can also show the arrangement of atoms or groups in space.

formula weight The relative molecular mass of a compound as calculated from its molecular formula.

fraction A mixture of liquids with similar boiling points collected by fractional distillation.

fractional crystallisation (a way or method of separation) It is a technique used for the purification of substances. It can be used to separate a less soluble substance from a more soluble substance present in a mixture. The substances are dissolved in a suitable solvent and then allowed to crystallize out. The less soluble substance crystallises out leaving more soluble substance in solution.

fractional distillation (also known as fractionation) A process of separating the components of a *mixture*. A *solvent* can be separated from a *solution* by the process of simple *distillation*. For a mixture of liquids with different *boiling points* it is usual to distil it and collect the products (*distillates*) which boil in definite *temperature* ranges. These distillates are termed *fractions*.

The exact temperature range of these fractions can be varied depending on the product which is in greatest demand. The distillation of whisky and brandy is an example of fractional distillation.

francium Symbol Fr. It is 'S' block element. A radioactive element belonging to group I of the periodic table; having a.n. 87;

r.d. 2.4; m.p. 27±1°C; b.p. 677±1°C. The element is found in uranium and thorium ores. All 22 known isotopes are radioactive, the most stable being francium –223. The existence of francium was confirmed by Marguerite Perey in 1939.

frasch process A method used for obtaining *sulphur* from deep underground. A double well is sunk and superheated water is passed down. This liquefies the sulphur which is then blown to the surface by compressed *air*.

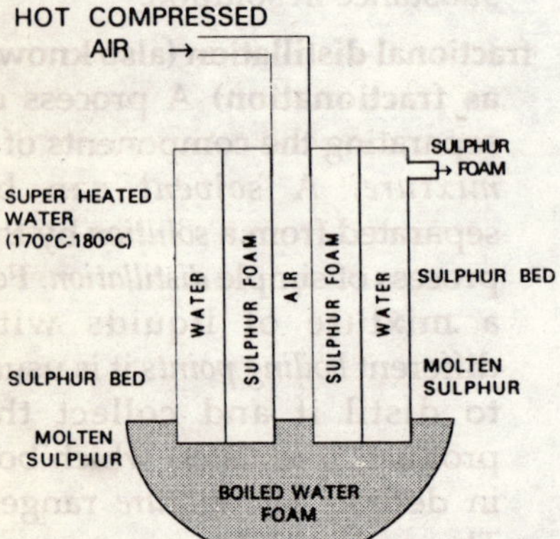

freezing The process by which a liquid is converted into a solid by cooling. This process is reverse of melting.

freeze drying It is a process used in dehydrating food, blood plasma, and other heat-sensitive substances. The product is deep-frozen and the ice trapped in it is removed by reducing the pressure and causing it to sublime. The water vapour is then removed, leaving an undamaged dry product.

freezing point It is a the temperature at which the equilibrium exists between a solid phase and the liquid phase at standard pressure. Below this temperature the liquid freezes or solidifies.

Frenkel defect *see* defect.

freundlich isotherms It is a graph between $\log\frac{x}{m}$ and log p. It is a straight line. Various forms are

$$\frac{x}{m} = kp' \text{(at low pressure)}$$

$$\frac{x}{m} = kp^{o} \text{ (at high pressure)}$$

$$\frac{x}{m} = kp^{\frac{1}{n}} \text{ (at intermediate pressure)}$$

$$\log = \frac{x}{m} \quad \log k + \frac{1}{n} \log p$$

$$\text{the slope of line} = \frac{1}{n}$$

$$\text{Intercept on } \log\frac{x}{m} \text{ axis} = \log k.$$

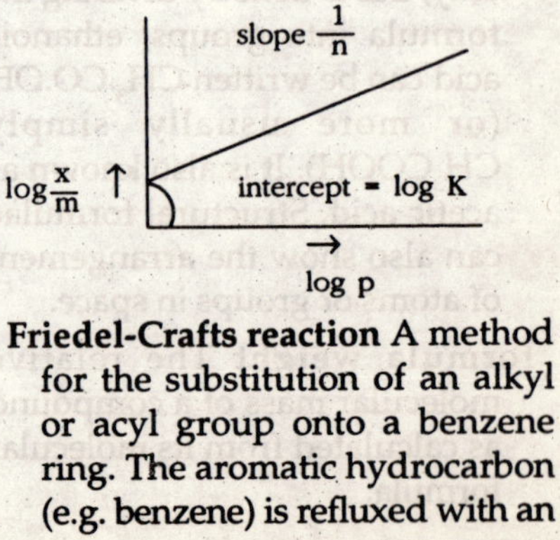

Friedel-Crafts reaction A method for the substitution of an alkyl or acyl group onto a benzene ring. The aromatic hydrocarbon (e.g. benzene) is refluxed with an alkyl halide or acyl halide using aluminium chloride catalyst. The product is an alkylarene, e.g.:

$$C_6H_6 + CH_3I \xrightarrow{\text{Anhd. AlCl}} C_6H_5CH_3 + HI$$

or a ketone, for example:

$$C_6H_6 + CH_3COCl \xrightarrow{\text{Anhd. AlCl}} C_6H_5COCH_3 + HCl$$

The aluminium chloride accepts a lone pair of electrons on the chlorine, polarizing the chloroalkane to produce positive charge on the carbon. Electrophilic substitution then occurs.

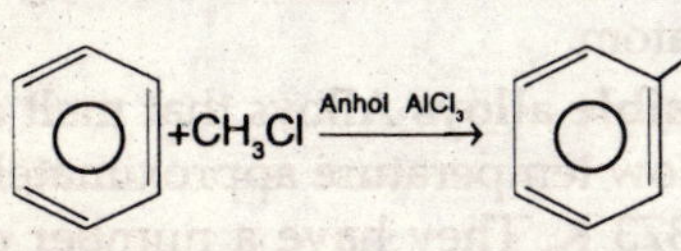

benzene chloromethane methylbenzene (toluene)

Friedel-Craftsmethylation

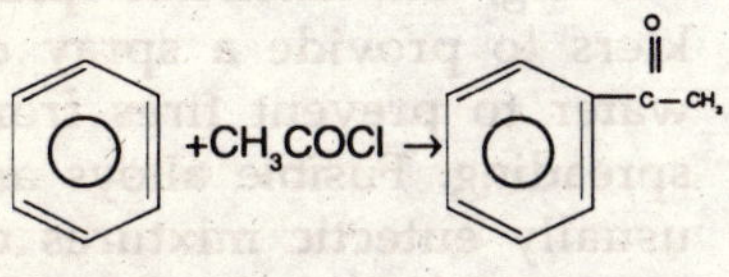

benzene acetyl chloride phenylmethylketone

Friedel-crafts acetylation

Friedel-Crafts acetylation

froth flotation A method of separating mixtures of solids, used industrially for separating ores from the unwanted gangue. The mixture is ground to a powder and water and a frothing agent added. Air is blown through the water. With a suitable frothing agent, the bubbles adhere only to particles of ore and carry them to the surface, leaving the gangue particles at the bottom.

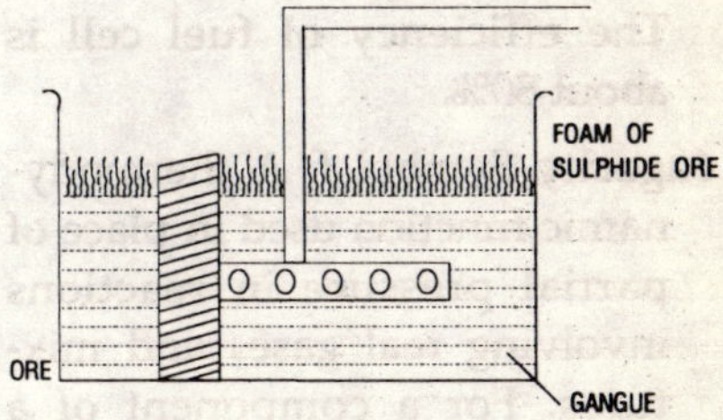

fructose ($C_6H_{12}O_6$) It is a sugar found in fruit juices, honey, and cane sugar. It is a ketohexose, existing in a pyranose form when free. In combination (e.g. in sucrose) it exists in the furanose form.

fuel cell It is a device used for conversion of chemical energy of a fuel directly into electrical energy.

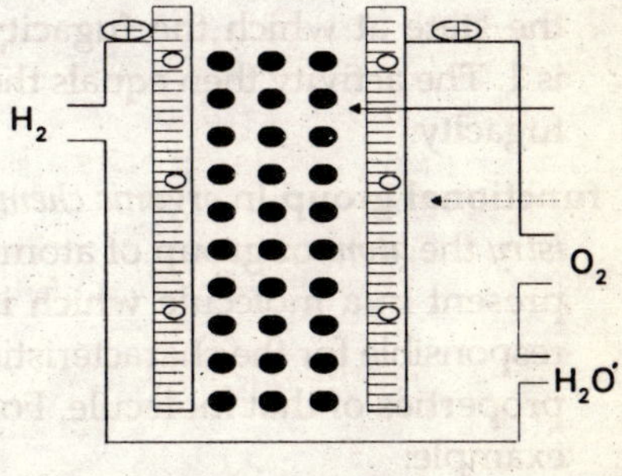

$H_2 - O_2$, fuel cell

Reaction in $H_2 - O_2$ fuel cell

Anode $H_2(g)+2OH^-(aq) \rightarrow$

$2H_2O(l)+2e^-] \times 2$

Cathode $O_2(g)+2H_2O(l)+4e^- \rightarrow 4OH^-(aq)$

Net reaction $2H_2(g) + O_2(g) \rightarrow 2H_2O(l)$

Such a cell is used to generate electrical power in Appolo space programme.

The efficiency of fuel cell is about 80%.

fugacity Symbol *f*. A thermodynamic function used in place of partial pressure in reactions involving real gases and mixtures. For a component of a mixture, it is defined by $d\mu = RTd(\ln f)$, where μ is the chemical potential. It has the same units as pressure and the fugacity of a gas is equal to the pressure if the gas is ideal. The fugacity of a liquid or solid is the fugacity of the vapour with which it is in equilibrium. The ratio of the fugacity to the fugacity in some standard state is the activity. For a gas, the standard state is chosen to be the state at which the fugacity is 1. The activity then equals the fugacity.

functional group In *organic chemistry* the *atom* or group of atoms present in a molecule which is responsible for the characteristic properties of that molecule. For example:

$-OH$	hydroxyl group
$-CO_2H$	carboxylic acid
$-CHO$	aldehyde
$-NH_2$	amine
$>C = O$	ketone

The 'functional groups' of organic chemistry correspond to the 'radicals' of *inorganic chemistry*.

fundamental units They are the units of length, mass, and time that form the basis of most systems of units. In SI, the fundamental units are the metre, the kilogram, and the second. *See also* base unit.

furanose A sugar having a five-membered ring containing four carbon atoms and one oxygen atom.

fusible alloys Alloys that melt at low temperature approximately 373 K. They have a number of uses, including constant-temperature baths, pipe bending, and automatic sprinklers to provide a spray of water to prevent fires from spreading. Fusible alloys are usually eutectic mixtures of bismuth, lead, tin, and cadmium. Wood's metal and Lipowitz's alloy are examples of alloys that melt at about 70°C.

fusion 1. It is the process in which solid changes to liquid (melting)

Solid → liquid.

2. *See* Neuclear fusion

G

Gabriel Phthalamide Synthesis It is used to prepare primary amine from potassium phthalimide.

gadolinium Symbol: Gd; m.p. 1313°C; b.p. 3266°C; r.d. 7.9; a.n. 64; r.a.m. 157.25. A member of lanthanoid series in 'f' block. A ductile malleable silvery element. It occurs in association with other lanthanoids. Gadolinium is used in alloys, magnets, and in the electronics industry.

galactose A simple sugar, having the formula $C_6H_{12}O_6$, stereoisomeric with glucose, that occurs naturally as one of the products of the enzymic digestion of milk sugar (lactose) and as a constituent of gum arabic.

galena It is a mineral form of lead(II) sulphide, PbS, crystallizing in the cubic system; the chief ore of lead. It usually occurs as grey metallic cubes, frequently in association with silver, arsenic, copper, zinc, and antimony. Important deposits occur in Australia (at Broken Hill), Germany, the USA (especially in Missouri, Kansas, and Oklahoma), and the UK.

gallic acid, $C_7H_6O_5$ It is 3, 4, 5-trihydroxy benzoic acid. It is sparingly soluble in water and alcohol. It is found in free state in many woody tissues, in gall nuts and in tea. It is a constituent of tannins. It is used in the manufacture of inks.

gallium Symbol Ga. A soft silvery metallic element belonging in group IIIA of the periodic table; a.n. 31; r.a.m. 69.72; r.d. 5.90 (20°C); m.p. 29.78°C; b.p. 2676 K. It occurs in zinc blende, bauxite, and kaolin, from which it can be extracted by fractional electrolysis. It also occurs in gallite, $CuGaS_2$, to an extent of 1%; although bauxite only contains 0.01%, this is the only commercial source. The two stable isotopes are gallium-69 and gallium-71; there are eight radioactive isotopes, all with short half-lives. The metal has only a few minor uses (e.g. as an activator in luminous paints), but gallium arsenide is extensively used as a semiconductor in many applications. Gallium corrodes most other metals because it rapidly diffuses into their lattices. Most gallium(I) and some gallium(II) compounds are unstable. The element was first identified by Francois Lecoq de Boisbaudran in 1875.

galvanized iron Iron or steel that has been coated with a layer of zinc to protect it from corrosion. Corrugated mild-steel sheets for roofing and mild-steel sheets for dustbins, etc., are usually galvanized by dipping them in molten zinc. The addition of small quantities of aluminium or magnesium prevents the formation of a brittle zinc-iron alloy. Wire is often galvanized by a cold electrolytic process as no alloy forms in this process. Galvanizing is an effective method of protecting steel because even if the surface is scratched, the zinc still protects the underlying metal.

galvanizing A process for coating steel with Zn by dipping in a bath of molten zinc, or by electrodeposition. The zinc protects the steel from corrosion.

gamma radiation It is the electromagnetic radiation emitted by excited atomic nuclei during the process of passing to a lower excitation state. Gamma radiation ranges in energy from about 10^{-15} to 10^{-11} joule (10 KeV to 100 MeV) corresponding to a wavelength range of about 10^{-10} to 10^{-14} metre.

gamma rays High energy electromagnetic waves having short wavelength produced during the decay of certain nuclei. Energy leaves as a packet of radiations and the nucleus becomes more stable.

Gamma rays can pass through matter very easily. They produce ionisation in gases. They can penetrate deep into the human body and may cause disorders such as cancer. Gamma radiography is used to examine the internal structure of metal objects such as air-craft engine components. Workers dealing with gamma-rays (γ-rays) be protected by lead and/or concrete shielding.

gas A *state of matter* in which *atoms* and *molecules* have few *bonds* between them and large intermolecular spaces and consequently have a large amount of freedom of movement. They move at high velocity and in random directions.

When *heat energy* is supplied to a *liquid*, the atoms or molecules are given increased *kinetic energy;* this may be sufficient to overcome the bonds which hold them together in the liquid state. If this happens the liquid boils and turns into a gas or *vapour*. In a gas, atoms or molecules fill the whole container and their collisions with the walls of the container exert a *pressure*.

gas constant It is denoted by 'R'. Its numerical value is 0.082 atm.

$dm^3\ mole^{-1}\ K^{-1}$, if P is measured in atmospheres and V in dm^3.

Its value is 8.314 J $mol^{-1}\ K^{-1}$ if P is measured in pascals and υ in m^{-1}.

R represents the work of expansion of one mole of gas for one degree increase in absolute temperature.

gaseous diffusion separation A technique for the separation of gases that relies on their slightly different atomic masses, e.g. the isotopes of uranium (^{235}U and ^{238}U) can be separated by first preparing uranium hexafluoride from uranium ore. If this is then made to pass through a series of fine pores, the molecules containing the lighter isotope of uranium will pass through more slowly. As the gases pass through successive 'diaphragms', the proportion of lighter molecules increases and a separation of over 99% is attainable. This method has also been applied for separating the isotopes of hydrogen.

gas laws These are the laws that describe the behaviour of gases. The two main ones are *Boyle's law* and *Charles' law.* If they are combined we realize that for a fixed mass of gas:

$$\frac{(\text{Pressure}) \times (\text{Volume})}{(\text{Temperature})} = \text{constant}$$

or,

$$\frac{PV}{T} = \text{constant (T is in Kelvin)}$$

gas thermometer A device used for measuring temperature in which the working fluid is a gas. It provides the most accurate method of measuring temperatures in the range 2.5 to 1337 K. Using a fixed mass of gas a *constant-volume thermometer* measures the pressure of a fixed volume of gas at relevant temperatures, usually by means of a mercury manometer and a barometer.

gauss Symbol G. The unit of magnetic flux density in the c.g.s. system. It is equal to 10^{-4} tesla.

Gattermann reaction Benzene diazonium chloride on treatment with Cu/HCl or Cu/HBr yields halobenzene. This reaction is called Gattermann reaction.

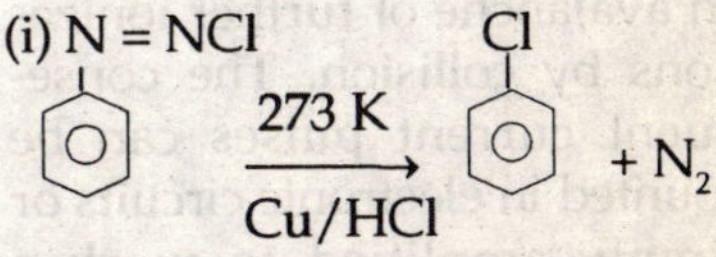

Chlorobenzene

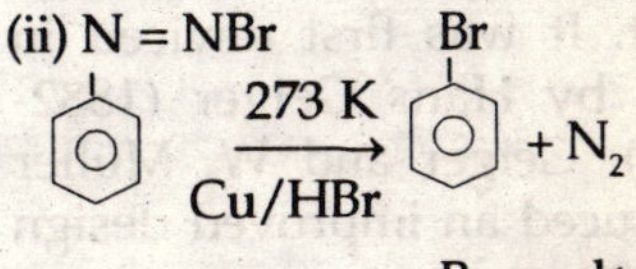

Bromobenzene

Gay Lussac's law It states that when gases combine chemically the volumes of the reactants and the volume of the product, if it is gaseous, bear simple relationships to each other when measured under the same conditions of temperature and pressure. The law was first stated in 1808 by J.L. Gay Lussac (1778-1850) and led to Avogadro's law.

Geiger counter (Geiger-Müller counter) A device used to detect and measure ionizing radiation. It consists of a tube containing a low-pressure gas (usually Ar or Ne and CH_4) and a cylindrical hollow cathode through the centre of which runs a fine-wire anode. A potential difference of about 1000 volts is maintained between the electrodes. An ionizing particle or photon passing through a window into the tube will cause an ion to be produced and the high p.d. will accelerate it towards its appropriate electrode, causing an avalanche of further ionizations by collision. The consequent current pulses can be counted in electronic circuits or simply amplified to work a small loudspeaker in the instrument. It was first deviced in 1908 by Hans Geiger (1882-1947). Geiger and W. Müller produced an improved design in 1928.

gel A lyophilic colloid that is normally stable but may be induced to coagulate partially under certain conditions (e.g. lowering the temperature). This produces a pseudo-solid or easily deformable jelly-like mass, called a gel, in which intertwining particles enclose the whole dispersing medium. Gels may be further subdivided into 2 types: elastic gels (e.g. gelatin) and rigid gels (e.g. silica gel).

gel filtration It is a type of column chromatography in which a mixture of liquids is passed down a column containing a gel. Small molecules in the mixture can enter pores in the gel and move slowly down the column; large molecules, which cannot enter the pores, move more quickly. Thus, mixtures of molecules can be separated on the basis of their size. The technique is used particularly for separating proteins but it can also be applied to other polymers and to cell nuclei, viruses, etc.

geometrical isomerism It arises due to restricted movement around a carbon-carbon double bond (C = C). This type of isomerism is shown by compounds with general formula $CA_2 B_2$. The two isomers (Cis- and trans-) can be written as under.

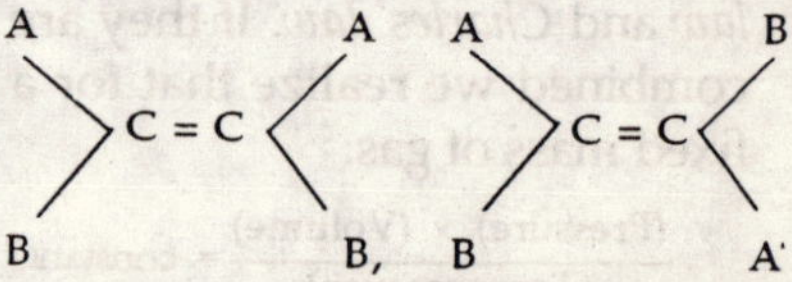

cis trans

cis = same Trans = opposite

germanium Symbol: Ge; m.p. 937.4°C; b.p. 3103 K; r.d. 5.32; a.n. 32; r.a.m. 72.59. A hard brittle grey metalloid element belonging to group IV, *'p'* block of the periodic table. It is found in sulphide ores such as argyrodite ($4Ag_2S.GeS_2$) and in zinc ores and coal. Germanium was extensively used in early semiconductor devices but has now been largely superseded by silicon. It is used as an alloying agent, catalyst, phosphor, and in infrared equipment.

German silver (nickel silver) An alloy of Cu, Zn and Ni often in the proportions 5:2:2. It resembles silver in appearance and is used in cheap jewellery and cutlery and as a base for silver-plated wire.

germicide It is a substance which is used to reduce or prevent the growth of micro-organisms. Germicides are used both in the home to deal with minor cuts and grazes, and in hospitals during treatment of wounds and in surgery. Many modern *compounds* are based on the molecule *phenol*. Antiseptics and *disinfectants* are kinds of germicide.

g factor It is the proportionality factor in the relation between the magnetic moment, μ, and the number of unpaired electrons.

$$\mu = g\sqrt{s(s+1)}$$

For a free electron g = 2.003

giant structure *Atoms* or *ions* that have large numbers of particles present in a *crystal lattice*. Each particle has a strong force of attraction for all the other particles which are near to it. In this way attractive forces are spead through the structure and giant structure tend to have high *melting* and *boiling points*. Like most elements ionic substances have giant structures, for example all *metals* and several *non-metals*.

Gibbs function (Gibbs free energy) Symbol *G*. A thermodynamic function defined by

$$G = H - TS$$

where *H* is the enthalpy, *T* the thermodynamic temperature, and *S* the entropy. It is useful for specifying the conditions of chemical equilibrium for reactions for constant temperature and pressure (*G* is a minimum).

glass Any noncrystalline solid; i.e. a solid in which the atoms are random and have no long-range ordered pattern. Glasses are often regarded as supercooled liquids. Characteristically they have no definite melting point, but soften over a range of temperatures.

The common glass used in windows, bottles, etc., is *soda glass*, which is made by heating a mixture of lime (CaO), soda (Na_2CO_3), and sand (SiO_2). It is a form of calcium silicate. Borosilicate glasses (e.g. *Pyrex*) are made by incorpora- ting some boron oxide, so that silicon atoms are replaced by boron atoms. They are tougher than soda glass and more resistant to temperature changes, hence their use in cooking utensils and laboratory apparatus. Glasses for special purposes (e.g. optical glass) have other elements added (for example B, Pb).

glass electrode It is a type of half cell having a glass bulb containing an acidic solution of fixed p^H, into which dips a platinum wire. The glass bulb is thin enough for hydrogen ions to diffuse through. If the bulb is placed in a solution containing hydrogen ions, the electrode potential depends on the hydrogen-ion concentration. Glass electrodes are used in p^H measurement.

glass fibres Melted glass drawn into thin fibre having diameter of about 0.005 mm-0.01 mm. The fibres may be spun into threads and woven into fabrics, which are then impregnated with resins to give a material that is both strong and corrosion resistant for use in car bodies and boat building.

Glauber's salt Sodium sulphate decahydrate, $Na_2SO_4.10\ H_2O$, used as a laxative. It is named after J.R. Glauber (1604-68).

glucose; $C_6H_{12}O_6$ A mono saccharide carbohydrate. It is produced during the process of photosynthesis. It is an important source of energy in both animal and plant cells.

$$6CO_2 + 6H_2O \xrightarrow{h\nu} C_6H_{12}O_6 + 6O_2$$

glyceride (acylglycerol) A fatty-acid ester of glycerol. Esterification can occur at one, two, or all three –OH groups of the glycerol molecule producing mono-, di-, and triglycerides respectively. Triglycerides are the major constituent of fats and oils found in living organisms. Alternatively, one of the –OH groups may be esterified with a phosphate group forming a phosphoglyceride (*see* phospholipid) or to a sugar forming a *glycolipid*.

glycerol It is also called glycerine. Its formula is

$$\begin{array}{c} CH_2OH \\ | \\ CH_2OH \\ | \\ CH_2OH \end{array}$$

It is a syrupy, colourless, sweet liquid.

glycogen (animal starch) A polysaccharide that is the main carbohydrate store of animals. It is composed of many glucose units linked in a similar way to starch. Glycogen is readily hydrolysed in a stepwise manner to glucose itself. It is stored largely in the liver and in muscle but is found widely distributed.

glycol Its formula is

$$\begin{matrix} CH_2OH \\ | \\ CH_2OH \end{matrix}$$

It is used as antifreezing material in radiators and is a diol.

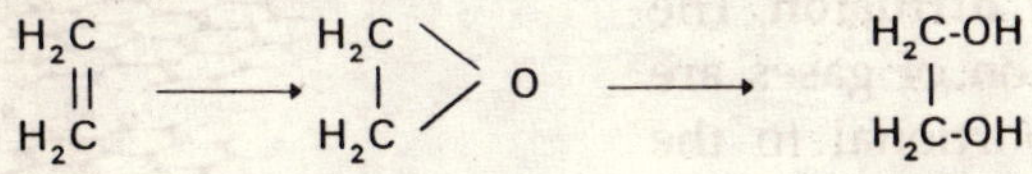

Ethene **epoxy ethane** **ethane 1,2, diol**

glycol Oxidizing ethene to obtain glycol.

goethite A yellow-brown mineral, having the molecular formula FeO.OH, crystallizing in the orthorhombic system. It is formed as a result of the oxidation and hydration of iron minerals or as a direct precipitate from marine or fresh water (e.g. in swamps and bogs). Most limonite is composed largely of cryptocrystalline goethite. Goethite is mined as an ore of iron.

gold Symbol Au. A soft yellow malleable metallic transition element; belongs to '*d*' block a.n. 79; r.a.m. 196.967; r.d. 19.32; m.p. 1064.43°C; b.p. 2807±2°C. It is found as the free metal in gravel or in quartz veins, and is also present in some lead and copper sulphide ores. It also occurs combined with silver in the telluride sylvanite, $(Ag,Au)Te_2$. It is used in jewellery, dentistry, and electronic devices. Chemically, it is unreactive, being unaffected by oxygen. It reacts with chlorine at 200°C to form gold(III) chloride. It forms a number of complexes with gold in the +1 and +3 oxidation states.

Goldschmidt process It is a method of extracting metals by reducing the oxide with aluminium powder, e.g.

$$Cr_2O_3 + 2Al \rightarrow 2Cr + Al_2O_3$$

The reaction can also be used to produce molten iron (*see* thermite). It was discovered by the German chemist Hans Goldschmidt (1861-1923).

gooch crucible A porcelain dish with a perforated base over which a layer of asbestos is placed. It is used for filtration in gravimetric analysis.

gram One thousandth of a kilogram. The gram is the

fundamental unit of mass in c.g.s. units and was formerly used in such units as the *gram-atom, gram-molecule,* and *gram-equivalent,* which have now been replaced by the mole. Its symbol is 'g'.

Grahm's law of diffusion The rates of diffusion of gases are inversely proportional to the square roots of their densities under similar conditions of temperature and pressure. Mathematically,

$$\frac{r_2}{r_1} = \sqrt{\frac{d_1}{d_2}} = \sqrt{\frac{M_1}{M_2}}$$

where r_1, r_2 are rates of diffusion, d_1, d_2 are densities and M_1, M_2 are molecular weights of two gases respectively.

graphite An allotropic form of *carbon.* It is found naturally as *plumbago. Charcoal* consists of small particles of graphite. It is a *giant structure* with the carbon *atoms* bonded together in a hexagonal arrangement in layers or planes.

There are strong *bonds* between the atoms in the planes but the bonds between the atoms in different planes are weak. It is possible for the planes to slip over each other.

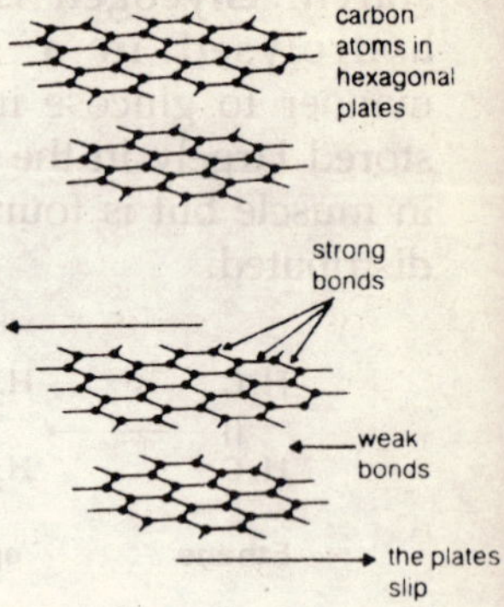

graphite The giant structure of bonded carbon atoms.

Because of this property, graphite is very useful as a lubricant and, in pencils where layers of graphite are left behind on the paper.

Since it is an electrical conductor, graphite also finds use as *electrodes* in the extraction of elements, e.g. *sodium, aluminium* and *chlorine.*

gravimetric analysis It is a process used for quantitative analysis. In it the ion to be estimated is converted to some compound of a definite composition which is precipitated, dried and weighed. From this the amount of ion is calculated.

greenhouse effect The increase in global temperature caused by the build-up of gases in the *Earth's atmosphere* which trap beneath them the Sun's energy reflected from the Earth. This trapped energy keeps the planet 313 K warmer than it would otherwise be. In doing this it is rather like a greenhouse—hence the term—but the mechanism for warming the Earth and keeping a greenhouse hot are quite different.

Grignard reagent A type of organometallic compound with the general formula RMgX, where R is an alkyl or aryl group and X is a halogen e.g. CH_3MgCl—Methyl magnesium chloride C_6H_5MgBr—Benzyl magnesium bromide. They are prepared by reacting the haloalkane or haloaryl compound with magnesium in dry ether:

$$CH_3Cl + Mg \rightarrow CH_3MgCl$$

Grignard reagents probably have the form $R_2Mg.MgCl_2$. They are used extensively in organic chemistry:

With formaldehyde a primary alcohol is produced:

$$RMgX + HCHO \rightarrow RCH_2OH + Mg(OH)X$$

Other aldehydes give secondary alcohols:

$$RMgX + R'CHO \rightarrow RR'CHOH + Mg(OH)X$$

Alcohols and carboxylic acids give hydrocarbons:

$$RMgX + R'OH \rightarrow RR' + Mg(OH)X$$

Water also gives a hydrocarbon:

$$RMgX + H_2O \rightarrow RH + Mg(OH)X$$

Solid carbon dioxide in acid solution gives a carboxylic acid:

$$RMg \times \xrightarrow[\text{(ii) } H_2O]{\text{(i) } CO_2} RCOOH+Mg(OH)X$$

ground state It refers to the lowest energy state of an atom, molecule etc.

group I elements A group of elements in the periodic table, divided into two subgroups: group IA (the main group, consists of alkali metals i.e. Li, Na, K, Rb, Cs and Fr) and group IB. Group IB consists of the coinage metals, copper, silver, and gold, which are usually classified with the transition elements.

group II elements A group of elements in the periodic table, divided into two subgroups: group IIA (the main group, consists of alkaline earth metals viz. Be, Mg, Ca, Sr, Ba and Ra) and group IIB. Group IIB consists of the three metals zinc (Zn), cadmium (Cd), and mercury (Hg), which have two *s*-electrons outside filled *d*-subshells. Moreover, none of their compounds have unfilled *d*-levels, and the metals are regarded as nontransition elements. They are sometimes called the *zinc group.* Zinc and cadmium are relatively electropositive metals, forming compounds containing divalent ions Zn^{2+} or Cd^{2+}. Mercury is more unreactive and also unusual in forming mercury(I) compounds, which contain the ion Hg_2^{2+}.

group III elements A group of elements in the periodic table, divided into subgroup IIIB (the main group) and subgroup IIIA. The IIIA subgroup consists of scandium (Sc) yttrium (Y), and lanthanum (La), which are generally classified with the lanthanoids, and actinium (Ac), generally classified with the actinoids. The term *group III elements* usually refers to the main group elements: boron (B), aluminium (Al), gallium (Ga), indium (In), and thallium (TI), which all have outer electronic configurations ns^2np^1 with no partly filled inner levels. They are the first members of the *p*-block. The group differs from the alkali metals and alkaline earth metals in displaying a considerable variation in properties as the group is descended.

Boron has a small atomic radius and a relatively high ionization energy. In consequence its chemistry is largely covalent and it is generally classed as a metalloid. It forms a large number of volatile hydrides, some of which have the uncommon bonding characteristic of electron deficient compounds. It also forms a weakly acidic oxide. In some ways, boron resembles silicon (*see* diagonal relationship).

As the group is descended, atomic radii increase and ionization energies are all lower than for boron. There is an increase in polar interactions and the formation of distinct M^3+ ions. This increase in metallic character is clearly illustrated by the increasing basic character of the hydroxides: boron hydroxide is acidic, aluminium and gallium hydroxides are amphoteric, indium hydroxide is basic, and thallium forms only the oxide. As the elements of group III have a vacant *p*-orbital they display many electron-acceptor properties. For example, many boron compounds form adducts with donors such as ammonia and organic amines (acting as Lewis acids). A large number of complexes of the type $[BF_4]^-$, $[AICI_4]^-$, $[InCI_4]^-$, $[TII_4]^-$ are known and the heavier members can expand their coordination number to six as in $[AIF_6]^{3-}$ and $[TICI_6]^{3-}$. This acceptor property is also seen in bridged dimers of the type Al_2Cl_6. Another feature of group III is the increasing stability of the monovalent state down the group. The electron configuration ns^2np^1 suggests that only one electron could be lost or shared in forming compounds. In fact, for the lighter members of the group the energy required to promote an electron from the *s*-subshell to a vacant *p*-subshell is small. It is more than compensated for by the resulting energy gain in forming three bonds rather than one. This energy gain is less important for the heavier members of the group. Thus, aluminium forms compounds of the type AlCl in the gas phase at high temperatures. Gallium similarly forms such compounds and gallium (I) oxide CGa_2O) can be isolated. Indium has a number of known indium (I) compounds (e.g. InCl, In_2O, In $[I_n{}'''Cl_6]$. Thallium has stable monovalent compounds. In aqueous solution, thallium(I) compounds are more stable than the corresponding thallium (III) compounds. *See* inert-pair effect.

group IV elements A group of elements in the periodic table; divided into the *main group* (subgroup IVB) consisting of carbon (C), silicon (Si), germanium (Ge), tin (Sn), and lead (Pb); and subgroup: IVA titanium (Ti), zirconium (Zr), and hafnium (Hf), which are transition metals. The main-group elements all have electronic structures with four outer electrons (s^2p^2) and no partly filled inner shells. The group shows the common trend towards metallic character with the heavier elements, thus carbon is a typical non-metal, silicon and germanium are metalloids, and tin and lead are characteristically metallic. As observed with other groups the first member of the group is quite different from the rest. The carbon atom is smaller and has a higher ionization potential, both favouring predominance of covalency, but additional factors are:

(1) The widespread nature of extensive catenation in carbon compounds.

(2) The possibility of strong overlap of *p* orbitals or *double bonding*.

(3) The inaccessibility of *d* orbitals in carbon compounds.

Some of the important differences are:

(1) Both oxides of carbon are gaseous, CO and CO_2, the other elements form solid oxides, e.g. SiO_2, Pb_3O_4.

(2) The heavier elements have no compounds analogous to aromatic compounds.

(3) The heavier elements have no compounds analogous to >C = C< or >C = O.

group V elements A group of elements in the periodic table, divided into subgroup VB (the main group) and subgroup VA. The VA subgroup consists of vanadium (V), niobium (Nb), and tantalum (Ta), which are generally classified with the transition elements. The term *group V elements* usually refers to the main-group elements; nitrogen (N), phosphorus (P), arsenic (As), antimony (Sb), and bismuth (Bi), which all have outer electronic configurations ns^2np^3 with no partly filled inner levels. The lighter elements (nitrogen and phosphorous) are non-metals; the heavier elements are metalloids. The lighter elements are electronegative in character and have fairly large ionization energies. Nitrogen has a valency of 3 and tends to form covalent compounds. The other elements have available *d*-sub-levels and can promote an *s*-electron into one of these to form compounds with the V oxidation state. Thus, they have two oxides P_2O_3, P_2O_5, Sb_2O_3, Sb_2O_5, etc. In the case of bismuth, the pentoxide Bi_2O_5 is difficult to prepare and unstable—an example of the increasing stability of the III oxidation state in going from phosphorus to bismuth. The oxides also show how there is increasing metallic (electropositive) character down the group. Nitrogen and phosphorus have oxides that are either neutral (N_2O, NO) or acidic. Bismuth trioxide (Bi_2O_3) is basic. Bismuth is the only member of the group that forms a well-characterized cation Bi^{2+}.

group VI elements A group of elements of the periodic table sometimes called the *chalcogens.* They are oxygen (O), sulphur (S), selenium (Se), tellurium (Te), and polonium (Po). The electronic configurations are all s^2p^4 with no vacant inner orbitals. These configurations are all just two electrons short of an inert gas structure, consequently they have high electron affinities and are almost entirely non-metallic in character.

The group shows the normal property of a trend towards metallic character as it is descended. Se, Te and Po have 'metallic' allotropes and polonium has generally metalloid-type properties where they have been studied (Po is very rare). Excluding oxygen, which forms some ionic metal-oxides, the compounds of group VI elements are practically all covalent in their bonding. All the elements combine with a large number of other elements, both metallic and non-metallic, but in contrast to compounds of the halogens they are more generally insoluble in water, and even where soluble they do not ionize readily.

Oxygen behaves like the first members of other groups in

having great differences from the rest of the group. For example, oxygen forms *hydrogen bonds* (which are very strong bonds) whereas sulphur and the others do not; oxygen cannot expand its outer shell and positive oxidation states are uncommon for oxygen (OF_2, O_2F_2, O_2+ PtF_6^-). Oxygen is paramagnetic. Excluding oxygen, group VI shows similar trends with increasing size to those in group V. For example, decreasing stability of H_2X, greater tendency to form complexes such as $SeBr_6^{2-}$, decreasing stability of high formal positive oxidation states, and marginal metallic properties (e.g. Po forms a hydroxide).

The variation of oxidation states, the variety of elements in combination, and in the case of sulphur the existence of many catenated species all combine to make the chemistry of group VI rather complex.

group VII elements A group of elements in the periodic table divided into two sub-groups: group VIIA and group VIIB. Group VIIB is the main group and consists of halogens (F, Cl, Br, I, At) and group VIIA consists of the elements manganese (Mn), technetium (Tc), and rhenium (Re), which are usually classified with the transition elements.

group VIII elements A group of nine elements in the periodic table consisting of the platinum metals—cobalt (Co), rhodium (Rh), iridium (Ir), nickel (Ni), palladium (Pd), and platinum (Pt)—together with iron (Fe), ruthenium (Ru), and osmium (Os). These metals are now classified with the transition elements.

gun-metal An alloys with approximate composition as follows.

Copper	90%
Tin	8-10%
Zinc	1-4%

gutta-percha It is an *isomer* of natural *rubber*.

gypsum $CaSO_4.2H_2O$ On being heated at 117°C, it changes to plaster of paris, $(CaSO_4)_2$. H_2O, i.e. hydrated calcium sulphate.

H

Haber's process It is a process for manufacture of ammonia. In it N_2 and H_2 combine directly to produce ammonia when the mixture of N_2 and H_2 in the ratio of 1:3 (by vol.) is heated to 400-450°C under a pressure of 250 atmospheres and in the presence of a catalyst (Fe + Al_2O_3). The ammonia formed is condensed and the unreacted gases are recirculated. The reaction can be written as follows:

$$N_2 + 3H_2 \rightleftharpoons 2NH_3$$

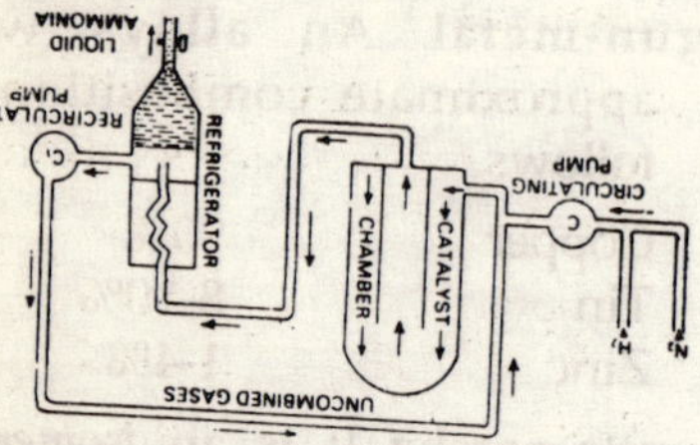

haematite It is a *mineral* form of iron(III) oxide (Fe_2O_3) which is one of the main raw materials for the production of *iron*.

haemoglobin One of the important constituent of blood. One of a group of globular proteins occurring widely in animals as oxygen carriers in blood. Vertebrate haemoglobin comprises two pairs of poly peptide chains (forming the *globin* protein) with each chain folded to provide a binding site for a haem group. Each of the four haem groups binds one oxygen molecule to form *oxyhaemoglobin*. Dissociation occurs in oxygen-depleted tissues: oxygen is released and haemoglobin is reformed. The haem groups also bind other inorganic molecules, including carbon monoxide. This binds more strongly than oxygen and competes with it (hence its toxicity). In vertebrates, haemoglobin is contained in the RBC (erythrocytes).

hafnium Symbol: Hf; m.p. 2493 K; b.p. 5503 K; r.d. 13.3; a.n. 72; r.a.m. 178.49. A transition metal found in zirconium ores. Hafnium is difficult to work and can burn in air. It is used in nuclear reactors.

half cell An electrode in contact with a solution of ions, forming part of a cell. Various types of half cell exist, the simplest consisting of a metal electrode immersed in a solution of metal ions. Gas half cells have a gold or platinum plate in a solution with gas bubbled over the metal plate. The commonest is the hydrogen half cell. Half cells can also be formed by a metal in contact with an insoluble salt or oxide and a solution. The calomel half cell is an example of this. Half cells are commonly referred to as *electrodes*.

half-life (half-life period) Symbol $t_{½}$. The time taken for half the nuclei of a sample of a radioactive nuclide to decay. The half-life of a nuclide is a measure of its stability. (Stable nuclei can be thought of as having infinitely long half-lives.) If N_0 is the original number of nuclei, the number remaining at the end of one half-life is $N_0/2$, at the end of two half-lives is $N_0/4$, etc.

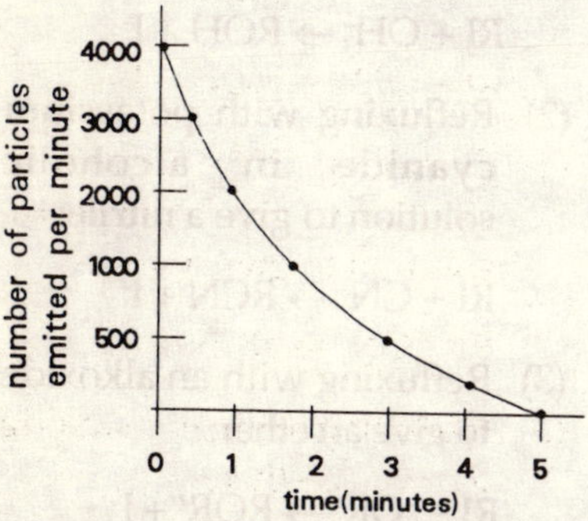

half-life The decay of an isotope with a half-life of 1 minute.

Isotope	*Half-life*
Carbon-14	5730 years
Oxygen-20	14 seconds
Copper-64	756 minutes
Uranium-234	250000 years

half-life The half-lives of different isotopes.

half-thickness It is the thickness of a specified material that reduces the intensity of a beam of radiation to half its original value.

halide A compound of a halogen with another element or group. The halides of typical metals are ionic, for example, sodium chloride, $Na^+ Cl^-$. Metals can also form halides in which the bonding is largely covalent (e.g. aluminium chloride, $AlCl_3$). Organic compounds are also sometimes referred to as halides; e.g. the alkyl halides (*see* haloalkanes) and the acyl halides. Halides are named *fluorides, chlorides, bromides,* or *iodides.*

halite (rock salt) It is naturally occurring sodium chloride (common salt, NaCl), crystallizing in the cubic system. It is chiefly colourless or white (sometimes blue) when pure but the presence of impurities may colour it grey, pink, red, or brown. Halite often occurs in association with anhydrite and gypsum.

Hall-Heroult cell An electrolytic cell used industrially for the extraction of aluminium from bauxite. The bauxite is first purified by dissolving it in sodium hydroxide and filtering off insoluble constituents. Aluminium hydroxide is then precipitated (by adding CO_2) and this is decomposed by heating to obtain pure Al_2O_3. In the Hall-Heroult cell, the oxide is mixed with cryolite (to lower its melting point) and the molten mixture electrolysed using graphite anodes. The cathode is the lining of the cell, also of graphite. The electrolyte is kept in a molten state (about 1123 K) by the current. Molten aluminium collects at the bottom of the cell and can be tapped off. Oxygen forms at the anode, and gradually oxidizes it away. The cell is named after the US chemist Charles Martin Hall (1863-1914), who discovered the process in 1886, and the French chemist Paul Heroult (1863-1914), who discovered it independently in the same year.

haloalkane (alkyl halide) A type of organic compound in which one or more hydrogen atoms of an alkane have been replaced by halogen atoms. Alkyl halides can be made by direct reaction of the alkane with a halogen.

Some of the other methods are:

(a) Reaction of an alcohol with the halogen acid (e.g. from NaBr + H_2SO_4) or with phosphorus halides (red phosphorus and iodine can be used):

$$ROH + HBr \rightarrow RBr + H_2O$$
$$ROH + PCl_5 \rightarrow RCl + POCl_3 + HCl$$

(b) Addition of an acid to an alkene:

$$RCH = CH_2 + HBr \rightarrow RCH_2CH_2Br$$

The haloalkanes are much more reactive than the alkanes, and are useful starting compounds for preparing a wide range of organic chemicals. In particular, they undergo nucleophilic substitutions in which the halogen atom is replaced by some other group (iodine compounds are the most reactive). Some reactions of alkyl halides are:

(1) Refluxing with aqueous potassium hydroxide to give an alcohol:

$$RI + OH^- \rightarrow ROH + I^-$$

(2) Refluxing with potassium cyanide in alcoholic solution to give a nitrile:

$$RI + CN^- \rightarrow RCN + I^-$$

(3) Refluxing with an alkoxide to give an ether:

$$RI + {}^-OR' \rightarrow ROR' + I^-$$

(4) Reaction with alcoholic ammonia solution (100°C in a sealed tube):

$$RI + NH_3 \rightarrow RNH_2 + HI$$

(5) Boiling with alcoholic potassium hydroxide, to eliminate an acid and produce an alkene:

$$RCH_2CH_2I + KOH \rightarrow KI + H_2O + RCH{:}CH_2$$

haloarenes These are also called aryl halides. In them the halogen atom is directly attached to carbon atom of the benzene ring e.g.

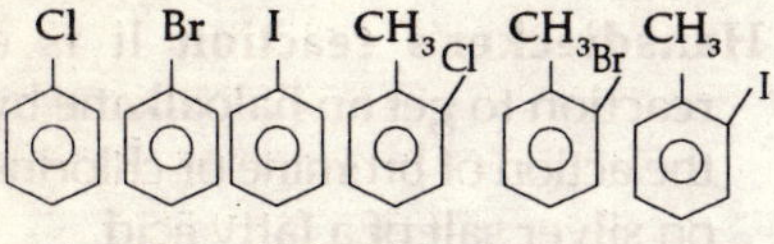

(I) (II) (III) (IV) (V) (VI)

(i) Chlorobenzene

(ii) Bromobenzene

(iii) Iodobenzene

(iv) 2-Chlorotoluene

(v) 2-Bromotoluene

(vi) 2-Iodotoluene

halogens (group VII elements) A group of elements in the periodic table (group VIIB): fluorine (F), chlorine (Cl), bromine (Br), iodine (I), and astatine (At). All have a characteristic electron configuration of noble gases but with outer ns^2np^5 electrons. The outer shell is thus one electron short of a noble-gas configuration. Consequently, the halogens are typical non-metals; they have high electronegativities—high electron affinities and high ionization energies. They form compounds by gaining an electron to complete the stable configuration; i.e. they are good oxidizing agents (they oxidise others and get themselves reduced). Alternatively, they share their outer electrons to form covalent compounds, with single bonds.

All are reactive elements with the reactivity decreasing down the group. The electron affinity decreases down the group and other properties also show a change from fluorine to astatine. Thus, the melting and boiling points increase; at 293 K, fluorine and chlorine are gases, bromine a liquid, and iodine and astatine are solids. All exist as diatomic molecules.

The name 'halogen' comes from the Greek 'salt-producer', and the elements react with metals to form ionic halide salts. They also combine with non-metals, i.e. '*p*' block elements, the activity decreasing down the group: fluorine reacts with all non-metals except nitrogen and the noble gases helium, neon, and argon; iodine does not react with any noble gas, nor with carbon, nitrogen, oxygen, or sulphur. The elements fluorine to iodine all react with hydrogen to give the acid, with the activity being greatest for fluorine, which reacts explosively. Chlorine and hydrogen react slowly at room temperature in the dark (sunlight causes a free-radical chain reaction). Bromine and hydrogen react if heated in the presence of a catalyst.

$$Br_2 + H_2 \xrightarrow{\Delta} 2HBr$$

Iodine and hydrogen react only slowly and the reaction is not complete. There is a decrease in oxidizing ability down the group from fluorine to iodine. As a consequence, each halogen will displace any halogen below it from a solution of its salt, for example:

$$Cl_2 + 2Br^- \rightarrow Br_2 + 2Cl^-$$

The halogens also form a wide variety of organic compounds in which the halogen atom is linked to carbon. In general, the aryl compounds are more stable than the alkyl compounds and there is decreasing resistance to chemical attack down the group from the fluoride to the iodide.

Fluorine has only a valency of 1, although the other halogens can have higher oxidation states using their vacant *d*-electron levels. There is also evidence for increasing metallic behaviour down the group. Chlorine and bromine form compounds with oxygen in which the halogen atom is assigned a positive oxidation state. Only iodine, however, forms positive ions, as in $I^+NO_3^-$.

hammer mills These are the devices used in the chemical industry for crushing and grinding solid materials at high speeds to a specified size. The impact between the particles, grinding plates, and grinding hammers pulverizes the particles. Hammer mills can be used for a greater variety of soft material than other types of grinding equipment. *Compare* ball mill.

Hansdiecker's reaction It is a reaction to get an haloalkane by the action of bromine or chlorine on silver salt of a fatty acid.

$$RCOOAg + Br_2 \rightarrow RBr + CO_2\uparrow + AgBr$$

$$CH_3CH_2COO\,Ag + Br_2 \xrightarrow{CCl_4} CH_3CH_2Br + CO_2 + Ag\,Br.$$

hardening of oils The process of converting unsaturated esters of fatty acids into (more solid) saturated esters by hydrogenation using a nickel catalyst. It is used in the manufacture of margarine from vegetable oils.

hardness of water The presence of dissolved calcium or magnesium ions in water forms a scum with soap and prevent the formation of a lather. The main cause of hard water is dissolved calcium hydrogencarbonate ($Ca(HCO_3)_2$), which is formed in limestone or chalk regions by the action of dissolved CO_2 on $CaCO_3$. This type is known as *temporary hardness* because it is removed by boiling:

$$Ca(HCO_3)_2(aq) \rightarrow CaCO_3(s) + H_2O(l) + CO_2(g)$$

The precipitated calcium carbonate is the 'fur' (or 'scale') formed in kettles, boilers, pipes, etc. In some areas, hardness also results from dissolved calcium sulphate ($CaSO_4$), which cannot be removed by boiling *(permanent hardness).*

Hard water is a considerable problem in washing, reducing the efficiency of boilers, heating systems, etc., and in certain industrial processes. Various methods of *water softening* are used. In public supplies, the temporary hardness can be removed by adding lime (calcium hydroxide), which precipitates calcium carbonate

$$Ca(OH)_2(aq) + Ca(HCO_3)_2(aq) \rightarrow 2CaCO_3(s) + 2H_2O(l)$$

hard water The water which contains the salts of calcium and magnesium dissolved in it. There are two distinct types of hard water:

(i) *Temporary hard water:* This contains dissolved calcium hydrogen carbonate $Ca(HCO_3)_2$. This can be removed by simply boiling the water.

(ii) *Permanent hard water:* This contains dissolved calcium sulphate ($CaSO_4$ and $MgSO_4$) and magnesium sulphate. They can be removed by adding washing soda.

heat capacity (thermal capacity) The ratio of the heat supplied to an object or specimen to its consequent rise in temperature. The *specific heat capacity* is the ratio of the heat supplied to unit mass of a substance to its consequent rise in temperature. The *molar heat capacity* is the ratio of the heat supplied to unit amount of a substance to its consequent rise in temperature. In practice, heat capacity (C) is measured in joules per kelvin, specific heat capacity (*c*) in $JK^{-1} kg^{-1}$, and molar heat capacity (C_m) in $JK^{-1} mol^{-1}$. For a gas, the values of *c* and C_m are commonly given either at *constant volume,* when only its internal energy is increased, or at *constant pressure,* which requires a greater input of heat as the gas is allowed to expand and do work against the surroundings. The symbols for the specific and molar heat capacities at constant volume are c_v and C_v, respectively; those for the specific and molar heat capacities at constant pressure are c_p and C_p.

heat energy All substances possess heat energy. It is directly proportional to the temperature of the substance. The higher their *temperature,* the more *energy* they possess. The source of this energy is the movement of atoms and molecules, i.e. their *kinetic energy.*

Heat energy is taken in during *endothermic reactions* and given out during *exothermic reactions.*

heat of atomisation It is the amount of heat that is required for dissociating one mole of substance into its constituent atoms.

heat of combustion The *heat energy* released when one *mole* of a substance is burnt in *oxygen*. There is no change in volume.

heat of formation The energy liberated or absorbed when one mole of a compound is formed from its constituent elements.

heat of neutralization The energy liberated when one mole of an acid or base is neutralized.

heat of reaction It is equal to the amount of heat evolved or absorbed as indicated by a balanced chemical equation.

heat of solution It is the energy change when one mole of a substance is dissolved in a given solvent to infinite dilution (in practice, to form a dilute solution).

heat of transition It is the amount of heat evolved or absorbed during transition of state (change from one state to another) by one mole of the substance e.g. heat of fusion, heat of sublimation etc.

hecto- Symbol h. A prefix used in the metric system to denote 100 times. For example, 100 coulombs = 1 hectocoulomb (hC).

Heisenberg's uncertainty principle It is not possible to determine simultaneously both the position and momentum of an electron with accuracy. Mathematically

$$\Delta x.\ \Delta p \simeq \frac{h}{2\pi}$$

where Δx and Δp are the uncertainties in position and momentum of the particle respectively, h is the Planck's constant (6.626196×10^{-34} Js)

helium Symbol He. A colourless, odourless gaseous non-metallic element belonging to group 0 *'p'* block of the periodic table. It is a noble gas; a.n. 2; r.a.m. 4.0026; d. 0.178 g dm^{-3}; m.p. –272.2°C (at 20 atm.); b.p. –268.93°C. The element has the lowest boiling point of all substances and can be solidified only under pressure. Natural helium is mostly helium-4, with a small amount of helium-3. There are also two short-lived radioactive isotopes: helium-5 and -6. It occurs in ores of uranium and thorium and in some natural-gas deposits. It has a variety of uses, including the provision of inert atmospheres for welding and semiconductor manufacture, as a refrigerant for superconductors, and as a diluent in breathing apparatus. It is also used in filling balloons. Chemically it is totally inert and has no known compounds. It was discovered in the solar spectrum in 1868 by Lockyer.

Helmholtz function (Helmholtz free energy) Symbol *A*. A thermodynamic function defined by

$$A = E - TS$$

where E is the internal energy, T the thermodynamic temperature, and S the entropy. It is a measure of the ability of a system to do useful work in an isothermal process.

hemihydrate A crystalline hydrate containing two molecules of compound per molecule of water (e.g. $2CaSO_4.H_2O$).

henry Symbol H. It is the SI unit of inductance equal to the inductance of a closed circuit in which an e.m.f. of one volt is produced when the electric current in the circuit varies uniformly at a rate of one ampere per second. It is named after Joseph Henry (1797-1878), a US physicist.

heptahydrate A crystalline hydrated compound containing one molecule of compound per seven molecules of water of crystallization.

heptane, C_7H_{16} An alkane found in petroleum. It has nine isomers.

hertz Symbol Hz. The SI unit of frequency equal to one cycle per second. It is named after Heinrich Hertz (1857-94), a German physicist.

Hess's law It states that, "The enthalpy change in a chemical or physical process is same whether the process is carried out in one step or multisteps."

In going from A to D, we have

$$\Delta H_4 + \Delta H_3 = \Delta H_1 + \Delta H_2$$

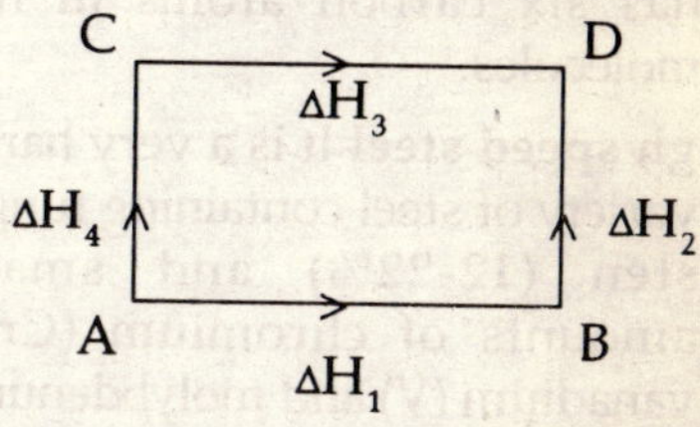

hetero atom The atoms, other than carbon, like O, N, S which form a part of a carbon ring in cyclic organic compounds are termed heteroatoms and such compounds are called heterocyclic compounds.

For instance, nitrogen is the hetero atom in pyridine.

Heterolytic fission The breaking of a bond in a compound in which the two fragments are oppositely charged ions. For example, $HCl \rightarrow H^+ + Cl^-$. *Compare* homolytic fission.

heusler alloys Ferromagnetic alloys containing no ferromagnetic elements. The original alloys contained copper (Cu) manganese (Mn) and tin (Sn) and were first made by Conrad Heusler (19th-century mining engineer).

hexadecanoic acid (palmitic acid) A crystalline carboxylic acid:

$$CH_3(CH_2)_{14}COOH$$

It is present as glycerides in fats and oils.

hexose A monosaccharide that has six carbon atoms in its molecules.

high speed steel It is a very hard variety of steel containing tungsten (12-22%) and small amounts of chromium (Cr), vanadium (V) and molybdenum (Mo). It is used for tools which remain hard even at red heat.

histochemistry The study of the distribution of the chemical constituents of tissues by means of their chemical reactions. It utilizes techniques such as staining, light and electron microscopy, autoradiography, and chromatography.

Hoffmann's bromamide reaction This method results in the formation of an amine having one carbon atom less than the amide which reacts with sodium hydroxide and bromine to give this reaction.

$$RCONH_2 + 4NaOH + Br_2 \rightarrow RNH_2 + 2NaBr + Na_2CO_3 + 2H_2O$$

It is also called *Hoffmann's degradation.*

Hoffmann's method It is a rather outmoded method for determining the vapour density of volatile liquids. A known weight of sample is introduced into a mercury barometer tube, which is surrounded by a heating jacket. The volume of vapour can thus be read off directly, the temperature is known, and the pressure is obtained by taking the atmospheric pressure minus the mercury height in the barometer (with corrections for the density of mercury at higher temperatures). The method's only advantage is that it may be used for samples that decompose at their normal boiling point.

holmium Symbol Ho. A soft silvery metallic element belonging to the lanthanoids; a.n. 67; r.a.m. 164.93; r.d. 8.795. (20°C); m.p. 1472°C; b.p. 2700°C. It occurs in apatite, xenotime, and some other rare-earth minerals. Three is one natural isotope, holmium-165; eighteen artificial isotopes have been produced. There are no uses for the element, which was discovered by P.T. Cleve and J.L. Soret in 1879.

homogeneous catalysis When the catalyst mixes homogeneously with the reactants and forms a single phase, the catalyst is said to be homogeneous. This kind of catalysis is known as homogeneous catalysis. For instance

$$SO_2(g) + O_2(g) \xrightarrow{\text{oxidation}} SO_3(g).$$

homologous series A series of compounds with the same *general formula*. For example:

(a) *alkanes* C_nH_{2n+2}
(b) *alkenes* C_nH_{2n}.

The compounds have the same *functional groups* and have the same chemical *properties*. The physical properties of the series of compounds change only gradually.

Alkanes: C_nH_{2n+2}

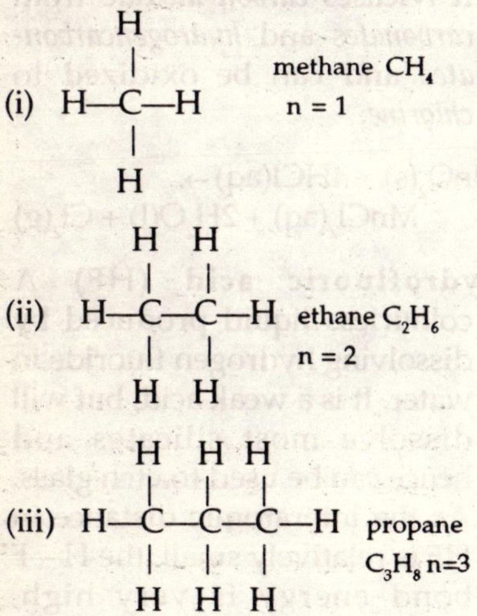

Alkenes : C_nH_{2n}

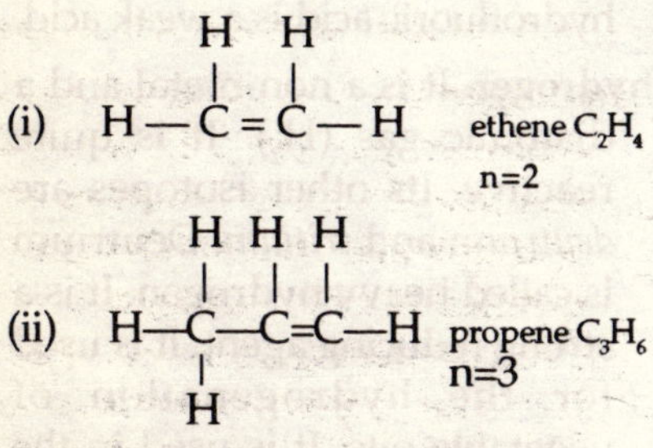

homologous series

hormone A substance that is manufactured and secreted in very small quantities into the bloodstream by an endocrine gland or a specialized nerve cell and regulates the growth or functioning of a specific tissue or organ in a distant part of the body. For example, the hormone insulin controls the rate and manner in which glucose is used by the body. Other examples of hormones are Luteotrophin, progesterone, testosterone etc.

Hückel Rule All aromatic compounds contain (4n+2) number of delocalised Ii electrons *see* Aromaticity.

Hund's rule of maximum multiplicity When electrons partially but not fully fill a subshell, they remain as unpaired as possible.

hydrate A substance formed by combination of a compound with water.

hydrated ion An ion that is surrounded by water molecules e.g. $[Cu(H_2O)_4]^{2+}$ etc.

hydrazine A colourless liquid or white crystalline solid, H_2N-NH_2; r.d. 1.01 (liquid); m.p. 1.4°C; b.p. 113.5°C. It is very soluble in water and soluble in ethanol. Hydrazine is prepared by the *Raschig synthesis* in which ammonia reacts with sodium(I) chlorate (sodium hypochlorite) to give NH_2Cl, which then undergoes further reaction with ammonia to give N_2H_4. Industrial production must be carefully controlled to avoid a side reaction leading to NH_4Cl. The compound is a weak base giving rise to two series of salts, those based on N^2H^{5+}, which are stable in water (sometimes written in the form $H_2N{-}NH_2.HCl$ rather than $N_2H_5{}^+Cl^-$), and a less stable and extensively hydrolysed series based on $N_2H_6^{2+}$. Hydrazine is a powerful reducing agent and reacts violently with many oxidizing agents, hence its use as a rocket propellant.

hydrazones These are organic compounds containing the group $>C=NNH_2$, formed by condensation of substituted hydrazines with aldehydes and ketones. *Phenyl-hydrazones* contain the group $>C=NNHC_6H_5$.

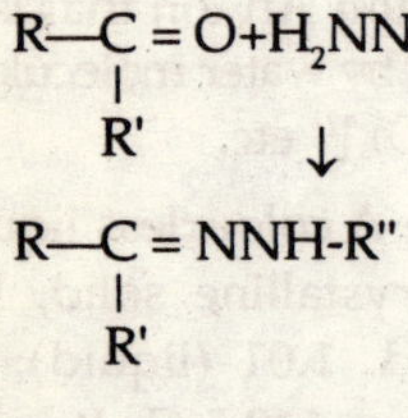

R' = (for aldehydges
= alkyl (for ketones
R" = H (for hydragine)
= C_6H_5 (for phenylhydrazine)

hydrochloric acid ($HCl(aq)$)[-1] A *solution* of *hydrogen chloride* in *water*; it contains *chloride* and *oxonium ions*. The maximum *concentration* of the solution is 36% (about 11 *mol/dm*^{3}). The *acid* is *monobasic* and produces *salts* called *chlorides*, e.g.

$$Fe(s) + 2HCl(aq) \rightarrow FeCl_2(aq) + H_2(g)$$
$$Mg(s) + 2HCl(aq) \rightarrow MgCl_2(aq) + H_2(g)$$
$$2Na(s) + 2HCl(aq) \rightarrow NaCl(s) + H_2(g)$$

It is a *strong acid* being fully dissociated into $Cl^-(aq)$ and $H_3O^+(aq)$ ions in dilute solution. It releases *carbon dioxide* from *carbonates* and *hydrogencarbonates* and can be oxidized to *chlorine*:

$$MnO_2(s) + 4HCl(aq) \rightarrow MnCl_2(aq) + 2H_2O(l) + Cl_2(g)$$

hydrofluoric acid (HF) A colourless liquid produced by dissolving hydrogen fluoride in water. It is a weak acid, but will dissolve most silicates and hence can be used to etch glass. As the interatomic distance in HF is relatively small, the H—F bond energy is very high, therefore it is unable to donate protons easily and hence hydrofluoric acid is a weak acid.

hydrogen It is a non-metal and a diatomic gas (H_2). It is quite reactive. Its other isotopes are *deutrium* and *tritium*. Deutrium is called heavy hydrogen. It is a strong reducing agent. It is used for the hydrogenation of vegetable oils. It is used in the synthesis of ammonia, methyl alcohol and methanal.

hydrogen bond It is a weak chemical *bond* formed between *hydrogen* atoms and *atoms* of *oxygen* or *nitrogen*. Although weaker than *covalent* or *ionic bonds*, hydrogen

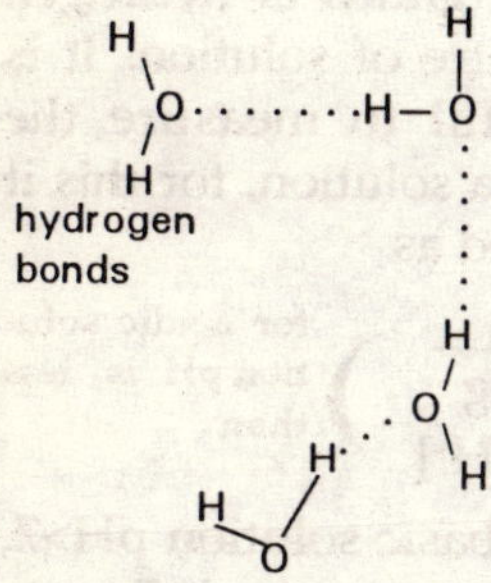

hydrogen bond Molecules in water and ice.

bonds affect the physical properties of *compounds. Molecules* in *water* and *ice* are extensively hydrogen-bonded to each other.

hydrogenation It is the process by which an unsaturated compound is converted to a saturated compound by the addition of hydrogen, e.g. Hydrogenation of butene to butane in presence of nickel as the catalyst.

$$CH_3 - CH = CH - CH_3 + H_2 \xrightarrow{Ni} CH_3 - CH_2 - CH_2 - CH_3$$

hydrogen bromide (HBr) A colourless sharp-smelling gas that is very soluble in water. It is produced by direct combination of hydrogen and bromine in the presence of a platinum catalyst

$$H_2 + Br_2 \longrightarrow 2HBr$$

or by the reaction of phosphorus tribromide with water.

$$PBr_3 + H_2O \rightarrow HBr + POBr_2$$

It dissolves in water to give hydrobromic acid. Hydrogen bromide is rather inactive chemically. It will not conduct electricity in the molten state, indicating that it is a molecular compound.

hydrogen chloride A colourless fuming gas, HCl; m.p. –114°C; b.p. –85°C. It can be prepared in the laboratory by heating sodium chloride with concentrated sulphuric acid

$$2NaCl + H_2SO_4\,(conc.) \rightarrow 2HCl + Na_2SO_4$$

hence the former name *spirits of salt*). Industrially it is made directly from the elements at high temperature and used in the manufacture of PVC and other chloro compounds. It is a strong acid and dissociates fully in solution *(hydrochloric acid)*.

hydrogen cyanide (hydrocyanic acid; prussic acid) A colourless liquid or gas, HCN, with a characteristic odour of almonds; r.d. 0.699 (liquid at 22°C); m.p. –14°C; b.p. 26°C. It is an extremely poisonous substance formed by the action of acids on metal cyanides. Industrially, it is made by catalytic oxidation of ammonia and methane with air and is used in producing acrylate plastics. Hydrogen cyanide is a weak acid (Ka = 2.1× 10^{-9} mol dm^{-3}). It forms cyanohydrins with organic carbonyl compounds.

hydrogen half cell (hydrogen electrode) A type of half cell in which a metal foil is immersed in a solution of hydrogen ions and hydrogen gas is bubbled over the foil. The standard hydrogen electrode, used in measuring standard electrode potentials, uses a platinum foil with a 1.0 M solution of hydrogen ions, the gas at 1 atmosphere pressure, and a temperature of 298 K. It is written Pt(s) | H_2(g), H^+(aq), the effective reaction being

$$H_2 \rightarrow 2H^+ + 2e.$$

hydrogen halides These are gaseous *compounds* formed between *hydrogen* and the *halogens*. They are *covalent* compounds which readily dissolve in *water* to form an acidic solution which contains the *halide ion*, e.g.

$$HBr(g) + H_2O(l) \rightarrow H_3O+(aq) + Br^-(aq)$$

Hydrogen fluoride	HF
Hydrogen chloride	HCl
Hydrogen bromide	HBr
Hydrogen iodide	HI

hydrogen ions (H+) It is a cation which is formed by loss of an electron from hydrogen atom.

$$H \rightarrow H^+ + e^-$$

It is quite reactive and in aqueous solution it combines with a molecule of water to form an oxonium ion.

$$H^+ + H_2O \rightarrow H_3O+$$

hydrogen ion concentration The number of grams of hydrogen ions per litre of solution. It is quite useful to measure the acidity of a solution, for this it is expressed as

$$pH\left(pH = \log\frac{1}{[H^+]}\right)$$ for acidic solution pH is less than 7 and for basic solution pH>7. The pH of pure water is 7 (neutral).

hydrogensulphate (bisul-phate) It is a salt containing the ion HSO_4^- or an ester of the type $RHSO_4$, where R is an organic group. It was formerly called *hydrosulphate*.

hydrogen sulphide (sulphu-retted hydrogen, H_2S) A colourless very poisonous gas with smell of rotten eggs. Hydrogen sulphide is prepared by reacting hydrochloric acid with iron(II) sulphide. It is tested for by mixing with lead nitrate, with which it gives a black precipitate. Its aqueous solution is weakly acidic. Hydrogen sulphide reduces iron(III) chloride to iron(II) chloride, forming hydrochloric acid and a yellow precipitate of sulphur. Hydrogen sulphide precipitates insoluble sulphides, and is used in qualitative analysis. It burns with a blue flame in oxygen to form sulphur (IV) oxide and water. North Sea gas contains some hydrogen sulphide, which is removed before supply to the consumer.

hydrolysis It is the term for the *decomposition* of a substance by the action of *water*. The water is also decomposed. *Esters* are hydrolysed as the example shows:

$$\underset{\text{ethylethanoate}}{CH_3COOC_2H_5} + H_2O \rightarrow \underset{\text{ethanoic}}{CH_3COOH} + \underset{\text{ethanol}}{C_2H_5OH}$$

hydromagnesite A mineral form of basic magnesium carbonate, $3MgCO_3.Mg(OH)_2.3H_2O$.

hydrophilic Having an affinity for water.

see also lyophilic

hydrophobic
see lyophobic

hydroquinone *see* 1, 4-dihydroxybenzene

hygroscopic A substance that has a tendency to absorb moisture from the atmosphere is called hygroscopic.

hypertonic A solution is said to be hypertonic as compared to another if its osmotic pressure is higher than that of the other.

hypotonic solution A solution that has a lower osmotic pressure than some other solution. *Compare* hypertonic solution with it.

hypoxanthine or sarkine or 6-hydroxypurin A crystalline powder which decomposes when heated at 150°C without melting. It is present in muscles, spleen and pancreas.

I

Ice *Solid*, crystalline *water*. Its *melting point* at a *pressure* of 1 *atmosphere* is 0°C. The regular, crystalline structure means that frozen water can take on the patterns that we see in snowflakes. Density of ice is less than that of water and it floats. See *crystal*.

ice point The temperature at which equilibrium between ice and water exists at standard atmospheric pressure (i.e. the freezing or melting point under standard conditions). It was used as a fixed point (0°) on the Celsius scale, but the kelvin and the International Practical Temperature Scale are based on the triple point of water.

ideal crystal A single crystal with a perfectly regular lattice without any impurities, imperfections, or other defects.

igneous rocks These are the rocks formed when molten rock *(magma)* cools and solidifies. Igneous rocks are crystalline, normally contain *minerals* and make up 90% of the earth's crust. Examples are *granite*, gabbro and basalt. See *crystallization, rock cycle*.

ignition temperature The temperature to which a substance must be heated before it will burn in air.

imperfections in solids At absolute zero there exists a perfectly ordered arrangement but as the temperature increases the crystals start deviating from their ordered arrangement. Any such deviation causes defect or imperfection in solid. Some defects in crystals arise due to presence of impurities. Due to these defects many a change is observed in the electrical conductivity, mechanical strength etc. of the solids. Such defects include:

(i) Electronic imperfections

(ii) Atomic imperfections

implosion It is an inward collapse of a vessel, especially as a result of evacuation.

indicator A compound that reversibly changes colour depending on the pH of the solution in which it is dissolved. The visual observation of this change is, therefore, a guide to the p^H of the solution and it follows that careful choice of indicators permits a wide range of end points to be detected in acid-base titrations.

Redox titrations require either specific indicators, which detect one of the components of the reaction (e.g. starch for iodine, potassium thiocyanate for Fe^{3+}) or true redox indicators in which the transition potential of the indicator between oxidized and reduced forms is important. The transition potential of a redox indicator is analogous to the transition pH in acid-base systems.

Complexometric titrations require indicators that complex with metal ions and change colour between the free state and the complex state.

indigo It is a dye which is blue in colour having general formula $C_{16}H_{10}N_2O_2$. It occurs as the glucoside *indican* in the leaves of plants of the genus *Indigofera,* from which it was formerly extracted. It is now made synthetically.

indium Symbol In. A soft silvery element belonging to group IIIA '*p*' block of the periodic table; a.n. 49; r.a.m. 114.82; r.d. 7.31 (20°C); m.p. 156.6°C; b.p. 2080±2°C. It occurs in zinc blende and some iron ores and is obtained from zinc flue dust in total quantities of about 40 tonnes per annum. Naturally occurring indium consists of 4.23% indium-113 (stable) and 95.77% indium-115 (half life 6 × 10^{14} years). There are a further five short-lived radioisotopes. The uses of the metal are small—some special-purpose electroplates and some special fusible alloys. Several semiconductor compounds are used, such as InAs, InP, and InSb. With only three electrons in its valency shell, indium is an electron acceptor; it forms stable indium(I), indium(II), and indium(III) compounds. The element was discovered in 1863 by Reich and Richter.

inductive effect It is the effect in which atoms or groups in a compound can attract (–1) or push away electrons (+1), forming polar bonds.

inert pair effect In case of heavy *p*-block elements such as Pb, Ti as correlation is found to exist between the oxidation states *n* and *(n-2)* and the s^2 configuration. e.g. in case of Pb we have Pb (II) and Pb (IV) states, in case of Tl we have Tl(I) and Tl(III) states. This is due to relatively inert ns^2 electrons and this is known as inert pair effect because of lesser tendency of these electrons to enter into bond formation.

inhibitor A substance which will slow down or stop a chemical *reaction.*

inhibition A reduction in the rate of a catalysed reaction by substances called *inhibitors.* In biochemical reactions, in which the enzymes, acts as catalysts if the inhibitor molecules resemble the substrate molecules they may bind to the active site of the enzyme, so preventing normal enzymatic activity. Alternatively they may form a complex with the substrate-enzyme intermediate or irreversibly destroy the enzyme configuration and active-site properties. The toxic effects of many substances are produced in this way. Inhibition by reaction products *(feedback inhibition)* is important in the control of enzyme activity.

initiator It is a substance which is used to start off a chemical *reaction* such as a *polymerization* or an *explosion.*

inner transition elements The elements having partly filled *f*-orbitals are called inner-transition elements. Inner transition elements contains two series known as *lanthanides and actinides.* These are placed at the bottom of the periodic table in two rows and are known as *f*-block elements, e.g.

Lanthanides: La, Ce, Gd, Tb etc.
Actinides: Ac, Th, U, Cf etc.

inorganic Inorganic substances are those which do not form part of living things and have no life, for example rocks and water.

inorganic chemistry It is the branch of chemistry concerned with elements other than carbon and with the preparation, properties, and reactions of their compounds. Certain simple carbon compounds are treated in inorganic chemistry, including the oxides, carbon disulphide, the halides, hydrogen cyanide, and salts, such as the cyanides, cyanates, carbonates, and hydrogencarbonates.

inorganic ion exchanges These are hydrated aluminium silicates $Na_2Al_2Si_2O_8.x\ H_2O$. It can be prepared by mixing soda ash (Na_2CO_3), sand (SiO_2) and alumina (Al_2O_3). It is also known as permutit. The portion $Al_2Si_2O_8.\ x\ H_2O$ is Zeolite (Z) and inorganic exchanger is represented by Na_2Z.

Zeolite removes Mg^{2+} and Ca^{2+} ions from hard water by exchanging it with Na^+ ions.

$$Na_2Z + CaCl_2 \rightarrow CaZ + 2\ NaCl$$

insoluble Describing a compound that has a very low solubility (in a specified solvent).

insulator A substance which is a poor *conductor* of either *heat* or electricity.

Non-metallic elements, most solid compounds and polymers are usually insulators.

insulin A hormone, secreted by the islets of Langerhans in the pancreas, that promotes the uptake of glucose by body cells and thereby controls its concentration in the blood. Underproduction of insulin results in the accumulation of large amounts of glucose in the blood and its subsequent excretion in the urine. This condition, known as *diabetes mellitus,* which can be treated successfully by insulin injections. Insulin is a protein, the whole structure of which is now known.

instrumentation It is the measurement of the conditions and the control of processes within a chemical plant. The instruments can be classified into three groups: those for current information using mercury thermometers, weighing scales, and pressure gauges; those for recording viscosity, fluid flow, pressure, and temperature; and those instruments that control and maintain the desired conditions including pH and the flow of materials.

intermetallic compound A compound consisting of two or more metallic elements present in definite proportions in an alloy.

internal conversion A process in which an excited atomic nucleus decays to the ground state and the energy released is transferred by electromagnetic coupling to one of the bound electrons of that atom rather than being released as a photon. The coupling is usually with an electron in the K-, L-, or M-shell of the atom, and this *conversion electron* is ejected from the atom with a kinetic energy equal to the difference between the nuclear transition energy and the binding energy of the electron. The resulting ion is itself in an excited state and usually subsequently emits an Auger electron or an X-ray photon.

internal energy Symbol *E.* The energy of a system that is the total of the kinetic and potential energies of its constituent particles (e.g. atoms and molecules). If the temperature of a substance is raised, by transferring energy to it, the internal energy increases (the particles move faster). Similarly, work down on or by a system results in an increase or decrease in the internal energy. The relationship between heat, work, and internal energy is given by the first law of thermodynamics. According to 1st law of thermodynamics, $E = q - W$ where 'q' is amount of heat 'W' is the work done. Sometimes the internal energy of a system is loosely spoken of as 'heat' or 'heat energy'. Strictly, this is incorrect; heat is the transfer of energy as a result of a temperature difference.

interstice It is a small space between the ions, atoms or molecules in a crystal lattice e.g. in steel, carbon atoms are present in interstices of the iron forming the lattice of the metal crystals.

interstitial compound A compound in which ions or atoms of a non-metal occupy interstitial positions in a metal lattice. Such compounds often have metallic properties. Examples are found in the carbides, borides, and silicides.

interstitial sites These are a number of certain hollows left vacant even in close packing of spheres. These holes or voids in the crystal are termed as interstitial sites. Tetrahedral sites and octahedral sites are the important interstitial sites.

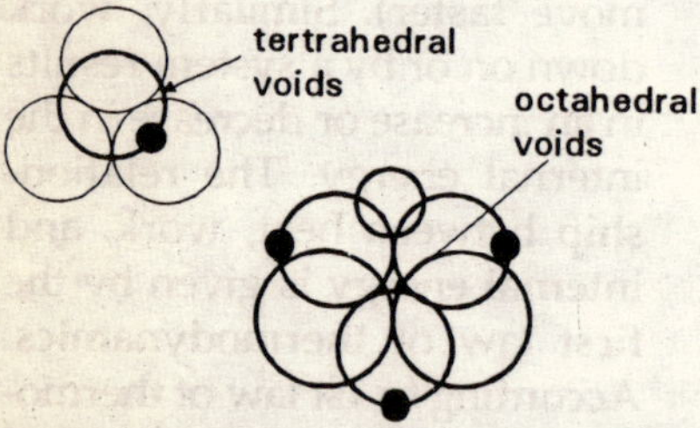

iodic acid Any of various oxoacids of iodine, such as iodic(V) acid and iodic(VII) acid. The term usually refers to iodic(V) acid (HIO_3) when the oxidation state is not specified.

iodine Symbol I. A dark violet non-metallic element belonging to group VII *'p'* block of the periodic table, a.n. 53; r.a.m. 126.9045; r.d. 4.94; m.p. 113.5°C; b.p. 183.45°C. The element is insoluble in water but soluble in ethanol and other organic solvents. When heated it gives a violet vapour that sublimes.

iodine monochloride (ICl) A dark red liquid made by passing chlorine over iodine $I_2 + Cl_2 \rightarrow 2ICl$ (dark red). It has properties similar to those of its constituent halogens. Iodine monochloride is used as a nonaqueous solvent and as an iodating agent in organic reactions.

iodine(V) oxide (iodine pentoxide) A white solid, I_2O_5; r.d. 4.79; decomposes at 583 K. It dissolves in water to give iodic(V) acid and also acts as an oxidizing agent.

iodine value It is the measure of the amount of unsaturation in a fat or vegetable oil (i.e. the number of double bonds). It is obtained by finding the percentage of iodine by weight absorbed by the sample in a given time under standard conditions.

iodoethane (ethyl iodide, C_2H_5I) A colourless liquid haloalkane made by reaction of ethanol with iodine in the presence of red phosphorus.

iodomethane (methyl iodide) A colourless liquid haloalkane CH_3I; r.d. 2.28; m.p. –66.45°C; b.p. 42.4°C. It can be made by reacting methanol with a mixture of iodine and red phosphorus.

ion An *atom* or group of atoms which possess an electrical charge. When an atom gains or loses an *electron* it becomes an *ion*. *Cations* have a positive charge, *anions* have a negative charge, e.g. sodium Na+, potassium K^+, chloride Cl^-, oxide O^{2-}. Atoms tend to gain or lose *electrons* to produce an ion with a *noble-gas* configuration. Groups of atoms (radicals) can also possess a charge. For example:

Sulphate SO_4^{2-}, Nitrate NO_3^-,
Hydroxide OH^-, Ammonium NH_4^+

They are also regarded as ions.

ion exchange A process that takes place in certain insoluble materials, which contain ions capable of exchanging with ions in the surrounding medium. Zeolites, the first ion exchange materials, were used for water softening. These have largely been replaced by synthetic resins made of an inert backbone material, such as polyphenylethene, to which ionic groups are weakly attached.

If the ions exchanged are cations, the resin is a cationic resin. An anionic resin exchanges anions. When all available ions have been exchanged (e.g. sodium ions replacing calcium ions) the material can be regenerated by passing concentrated solutions (e.g. sodium chloride) through it. The calcium ions are then replaced by sodium ions. Ion-exchange techniques are used for a vast range of purification and analytical purposes.

For example, solutions with ions that can be exchanged for OH^- and H^+ can be estimated by titrating the resulting solution with an acid or a base.

ionic crystal The crystal of NaCl, CsCl, KCl etc. which are formed because of electrostatic attraction between +vely charged and –vely charged ions (i.e. cations and anions respectively) are known as ionic crystals.

ionic product It is the product of the concentrations of ions present in a given solution taking the stoichiometry into account. For a sodium chloride solution the ionic product is $[Na^+][Cl^-]$; for a calcium chloride solution it is $[Ca^{2+}][Cl^-]^2$. In pure water, there is an equilibrium with a small amount of self-ionization:

$$H_2O \rightleftharpoons H^+ + OH^-$$

The equilibrium constant of this dissociation is given by

$$K_w = [H^+][OH^-]$$

since the concentration $[H_2O]$ can be taken as constant. K_w is referred to as the ionic product of water. It has the value 10^{-14} $mol^2\ dm^{-6}$ at 25°C. In pure water (i.e. no added acid or added alkali) $[H^+] = [OH^-] = 10^{-7}$ mol dm^{-3}.

ionic radius A measure of the effective radius of an ion in a compound is called the ionic radius. For an isolated ion, the concept is not very meaningful, since the ion is a nucleus surrounded by an 'electron cloud'. Values of ionic radii can be assigned, however, based on the distances between ions in crystals.

Different methods exist for determining ionic radii and often different values are quoted for the same ion. The two main methods are those of Goldschmidt and of Pauling. The Goldschmidt radii are determined by substituting data from one compound to another, to produce a set of ionic radii for different ion. The Pauling radii are assigned by a more theoretical treatment for apportioning the distance between an anion and a cation.

ionic strength The ionic strength of an electrolyte solution is given by

$$I = \frac{1}{2} \Sigma m_i z_i^2$$

where (z) is the charge on ionic species and (m) is the molal concentration, the summation being continued over all the different ionic species in the solution.

ionization It is the process by which an *atom* loses or gains *electrons* and becomes an *ion*. e.g

$$Na \rightarrow Na^+ + 1e^-$$
$$Mn \rightarrow Mn^{2+} + 2e^- \text{ etc.}$$

ionisation energy (I.E.) It is the energy required to remove the most loosely bound electron from an isolated gaseous atom.

$$M(g) \xrightarrow{\text{I.E,}} M^+ + e^-$$

Variation in I.E.

In a period Increases on moving from left to right. and In a group decreases on moving from top to bottom

It is measured in electron volts (ev).

ionizing radiation It is the radiation of sufficiently high energy to cause ionization in the medium through which it passes. It may consist of a stream of high-energy particles (e.g. electrons, protons, alpha-particles) or short-wavelength electromagnetic radiation (ultraviolet, X-rays, gamma-rays). This type of radiation can cause extensive damage to the molecular structure of a substance either as a result of the direct transfer of energy to its atoms or molecules or as a result of the secondary electrons released by ionization. In biological tissue the effect of ionizing radiation can be very serious, usually as a consequence of the ejection of an electron from a water molecule and the oxidizing or reducing effects of the resulting highly reactive species:

$$H_2O \rightarrow e^- + H_2O^* + H_2O^+ \rightarrow {}^\circ OH + H_3O^+ + {}^\circ H,$$

where the dot before a radical indicates an unpaired electron and an* denotes an excited species.

iridium Symbol: Ir; m.p. 2450°C: b.p. 4130°; r.d. 22.4; a.n. 77; r.a.m. 192.22. It belongs to *'d'* block of periodic table. A white transition metal that is highly resistant to corrosion. It is used to harden platinum for electrical contacts and in jewellery.

iron Symbol Fe. A silvery malleable and ductile metallic transition element; a.n. 26; r.a.m. 55.847; r.d. 7.87; m.p. 1535°C; b.p. 2750°C. The main sources are the ores haematite (Fe_2O_3), magnetite (Fe_3O_4), limonite ($FeO(OH)_nH_2O$), ilmenite ($FeTiO_3$), siderite ($FeCO_3$), and pyrite (FeS_2). The metal is smelted in a blast furnace to give impure pig iron, which is further processed to give cast iron, wrought iron, and various types of steel. The pure element has three crystal forms: *alpha-iron,* stable below 1179K with a body-centred-cubic structure; *gamma-iron,* stable between 1179K and 1676K with a non-magnetic face-centred-cubic structure; and *delta-iron,* which is the body-centred-cubic form above 1676 K. Alpha-iron is ferromagnetic up to its Curie point 1041K. The element has nine isotopes (mass numbers 52-60), and is the fourth most abundant in the earth's crust. It is required as a trace element (essential element) by living organisms. Iron is quite reactive, being oxidized by moist air, displacing hydrogen from dilute acids, and combining with non-metallic elements. It forms ionic salts and numerous complexes with the metal in the +2 or +3 oxidation state. Iron (VI) also exists in the ferrate ion FeO_4^{2-}, and the element also forms complexes in which its oxidation number is zero (e.g. $Fe(CO)_5$).

iron (II) chloride (ferrous chloride, $FeCl_2$) A compound prepared by passing dry hydrogen chloride gas over heated iron.

$$\underset{(dry)}{2HCl} + Fe \xrightarrow{\Delta} FeCl_2 + H_2.$$

White feathery anhydrous crystals are produced. Hydrated iron(II) chloride ($FeCl_2.6H_2O$) is prepared by reacting excess iron with dilute or concentrated hydrochloric acid. Green crystals of the hexahydrate are obtained on crystallization from solution. Iron(II) chloride is readily soluble in water, producing an acidic solution due to salt hydrolysis.

iron (III) chloride A black-brown solid, $FeCl_3$: hexagonal; r.d. 2.9; m.p. 306°C; decomposes at 315°C. It also exists as the hexahydrate $FeCl_3.6H_2O$, a brown-yellow deliquescent crystalline substance (m.p. 37°; b.p. 280-285°C). Iron(III) chloride is prepared by passing dry *chlorine* over iron wire or steel wool. $2Fe + 3Cl_2 \rightarrow 2FeCl_3$. The reaction proceeds with incandescence when started and iron(III) chloride sublimes as almost black iridescent scales. The compound is rapidly hydrolysed in moist air. In solution it is partly hydrolysed; hydrolysis can be suppressed by the addition of hydrochloric acid. The compound dissolves in many organic solvents, forming solutions of low electrical conductivity: in ethanol, ethoxyethane, and pyridine the molecular weight corresponds to $FeCl_3$ but is higher in other solvents corresponding to Fe_2Cl_6. The vapour is also dimerized. In many ways the compound resembles aluminium choride, which it may replace in Friedel-Crafts reactions.

iron (II) oxide A black solid, FeO: cubic; r.d. 5.7; m.p. 642K. It can be obtained by heating iron(II) oxalate; the carbon monoxide formed produces a reducing atmosphere thus preventing oxidation to iron (III) oxide. The compound has the sodium chloride structure, indicating its ionic nature, but the crystal lattice is deficient in iron(II) ions and it is nonstoichiometric. Iron(II) oxide dissolves readily in dilute acids.

iron(III) oxide A red-brown to black insoluble solid, Fe_2O_3: trigonal; r.d. 5.24; m.p. 1838K. There is also a hydrated form, $Fe_2O_3xH_2O$, which is a red-brown powder; r.d. 2.44-3.60. (*see* rusting)

Iron(III) oxide occurs naturally as haematite and can be prepared by heating iron(III) hydroxide or iron(II) sulphate. It is readily reduced on heating with carbon or in a stream of carbon monoxide, hydrogen, or coal gas:

$$Fe_2O_3 + 3C \rightarrow 2Fe + 3CO$$

iron(II) sulphate (ferrous sulphate, green vitriol having molecular formula. $FeSO_4$. $7H_2O$) A compound that occurs in nature as the mineral melanterite (or copperas). It is made industrially from iron pyrites. In the laboratory iron (II) sulphate is prepared by dissolving excess iron in dilute sulphuric acid. On crystallization, green crystals of the heptahydrate i.e. seven water molecules are obtained. Careful heating of the hydrated salt yields anhydrous iron(II) sulphate; on further heating the sulphate decomposes to give iron(III) oxide, sulphur(IV) oxide, and sulphur(VI) oxide. The hydrated crystals oxidize easily on exposure to air owing to the formation of basic iron (III) sulphate. A freshly prepared solution of iron(II) sulphate absorbs nitrogen(II) oxide (brown-ring test). iron(II) sulphate crystals are isomorphous with the sulphates of zinc, magnesium, nickel, and cobalt.

iron(III) sulphate A yellow hygroscopic compound. $Fe_2(SO_4)_3$: rhombic: r.d. 3.097; decomposes above 753K. It is obtained by heating an aqueous acidified solution of iron- (II) sulphate with hydrogen peroxide:

$$2FeSO_4 \times H_2SO_4 + H_2O_2 \rightarrow Fe_2(SO_4)_3 + 2H_2O$$

On crystallizing the hydrate $Fe_2(SO_4)_3 . 9H_2O$ is formed. The acid sulphate $Fe_2(SO_4)_3 . H_2SO_4 \text{-} 8H_2O$ is deposited from solutions containing a sufficient excess of sulphuric acid.

irreversible process A process that can be carried out so slowly that the system remains almost in a state of equilibrium at every stage is called a reversible process and if any process does not satisfy the above condition then it is called an irreversible process. An irreversible process can be reversed only with the help of an external agency, e.g.

$$Fe_2O_3 + 3C \rightarrow 2Fe + 3CO$$

isentropic process Any process that takes place without a change of entropy is known as isentropic process. The quantity of heat transferred, $T\delta S$, in a reversible process is proportional to the change in entropy, δS, i.e. $\delta Q = T\delta S$, where T is the thermodynamic temperature. Therefore, a reversible adiabatic process is isentropic, i.e. when $\delta Q = 0, \delta S$ also equals 0.

isobar Atoms of different elements having same mass number but different atomic numbers are known as isobars e.g. K-40 and Ar-40.

isocyanide test A test for primary amines by reaction with an alcoholic solution of potassium hydroxide and chloroform

$$RNH_2 + 3KOH + CHCl_3 \rightarrow RNC + 3KCl + 3H_2O$$

isomers Two or more different *compounds* having the same *molecular formula.* Because the compounds are different, they have different *properties.*

C_2H_5OH	$H_3C\text{-}O\text{-}CH_3$
ethanol	methoxymethane

isomer Ethanol and methoxymethane have the same molecular formula (C_2H_6O) but different properties.

isomer Ethanol and methoxy

methane have the same molecular formula (C_2H_6O) but different properties.

isomerism The phenomenon of the existence of chemical compounds (*isomers*) that have the same molecular formulae but *different* molecular structures or different arrangements of atoms in space. In *structural isomerism* the molecules have different molecular structures: i.e. they may be different types of compound or they may simply differ in the position of the functional group in the molecule. Structural isomers generally have different physical and chemical properties. In *stereoisomerism,* the isomers have the same formula and functional groups, but differ in the arrangement of groups in space. Optical isomerism is one form of this. Another type is *cis-trans isomerism* (formerly *geometrical isomerism),* in which the isomers have different positions of groups with respect to a double bond or central atom (see illustration).

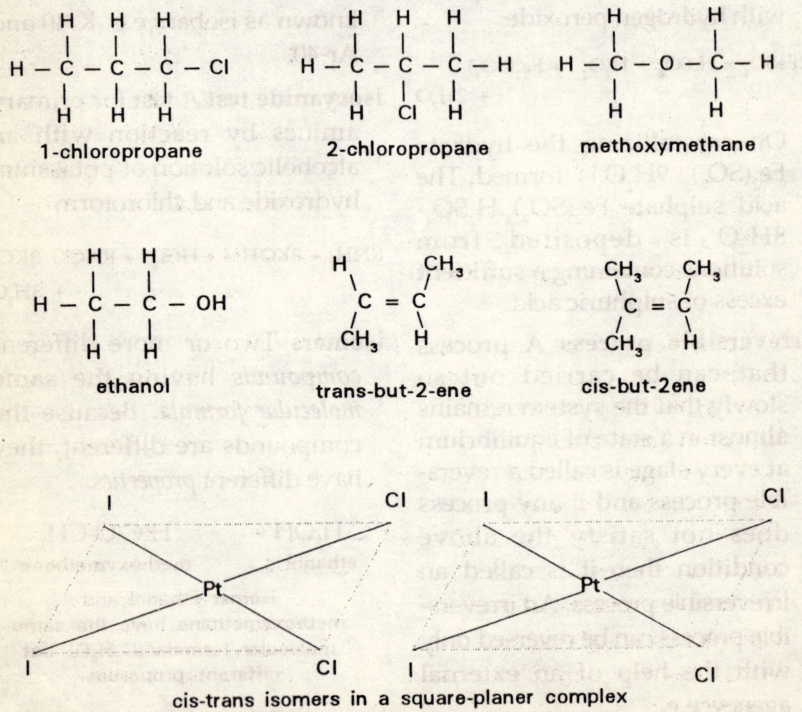

Isomerism

isomorphism The existence of compounds with the same crystal structure is known as isomorphism.

isonitrile Also known as isocyanide/carbylamine. An organic compound containing the group —NC, in which the bonding is to the nitrogen atom.

isothermal process It is the process that takes place at constant temperature. In such a process heat is, if necessary, supplied or removed from the system at just the right rate to maintain constant temperature.

isotonic Solutions that have the same osmotic pressure are called isotonic.

isotopes *Atoms* of the same *element* containing different numbers of *neutrons.* Atoms of an element having same atomic number. However they may have different atomic mass number.

isotopic mass (isotopic weight) It is the mass number of a given isotope of an element.

isotopic number (neutron excess) It is the difference between the number of neutrons in an isotope and the number of protons.

isotropy It is the property of a substance which have, various physical properties such as electrical conductivity, refractive index, thermal expansion etc., same in all directions. This is characteristic of amorphous solids.

IUPAC International union of pure and applied chemistry. This international body establishes commissions that develop agreements on nomenclature, symbols, units and sign conventions.

J

Jade A hard semiprecious stone consisting either of jadeite or nephrite. *Jadeite,* the most valued of the two, is a sodium aluminium pyroxene, $NaAlSi_2O_6$. It is prized for its intense translucent green colour but white, green and white, brown, and orange varieties also occur. The only important source of jadeite is in the Mogaung region of upper Burma. *Nephrite* is one of the amphibole group of rock-forming minerals. It occurs in a variety of colours, such as green, yellow, white, and black. Important sources include Russia, New Zealand, Alaska, China, and the USA.

jasper It is a coloured impure form of natural silica, SiO_2.

jet A variety of coal that can be cut and polished and it is used for jewellery, ornaments, etc.

jeweller's rouge Iron(III) oxide (Fe_2O_3), used as a mild abrasive.

John-Teller effect John-Teller theorem states that, if in any degenerate electronic state the electrons are present in such a way that all the degenerate orbitals are not fully filled, then the geometry of the species will change in such a way as to form non-degenerate orbitals. This theorem is applicable mostly in cases of compounds of transition metals, e.g. Cu (II) has a distorted octahedral coordination.

joule The *SI unit* of *energy* and work. It has the *symbol* J. In scientific usage the kilojoule (kJ) is common.

Joule-Thomson effect It refers to the change in temperature (lowering of temp., cooling effect) when a gas under high pressure is allowed to pass through a porous plug into a region of lower pressure.

Joule's law It states that the internal energy of a given mass of gas is independent of its volume and pressure, being a function of temperature alone. This law applies only to ideal gases (for which it provides a definition of thermodynamic temperature) as in a real gas intermolecular forces would cause changes in the internal energy, should a change of volume occur. *See also* Joule-Thomson effect.

K

Kalinite A mineral form of aluminium potassium sulphate ($Al_2(SO_4)_3$, $K_2SO_4 \cdot 24H_2O$).

kaolin (china clay) A soft white clay that is composed chiefly of the mineral kaolinite (*see* clay minerals). It is formed during the weathering and hydrothermal alteration of other clays or feldspar. Kaolin is mined in the UK, France, Czechoslovakia and USA. It plays a vital role in ceramics industry. It is also used extensively as a filler in the manufacture of rubber, paper, paint, and textiles and as a constituent of medicines.

katharometer An instrument for comparing the thermal conductivities of two gases by comparing the rate of loss of heat from two heating coils surrounded by the gases. The instrument can be used to detect the presence of a small amount of an impurity in air. It is also used as a detector in gas chromatography.

Kekule structure A proposed structure of benzene in which the molecule has a hexagonal ring of carbon atoms linked by alternating double and single bonds. It was suggested in 1865 by Friedrich August Kekule (1829-69).

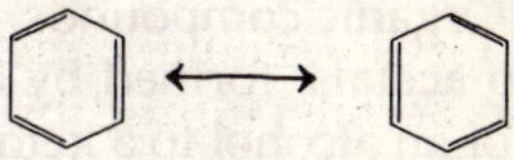

Kekule structure of C_6H_6

Kelvin temperature scale The Kelvin is the *SI unit* of *temperature*. The Kelvin (K) is the same as one degree *Celsius*. Absolute zero is 0 K.

Kelvin	0	273	310	373	K
Celsius	-273	0	37	100	°C
	absolute zero	freezing point of water	blood heat	boiling point of water	

Kelvin temperature scale A comparison with the Celsius scale.

Note: A temperature in Kelvin does not include a degree sign (°), thus the b.p. of water is simply 373 K.

Named after the Scottish physicist William Thomson Kelvin, 1824-1907, famous for his work in thermodynamics and electricity.

keratin It is a group of fibrous proteins occurring in hair, feathers, hooves and horns. Keratins have coiled polypeptide chains that combine to form supercoils of several polypeptides linked by disulphide bonds between adjacent cysteine amino acids.

kerosine A product of *petroleum* refining. Its uses include *fuel* for jet aircraft and also household paraffin which can be used for heating and lighting. Kerosines boil between 433K and 523 K.

ketals Organic compounds, similar to acetals, formed by addition of an alcohol to a ketone. If one molecule of ketone (RR'CO) reacts with one molecule of alcohol R"OH, then a *hemiketal* is formed. The rings of ketose sugars are hemiketals. Further reaction produces a full ketal ($RR'C(OR'')_2$), e.g.

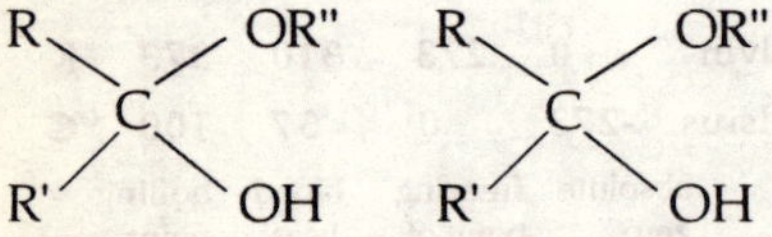

Hemiketal Ketal

keto-enol tautomerism It is an equilibrium between two isomers in which one isomer is a ketone (the *keto form)* and the other an enol. The equilibrium is by transfer of a hydrogen atom between the oxygen atom of the carbonyl group and an adjacent carbon atom.

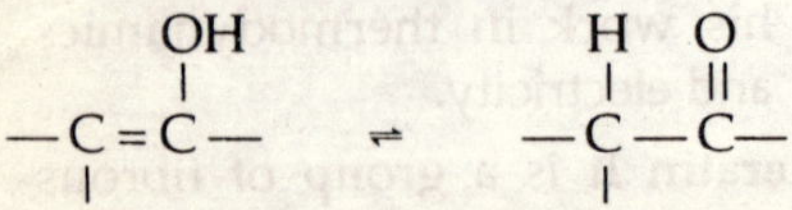

enol form keto-form

Keto-enol tautomerism

ketone body Any of three compounds, acetoacetic acid (3-oxobutanoic acid, CH_3COCH_2COOH), *β*-hydroxybutyric acid (3-hydroxybutanoic acid, CH_3CH-(OH) CH_2COOH), and acetone or (propanone, CH_3COCH_3), produced by the liver as a result of the metabolism of body fat deposits. Ketone bodies are normally used as energy source by peripheral tissues.

ketone A type of organic compound with the general formula

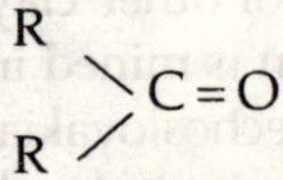

having two alkyl or aryl groups bound to a carbonyl group. They are made by oxidizing secondary alcohols

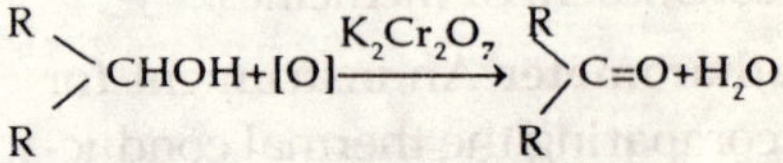

Secondary alcohol Ketone

e.g.

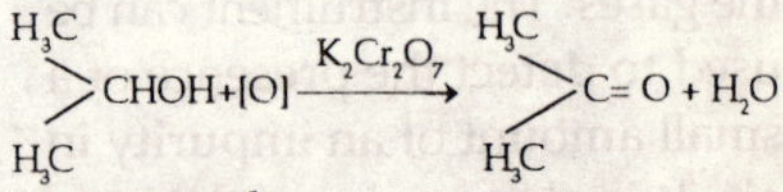

iso-propanol acetone

(just as aldehydes are made from primary alcohols). Simple examples are propanone (acetone, CH_3COCH_3) and butanone (methylethyl ketone, $CH_3COC_2H_5$).

The chemical reactions of ketones are similar in many ways to those of aldehydes. The carbonyl group is polarized, with positive charge on the carbon and negative charge on the oxygen. Thus nucleophilic addition can occur at the carbonyl group. Ketones thus:

(1) Undergo addition reactions with hydrogen cyanide and hydrogensulphite ions.

(2) Undergo condensation reactions with hydroxylamine, hydrazine, and their derivatives.

(3) Are reduced to (secondary) alcohols. They are not, however, easily oxidized. Strong oxidizing agents give a mixture of carboxylic acids. They do not react with Fehling's solution or Tollen's reagent, and do not easily polymerize.

kieselguhr It is a soft fine-grained deposit consisting of the siliceous skeletal remains of diatoms, formed in lakes and ponds. Kieselguhr is used as an absorbent, filtering material, filler, and insulator.

killed spirits Zinc(II) chloride solution used as a flux for solder. It is called killed spirits because it is made, by adding zinc to hydrochloric acid ('spirits of salt').

kimberlite It is a rare igneous rock that often contains diamonds. It occurs as narrow pipe intrusions but is often altered and fragmented. It consists of olivine and phlogopite mica, usually with calcite, serpentine, and other minerals. The chief occurrences of kimberlite are in South Africa, especially at Kimberley (after which the rock is named), and in the Yakutia area of Siberia.

kinematic viscosity Symbol *v*. The ratio of the viscosity of a liquid to its density is called kinematic viscosity. The SI unit is $m^2 s^{-1}$.

kinetics It is a branch of physical chemistry concerned with the study of rates of chemical reations and the effect of physical conditions that influence the rate of reaction, e.g. temperature, light, concentration, etc. The measurement of these rates under different conditions gives information on the mechanism of the reaction; i.e. on the sequence of processes by which reactants are converted into products.

kinetic energy The energy possessed by a body because of its motion. The greater its *velocity* (speed) the more energy it has. The kinetic energy of a particle is ½ mv^2 where m is its *mass* and v its velocity. If the mass is measured in kilograms and the velocity in metres/second the kinetic energy is measured in *joules*.

kinetic theory It is the theory explaining physical properties in terms of the motion of particles. The kinetic theory of gases assumes that the molecules or atoms of a gas are in continuous random motion and the pressure (p) exerted on the walls of a containing vessel arises from the bombardment by these fast moving particles. When the temperature is raised the speeds increase; so consequently does the pressure. If more particles are introduced or the volume is reduced there are more particles to bombard unit area of the walls and the pressure also increases. When a particle collides with the wall it experiences a rate of change of momentum, which is proportional to the force exerted. For a large number of particles this provides a steady force per unit area (or pressure) on the wall.

Following certain additional assumption, the kinetic theory leads to an expression for the pressure exerted by an ideal gas. The main assumptions of this theory are:

(1) The particles behave as if they are hard smooth perfectly elastic points.

(2) They do not exert any appreciable force on each other except during collisions.

(3) The volume occupied by the particles themselves is a negligible fraction of the volume of the gas.

(4) The duration of each collision is negligible compared with the time between collisions.

By considering the change in momentum on impact with the walls it can be shown that

$$p = \rho c^{2/3}$$

where ρ is the density of the gas and c is the root-mean-square speed of the molecules. The mean-square speed of the molecules is proportional to the absolute temperature:

$$Nmc^2 = RT$$

Kinetic equation of an ideal gas

$$PV = 1/3\ mn\ c^2$$

where m = mass of each molecule of gas
n = number of molecules in a gas
V = Volume of gas
P = pressure exerted by the gas
c = root mean square velocity of gas

Kipp's apparatus This apparatus is made of glass or polythene and consists of three receptacles. The top one is a reservoir for the liquid and it is connected with the help of large stem to the bottom container. The middle part of the apparatus contains the solid and is provided with a tap to take out gases produced. In the laboratory it is used to prepare

H_2S gas used in qualitative analysis.

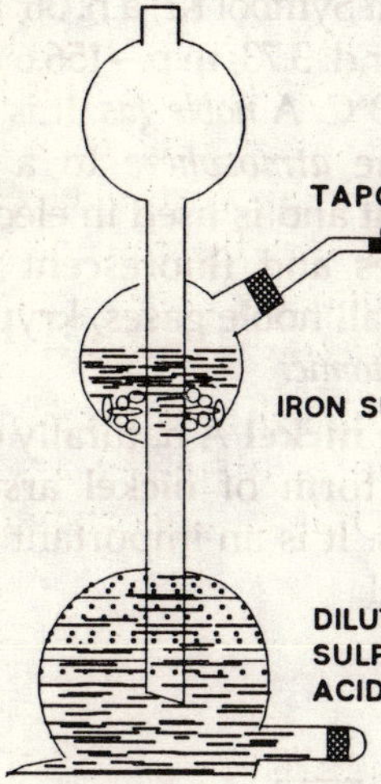

Kohlrausch's law It states that if a salt is dissolved in water, the conductivity of the (dilute) solution is the sum of two values—one depending on the positive ions and the other on the negative ions. The law, which depends on the independent migration of ions, was deduced experimentally by the German chemist Friedrich Kohlrausch (1840-1910).

Kolbe's electrolytic reaction It is a method of preparing alkanes. In it alkanes are obtained by the electrolysis of sodium salt of carboxylic acid. e.g.

$$2\,CH_3COONa \rightarrow 2\,CH_3COO^- + 2Na^+$$

At anode, $2\,CH_3COO^- \rightarrow CH_3-CH_3 + 2CO_2 + 2e^-$

At cathode $2Na^+ + 2e^- \rightarrow 2Na$

$$2Na + 2H_2O \rightarrow 2NaOH + H_2\uparrow$$

Krebs cycle (citric acid cycle; tricarboxylic acid cycle; TCA cycle) A cyclical series of biochemical reactions that is fundamental to the metabolism of aerobic organisms, i.e. animals, plants, and many microorganisms. It takes place in mitochondria. The enzymes of the Krebs cycle are in close association with the components of the electron transport chain. The two-carbon acetyl coenzyme A (acetyl CoA) reacts with the four-carbon oxaloacetate to form the six-carbon citric acid. In a series of seven reactions, this is reconverted to oxaloacetate and produces two molecules of carbon dioxide. Most importantly, the cycle generates one molecule of guanosine triphosphate (GTP—equivalent to 1 ATP) and reduces three molecules of the coenzyme NAD to NADH and one molecule of the coenzyme FAD to $FADH_2$. NADH and $FADH_2$ are then oxidized by the electron transport chain to generate three and two molecules of ATP respectively. This gives a net yield of 12 molecules of ATP per molecule of acetyl CoA.

Acetyl CoA can be derived from carbohydrates (via glycolysis), fats, or certain aminoacids. (Other amino acids may enter the cycle at different stages.) Thus the Krebs cycle is the central 'crossroads' in the complex system of metabolic pathways and is involved not only in degradation and energy production but also in the synthesis of biomolecules. It is named after its principal discoverer, Sir Hans Adolf Krebs (1900-81).

Kroll process It is a process for reduction of metal halides using magnesium (Mg), sodium (Na) or calcium (Ca) as reducing agents e.g. reduction of $TiCl_4$ by Mg in the metallurgy of titanium.

$$TiCl_4 + 2Mg \rightarrow 2MgCl_2 + Ti$$

krypton Symbol Kr; a.n. 36; r.a.m. 83.8; r.d. 3.73; m.p. –156.6°C; b.p. 15.2.3°C. A *noble gas*. It is found in the *atmosphere* to a small extent and is used in electronic valves and fluorescent tubes. Like all noble gases, krypton is *monatomic*.

Kupfer nickel A naturally occurring form of nickel arsenide, NiAs. It is an important ore of nickel.

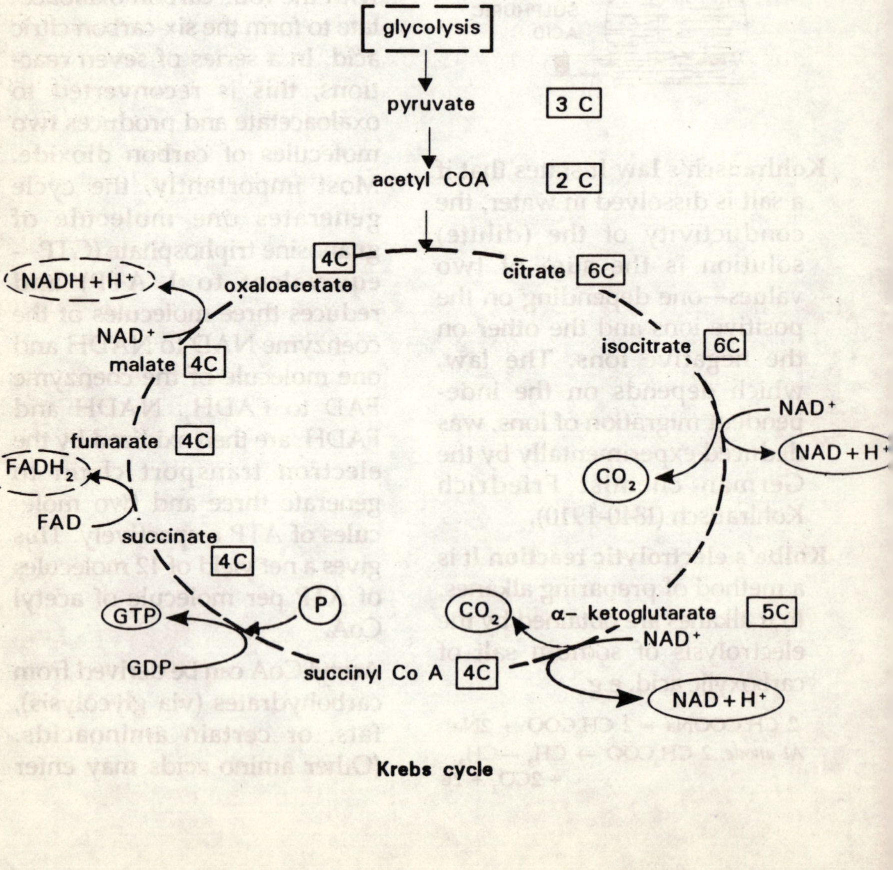

Krebs cycle

L

L It is the symbol for the *Avogadro constant*. It is the number of particles in one *mole* of a substance. Its value is 6×10^{23} particles per mole.

labelling The process of replacing a stable atom in a compound with a radioisotope of the same element to enable its path through a biological or mechanical system to be traced by the radiation it emits. In some cases a different stable isotope is used and the path is detected by means of a mass spectrometer. A compound containing either a radioactive or stable isotope is called a *labelled compound.* If a hydrogen atom in each molecule of the compound has been replaced by a tritium atom, the compound is called a *tritiated compound.* A radioactive labelled compound will behave chemically and physically in the same way as an otherwise identical stable compound, and its presence can easily be detected using a Geiger counter. This process of *radioactive tracing* is widely used in chemistry, biology, medicine, and engineering. For example, it can be used to follow the course of the reaction of a carboxylic acid with an alcohol to give an ester, e.g.

$$\underset{\text{acetic acid}}{CH_3COOH} + \underset{\text{Ethanol}}{C_2H_5OH} \rightarrow \underset{\text{Ethyl acetate}}{C_2H_5COOCH_3} + H_2O$$

To determine whether the noncarbonyl oxygen in the ester comes from the acid or the alcohol, the reaction is performed with the labelled compound $CH_3CO\,^{18}OH$ in which the oxygen in the —OH group of the acid has been 'labelled' by using the ^{18}O isotope. It is then found that water product is $H_2\,^{18}O$ i.e. the oxygen in the ester comes from the alcohol, not the acid.

labile It is a complex that can exchange ligands at a rapid rate.

lactams Organic compounds containing a ring of atoms in which the group —NH.CO.—forms part of the ring. Lactams can be formed by reaction of an amino group in one part of a molecule with a carboxylic group in the other to give a cyclic amide. They can exist in an alternative tautomeric form, the *lactim* form, in which the hydrogen atom on the nitrogen has migrated to the oxygen of the carbonyl to give -N = C(OH)= The pyrimidine base uracil is an example of a lactam.

Lactam

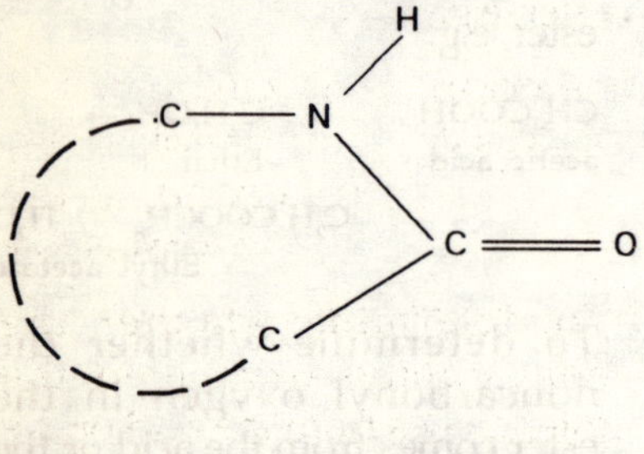

lactate It is a salt or ester of lactic acid i.e. a 2-hy droxypropanoate.

lactic acid, CH_3 CH (OH) COOH It is an optically active compound. It is α-hydroxy acid. It is the main constituent of milk. It can be prepared by the action of dil. HCl on acetal dehyde cyanohydrin.

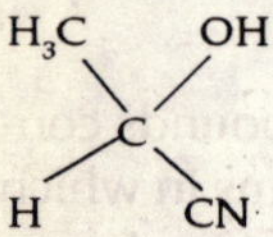

acetaldehyde cyanohydrin

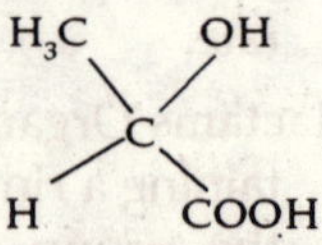

lactic acid

lattice It is a regular arrangement of *molecules, atoms* or *ions* within a crystalline *solid*. Lattices contain large numbers of particles which are arranged in very particular ways. See *crystal*.

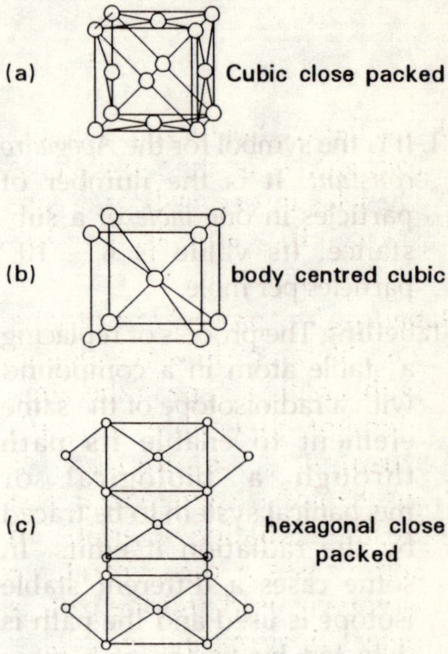

lattice Small sections of three lattices: (a) aluminium, (b) sodium, (c) magnesium.

lactose Also known as milk sugar. A sugar comprising one glucose molecule linked to a galactose molecule. Lactose is manufactured by the mammary gland and occurs only in milk. For example, cow's milk contains about 4.7% lactose. It is less sweet than sucrose (cane sugar).

Ladenburg benzene An (erroneous) structure for benzene. It was proposed by Albert Ladenburg (1842-1911), in which the six carbon atoms were arranged at the corners of a triangular prism and linked by single bond to each other and to the six hydrogen atoms.

laevorotatory An optically active that compound that rotates the plane polarized light towards left. Such a compound is designated as *l* - or (-). *see* optical activity.

lake A pigment made by combining an organic dyestuff with an inorganic compound (e.g. an oxide).

Lamb shift A small energy difference between two levels ($^2S_{1/2}$ and $^2P_{1/2}$) in the hydrogen spectrum. The shift results from the quantum interaction between the atomic electron and the electromagnetic radiation. It was first explained by Willis Eugene Lamb (1913-).

lamellar compound It is a compound with a crystal structure composed of thin plates or layers. Silicates form many compounds with distinct layers. Examples are talc ($Mg_3(OH)_2Si_4O_{10}$(OH)) and pyrophyllite ($Al_2(OH)_2Si_4O_{10}$). (intercallation compound).

lamellar solids These are the solid substances in which the crystal structure has distinct layers (i.e. has a layer lattice). The micas are an example of this type of compound. *Intercalation compounds* are lamellar compounds formed by interposition of atoms, ions, etc., between the layers of an existing element or compound. For example, graphite is a lamellar solid. With strong oxidizing agents (e.g. a mixture of concentrated sulphuric and nitric acids) it forms a non-stoichiometric 'graphitic oxide', which is an intercalation compound having oxygen atoms between the layers of carbon atoms.

lamp black It is a black pigment and a finely divided form of carbon formed by incomplete combustion of an organic compound.

lanolin An emulsion of purified wool fat in water, containing cholesterol and certain terpene alcohols and esters. It is used in cosmetics.

lanthanoids (lanthanides; lanthanons; rare-earth elements) A series of elements belonging to '*f*' block orbital in the periodic table, generally considered to range in proton number from cerium having atomic number 58 to lutetium having atomic number 71 inclusive. The lanthanoids all have two outer *s*-electrons (a $6s^2$ configuration), follow lanthanum, and are classified together because an increasing proton number corresponds to increase in number of $4f$ electrons. In fact, the $4f$ and $5d$ levels are close in energy and the filling is not smooth. The outer electronic configurations has been given as follows:

57 lanthanum (La) $5d^1 6s^2$
58 cerium (Ce) $4f5d^1 6s^2$ (or $4f^2 6s^2$)
59 praseodymium (Pr) $4f^3 6s^2$
60 neodymium (Nd) $4f^4 6s^2$
61 promethium (Pm) $4f^5 6s^2$
62 samarium (Sm) $4f^6 6s^2$
63 europium (Eu) $4f^7 6s^2$
64 gadolinium (Gd) $4f^8 5d^1 6s^2$
65 terbium (Tb) $4f^9 6s^2$
66 dysprosium (Dy) $4f^{10} 6s^2$
67 holmium (Ho)$4f^{11} 6s^2$
68 erbium (Er) $4f^{12} 6s^2$
69 thulium (Tm) $4f^{13} 6s^2$
70 ytterbium (Yb) $4f^{14} 6s^2$
71 lutetium (Lu) $4f^{14} 5d^1 6s^2$

Note that lanthanum itself does not have a 4*f* electron but it is generally classified with the lanthanoids because of its chemical similarities, as are yttrium (Yt) and scandium (Sc). Scandium, yttrium, and lanthanum having atomic number 21, 39 and 57 respectively are *d*-block elements; the lanthanoids and actinoids make up the *f*-block.

The lanthanoids are sometimes simply called the *rare earths,* although strictly the 'earths' are their oxides. Nor are they particularly rare: they occur widely, usually together. All are silvery very reactive metals. The *f*-electrons do not penetrate to the outer part of the atom and there is no *f*-orbital participation in bonding (unlike the *d*-orbitals of the main transition elements) and the elements form few coordination compounds. The main compounds contain M^{3+} ions. Cerium also has the highly oxidizing Ce^{4+} state and europium and ytterbium have a M^{2+} state.

The 4*f* orbitals in the atoms are not very effective in shielding the outer electrons from the nuclear charge. In going across the series the increasing nuclear charge causes a contraction in the radius of the M^{3+} ion—from 0.1061 nm in lanthanum to 0.0848 nm in lutetium.

lanthanide contraction In case of lanthanides there occurs a decrease in atomic radii as we go form La/La^{3+} to Lu/Lu^{3+}. This phenomenon of decrease in atomic/ionic radii is known as lanthanide contraction.

lanthanum Symbol La. A silvery metallic element belonging to group IIIB *p* of the periodic table and often considered to be one of the lanthanoids: atomic number 57; r.a.m. 138.91; r.d. 6.146 (20°C); m.p. 918°C; b.p. 3464°C. Its principal ore is bastnasite, from which it is separated by an ion-exchange process. There are two natural isotopes, lanthanum-139 (stable) and lanthanum-138 (half-life 10^{10}-10^{15} years). The metal, being pyrophoric, is used in alloys for lighter flints and the oxide is used in some optical glasses. The largest use of lanthanum, however, is as a catalyst in cracking crude oil. Its chemistry resembles that of the lanthanoids. The element was discovered by C.G. Mosander in 1839.

law of constant composition According to this law, "A chemical compound is always made up of the same element combined together in the same ratio by weight." H_2O, water is made up of hydrogen and oxygen combined in the ratio of 1: 8 by mass.

law of mass action It states that at constant temperature, the rate of a chemical reaction is directly proportional to the active mass of the reactants, the active mass being taken as the concentration in mol dm^{-3}. In general, the rate of reaction decreases steadily as the reaction proceeds; a measure of the concentration of any of the reactants will give a measure of the rate of reaction.

For the general reaction,

$$A + B \rightarrow \text{products},$$

the law of mass action states that

$$\text{rate} = K[A][B]$$

where [A] represents the concentration of A in mol dm^{-3} and K is the rate constant. The term *active mass* can only equal the concentration in mol dm^{-3} if there is no interaction or interference between the reacting molecules. Many systems exhibit interactions and interference and consequently the concentration in mol dm^{-3} has to be multiplied by an activity coefficient in order to obtain the effective active mass.

law of multiple proportions It states that if two elements form more than one compound then there is a simple relationship between the masses of one of the elements that combine with a fixed mass of the other elements, e.g. Hydrogen and oxygen combine to form water (H_2O) and hydrogen peroxide (H_2O_2), the masses of oxygen that combine with a fixed mass (2g) of hydrogen and these bear a simple ratio of 16:32 (or 1:2).

lawrencium Symbol Lr. A radioactive metallic transuranic element belonging to the actinoids '*f*' block; a.n. 103; mass number of only known isotope 257 (half-life 8 seconds). The element was identified by A. Ghiorso and associates in 1961. The alternative name *unniltrium* has been proposed.

layer lattice It is a crystal structure in which the atoms are chemically bonded in plane layers, with relatively weak forces between atoms in adjacent layers. Graphite and micas are examples of substances having layer lattices (i.e. they are lamellar solids).

LCAO method The full form of LCAO is linear combination of atomic orbitals. It is one of the methods of explaining the formation of molecules and the overlap of orbitals during the formation of molecules.

leaching The process of extraction of soluble components of a solid mixture by percolating a solvent through it.

lead (Pb) a.n. 82. A metallic element of group 14 '*P*' block of the periodic table. It is soft grey metal and has a high density. Its important ore is galena (PbS). Lead and its compounds are used in various ways like making lead storage batteries, covering cables, tetraethyl lead (TEL), pigments in paints, as solder and as a type metal.

lead-acid accumulator An accumulator in which the electrodes are made of lead and the electrolyte consists of dilute sulphuric acid. The electrodes are usually cast from a lead alloy containing 7-12% of antimony (to give increased hardness and corrosion resistance) and a small amount of tin (for better casting properties). The electrodes are coated with a paste of lead(II) oxide (PbO) and finely divided lead; after insertion into the electrolyte a 'forming' current is passed through the cell to convert the PbO on the cathode into a sponge of finely divided lead. On the anode the PbO is converted to lead (IV) oxide (PbO_2). The equation for the overall reaction during discharge is:

$$PbO_2 + 2H_2SO_4 + Pb \rightarrow 2PbSO_4 + 2H_2O$$

The reaction is reversed during charging. Each cell gives an e.m.f. of about 2 volts and in motor vehicles a 12-volt battery of six cells is usually used. The lead-acid battery produces 80-120 kJ per kilogram.

lead(II) carbonate A white solid, having molecular formula $PbCO_3$, insoluble in water; rhombic; r.d. 6.6. It occurs as the mineral cerussite, which is isomorphous with aragonite and may be prepared in the laboratory by the addition of cold ammonium carbonate solution to a cold solution of a lead(II) salt (acetate or nitrate). It decomposes at 588K to lead(II) oxide and carbon dioxide.

lead(II) carbonate hydroxide (white lead, having molecular formula $2PbCO_3 . Pb(OH)_2$) It is the most important basic lead carbonate. It can be manufactured electrolytically. It has been used as a pigment in white and coloured paints but it has the considerable drawback that it is poisonous.

lead-chamber process It is a process used for the manufacture of sulphuric acid. In it sulphur is heated to give SO_2 which is oxidised by NO_2 (oxides of nitrogen) to SO_3; SO_3 when dissolved in water gives H_2SO_4. This process is carried out in various lead chambers.

lead(II) ethanoate (lead(II) acetate) A white crystalline solid, molecular formula $Pb(CH_3COO)_2$, soluble in water and slightly soluble in ethanol. It exists as the anhydrous compound (r.d. 3.25; m.p. 553K), as a trihydrate, $Pb(CH_3COO)_2.3H_2O$ monoclinic; (r.d. 2.55; loses water at 75°C), and as a decahydrate, $Pb(CH_3COO)_2.10H_2O$ (rhombic; r.d. 1.69). The common form is the trihydrate. Its chief interest stems from the fact that it is soluble in water and it also forms a variety of complexes in solution. It was once known as *sugar of lead* because of its sweet taste.

lead(IV) ethanoate (lead tetraacetate) A colourless solid, $Pb(CH_3COO)_4$, which decomposes in water and is soluble in pure ethanoic acid; monoclinic; r.d. 2.228; m.p. 448K. It may be prepared by dissolving dilead(II) lead(IV) oxide in warm ethanoic acid. In solution it behaves essentially as a covalent compound (no measurable conductivity) in contrast to the lead(II) salt, which is a weak electrolyte.

lead(II) oxide (lead monoxide, PbO) A yellow crystalline powder formed by roasting molten lead in air. *Litharge,* the most common form, is obtained when lead(II) oxide is heated above its m.p. If prepared below its melting point, another form, called *massicot,* is obtained. Litharge is used in the rubber industry, in the manufacture of paints and varnishes, and in the manufacture of lead glazes for pottery.

lead(IV) oxide (lead dioxide) A dark brown or black solid with a rutile lattice, PbO_2, which is insoluble in water and sparingly soluble in concentrated sulphuric and nitric acids; r.d. 9.375; decomposes at 290°C. Lead(IV) oxide may be prepared by the oxidation of lead(II) oxide by heating with alkaline chlorates or nitrates, or by anodic oxidation of lead (II) solutions. It is an oxidizing agent and readily reverts to the lead(II) oxidation state, as illustrated by its conversion to Pb_3O_4 and PbO on heating. It reacts with hydrochloric acid to evolve chlorine. Lead(IV) oxide has been used in the manufacture of safety matches.

lead(II) sulphate A white crystalline solid, $PbSO_4$, which is virtually insoluble in water and soluble in solutions of ammonium salts; r.d. 6.2; m.p. 1443K. It occurs as the mineral *anglesite;* it may be prepared in the laboratory by adding any solution containing sulphate ions to solutions of lead(II) ethanoate. The material known as *basic lead (II) sulphate* may be made by shaking together lead(II) sulphate and lead(II) hydroxide in water. This material has been used in white paint in preference to lead(II) carbonate hydroxide, as it is not so susceptible to discoloration through reaction with hydrogen sulphide. The toxicity of lead compounds has led to a decline in the use of these compounds.

lead(II) sulphide (PbS) A black solid occuring naturally as the mineral galena. It can be prepared as a precipitate by reacting a solution of a soluble lead(II) salt with hydrogen sulphide or with a solution of a soluble sulphide. Lead(II) sulphide is useful as a rectifier in electrical components.

lead tetraethyl(IV) (tetraethyl lead) A colourless liquid, $Pb(C_2H_5)_4$, insoluble in water, soluble in benzene, ethanol, ether, and petroleum; r.d. 1.659; m.p. –137°C; b.p. 200°C. It may be prepared by the reaction of hydrogen and ethene with lead but a more convenient laboratory and industrial method is the reaction of sodium-lead alloy with chloroethane. A more recent industrial process is the electrolysis of C_2H_5MgCl (the Grignard reagent) using a lead anode and slowly running additional chloroethane onto the cathode. Lead tetraethyl is used in fuel for internal-combustion engines (along with 1,2-dibromoethane) to increase the octane number and reduce knocking. Mounting pressure from groups concerned about environmental pollution has led to a reduction of permitted levels of lead tetraethyl in many countries.

Le Chatelier's principle According to this principle if a reaction is at *equilibrium* and any of the conditions are changed, further reaction will occur to counter the changes and re-establish equilibrium. For example; in the *Haber process:*

$$N_2(g) + 3H_2(g) \rightarrow 2NH_3(g)$$

If extra *nitrogen* or *hydrogen* is added to an equilibrium *mixture* then more *ammonia* will be formed and the equilibrium will be re-established. Similarly, if extra ammonia is added, more nitrogen and hydrogen will be formed.

If the *pressure is increased* more ammonia will be formed. This is because forming more ammonia leads to a *lowering* of the pressure owing to an overall reduction in the number of gas molecules present. In this way equilibrium is re-established.

A change of *temperature* leads to a change in the proportions of the equilibrium mixture. For *exothermic* reactions i.e. heat is evolved (e.g. Haber process) *raising* the temperature favours the *right* → *left* reaction (ammonia would react to form more nitrogen and hydrogen). This is because the right → left reaction is *endothermic*, i.e. heat is absorbed. It, therefore, counters the rise in temperature by absorbing heat.

Named after the French chemist Henri Le Chatelier, 1850-1936.

Leclanche cell It is a primary voltaic cell consisting of a carbon rod (the anode) and a zinc rod (the cathode) dipping into an electrolyte of a 10-20% solution of ammonium chloride. Polarization is prevented by using a mixture of manganese dioxide mixed with crushed carbon, held in contact with the anode by means of a porous bag or pot; this reacts with the hydrogen produced. This wet form of the cell, devised in 1867 by Georges Leclanche (1839-82), has an e.m.f. of about 1.5 volts. The dry cell based on it is widely used in torches, radios, and calculators.

Lewis acid *See* acid

Lewis base *See* base

Liebig condenser A laboratory condenser having a straight glass tube surrounded by a coaxial glass jacket through which cold water is passed. It is named after the German organic chemist Justus von Liebig (1803-73).

ligand It is an ion or molecule that donates a pair of electrons to a metal atom or ion in forming a coordination complex. Molecules that function as ligands are acting as Lewis bases. For example, in the complex hexaquocopper(II) ion $[Cu\text{-}(H_2O)_6]^{2+}$ six water molecules coordinate to a central Cu^{2+} ion. In the tetrachloroplatinate(II) ion $[PtCl_4]^{2-}$, four Cl-ions are coordinated to a central Pt^{2+} ion. A feature of such ligands is that they have lone pairs of electrons, which they donate to empty metal orbitals. A certain class of ligands also have empty *p*- or *d*-orbitals in addition to their lone pair of electrons and can produce complexes in which the metal has low oxidation state. A double bond is formed between the metal and the ligand: a sigma bond by donation of the lone pair from ligand to metal, and a pi bond by *back donation* of electrons on the metal to empty *d*-orbitals on the ligand. Carbon monoxide is the most important such ligand, forming metal carbonyls (e.g. $Ni(CO)_4$).

The examples given above are examples of *monodentate* ligands (literally: 'having one tooth'), in which there is only one point on each ligand at which coordination can occur. Some ligands are *polydentate;* i.e. they have two or more possible coordination points. For instance, 1,2-diaminoethane, $H_2NC_2H_4NH_2$, is a *bidentate* ligand, having two coordination points. Certain polydentate ligands can form chelates.

light (visible radiation) A form of electromagnetic radiation able to be detected by the human eye. Its wavelength range is between about 400 nm (far 'red') and about 700 nm (far 'violet'). The boundaries are not distinct as individuals vary in their ability to detect extreme wavelengths; this ability also declines with age.

lime (also called as quicklime) Another name for *calcium oxide,* produced by heating *limestone* above 900°C. The reaction is *endothermic*: i.e.

$$\Delta H = +ve$$

$$CaCO_3(s) \rightarrow CaO(s) + CO_2(g)$$

This is an important industrial chemical which is used in:

(a) *Metal* production;

(b) *Refractory* materials;

(c) *Fertilizers;*

(d) Production of other chemicals;

(e) Building materials.

It is used to make *slaked lime* and is responsible for turning impurities in the *blast furnace* into *slag*. In the laboratory it is a useful drying agent for *ammonia.*

limestone It is a sedimentary rock that is composed largely of carbonate minerals, especially carbonates of calcium and magnesium. Calcite and aragonite are the chief minerals; dolomite is also present in the dolomitic limestones. There are many varieties of limestones but most are deposited in shallow water. *Organic limestones* (for example chalk) are formed from the calcareous skeletons of organisms; *precipitated limestones* include oolite, which is composed of ooliths-spherical bodies formed by the precipitation of carbonate around a nucleus; and *clastic limestones* are derived from fragments of pre-existing calcareous rocks.

lime water It is a solution of calcium hydroxide, $Ca(OH)_2$ in water. When CO_2 is passed through it, turns milky.

limonite It is a generic term for a group of hydrous iron oxides, mostly amorphous. Goethite and haematite are important constituents, together with colloidal silica, clays, and manganese oxides. Limonite is formed by direct precipitation from marine or fresh water in shallow seas, lagoons, and bogs (thus it is often called *bog iron ore)* and by oxidation of iron-rich minerals. It is used as an ore of iron and as a pigment.

Lindane gamma isomer of BHC having high insecticidal property.

See benzenehexachloride.

line defect It is a crystal defect. It includes edge dislocation and screw dislocation.

line spectrum A spectrum composed of numerous discrete lines corresponding to single wavelengths of emitted or absorbed radiation. Line spectra are produced by atoms or simple (monatomic) ions in gases. Each line corresponds to a change in electron orbit, with emission or absorption of radiation.

lipid Any of a diverse group of organic compounds, occurring in living organisms, that are insoluble in water but soluble in organic solvents, such as $CHCl_3$ and C_6H_6 etc. Lipids are broadly classified into two categories: *complex lipids,* which are esters of long-chain fatty acids and include the glycerides (which constitute the fats and oils of animals and plants), glycolipids, phospholipids, and waxes; and *simple lipids*, which do not contain fatty acids and include the steroids and terpenes.

Lipids have various functions in living organisms. Fats and oils are a convenient and concentrated means of storing food energy in plants and animals. Phospholipids and sterols, such as cholesterol, are major components of cell membranes. Waxes provide vital waterproofing for body surfaces. Terpenes include vitamins A, E and K, and phytol (a component of chlorophyll) and occur in essential oils, such as menthol and camphor. Steroids include the adrenal hormones, sex hormones, and bile acids.

Lipids can combine with proteins to form *lipoproteins,* e.g. in cell membranes. In bacterial cell walls, lipids may associate with polysaccharides to form *lipopolysaccharides.*

lipoic acid A vitamin of the vitamin B complex. It is one of the coenzymes involved in the decarboxylation of pyruvate by the enzyme pyruvate dehydrogenase. Liver and yeast are the good sources of lipoic acid.

lipolysis It is the process of the breakdown of storage lipids in living organisms. Most long-term energy reserves are in the form of triglycerides in fats and oils. When these are needed, e.g. during starvations, lipase enzymes convert the triglycerides into glycerol and the component fatty acids. These are then transported to tissues and oxidized to provide energy.

liquefaction It is the process which involves changes of a gas into the liquid state.

liquefied petroleum gas Commonly known as LPG. Various petroleum gases, principally propane and butane, stored as a liquid under pressure. It is used as an engine fuel and has the advantage of causing very little cylinder-head deposits.

liquefied natural gas (LNG) is a similar product and consists mainly of methane. However, it cannot be liquefied simply by pressure as it has a low critical temperature of 190 K and must, therefore, be cooled to below this temperature before it will liquefy. Once liquefied it has to be stored in well-insulated containers. It provides a convenient form in which to ship natural gas in bulk from oil wells to users. It is also used as an engine fuel.

liquid It is a state of matter in which particles are bonded by intramolecular forces. Liquids have definite volume but no definite shape. They take the shape of container.

liquid air A pale blue liquid. It is a mixture of liquid oxygen (b.p —182.9°C) and liquid nitrogen (b.p. –195.7°C).

lithium Symbol: Li, a.n. 3 r.a.m. 6.93; r.d. 0.53; m.p. 180.5°C; b.p. 1340°C. A group I metal. It is the least reactive element in the group. Nevertheless it is stored under oil because of its reactivity towards *air* and *water*. It is soft, and can be cut with a knife, revealing a silvery surface which tarnishes readily. It has a steady reaction with water but reacts vigorously with acids.

$$2Li(s) + 2H_2O\ (l) \rightarrow 2LiOH(aq) + H_2(g)$$

It is possible that the metal will be very important in the future if electricity can be generated by *nuclear fusion* reactions. The metal ion gives a red *flame test*.

lithium aluminium hydride see lithium tetrahydridoaluminate (III)

lithium carbonate, Li_2CO_3 A white ppt. obtained by adding ammonium carbonate to the solution of soluble lithium salt. It is used in glass industry.

lithium chloride (LiCl) A white solid produced by dissolving lithium carbonate or oxide in dilute hydrochloric acid and crystallizing the product. Below 292K the dihydrate ($LiCl.\ 2H_2O$) is obtained; at 292 K the chloride loses one molecule of water and becomes anhydrous at 366.5K. Lithium chloride is used as a flux in welding aluminium.

The compound forms cubic crystals; the anhydrous salt is isomorphous with sodium chloride. It dissolves in such organic solvents as alcohols, ketones, and esters.

lithium hydride A white solid, LiH; cubic; r.d. 0.82; m.p. 686°C; decomposes at about 850°C. It is produced by direct combination of the elements at temperatures above 500°C. The bonding in lithium hydride is believed to be largely ionic; i.e. Li^+H^- as supported by the fact that hydrogen is released from the anode on electrolysis of the molten salt. The compound reacts violently and exothermically with water to yield hydrogen and lithium hydroxide. It is used as a reducing agent to prepare other hydrides and the ^2H isotopic compound, *lithium deuteride*, is particularly valuable for deuterating a range of organic compounds. Lithium hydride is used as a shielding material for thermal neutrons.

lithium hydrogen carbonate; $LiHCO_3$ Exists only in solution. It is obtained when carbon dioxide is passed through a suspension of lithium carbonate.

$$Li_2CO_3 + H_2O + CO_2 \rightarrow LiHCO_3$$

The solution is known as *Lithia water* and is used in medicines for treatment of goat.

lithium hydroxide A white crystaline solid, LiOH, soluble in water, slightly soluble in ethyl alcohol and insoluble in ether. It is known as the monohydrate (monoclinic; r.d. 1.51) and in the anhydrous form (tetragonal, r.d. 1.46; m.p. 450°C; decomposes at 924°C). The compound is made by reacting lime with lithium salts or lithium ores. Lithium hydroxide is basic but has a closer resemblance to group II hydroxides than to the other group I hydroxides (an example of the first member of a periodic group having a typical properties).

lithium oxide (lithia) A white crystalline compound, Li_2O; cubic; r.d. 2.01; m.p. 1700°C. It can be obtained from a number of lithium ores; the main uses of lithium oxide are in lubricating greases, ceramics, glass and refractories, alkaline storage batteries, and as a flux in brazing and welding.

lithium sulphate (Li_2SO_4) A white solid prepared by the addition of excess Li_2O or Li_2CO_3 to a solution of sulphuric acid. It is readily soluble in water from which it crystallizes as the monohydrate. In contrast to the other group I sulphates it does not form alums and it is not isomorphous with these other sulphates.

lithium tetrahydridoaluminate (III), $LiAlH_4$ It is generally called lithium aluminium hydride. It is a powerful reducing agent and is obtained by the action of anhydrous $AlCl_3$ on LiH in ethereal solution.

$$4LiH + AlCl_3 \rightarrow LiAl\,H_4 + 3LiCl$$

Lithium Aluminium hydride

It reduces aldehydes and ketones to primary and secondary alcohols respectively.

litmus A substance which is extracted from lichen that is used as an *acid-base indicator;* according to the pH scale:

acidic solution	pH 7	alkaline solution
red	purple	blue

litre Symbol: l. It is the unit of volume now defined as 10^3 cubic centimetre^3; i.e. 1000 cm^3. The millilitre (ml) is thus the same as the cubic centimetre (cm^3). However, the name is not recommended for precise measurements since the litre was formerly defined as the volume of one kilogram of pure water at 4°C and standard pressure. On this definition, one litre is the same as 1000.028 cubic centimetres.

lixiviation The separation of mixtures by dissolving soluble constituent in water is called lixiviation.

localized bond A chemical bond in which the electrons forming the bond remain between (or close to) the linked atoms.

lone pair A pair of valence electrons having opposite spin that are located together on one atom, i.e. are not shared as in a covalent bond. Lone pairs occupy similar positions in space to bond pairs and account for the shapes of molecules. A molecule with a lone pair can donate this to an electron acceptor, such as H^+ or a metal ion, to form coordinate bonds. (complex) Lewis base.

Loschmidt's number It is the number of molecules of an ideal gas in unit volume at standard temperature and pressure. It is equal to 2.687×10^{19} per cm^3.

lowering of vapour pressure A reduction in the saturated vapour pressure of a pure liquid when a solute is introduced. If the solute is a solid of low vapour pressure, the decrease in vapour pressure of the liquid is directly proportional to the concentration of particles of solute; i.e. to the number of dissolved molecules or ions per unit volume. To a first approximation, it does not depend on the nature of the particles.

lumen Symbol lm. The SI unit of luminous flux equal to the flux emitted by a uniform point source of 1 candela in a solid angle of 1 steradian.

luminescence It is the phenomenon the emission of light by a substance for any reason other than a rise in its temperature. In general, atoms of substances emit photons of electromagnetic energy when they return to the ground state after having been in an excited state. The causes of the excitation are various. If the exciting cause is a photon, the process is called *photoluminscence;* if it is an electron it is called *electroluminescence. Chemiluminescence* is luminescence resulting from a chemical reaction (such as the slow oxidation of phosphorus); *bioluminescence* is the luminescence produced by a living organism (such as firefly). If the luminescence persists significantly after the exciting cause is removed it is called *phosphorescence;* if it does not it is called *fluorescence.* This distinction is arbitrary since there must always be some delay; in some definitions a persistence of more than 10 nanoseconds (10^{-8} s) is treated as phosphorescence.

lutetium Symbol Lu. A silvery metallic element belonging to the lanthanoids: '*f*' block element having atomic number 71; r.a.m. 174.97; r.d. 9.842 (20°C); m.p. 1663°C; b.p. 3402°C. Lutetium is the least abundant of the elements and the little quantities that are available have been obtained by processing other metals. There are two natural isotopes, lutetium-175 (stable) and lutetium–176 (half-life 2.2×10^{10} years). There are no uses for the element, which was first identified by G. Urban in 1907.

lux Symbol lx the SI unit of illumination, equal to the illumination produced by a luminous flux of one lumen falling on a surface of one square metre. 1 l × = 1 lm^{-2}.

lyophilic The affinity for the solvent (i.e. solvent loving); if the solvent is water the term *hydrophilic* is used. Lyophilic colloids are those in which particles of dispersed phase have a great affinity (or love) for the dispersion medium e.g. glue, gelatin, starch etc.

lyophobic Those lacking any affinity for a solvent ('solvent-hating; if the solvent is water the term *hydrophobic* is used).

M

Macromolecule Refers to a large molecule with molecular mass more than 1000. e.g. polymers likes carbohydrates, proteins, nucleic acids, plastics, rubber etc.

macromolecular crystal A crystalline solid in which the atoms are all linked together by covalent bonds. Carbon (in diamond), boron nitride, and silicon carbide are examples of substances that have macromolecular crystals. In effect, the crystal is a large molecule. (hence the alternative description *giant-molecular*), which accounts for the hardness and high m.p. of such materials.

macroscopic system It refers to a system that contains a large number of chemical species (atoms, ions or molecules).

magnadur Tradename for a ceramic material which is used to make permanent magnets. It consists of sintered iron oxide and barium oxide.

magnesium Symbol : Mg, a.n. 12; r.a.m. 24.32; r.d. 1.74, m.p. 651°C; b.p. 1107°C. A shiny grey *group* II *metal* belonging to *'s'* block. It is quite reactive giving vigorous *reactions* towards *acids*. It burns vigorously in air with a bright white light, hence its use in flares, fireworks and flash bulbs. It also burns in *carbon dioxide gas*, and will react with *steam* to release *hydrogen*. The metal is obtained by the *electrolysis* of molten magnesium chloride. Much of this is extracted from seawater.

The chief use of magnesium is in the production of low density *alloys* for use in the aircraft industry. There is no production of the metal in the U.K. Much of the European production takes place in Norway because of the availability of hydroelectricity. Magnesium is also used in the production of *steel*, as a *reducing agent* in the chemical industry, and as *sacrificial anodes* in the protection of other metals.

magnesium chloride, $MgCl_2$ It is extracted from sea water. The crystalline magnesium chloride is hexahydrate ($MgCl_2 . 6H_2O$) and is quite deliquescent. It is used as lubricant for thread, in spinning and weaving industry. It is also used for making 'Sorel's cement'. Sorel's cement is a paste of magnesium chloride ($MgCl_2$) and magnesium oxide

(MgO) which sets into a stone like mass due to the formation of the oxychloride. Sorel's cement is used for making artificial teeth and as a cement for teeth.

magnesium hydrogencarbonate (Also known as magnesium bicarbonate, Mg $(HCO_3)_2$) The solid hydrogencarbonate is unknown at room temperature. The compound is produced in solution when water containing carbon dioxide dissolves magnesium carbonate:

$$MgCO_3 + H_2O + CO_2 \rightarrow Mg(HCO_3)_2$$

It is a cause of temporary hardness in water.

magnesium hydroxide A white solid compound, $Mg(OH)_2$; trigonal; r.d. 2.36; decomposes at 623K. Magnesium hydroxide occurs naturally as the mineral *brucite* and can be prepared by reacting magnesium sulphate or chloride with sodium hydroxide solution.

$$MgCl_2 + 2NaOH \rightarrow Mg(OH)_2 + 2NaCl$$
$$MgSO_4 + 2NaOH \rightarrow Mg(OH)_2 + Na_2SO_4$$

It is used in the refining of sugar and in the processing of uranium. Medicinally it is important as an antacid *(milk of magnesia)* and as a laxative.

magnesium iodide, MgI_2 A white hygroscopic unstable substance that decomposes liberating iodine.

magnesium oxide (magnesia) A white compound, MgO; cubic; r.d. 3.58; m.p. 2800°C. It occurs naturally as the mineral *periclase* and is prepared commercially by thermally decomposing the mineral magnesite:

$$MgCO_3(s) \rightarrow MgO(s) + CO_2(g)$$

It has various uses, including reflective coatings on optical instruments and aircraft windscreens and in semi-conductors. Its high m.p. makes it useful as a refractory lining in metal and glass furnaces.

magnesium peroxide having molecular formula (Mg_2O_2) A white insoluble solid prepared by reacting sodium or barium peroxide with a concentrated solution of a magnesium salt. Magnesium peroxide is used as a bleach for dyestuffs and silks.

magnesium sulphate, $MgSO_4 . 7H_2O$ (hydrated magnesium sulphate) It is called *Epsom salt.* It is used as a fire proofing chemical. It is used as a purgative in medicines, a mordant in dying, in the manufacture of paints and soaps, as a catalyst carrier in the manufacture of H_2SO_4 acid in Grillo's converter.

magnetic moment The ratio between the maximum torque (T_{max}) exerted on a magnet, current-carrying coil, or moving charge situated in a magnetic field and the strength of that field. It is thus a measure of the strength of a magnet or current-carrying coil. In the Sommerfeld approach this quantity (also known as *electromagnetic moment* or *magnetic area moment*) is the ratio T_{max}/B. In the Kennelly approach the quantity (also known *magnetic dipole moment*) is T_{max}/H.

In the case of a magnet placed in a magnetic field of field strength H, the maximum torque T_{max} occurs when the axis of the magnet is perpendicular to the field. In the case of a coil of N turns and area A carrying a current I, the magnetic moment can be shown to be $m=T/B = NIA$ or $m=T/H = \mu NIA$. Magnetic moments are measured in A m^2.

An orbital electron has an orbital magnetic moment IA, where I is the equivalent current as the electron moves round its orbit. It is given by $I = q\omega/2\pi$, where q is the electronic charge and ω is its angular velocity. The orbital magnetic moment is therefore $IA = q\omega A/2\pi$, where A is the orbital area. If the electron is spinning there is also a spin magnetic moment; atomic nuclei also have magnetic moments.

magnetism A group of phenomena associated with magnetic fields. Whenever an electric current flows a magnetic field is produced; as the orbital motion and the spin of atomic electrons are equivalent to tiny current loops, individual atoms create magnetic fields around them, when their orbital electrons have a net magnetic moment as a result of their angular momentum. The magnetic moment of an atom is the vector sum of the magnetic moments of the orbital motions and the spins of all the electrons in the atom. The macroscopic magnetic properties of a substance arise from the magnetic moments of its component atoms and molecules. Different materials have different characteristics in an applied magnetic field; there are four main types of magnetic behaviour:

(i) In *diamagnetism* (paired electrons) the magnetization is in the opposite direction to that of the applied field, i.e., the susceptibility is negative. Although all substances are diamagnetic, it is a weak form of magnetism and may be masked by other stronger forms. It results from changes induced in the orbits of electrons in the atoms of a substance by the applied field, the direction of the change opposing the applied flux. There is thus a weak negative susceptibility (of the order of -10^{-8} m^3 mol^{-1}) and a relative permeability of slightly less than one.

(ii) In *paramagnetism* (unpaired electrons) the atoms or

molecules of the substance have net orbital or spin magnetic moments that are capable of being aligned in the direction of the applied field. They, therefore, have a positive (but small) susceptibility and a relative permeability slightly in excess of one. Paramagnetism occurs in all atoms and molecules with unpaired electrons; for example free atoms, free radicals, and compounds of transition metals containing ions with unfilled electron shells. It also occurs in metals as a result of the magnetic moments associated with the spins of the conducting electrons.

(iii) In *ferromagnetic* substances, within a certain temperature range, there are net atomic magnetic moments, which line up in such a way that magnetization persists after the removal of the applied field. Below a certain temperature, called the *Curie point* (or Curie temperature) an increasing magnetic field applied to a ferromagnetic substance will cause increasing magnetization to a high value, called the *saturation magnetization*. This is because a ferromagnetic substance consists of small (1-0.1 mm across) magnetized regions called *domains*. The total magnetic moment of a sample of the substance is the vector sum of the magnetic moments of the component domains. Within each domain the individual atomic magnetic moments are spontaneously aligned by *exchange forces,* related to whether or not the atomic electron spins are parallel or anti-parallel. However, in an unmagnetized piece of ferromagnetic material the magnetic moments of the domains themselves are not aligned; when an external field is applied those domains that are aligned with the field increase in size at the expense of the others. In a very strong field all the domains are lined up in the direction of the field and provide the high observed magnetization. Iron (Fe), Cobalt (Co) and Nickel (Ni) and their alloys are ferromagnetic. Above the Curie point, ferromagnetic materials become paramagnetic.

(iv) Some metals, alloys, and transition-element salts exhibit another form of magnetism called *anti-ferromagnetism*. This occurs below a certain temperature, called the *Néel temperature,* when an ordered array of atomic magnetic moments spontaneously forms in which alternate moments have opposite directions. There is, therefore, no net resultant magnetic moment in the absence of an applied field. In manganese fluoride, for example, this anti-parallel arrangement occurs below a Néel temperature of –201°C. Below this temperature the spontaneous ordering opposes the normal tendency of the magnetic moments to align with the applied field. Above the Néel temperature the substance is paramagnetic.

A special form of anti-ferromagnetism is *ferrimagnetism*, a type of magnetism exhibited by the ferrites. In these materials the magnetic moments of adjacent ions are anti-parallel and of unequal strength, or the number of magnetic moments in one direction is greater than those in the opposite direction.

magnetite It is a naturally occurring black oxide of iron, having formula Fe_3O_4. It is a magnetic iron ore.

magnetochemistry It may be defined as the branch of physical chemistry concerned with measuring and investigating the magnetic properties of compounds. It is used particularly for studying transition-metal complexes, many of which are paramagnetic (having unpaired electrons) because they have unpaired electrons. Measurement of the magnetic susceptibility allows the magnetic moment of the metal atom to be calculated, and this gives information about the bonding in the complex.

magneton It is used as a unit for measuring the magnetic moments of atomic particles. The Bohr magneton (B.M.), μ_E, is equal to

$$\frac{e\,h}{4\pi\, m_e} = 9.2741 \times 10^{-24} \text{ ampere metre}^2$$

Various symbol are denoted as

e = charge of electron

m_e = mass of electron

h = plank's constant

The nuclear magneton, μ_N, is equal to

$\mu_p\, m_c/m_v = 5.05 \times 10^{-27}$ ampere metre²

where m_v = mass of proton.

malachite A green mineral consisting of copper(II) carbonate and hydroxide ($CuCO_3.Cu(OH)_2$). It is used as an ore and a pigment.

maleic acid, $C_4H_4O_4$ It is a colourless crystalline solid, used in the production of polymers. It is

malleable Malleable substances are those which can be beaten or hammered into different shapes. The larger the *crystals* in a substance, the more malleable it is. *Materials* which are malleable are usually also *ductile*. *Metals* and *alloys* have these properties.

malic acid,

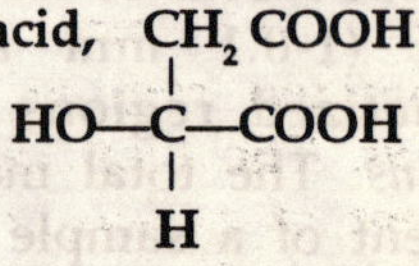

It is a colourless, crystalline solid, quite deliquescent. In place of citric acid and tartaric acid it is used in beverages. It is used as a remedy for sore-throat and also as a purgative.

maltose (malt sugar) A sugar consisting of two linked glucose molecules that results from the action of the enzyme amylase on starch. Maltose occurs in barley seeds following germination and drying, which is the basis of the malting process used in the manufacture of beer and malt whisky.

manganate (VI) A salt containing the ion MnO_4^{2-}.

manganate(VII) (permanganate) A salt containing the ion MnO_4^-. Manganate(VII) ions are dark purple and strong oxidizing agents, i.e. it oxidises others and get itself reduced easily.

manganese Symbol: Mn; a.n. 25; r.a.m. 54.94; r.d. 7.4; m.p. 1244°C; b.p. 2040°C. A *transition metal.* It is found naturally as the oxide (MnO_2) and is extracted either by *electrolysis* of the sulphate or by a *thermal reaction.* The chief use of the metal is in *alloys,* e.g. *steels* and *bronzes.*

manganese(IV) oxide (manganese dioxide) A black oxide made by heating manganese(II) nitrate. The compound also occurs naturally as pyrolusite. It is a strong oxidizing agent. It is used as a depolarizing agent in voltaic cells.

manganese(III) oxide (also known as manganic oxide, manganese sesquioxide, Mn_2O_3), a black powder obtained by igniting manganese (IV) oxide or a manganese(II) salt in air at 1073 K. It reacts slowly with cold dilute acids to form manganese(III) salts. Manganese (III) oxide occurs in nature as braunite ($3Mn_2O_3.MnSiO_3$), and the monohydrate ($Mn_2O_3.H_2O$) occurs in the mineral manganite. The manganese(III) oxide crystal lattice contains Mn^{3+} and O^{2-} ions. With concentrated alkalis, such as NaOH, KOH etc. it undergoes disproportionation to give manganese(II) and manganese (IV) ions.

manganous compounds Compounds of manganese in its +2 oxidation state; for example manganous oxide is manganese(II) oxide, MnO.

mannitol A polyhydric alcohol, $CH_2OH(CHOH)_4CH_2OH$, found in some plants. It is used as a sweetener in certain foodstuffs.

mannose ($C_6H_{12}O_6$) A simple sugar found in many polysaccharides. It is an aldohexose, isomeric with glucose.

manometer A device for measuring pressure differences, usually by the difference in height of two liquid columns. The simplest type is the U-tube manometer, which consists of a glass tube bent into the shape of a U. If a pressure to be measured is fed to one side of the U-tube and the other is open to the atmosphere, the difference in level of the liquid in the two limbs gives a measure of the unknown pressure.

marble A dense mineral form of calcium carbonate ($CaCO_3$), formed from limestone.

Markownikoffs' rule It governs the addition to unsymmetrical multiple bond. It states, "Whenever addition takes place to an unsymmetrical multiple bond, the negative part of addendum goes to the carbon atom with lesser number of hydrogen atoms while positive part goes to the other carbon atom." e.g. Reaction of propene with hydrogen bromide forming 2-bromo propane.

$$CH_3CH = CH_2 + HBr \rightarrow CH_2 - \underset{\displaystyle Br}{\underset{|}{CH}} - CH_3$$

$$CH_3CH{=}CH_2 + HO^{\delta-}Cl^{\delta+} \rightarrow CH_3\ \underset{\displaystyle OH}{\underset{|}{CH}} - \underset{\displaystyle Cl}{\underset{|}{CH_2}}$$

Marsh's test A chemical test for arsenic in which HCl acid and Zn are added to the sample, arsine being produced by the nascent hydrogen generated. Gas from the sample is led through a heated glass tube and, if arsine is present, it decomposes to give a brown deposit of arsenic metal. The arsenic is distinguished from antimony (which gives a similar result) by the fact that antimony does not dissolve in sodium chlorate(I) (hypochlorite). The test was devised in 1836 by the British chemist James Marsh.

martensite It is a hard and brittle constituent of steel. It is produced when the material is cooled from its hardening temperature at a greater rate than its critical cooling rate.

mass It is the measure of a body's inertia, i.e. its resistance to acceleration. According to Newton's laws of motion, if two unequal masses, m_1 and m_2, are allowed to collide, in the absence of any other forces both will experience the same force of collision. If the two bodies acquire accelerations a_1 and a_2 as a result of the collision, then $m_1a_1 = m_2a_2$. This equation enables two masses to be compared. If one of the masses is regarded as a standard of mass, the mass of all other masses can be measured in terms of this standard. The body used for this purpose is a 1-kg cylinder of platinum-iridium alloy, called the international standard of mass.

masurium Technetium was earlier known by this name.

Maxwell's Boltzmann distribution of velocities It is a curve representing the distribution of molecular velocities in a gaseous sample at any specified temperature.

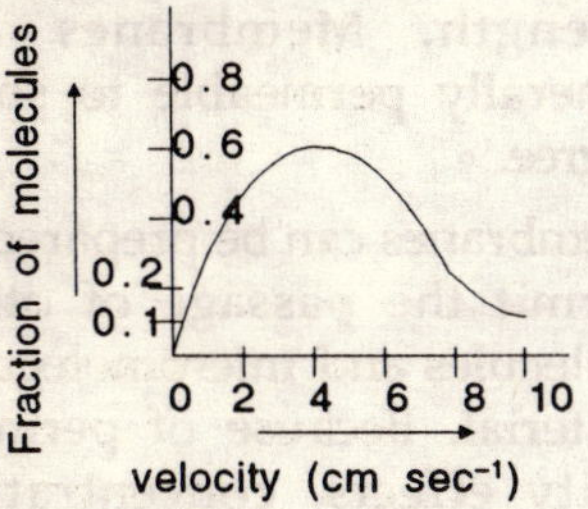

From the curve it can be easily seen that the number of molecules having very low or very high velocities is very small.

McLeod gauge A vacuum pressure gauge in which a relatively large volume of a low-pressure gas is compressed to a small volume in a glass apparatus. The volume is reduced to an extent that causes the pressure to rise sufficiently to support a column of fluid high enough to read. This simple device, which works on Boyle's law, is suitable for measuring pressure in the range 10^3 to 10^{-3} pascal.

mean free path It is the average distance covered by a gaseous molecule between two successive collisions. In case of hydrogen molecule, it is found to be 1.8×10^{-6} cm at S.T.P.

mean free time It is the average time that elapses between the collisions of the molecules in a gas, the electrons in a crystal, the neutrons in a moderator, etc. (mean free path).

mechanism A step-by-step description of the events taking place in a chemical reaction. It is a theoretical framework accounting for the fate of bonding electrons and illustrates which bonds are broken and which are formed. For example, in the chlorination of methane to give chloromethane.

step 1
$$Cl{:}Cl \rightarrow 2Cl$$
step 2
$$Cl + CH_4 \rightarrow HCl + CH_3$$
step 3
$$CH_3 + Cl{:}Cl \rightarrow CH_3Cl + Cl$$

mega Symbol M. A prefix used in the metric system to denote one million times. For example, 10^6 volts = 1 megavolt (MV).

melamine A colourless, crystalline compound produced from *urea*. It undergoes *condensation polymerization* with formaldehyde to produce melamine resins. These are heat and light-resistant, colourless and shatter-resistant. They are widely used as picnic-ware and as kitchen worktops.

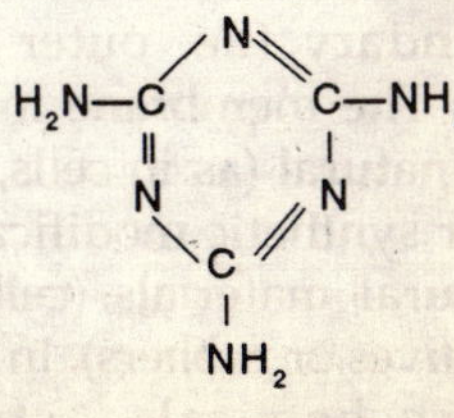

melamine

melamin-formaldehyde resin Melamine and formaldehyde copolymerise to form this polymer. It is quite hard and is used in making plastic crockery.

melting The process by which a solid is converted into a liquid by heat or pressure is known as melting (or fusion).

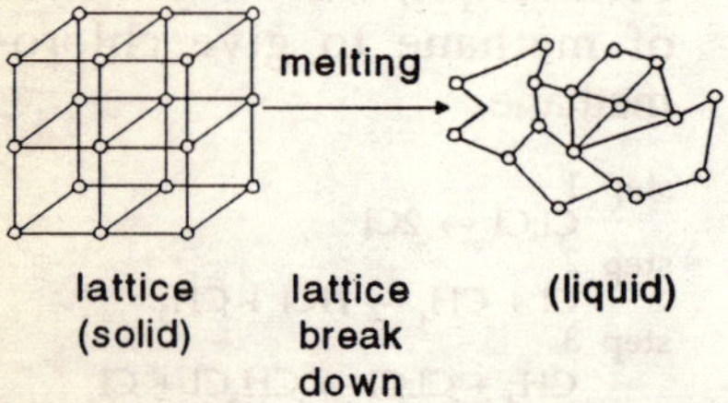

melting point (m.p.) It may be defined as the temperature at which a solid changes into a liquid. A pure substance under standard conditions of pressure (usually 1 atmosphere) has a single reproducible melting point. If heat is gradually and uniformly supplied to a solid the consequent rise in temperature stops at the m.p. until the melting process is complete.

membrane A thin pliable sheet of tissue or other material acting as a boundary (i.e. outer most layer). The membrane may be either natural (as in cells, skin, etc.) or synthetic modifications of natural materials (cellulose derivatives or rubbers). In many physicochemical studies membranes are supported on porous materials, such as porcelain, to provide mechanical strength. Membranes are generally permeable to some degree.

Membranes can be prepared to permit the passage of other molecules and micromolecular material. Because of permeability effects, concentration differences at a membrane give rise to a whole range of membrane-equilibrium studies, of which osmosis, dialysis, and ultra-filtration are examples.

Mendelvium. Symbal Md. Refers to a radioactiive metallic transuranic element which belongs to the actinoids; a.n. 101; mass number of the only known isotope 256 (halflife 1.3 hours). It was first identified by A. Ghiorso, G.T. Seaborg in 1955.

mercuric compounds They are compounds of mercury in its +2 oxidation state; e.g. mercuric chloride is mercury(II) chloride, $HgCl_2$.

mercurous compounds These are compounds of mercury in its +1 oxidation state; e.g. mercury(I) chloride is mercurous chloride, HgCl.

mercury Symbol: **Hg**; m.p. 192 K; b.p. 630 K; r.d. 13.5; a.n. 80; r.a.m. 200.59. A transition metal occurring naturally as cinnabar (mercury(II) sulphide). The vapour is very poisonous.

Mercury is used in thermometers, special amalgams for dentistry, and in scientific apparatus. Mercury compounds are used as fungicides, timber preservatives, and explosives.

mercury cell A primary voltaic cell consisting of a zinc anode and a cathode of mercury(II) oxide (HgO) mixed with graphite. The electrolyte is potassium hydroxide (KOH) saturated with ZnO, the overall reaction being:

$$Zn + HgO \rightarrow ZnO + Hg$$

The e.m.f. is 1.35 volts and the cell will deliver about 0.3 ampere-hour per cm^3.

mercury(I) chloride It is a white salt, Hg_2Cl_2; r.d. 7.0; m.p. 575 K; b.p. 657 K. It is made by heating mercury(II) chloride with mercury and is used in calomel cells (so called because the salt was formerly called *calomel*) and as a fungicide.

mercury(II) chloride (mercuric chloride, $HgCl_2$) A colourless crystalline compound prepared by direct combination of mercury with cold dry chlorine. $HgCl_2$ is soluble in water; it also dissolves in concentrated hydrochloric acid due to the formation of complex ions, $HgCl_4^{2-}$ and $HgCl_3^-$. On heating, mercury(II) chloride sublimes forming a white translucent mass. It is extremely poisonous, but in dilute solution (1:1000) it is used as an antiseptic.

mercuric iodide, molecular formula HgI_2 A yellow precipitate formed by adding calculated amount of potassium iodide to mercuric chloride solution.

$$HgCl_2 + 2KI \rightarrow HgI_2 \downarrow + 2KCl$$

It is used to prepare Nessler's reagent, in preparation of ointments etc.

$$HgI_2 + 2KI \rightarrow \underset{\text{Nessler's reagent}}{K_2HgI_2}$$

mercury(II) oxide A yellow or red oxide of mercury, HgO. The red form is made by heating mercury in oxygen at 623 K, the yellow form, which differs from the red in particle size, is precipitated when sodium hydroxide solution is added to a solution of mercury(II) nitrate. Both forms decompose to the elements at high temperature. The black precipitate formed when sodium hydroxide is added to mercury(I) nitrate solution is sometimes referred to as mercury(I) oxide (Hg_2O) but is probably a mixture of HgO and free mercury.

mercury(II) sulphide A red or black compound, having formula HgS, occurring naturally as the minerals cinnabar (red) and metacinnabar (black). It can be obtained as a black precipitate by bubbling hydrogen sulphide through a solution of mercury(II) nitrate. The red form is obtained by sublimation. The compound is also called *vermilion* (used as a pigment).

mesitylene,

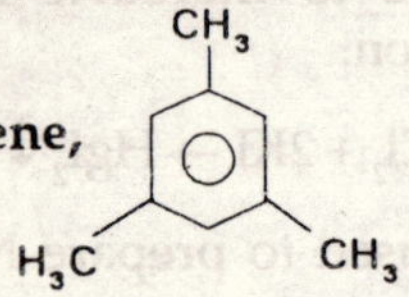

It is a colourless, pleasent smelling liquid.

meta 1. Prefix designating a benzene compound in which two substituents are in the 1,3 positions on the benzene ring. The abbreviation *m*- is used; for example, *m*-xylene is 1,3-dimethylbenzene.

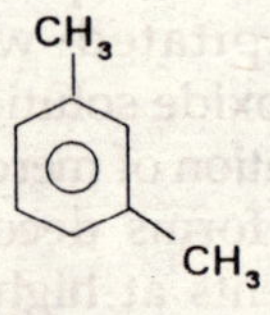

(meta-xylene)

Compare ortho-; para-. **2.** Prefix designating a lower oxo acid, e.g. metaphosphoric acid.

metabolism The sum of the chemical reactions that occur within living organisms. The various compounds that take part in or are formed by these reactions are called *metabolites.* In animals many metabolites are obtained by the digestion of food, whereas in plants only the basic starting materials (CO_2, H_2O and minerals) are extremely derived. The synthesis (anabolism) and breakdown (catabolism) of most compounds occurs by a number of reaction steps, the reaction sequence being termed a *metabolic pathway*. Some pathways (e.g. glycolysis) are linear; others (e.g. the Krebs cycle) are cyclic.

metal Many elements (Approx 17%) are metals. Metals are good conductors of heat and electricity and their conductivity decreases with increase in temperature. They are generally malleable and ductile. Pure metals are rarely used. Most metals are used in the form of alloys.

metal carbonyls The compounds of certain metals formed with carbon monoxide (CO). e.g.

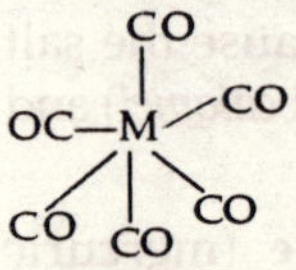

$M(CO)_6$; where M=Cr, Mo etc.

$M(CO)_5$, where M=Fe

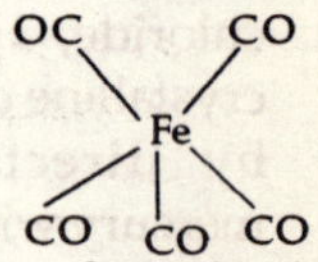

Iron carboxyl

$M(CO)_4$, where M = Ni

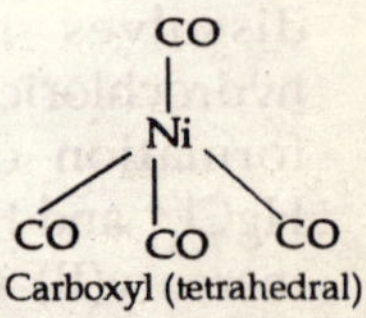

Nickel Carboxyl (tetrahedral)

M—C bond is metal carboxyls has a σ (sigma) as well as a π (pi)-character.

metaldehyde A solid compound, $C_4O_4H_4(CH_3)_4$, formed by polymerization of ethanal (acetaldehyde) in dilute acid solutions below 0°C. The compound, a tetramer of acetaldehyde is used in slug pellets and as a fuel for portable stoves.

Metathesis double substitution or double replacement or double decomposition reactions e.g. $AgNO_3$+Nacl⟶ AgCl+ $NaNO_3$ are referred as Metathesis reaction.

metallic bond It is a bond formed between atoms of a metallic element in its zero oxidation state and in an array of similar atoms. The outer electrons of each atom are regarded as contributing to an 'electron gas', which occupies the whole crystal of the metal. It is the attraction of the positive atomic cores for the negative electron gas that provides the strength of the metallic bond.

The quantum mechanical treatment of the electron gas restricts its energy to a series of 'bands'. It is the behaviour of electrons in these bands that gives rise to semiconductors.

metallic crystal A crystalline solid in which the atoms are held together by metallic bonds is known as metallic crystal. Metallic crystals are found in some interstitial compounds as well as in metals and alloys.

metallocene A sandwich compound in which a metal atom is coordinated to two cyclopentadienyl ions. Ferrocene ($Fe_(C_5H_5)2$) is the commonest example.

metalloid *Elements* that are neither *metals* nor *non-metals*. They are also known as *semi-metals*.

The best examples are germanium and *arsenic*. Such substances tend to have the physical properties of metals, in that they have a shiny appearance and a high m.p. and b.p. but the chemical properties of non-metals, e.g. do not react with *acids*. They are useful as *semiconductors*.

metallurgy The branch of applied science concerned with the production of metals from their ores, the purification of metals, the manufacture of alloys, and the use and performance of metals in engineering practice. *Process metallurgy* deals with the extraction and production of metals, while *physical metallurgy* deals the mechanical behaviour of metals.

metastable species An excited state of an atom, ion, or molecule, that has a relatively long lifetime before reverting to the ground state. Metastable species are intermediates in some reactions.

metastable state A condition of a system in which it has a precarious stability that can easily be disturbed. It is unlike a state of stable equilibrium in that a minor disturbance will cause a system in a metastable state to fall to a lower energy level. A book lying on a table is in a state of stable equilibrium; a thin book standing on edge is in metastable equilibrium. Supercooled water is also in a metastable state. It is liquid below 273 K; a grain of dust or ice introduced into it will cause it to freeze. An excited state of an atom or nucleus that has an appreciable lifetime is also metastable.

methacrylate A salt or ester of methacrylic acid (2-methyl-propenoic acid).

methanal Also known as formaldehyde, a toxic gas belonging to the family of *organic* compounds called *aldehydes*. Methanal is produced by the *oxidation of methanol*.

$$CH_3OH + [O] \xrightarrow{K_2Cr_2O_7} HCHO + H_2O$$

It is an important chemical in the production of *thermosetting polymers*. (*Urea/methanal resins, phenol*/methanal resins and *melamine*).

methanal trimer A cyclic trimer of methanal, (formaldehyde) C_3O_3H6, obtained by distillation of an acidic solution of methanal. It has a six-membered ring of alternating –O– and $–CH_2–$ groups).

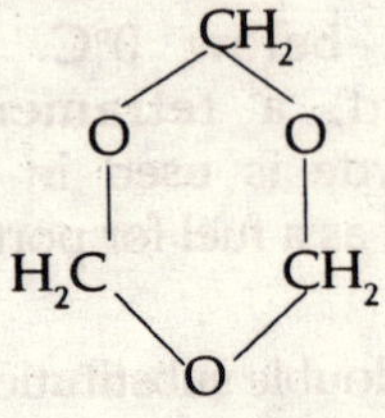

methanal trimer

methane A colourless odourless gas, CH_4; m.p. –182·5°C; b.p. –161°C. Methane is the simplest hydrocarbon, being the first member of the alkane series. It is the main constituent of natural gas (~99%) and as such is an important raw material for producing other organic compounds. It can be converted into methyl alcohol by catalytic oxidation.

methanamide, having molecular formula $HCONH_2$. It is also called formamide. It is a hygroscopic liquid. It dissolves in water as also in alcohol. It is used as a solvent and also as a plasticizer.

methanoate (formate) A salt or ester of methanoic acid.

methanoic acid (formic acid) A colourless pungent liquid, HCOOH; r.d. 1.2; m.p. 8°C; b.p. 101°C. It can be made by the action of concentrated sulphuric acid on the sodium salt (sodium methanoate). It can also be prepared by action of NaOH on carbon monoxide.

$$NaOH + XO \xrightarrow[473\ K]{6\text{-}10\ atm} HCOON\alpha \xrightarrow{HCl} \underset{\text{Methanoic acid}}{HCOOH} + NaCl$$

and occurs naturally in ants and stinging nettles. Methanoic acid is the simplest of the carboxylic acids.

methanol (Methyl alcohol; CH_3OH) An *alcohol*. It is a colourless *poisonous liquid*. Methanol is produced in large quantities from *synthesis gas* at high *temperature* and *pressure*:

$$CO(g) + 2H_2(g) \rightarrow CH_3OH(g)$$
$$CO_2(g) + 3H_2(g) \rightarrow CH_3OH(g) + H_2O(g)$$

Methanol is used in several ways:

(a) As a solvent;
(b) To produce *ethanoic acid;*
(c) To produce *methanal* and *thermosetting polymers;*
(d) As an *additive* to *unleaded petrol;*
(e) In the production of *methylated spirit*

methoxy group The organic group CH_3O–.

methylated spirits *A mixture* of *ethyl alcohol* (90%), *methyl alcohol* (9.5%), pyridine (0.5%) and traces of a purple *dye*. This mixing is done to make the *ethanol* unfit for drinking. There is no excise tax on the mixture and so it is inexpensive. It is used as *a fuel* and *a solvent*.

methylation A chemical reaction in which a methyl group (CH_3–) is introduced in a molecule. A particular example is the replacement of a hydrogen atom by a methyl group, as in a Friedel-Crafts reaction.

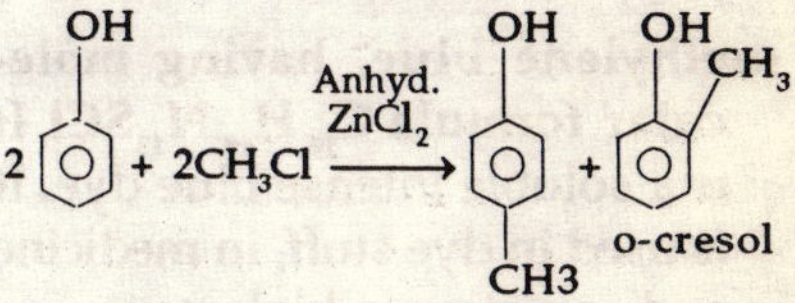

o-cresol

p-cresol

methylbenzene, also known as toluene. C_7H_8 It is used as a solvent. It is used to obtain T.N.T. (an explosive).

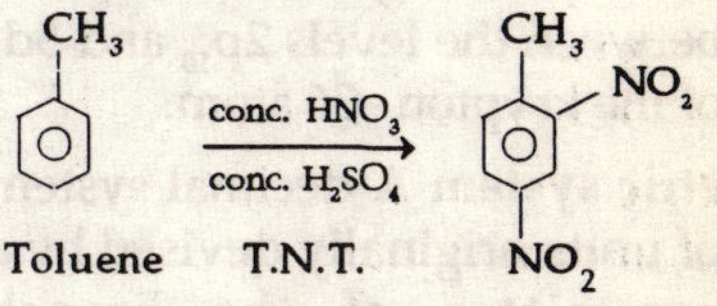

methyl ethanoate (methyl acetate) A colourless volatile fragrant liquid, CH_3COOCH_3; r.d. 0.92; m.p. –98°C; b.p. 54°C. A typical ester, it can be made from methanol and methanoic acid

$$CH_3OH + CH_3COOH \xrightarrow{HCl} CH_3COOCH_3 + H_2O$$

is used mainly as a solvent.

methyl orange An acid-base indicator that is red in solutions below a pH of 3 and yellow above a pH of 4.4. As the transition range is clearly on the acid side, methyl orange is suitable for the titration of an acid with a moderately weak base, such as sodium carbonate (Na_2CO_3).

methyl red An organic dye similar in structure and use to methyl orange. It changes from red below pH 4.4 to yellow above pH 6.0 (at 25°C).

methylene blue, having molecular formula $C_{16}H_{18}N_{13}SCl$ It is a soluble intense blue dye. It is used in dye stuff, in medicine and as a stain in biology.

metre Symbol: m It is the SI base unit of length, defined as the length equal to 1 650 763.73 wavelengths in vacuum corresponding to the transition between the levels $2p_{10}$ and $5d_5$ of the krypton –36 atom.

metric system A decimal system of units originally devised by a committee of the French Academy, which included J.L. Lagrange and P.S. Laplace, in 1791. It was based on the metre, the gram defined in terms of the mass of a cubic centimetre of water, and the second. This centimetre-gram-second system (*see* c.g.s. units) later gave way for scientific work to the metre-kilogram-second system (*see* m.k.s. units) on which SI units are based.

mica Any of a group of silicate minerals with a layered structure. Micas are composed of linked SiO_4 tetrahedra with positive ions and hydroxyl groupings between the layers. The general formula is $X_2Y_{4-6}Z_8O_{20}(OH,F)_4$, where X = K,Na,Ca; Y = Al,Mg,Fe,Li; and Z = Si,Al. The three main mica minerals are muscovite,

$K_2Al_4(Si_6Al_2O_{20})$-$(OH,F)_4$

biotite, $K_2(Mg,Fe^{2+})_{6-4}(Fe^{3+},$ $-Al,Ti)_{0-2}(Si_{6-5}Al_{2-3}O_{20})(OH,F)_4$

lepidolite, $K_2(Li,Al)_{5-6}(Si_{6-7}$-$Al_{2-1}O_{20})(OH,F)_4$

Micas have perfect basal cleavage and the thin cleavage flakes are flexible and elastic. Flakes of mica are used as electrical insulators and as the dielectric in capacitors.

micelle An aggregate of molecules in a colloid. For example, when soap or other detergents dissolve in water they do so as micelles—small clusters of molecules in which the nonpolar hydrocarbon groups are in the centre and the hydrophilic polar groups are on the outside solvated by the water molecules.

micro- Symbo μ. A prefix used in the metric system to denote one millionth. For example, 10^{-6} metre = 1 micrometre (mm).

microbalance A sensitive balance capable of weighing masses of the order 10^{-6} to 10^{-9} kg.

micron Symbol: μm A unit of length equal to 10^{-6} metre.

microscope A device for forming a magnified image of a small object. The *simple microscope* consists of a biconvex magnifying glass or an equivalent system of lenses, either hand-held or in a simple frame. The *compound microscope* uses two lenses or systems of lenses, the second magnifying the real image formed by the first. The lenses are usually mounted at the opposite ends of a tube that has mechanical controls to move it in relation to the object. An optical condenser and mirror, often with a separate light source, provide illumination of the object. The widely used binocular *microscope* consists of two separate instruments fastened together so that one eye looks through one while the other eye looks through the other. This gives stereoscopic vision and reduces eye strain.

microwaves These are the electromagnetic radiations in the frequency range 10^{10}-10^{12} hertz (Hz).

migration 1. The movement of a group, atom, or double bond from one part of a molecule to another. **2**. The movement of ions under the influence of an electric field.

milli Symbol: m A prefix denoting 10^{-3}. For example, 1 millimetre (mm) = 10^{-3} metre (m).

mineral A naturally occurring substance that has a characteristic chemical composition and, in general, a crystalline structure is known as mineral.

Mineral	*Use*
Clay	Building materials
Fluospar	Plastics
Gypsum	Cement
Limestone	Cement, glass, paper, rubber, building materials
Phosphates	Fertilizers, detergents
Potash	Potassium chemicals, fertilizers
Rock salt	Detergents, soaps, food, textiles, paper, plastics, bleaches
Sand	Building materials, cement, glass, catalysts
Sulphur	Explosives, paints, plastics, dyes, fertilizers

mineral acid A common inorganic acid, such as HCl, H_2SO_4 or HNO_3.

mineral processing It is the techniques of changing *mineral*s and metallic *ore*s into more useful forms. They are processed in standard ways. For example:

(a) Extraction;
(b) Crushing and grinding to a powder;
(c) Sorting according to size and properties;
(d) Removal of impurities;
(e) Chemical purification.

Mitscherlich's law (law of isomorphism) The law states

that substances that crystallize in isomorphous forms (i.e. have identical crystalline forms and form mixed crystals) have similar chemical compositions. The law can be used to indicate the formulae of compounds. For instance, the fact that chromium oxide is isomorphous with Fe_2O_3 and Al_2O_3 implies that its formula is Cr_2O_3.

mixture It is the system of two or more distinct chemical substances. *Homogeneous mixtures* are those in which the atoms or molecules are interspersed, as in a mixture of gases or in a solution. *Heterogeneous mixtures* have distinguishable phases, e.g. a mixture of iron filings and sulphur. In a mixture there is no redistribution of valence electrons, and the components retain their individual chemical properties. Unlike compounds, mixtures can be separated by physical means (distillation, crystallization, etc.).

mm Hg (millimetre of mercury) A former unit of pressure defined as the pressure that will support a column of mercury one millimetre high under specified conditions. It is equal to 133.3224 Pa, and is almost identical to the torr.

molal elevation constant (Kb) It is the elevation in boiling point of a molal (1m) solution.

The molal elevation constant is also called ebulioscopic constant.

Ebulioscopic constants for some liquids are as follows

Water	0.52°C	Acetone	1.72°C
Benzene	2.47°C	Ethanol	1.15°C
Ether	2.11°C	Trichloro methane	3.88°C

Molality The concentration of a solution expressed in terms of the number of moles of solute dissolved in one litre of solvent.

molar Denoting that an extensive physical property is being expressed per amount of substance, usually per mole. For example, the molar heat capacity of a compound is the heat capacity of that compound per unit amount of substance; in SI units it would be expressed in $J\,K^{-1}\,mol^{-1}$.

molarity (M) The number of moles of the solute dissolved per litre of solution is called molarity. It is represented by M.

$$\text{Molarity (M)} = \frac{n_B}{V} = \frac{\text{number of moles of solute}}{\text{volume in litres of solution}}$$

mole The amount of a substance (*element* or *compound*) which contains L particles (L is the *Avogadro constant*).

L is defined as the number of *atoms* there are in 12 g of the *carbon*-12 *isotope*. It follows that the *mass* of one mole of an element or compound is the *relative atomic mass* (expressed in grammes). For example, one mole of

Oxygen	(O_2)	is 16 + 16	= 32 g
Water	(H_2O)	is 2(1) + 16	= 18 g
Ammonia	(NH_3)	is 14 + 3(1)	= 17 g
Ethene	(C_2H_4)	is 2(12) + 4(1)	= 28 g

mole fraction Represented by x. It is the ratio of number of moles of one component to the total number of moles present in solution

Mole fraction of solute (X_A)

$$= \frac{\text{Moles of solute}}{\text{Moles of solute} + \text{Moles of solvent}}$$

$$= \frac{n_A}{n_A + n_B}$$

Mole fraction of solvent (X_B)

$$= \frac{\text{Moles of solvent}}{\text{Moles of solute} + \text{Moles of solvent}}$$

$$= \frac{n_B}{n_A + n_B}$$

whereas, $X_A + X_B = 1$.

molecular beam A beam of atoms, ions, or molecules at low pressure, in which all the particles travel in the same direction and there are few collisions between them. They are formed by allowing a gas or vapour to pass through an aperture into an enclosure, which acts as a collimator by containing several additional apertures and vacuum pumps to remove any particles that do not pass through the apertures. Molecular beams are used in studies of surfaces and chemical reactions and in spectroscopy.

molecular distillation Distillation in high vacuum (about 0.1 pascal) with the condensing surface so close to the surface of the evaporating liquid that the molecules of the liquid travel to the condensing surface without collisions. This technique enables very much lower temperatures to be used than are used with distillation at atmospheric pressure and therefore heat-sensitive substances can be distilled. Oxidation of the distillate is also eliminated as there is no oxygen present.

molecularity The total number of reacting molecules in the individual steps of a chemical reaction. Thus, a unimolecular step has molecularity 1, a bimolecular step 2, etc. Molecularity is always an integer, whereas the order of a reaction need not necessarily be so. The molecularity of a reaction gives no information about the mechanism by which it takes place, for example, in the reaction

$N_2 + 3H_2 \rightarrow 2NH_3$, molecularity is 4.

molecular formula It is the formula which shows the number and types *of atoms* in the *molecule*. It tells us nothing about how the atoms are arranged, e.g. $C_4H_{10}O$ is the molecular formula of butanol and *ether* (ethoxyethane). *(empirical formula, structural formula.)*

molecular mass The number of times a mole of the compound is heavier than 1/12th of the mass of carbon-12, is known as molecular mass. It is equal to the sum of the atomic masses of all the atoms present in one molecule of the substance. e.g. molecular mass of hydrogen (H_2) is two and that of H_2O (water) is 18. Molecular mass of oxygen (O_2) is 32.

molecular sieve Porous crystalline substances, especially aluminosilicates, that can be dehydrated with little change in crystal structure. As they form regularly spaced cavities, they provide a high surface area for the absorption of smaller molecules. The general formula of these substances is $M_nO.Al_2O_3.xSiO_2.yH_2O$, where M is a metal ion and n is twice the reciprocal of its valency. Molecular sieves are used as drying agents and in the separation and purification of fluids. They can also be loaded with chemical substances, which remain separated from any reaction that is taking place around them, until they are released by heating or by displacement with a more strongly absorbed substance. They can thus be used as cation exchange medium and as catalysts and catalyst supports.

molecular spectroscopy As in case of atoms, energy can be emitted or absorbed by molecules in order to pass through various quantised states. In contrast to line spectrum obtained in case of atoms, we generally obtain a band spectrum in case of molecules. Each molecule is characterised by its band spectrum. Molecular spectroscopy is mainly concerned with the study of interaction between radiant energy and the molecule. In general it is absorption spectroscopy. Each type of interaction produces an absorption spectrum that lies in some characteristic spectral zone. Some important zones are:

Zones	*Type of transition*
(i) Far infra red	Between rotational states within same electronic state.
(ii) Near infra-red	Between vibrational states within the same electronic state.
(iii) Visible/u.v.	Between different electronic states and contemporary vibrational transitions.

molecular spectrum It is the absorption or emission spectrum that is characteristic of a molecule. Molecular spectra are usually band spectra.

molecule The smallest particle of *an element* or *compound* which exists independently. It contains *atoms* bonded together in a fixed whole number ratio:

Oxygen O_2	Phosphorus P_4
Nitrogen N_2	Carbon dioxide CO_2
Neon Ne	Water H_2O
Sulphur S	Hydrogen chloride HCl
Hydrogen H_2	

All organic compounds except *polymers* are molecules.

mole fraction It is denoted by 'X'. A measure of the amount of a component in a mixture. The mole fraction of component A is given by $X_A = n_A/N$, where n_A is the amount of substance of A (for a given entity) and *N* is the total amount of substance of the mixture (for the same entity).

molybdenum Symbol: Mo; m.p. 2620°C; b.p. 4800°C; r.d. 10.2; a.n. 42; r.a.m. 95.94. A transition element that occurs naturally in molybdenite (MoS_2). It is used in alloy steels and in lamp bulbs. The compound ammonium molybdate, dissolved in HNO_3 is used as a test for phosphates(V).

monatomic molecule A *molecule* which only contains one *atom*. Only the *noble gases* are monatomic. Because of their *electronic configurations* it is difficult for *noble* gas atoms to form *bonds*, and so they exist in the monatomic form. e.g. He, Ne, Ar, Kr, Xe, Rn.

monel metal An alloy of nickel (60-70%), copper (25-35%), and small quantities of iron, manganese, silicon, and carbon. It is used in manufacture of acid-resisting equipment in the chemical industry.

monosaccharide A sugar that cannot be hydrolysed to simpler carbohydrates of smaller carbon content. Glucose and fructose are examples.

monotropy The existence of a single allotrope of an element that is always more stable than the other(s) independent of temperature; phosphorus, for example, exhibits monotropy. The phase diagram for a monotropic element shows that one allotrope always has a lower vapour pressure than the other(s) at all temperatures; this is the stable allotrope.

mordant A substance used in certain dyeing processes. Mordants are often inorganic oxides or salts, which are absorbed on the fabric. The dyestuff then forms a coloured complex with the mordant. The colour depends on the mordant used as well as the dyestuff.

morphine An alkaloid present in opium. It is an analgesic and narcotic. It is used medically for the relief of severe pain.

Moseley's law Lines in the X-ray spectra of elements have frequencies that depend on the proton number of the element. For a set of elements, a graph of the square root of the frequency of X-ray emission against proton number is a straight line (for spectral lines corresponding to the same transition).

mother liquor It refers to the solution that is left after the formation of crystals during crystallisation.

multiplet 1. A spectral line formed by more than two (doublet) closely spaced lines. 2. A group of elementary particles that are identical in all respects except that of electric charge.

multicentre bond It is a bond formed by a bonding molecular orbital between three or more atoms containing a single pair of electrons e.g. as in case of boron hydrides (B2 H6 etc.)

mumetal (*Trademark*) A magnetic alloy containing about 75% Ni, the remainder being Fe, Cu and Cr and sometimes Mo. It is easily magnetized and demagnetized, has a high permeability, and is used in transformer cores and electromechanical equipment.

Muntz metal A form of brass containing 60% Cu, 39% Zn, and small amounts of Pb and Fe. Stronger thav a-brass it is used for hot forgings, brazing rods, and large nuts and bolts. It is named after G.F. Muntz (1794-1857).

muscovite (also known as white mica; potash mica) A mineral form of potassium aluminosilicate, $K_2Al_4(Si_6Al_2)O_{20}$ $(OH,F)_4$; one of the most important members of the mica group of minerals. It is chemically complex and has a sheet like crystal structure. It is usually silvery-grey in colour, sometimes tinted with green, brown, or pink. Muscovite is a common constituent of certain granites and pegmatites. It is also common in metamorphic and sedimentary rocks. It is widely used in industry, for example, in the manufacture of electrical equipment and as a filler in roofing materials, wallpapers, and paint.

mustard gas A highly poisonous gas, $(ClCH_2CH_2)_2S$; dichlorodiethyl sulphide. It is made from ethene ($H_2C=CH_2$) and disulphur dichloride (S_2Cl_2), and used as a war gas.

mutarotation Change of optical activity with time as a result of spontaneous chemical reaction.

myoglobin It is a globular protein occurring widely in muscle tissue as an oxygen carrier. It comprises a single polypeptide chain and a haem group, which reversibly binds a molecule of oxygen. This is only relinquished at relatively low external oxygen concentrations, e.g. during strenuous exercise when muscle oxygen demand outpaces supply from the blood. Myoglobin thus acts as an emergency oxygen store.

N

NAD (nicotinamide adenine dinucleotide) A coenzyme, derived from the B vitamin nicotinic acid, that participates in many biological dehydrogenation reactions. NAD is characteristically loosely bound to the enzymes concerned. It normally carries a positive charge and can accept one hydrogen atom and two electrons to become the reduced form, NADH. NADH is generated during the oxidation of food; it then gives up its two electrons (and single proton), to the electron transport chain, thereby reverting to NAD^+ and generating three molecules of ATP per molecule of NADH.

NADP (nicotinamide adenine dinucleotide phosphate) differs from NAD only in possessing an additional phosphate group. It functions in the same way as NAD although anabolic reactions (anabolism) generally use NADPH (reduced NADP) as a hydrogen donor rather than NADH. Enzymes tend to be specific for either NAD or NADP as coenzyme.

naphtha It is obtained from paraffin oil, coal tar etc. It is a mixture of hydrocarbons. *Wood naphtha* is impure methanol and is obtained by destructive distillation of wood.

naphthols Two phenols derived from naphthalene with the formula $C_{10}H_7OH$, differing in the position of the –OH group. The most important is naphthalen-2-ol (β-naphthol), with the –OH in the 2-position. It is a white solid (r.d. 1.2; m.p. 395 K, b.p. 558 K) used in rubber as an antioxidant. Naphthalen-2-ol will couple with diazonium salts at the 1-position to form red azo compounds, a reaction used in testing for primary amines (by making the diazonium salt and adding naphthalen-2-ol).

naphthalene A white volatile solid, $C_{10}H_8$; r.d. 1.14; m.p. 80.2°C; b.p. 218°C. Naphthalene is an aromatic hydrocarbon with an odour of mothballs and is obtained from crude oil.

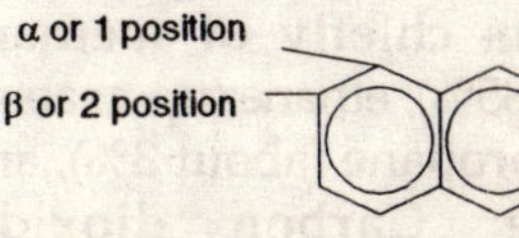

Naphthalene

It is a raw material for making certain synthetic resins.

nascent hydrogen A particularly reactive form of hydrogen, which is believed to exist briefly between its generation (e.g. by the action of dilute acid on magnesium)

$$\underset{}{Mg} + \underset{(dil)}{H_2SO_4} \longrightarrow MgSO_4 + \underset{\text{Nascent hydrogen}}{2[H]}$$

and its appearance as bubbles of normal hydrogen gas. It is thought that part of the free energy of the production reaction remains with the hydrogen molecules for a short time. Nascent hydrogen may be used to produce the hydrides of phosphorus, arsenic, and antimony, which are not readily formed from ordinary hydrogen.

natural fibres *Fibr*es which are produced from either animal or plant sources *cotton, flax*, hemp, jute are the examples of fibres produced from plants while silk and wool are the fibres produced from animals.

natural gas A naturally occurring mixture of gaseous hydrocarbons that is found in porous sedimentary rocks in the earth's crust, usually in association with petroleum deposits. It consists chiefly of methane (about 85%), ethane (up to about 10%), propane (about 3%), and butane. Carbon dioxide, nitrogen, oxygen, hydrogen sulphide, and sometimes helium may also be present. Natural gas, like petroleum, originates in the decomposition of organic matter. It is widely used as a fuel and also to produce carbon black and some organic chemicals. Natural gas occurs on every continent, USSR, USA, Algeria, Canada, and the Middle East are the major reserves of natural gas.

natural radioactivity If a substance emits radiations by itself, it is said to possess natural radioactivity.

neodymium Symbol: Nd; m.p. 1021°C; b.p. 3068°C; r.d. 6.8 or 7.0; a.n. 60; r.a.m. 144.24. It is an '*f*' block element. A toxic silvery element having two allotropic forms and belonging to the lanthanoid series of metals.

It occurs in association with other lanthanoids. Neodymium is used in various alloys, as a catalyst, and in compound form in carbon-arc searchlights, etc., and in the glass industry.

neon Symbol: Ne; a.n. 10; r.a.m. 20.79; r.d. 0.9; m.p. –248.6°C; b.p. –246°C. Belongs to 'p' block in periodic table. *A noble g*as which is found in the *atmosphe*re to a small extent. It forms no known *compounds* but is used to fill fluorescent tubes. A red glow is produced. Neon lights are often used for advertising signs.

neoprene A synthetic rubber made by polymerizing the

compound 2-chlorobuta-1, 3-diene

$$H_2C=\underset{\displaystyle Cl}{\underset{|}{C}}-CH=CH_2$$

Neoprene is often used instead of natural rubber in applications requiring resistance to chemical attack.

neptunium Symbol: Np; m.p. 640°C; b.p. 3902°C (est.); r.d. 20.25; a.n. 93; stablest isotope 237Np (half-life 2.2´ 106 years). It is the member of 'f' block of periodic table. A toxic radioactive silvery element of the actinoid series of metals that was the first transuranic element to be synthesized (1940). Found on earth only in minute quantities in uranium ores, it is obtained as a by-product in plutonium-239 production.

Nernst heat theorem A statement of the third law of thermodynamics in a restricted form. It states that if a chemical change takes place between pure crystalline solids at absolute zero, there is no change of entropy.

Nessler's reagent A solution of mercury(II) iodide (HgI_2) in KI and KOH. It is used in testing for ammonia, with which it forms a brown coloration or precipitate.

neutral Describing a compound or solution that is neither acidic nor basic. A neutral solution is one that contains equal numbers of both protonated and deprotonated forms of the solvent.

neutralisation It is the process in which an acid and a base react to produce salt and water.

$$\text{(i)}\ \underset{\text{acid}}{HCl\,(aq)} + \underset{\text{base}}{NaOH\,(aq)} \rightarrow \underset{\text{salt}}{NaCl\,(aq)} + \underset{\text{water}}{H_2O\,(l)}$$

$$\text{(ii)}\ \underset{\text{acid}}{H_2SO_4(aq)} + \underset{\text{base}}{NaOH(aq)} \rightarrow \underset{\text{salt}}{Na_2SO_4(aq)} + \underset{\text{water}}{H_2O\,(l)}$$

A neutralisation reaction corresponds to

$$H^+ OH^- \rightarrow H_2O$$

neutron A neutral hadron that is stable in the atomic nucleus but decays into a proton, an electron, and an antineutrino with a mean life of 12 minutes outside the nucleus. Its rest mass is slightly greater than that of the proton, being 1.674 92 × 10^{-27} kg. Neutrons occur in all atomic nuclei except normal hydrogen. The neutron was first reported in 1932 by James Chadwick (1891—1974).

neutron activation analysis It is a method of detection of trace quantities of a substance present in a sample. For this a non-radioactive sample is bombarded so as to convert the element of interest into a radioactive isotope. The radioactivity of this isotope is measured and from this the concentration can be found out. This technique is useful in detecting even one part of the element per billion parts of the sample.

Nickel, Symbol, **Ni;** a.n. 28; r.a.m. 58.7; r.d. 8.9; m.p. 14⁵0oC; b.p. 2840°C. A silvery white transition element. Its important ores are Nickelite (Ni-As), Nickel blends (NiS) and Nickel glance (NiAsS). It is used in making alloys, in electroplating etc.

nickel carbonyl A colourless volatile liquid, $Ni(CO)_4$; m.p. –25°C; b.p. 43°C. It is formed by direct combination of nickel metal with carbon monoxide at 50-60°C.

$$Ni + 4CO \xrightarrow{50\text{-}60°C} Ni\,(CO)_4$$

The reaction is reversed at higher temperatures, and the reactions are the basis of the Mond process for purifying nickel. The nickel in the compound has an oxidation state of zero, and the compound is a typical example of a complex with pi-bonding ligands, in which filled *d*-orbitals on the nickel overlap with empty p-orbitals on the carbon.

nickel-iron accumulator (Edison cell; NIFE cell) A secondary cell devised by Thomas Edison (1847-1931) having an anode of nickel oxide and a cathode of iron both immersed in an electrolyte of potassium hydroxide. The reaction on discharge is

$$2NiOOH.H_2O + Fe \rightarrow 2Ni(OH)_2 + Fe(OH)_2,$$

the reverse occurring during charging. Each cell gives an e.m.f. of about 1.2 volts and produces about 100 kJ per kilogram during each discharge.

nickel(II) oxide A green powder, NiO; r.d. 6.6. It can be made by heating nickel(II) nitrate or carbonate with air excluded.

nickel(III) oxide also known as (nickel peroxide; nickel sesquioxide) A black or grey powder, Ni_2O_3; r.d. 4.8. It is made by heating nickel(II) oxide in air and used in nickel-iron accumulators.

niobium Symbol Nb. A soft ductile grey-blue metallic transition element; a.n. 41; r.a.m. 92.91; r.d. 8.57; m.p. 2468°C; b.p. 4742°C. It occurs in several minerals, including niobite ($Fe(NbO_3)_2$), and is extracted by several methods including reduction of the complex fluoride K_2NbF_7 using sodium. It is used in special steels and in welded joints (to increase strength). Niobium-zirconium alloys are used in superconductors. Chemically, the element combines with the halogens and oxidizes in air at 473K. It forms a number of compounds and complexes with the metal in oxidation states 2, 3 or 5. The element was discovered by Charles Hatchett in 1801 and first isolated by Blomstrand in 1864. Formerly, it was called *columbium*.

nitrate It is the *salt of nitric acid*, containing the $-NO_3$ group and with *a valency* of 1. A nitrate can be made by treating a metal *carbonate* or *oxide* with the dilute *acid*:

$$CuCO_3(s) + 2HNO_3(aq) \rightarrow Cu(NO_3)_2(aq) + CO_2(g) + H_2O(l)$$
$$ZnO(s) + 2HNO_3(aq) \rightarrow Zn(NO_3)_2(aq) + H_2O(l)$$

Nitrates are easily decomposed by heat. There are three kinds of reaction:

(a) $2KNO_3(s) \rightarrow 2KNO_2(s) + O_2(g)$

examples: sodium, potassium.

(b) $2Cu(NO_3)_2(s) \rightarrow 2CuO(s) + O_2(g) + 4NO_2(g)$

all metal nitrates other than shown in (a) and (c).

(c) $2AgNO_3(s) \rightarrow 2Ag(s) + 2NO_2(g) + O_2(g)$

examples are Ag, Hg

Nitrates are important *fertilizers*, e.g. *sodium nitrate* and *ammonium nitrate*. If used incorrectly they can lead to serious water pollution.

nitre (saltpetre) Commercial potassium nitrate (KNO_3); the name was formerly applied to natural crustlike efflorescences, occurring in some arid regions.

nitric acid (HNO_3) A colourless fuming corrosive liquid that is a strong acid. Nitric acid can be made in a laboratory by the distillation of a mixture of an alkali metal nitrate and concentrated sulphuric acid. Commercially it is prepared by the catalytic oxidation of ammonia and is supplied as concentrated nitric acid, which contains 68% of the acid and is often coloured yellow by dissolving oxides of nitrogen. Nitric acid is a strong oxidizing agent. Most metals are converted to their nitrates with the evolution of oxides of nitrogen (the composition of the mixture of the oxides depends on the temperature and on the concentration of the nitric acid used). Some non-metals (e.g. sulphur and phosphorus) react to produce oxyacids. Organic substances (e.g. sawdust and ethanol) react violently, but the more stable aromatic compounds, such as benzene and toluene, can be converted to nitro compounds in controllable reactions.

nitrides Compounds of nitrogen with a more electropositive element. Boron nitride is a covalent compound having macromolecular crystals. Certain electropositive elements, such as lithium, magnesium, and calcium, react directly with nitrogen to form ionic nitrides containing the N^{3-} ion. Transition elements form a range of interstitial nitrides (e.g. Mn_4N, W_2N), which can be produced by heating the metal in ammonia.

nitrile A class of organic compounds with general formula RCN where 'R' is an alkyl or an aryl group and functional group –CN. They are also known as cyanides. They are generally liquids having a pleasant odour, e.g.

CH_3CN	Methyl Cyanide
C_6H_5CN	Benzonitrile

nitrites *Salts* of nitrous acid (HNO_2). The *sodium* and *potassium* salts can be made by heating the nitrate:

$$2NaNO_3(s) \rightarrow 2NaNO_2(s) + O_2(g)$$

They are used in the *curing* of meats.

nitrobenzene A yellow oily liquid, $C_6H_5NO_2$; r.d. 1.2; m.p. 6°C; b.p. 211°C. It is made by the nitration of benzene using a mixture of nitric and sulphuric acids.

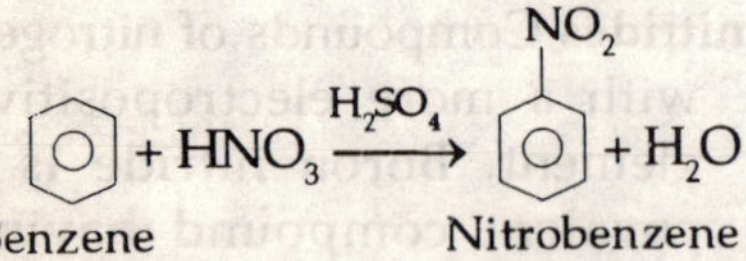

Benzene Nitrobenzene

nitrogen (N) a.n. 7; r.a.m. 14; d 1.2506; gdm^{-3}; m.p.–209°C; b.p. –195·8oC. A non-metallic *element* in group V of the periodic table. It is an unreactive, *diatomic* gas which forms about 78% of the *atmosphere*. It is produced by the *fractional distillation* of liquid *air*.

Nitrogen is an important chemical because of the need for *nitric acid* and *ammonia*. It is *fixed* from the atmosphere in the *Haber process*.

Nitrogen gas is used to provide an *inert* atmosphere, for example, in:

(a) *Annealing steel*;

(b) *Silicon* chip production;

(c) Food packaging;

(d) *Glass* production.

nitrogen cycle One of the major cycles of chemical elements in the environment. Nitrates in the soil are taken up by plant roots and may then pass along food chains into animals. Decomposing bacteria convert nitrogen-containing compounds (especially ammonia) in plant and animal wastes and dead remains back into nitrates, which are released into the soil and can again be taken up by plants (nitrification). Though nitrogen is essential to all forms of life, the huge amount present in the atmosphere is not directly available to most organisms. It can, however, be assimilated by some specialized bacteria and algae (nitrogen fixation) and is thus made available to other organisms indirectly. Lightning flashes also make some nitrogen available to plants by causing the combination of atmospheric

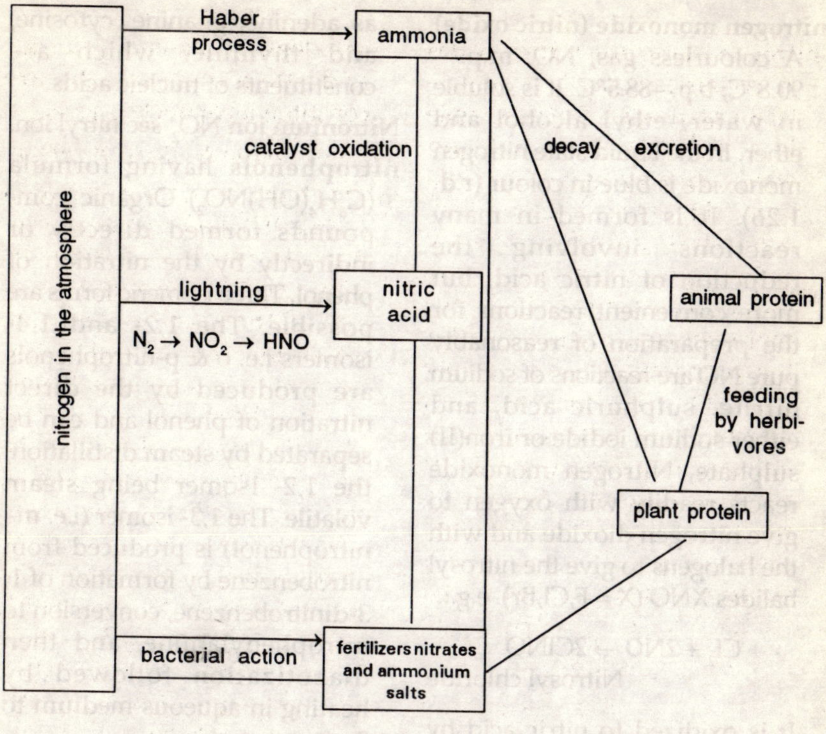

nitrogen cycle

nitrogen and oxygen to form oxides of nitrogen, which enter the soil and form nitrates. Some nitrogen is returned from the soil to the atmosphere by denitrifying bacteria (denitrification).

nitrogen fixation It is a chemical process in which atmospheric nitrogen is assimilated into organic compounds in living organisms and hence into the nitrogen cycle (explained earlier). The ability to fix nitrogen is limited to certain bacteria (e.g. *Azotobacter*) and blue-green algae (for example *Anabaena*). *Rhizobium* bacteria are able to fix nitrogen in association with cells in the roots of leguminous plants such as peas and beans, in which they form characteristic root nodules; cultivation of legumes is, therefore, one way of increasing soil nitrogen. Various chemical processes are used to fix atmospheric nitrogen in the manufacture of fertilizers. These include the Birkeland-Eyde process, the cyanamide process (calcium dicarbide), and the Haber process.

nitrogen monoxide (nitric oxide) A colourless gas, NO; m.p. –90.8°C; b.p. –88.5°C. It is soluble in water, ethyl alcohol and ether. In the liquid state nitrogen monoxide is blue in colour (r.d. 1.26). It is formed in many reactions involving the reduction of nitric acid, but more convenient reactions for the preparation of reasonably pure NO are reactions of sodium nitrite, sulphuric acid, and either sodium iodide or iron(II) sulphate. Nitrogen monoxide reacts readily with oxygen to give nitrogen dioxide and with the halogens to give the nitrosyl halides XNO (X = F,Cl,Br). e.g.:

$$Cl_2 + 2NO \rightarrow 2ClNO$$

Nitrosyl chloride

It is oxidized to nitric acid by strong oxidizing agents and reduced to dinitrogen oxide by reducing agents. The molecule has one unpaired electron, which accounts for its paramagnetism and for the blue colour in the liquid state. This electron is relatively easily removed to give the *nitrosyl ion* NO^+, which is the ion present in such compounds as $NOClO_4$, $NOBF_4$, $NOFeCl_4$, $(NO)_2PtCl_6$ and a ligand in complexes such as $Co(CO)_3NO$.

nitrogenous base A basic compound containing nitrogen. The term is used especially of organic ring compounds, such as adenine, guanine, cytosine, and thymine, which are constituents of nucleic acids.

Nitronium ion NO_2^+ see nitryl ion.

nitrophenols having formula ($C_6H_4(OH)NO_2$) Organic compounds formed directly or indirectly by the nitration of phenol. Three isomeric forms are possible. The 1,2- and 1,4-isomers i.e. o & p-nitrophenols are produced by the direct nitration of phenol and can be separated by steam distillation, the 1,2- isomer being steam volatile. The 1,3- isomer (i.e. m–nitrophenol) is produced from nitrobenzene by formation of 1, 3-dinitrobenzene, conversion to nitrophenylamine, and then diazotization followed by heating in aqtueous medium to 3-nitrophenol.

It has the following structure :

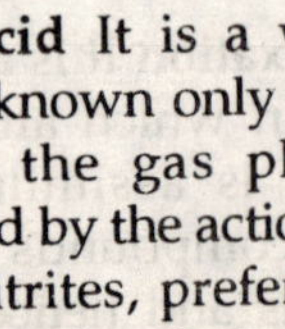

3 Nitrophenol

nitrous acid It is a weak acid, HNO_2, known only in solution and in the gas phase. It is prepared by the action of acids upon nitrites, preferably using a combination that removes the salt as an insoluble precipitate (e.g. $Ba(NO_2)_2$ and H_2SO_4). The solutions are unstable and decompose on heating to give nitric acid and nitrogen monoxide. Nitrous acid can function both as an oxidizing agent (forms NO) with I– and Fe^{2+}, or as a reducing agent (forms NO_3^-) with, for example, Cu^{2+}; the latter is most common. It is widely used (prepared *in situ*) for the preparation of diazonium compounds in organic chemistry. The full systematic name is *dioxonitric(III) acid*.

nitryl ion also known as (*nitronium ion*) The ion NO_2^+, found in mixtures of nitric acid and sulphuric acid and solutions of nitrogen oxides in nitric acid. Nitryl salts, such as $NO_2ClO_4^-$, can be isolated but are extremely reactive. Nitryl ions generated *in situ* are used for nitration in organic chemistry.

Symbol: No; a.n. 102.

nobelium A radioactive transuranic element of the actinoid series, 'f' block element not found naturally on Earth. Several very short-lived isotopes have been synthesized.

noble gases They are the members of group 18 'p' block element of the periodic table e.g. He, Ne, Ar, Kr, Xe, Rn. They have eight electrons in the outermost shell except helium which has only two electrons. Their general electronic configuration is ns^2p^6 (for He is $1s^2$). They are quite inert and have no tendency to gain or lose electrons. They are monoatomic. They are also known as *inert gases*.

Only weak vander Waals forces are present between the atoms of noble gases in liquid or in solid state. These vander Waals forces increase with size of the atoms and so their m.p. and b.p. increase from He to Rn.

non-metals *Elements* which have either molecular structures, and thus are *gases at room temperature*, or are *solids* or *liquids* with *low melting* and *boiling points*; or *giant structures* with *covalent* bonding. Typical properties of non-metals are as follows:

(a) They have poor *conductivity*.

(b) They do not react with *acids*.

(c) They produce *acidic oxides*.

(d) They form *covalent* compounds.

(e) They give rise to *anions*.

Examples include; the *halogens* (Cl, Br, I, F), the *noble gases* (He, Ne, Ar etc.), *oxygen*, *sulphur*, *carhon*, *nitrogen*.

non-polar compound A compound that has covalent molecules with no permanent dipole moment. Examples of nonpolar compounds are methane (CH_4) and benzene (C_6H_6).

non-polar solvent A solvent that does not possess a permanent electric dipole moment and consequently has no drive towards intermolecular association with polar species. Non-polar solvents are usually good solvents for non-polar solutes. For example, carbon tetrachloride (CCl_4), hexane, and benzene (C_6H_6) are good solvents for iodine.

Solvation energies are usually low and the driving force for dissolution by non-polar solvents is the increased disorder of the solution.

normal hydrogen electrode It is a standard reference electrode. Its electrode potential is taken as zero at all temperatures. A N.H.E. (normal hydrogen electrode) consists of a platinum foil coated with platinum dipped in IMH$^+$ ions and hydrogen gas at 1 atmospheric pressure is constantly bubbled over it. It can be represented as

$$Pt_1, H_2 \text{ (1 atmo)} \parallel H^+ \text{ (1M)}$$

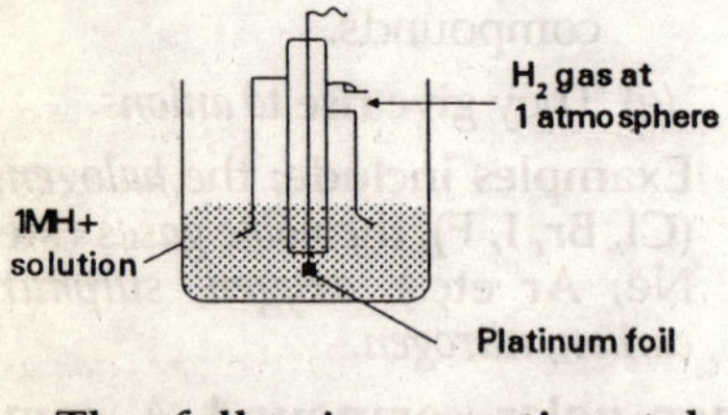

The following reaction takes place

$$H^+ (aq) + e \rightarrow \frac{1}{2} H_2(g)$$

$$\text{or } \frac{1}{2} H_2(g) \rightarrow (aq) + e$$

normality (N) It is the number of gram equivalents of the solute dissolved per litre of solution. It is denoted by N

$$\text{Normality, N} = \frac{\text{Number of gram equivalents of solute}}{\text{Volume in litres of solution}}$$

normal Having a concentration of one gram equivalent per dm^3.

nuclear fission The division of a nucleus into two approximately equal parts is called nuclear fission.

$^{235}_{92}$U undergoes fission as follows:

$$^{235}_{93}U + {}^1_0n \rightarrow U \rightarrow \begin{cases} ^{140}_{56}Ba + {}^{93}_{36}Kr + 3\,{}^1_0n \\ ^{144}_{54}Xe + {}^{90}_{38}Sr + 2\,{}^1_0n \\ ^{144}_{55}Cs + {}^{95}_{36}Rb + 3\,{}^1_0n \end{cases}$$

A large amount of energy is released during nuclear fission.

nucleons Particles found in the *nucleus* of the *atom*, that is, *protons* and *neutrons*.

nucleon number (mass number) Symbol: A The number of nucleons (protons plus neutrons) in an atomic nucleus.

nucleophile An ion or molecule that can donate electrons. Nucleophiles are often oxidizing agents and Lewis bases. They are either negative ions (e.g. Cl^-) or molecules that have electron pairs (e.g. NH_3). In organic reactions they tend to attack positively charged parts of a molecule.

nucleophilic addition A type of addition reaction in which the first step is attachment of a nucleophile to a positive (electron-deficient) part of the molecule. Aldehydes and ketones undergo reactions of this type because of polarization of the carbonyl group (carbon positive). e.g.:

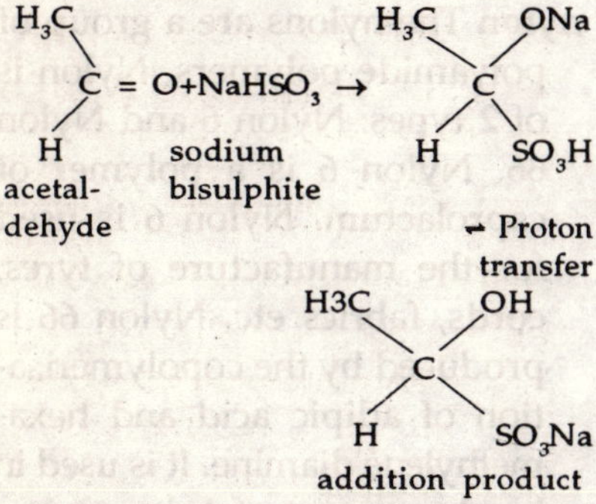

nucleophilic substitution (Nucleus loving) A reaction involving the substitution of an atom or group of atoms in an organic compound with a nucleophile as the attacking substituent. Since nucleophiles are electron-rich species, nucleophilic substitution occurs in compounds in which a strongly electronegative atom or group leads to a dipolar bond. The electron-deficient centre can then be attacked by the electron-rich nucleophile causing the electronegative atom or group to be displaced. In general terms:

$$R\text{-}Le + Nu^- \rightarrow R\text{-}Nu + Le^-$$

where Nu^- represents the incoming nucleophile and Le^- represents the leaving group.

There are two possible mechanisms for nucleophilic substitution. In the S_N^1 (Nucleophilic unimolecular substitution) reaction the molecule first forms a carbonium ion; for example:

$$RCH_2Cl \rightarrow RCH_2^+ + Cl^-$$

The nucleophile then attaches itself to this carbonium ion:

$$RCH_2^+ + OH^- \rightarrow RCH_2OH$$

In the S_N2 (Nucleophilic bimolecular substitution) reaction the nucleophile approaches as the other group leaves, forming a transition state in which the carbon has five attached groups.

The preferred mechanism depends on several factors:

(a) The stability of the intermediate in the S_N1 mechanism.

(b) Steric factors affecting the formation of the transition state in the S_N2 mechanism.

(c) The solvent in which the reaction occurs: polar solvents will stabilize polar intermediates and so favour the S_N1 mechanism.

In practice, however, both routes or some intermediate mechanism is thought to operate in many cases.

nucleotide It is an organic compound consisting of a nitrogen-containing purine or pyrimidine base linked to a sugar (ribose or deoxyribose) and a phosphate group. DNA and RNA are made up of long chains of nucleotides (i.e. *polynucleotides).*

nucleus The part of an *atom* where the *mass* is concentrated. It contains *protons* and *neutrons* and is usually pictured as being the compact centre of a spherical atom.

Electrons move around the nucleus. The nucleus has a positive charge and in the neutral atom this is balanced by the charges on the electrons.

The hydrogen-1 *isotope* is the only atom whose nuclei contain no neutrons. See diagram.

a nucleus of carbon-12 contains 6 protons and 6 neutrons

a nucleus of carbon 14 contains 6 protons and 8 neutrons

nucleus Different isotopes showing different nuclei.

nuclide 1. An atomic nucleus as characterized by its atomic number and its neutron number. An isotope refers to a series of different atoms that have the same atomic number but different neutron numbers (e.g. uranium-238 and uranium-235 are isotopes of uranium), whereas a nuclide refers only to a particular nuclear species (e.g. the nuclides uranium-235 and plutonium-239 are fissile). 2. The atom to which a specified nucleus belongs.

nylon The nylons are a group of polyamide polymers. Nylon is of 2 types: Nylon 6 and Nylon 66. Nylon 6 is a polymer of caprolactum. Nylon 6 is used for the manufacture of tyres, cords, fabrics etc. Nylon 66 is produced by the copolymerisation of adipic acid and hexamethylene diamine. It is used in brushes, carpets, fabrics etc.

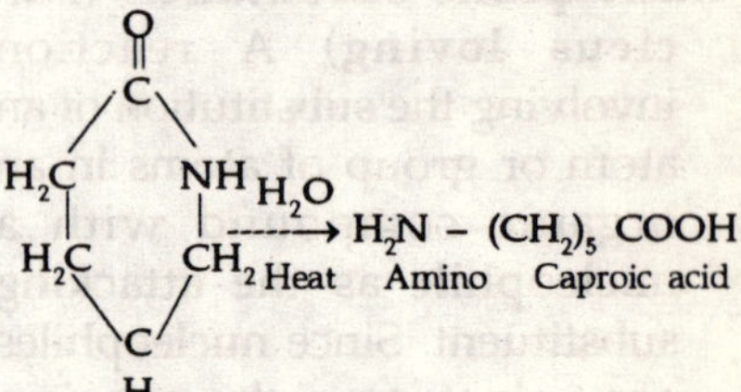

Caprolactum

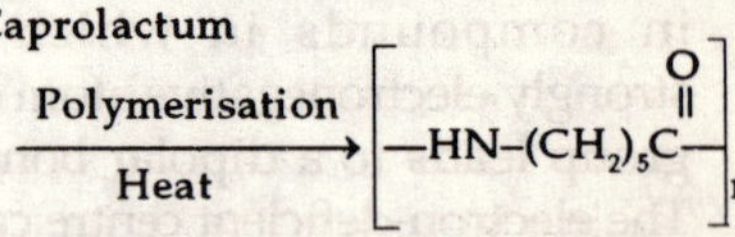

Nylon–6 (Type I)

$$n\,H_2N\,(CH_2)_6-NH_2 + n\,HO-\overset{O}{\overset{\|}{C}}-(CH_2)_4-\overset{O}{\overset{\|}{C}}-OH$$

Hexamethylene Adipic acid

$$\downarrow$$

$$\left[-\overset{H}{\overset{|}{N}}-(CH_2)_6-\overset{H}{\overset{|}{N}}-C-(CH_2)_4-\overset{O}{\overset{\|}{C}}-\right]_n + n\,H_2O$$

Nylon 66 (Type II)

Nylon fibres has great strength. It is useful because it will not rot, is hard wearing and does not absorb water, however it does stretch.

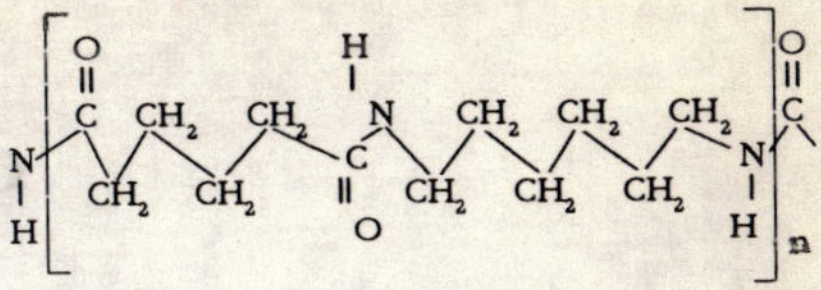

nylon The most common nylon, nylon 6.6.

O

Occlusion (a) The trapping of small pockets of liquid in a crystal during crystallization. (b) The absorption (surface phenomenon) of a gas by a solid such that atoms or molecules of the gas occupy interstitial positions in the solid lattice. Palladium, for example, can occlude hydrogen.

occultation It is the process of cutting off the light or radio emission from one celestial body when another is interposed between it and the observer e.g. the invisibility of a star to an optical or radio telescope when it is hidden behind the moon.

ochre A yellow or red mineral form of iron(III) oxide, Fe_2O_3, used as a pigment.

octadecanoic acid also known as (stearic acid, having moleculor formula $CH_3(CH_2)_{16}COOH$) A solid carboxylic acid present in fats and oils as the glyceride.

octadecenoic acid A straight-chain unsaturated fatty acid with the formula $C_{17}H_{33}COOH$. *Cis-octadec-9-enoic acid* has the formula

$CH_3(CH_2)_7CH{:}CH(CH_2)_7COOH$; natural fats and oils contain glycerides of this acid.

octane, C_8H_{18} An alkane, a colourless liquid, exists in a number of isomeric forms, for example, n-octane, iso-octane etc.

octane number It refers to a number that provides a measure of the ability of a fuel to resist knocking when it is burnt in a spark-ignition engine. It is the percentage by volume of iso-octane (C_8H_{18} 2, 2,4 trimethyl-pentane) in a blend with normal heptane (C_7H_{16}) that matches the knocking behaviour of the fuel being tested in a single cylinder four-stroke engine of standard design.

octane rating A rating for the performance of petrol in interal-combustion engines. The octane rating measures the freedom from 'knocking' - that is preignition of the fuel in the engine. This depends on the relative proportions of branched-chain and straight-chain hydrocarbons present. High proportions of branched-chain alkanes are better in high-performance engines. In rating fuels, 2,2,4-trimethylpentane (isooctane) is given a value of 100 and heptane is given a value 0. The performance of a fuel is compared with a mixture of these hydrocarbons.

octanoic acid (caprylic acid) A colourless liquid straight-chain saturated carboxylic acid having formula $CH_3(CH_2)_6COOH$; b.p. 237°C.

ohm (Ω) It is S.I. unit of electrical resistance.

1 ohm = 1 volt × 1 ampere.

1 ohm is the resistance offered to a current of 1 ampere when the potential difference is 1 volt.

oil It is a liquid fat, for example, oil of anise, olive oil etc. It also refers to petroleum (a mixture of naturally occurring hydrocarbons).

oil sand as (tar sand; bituminous sand) It is a sandstone or porous carbonate rock that is impregnated with hydrocarbons. The largest deposit of oil sand occurs in Alberta, Canada (the Athabasca tar sands); there are also deposits in the Orinoco Basin of Venezuela, the USSR, USA, Madagascar, Albania, Trinidad, and Romania.

oil shale It refers to a very fine-grained carbonaceous sedimentary rock from which oil can be extracted. The rock contains organic matter—*kerogen*—which decomposes to yield oil when heated. Deposits of oil shale occur on every continent, the largest known reserves occurring in Colorado. Utah, and Wyoming in the USA. Commercial production of oil from oil shale is generally considered to be uneconomic unless the price of petroleum rises above the recovery costs for oil from oil shale. However, threats of declining conventional oil resources have resulted in considerable interest and developments in recovery techniques.

oleum also known as phyrosulphuric acid, having formula $H_2S_2O_7$); A colourless fuming liquid formed by dissolving sulphur(VI) oxide in concentrated sulphuric acid. It gives sulphuric acid on diluting with water.

onium ion An ion formed by adding a proton to a neutral molecule, is called an onium ion. e.g. the hydroxonium ion (H_3O^+) or the ammonium ion (NH_4^+).

opal A hydrous amorphous form of silica. Many varieties of opal occur, some being prized as gemstones. Common opal is usually milk white but the presence of impurities may colour it yellow, green, or red. Precious opals, are used as gemstones. They display the property of *opalescence*—a characteristic internal play of colours resulting from the interference of light rays within the stone. Black opal has a black background against which the colours are displayed. The chief sources of precious opals are Australia and Mexico. Geyserite is a variety deposited by geysers or hot springs. Another variety, diatomite, is made up of the skeletons of diatoms.

open-hearth process A process of making steel by heating pig iron in an open-hearth furnace by burning a mixture of gas and air. Oxygen is injected through pipes to oxidize impurities and burn off carbon, and lime is used to form a slag.

open system A system in which exchange of both mass and energy between the system and the surroundings is possible, is called an open system.

optical activity The ability of certain substances to rotate the plane of plane-polarized light passing through a crystal, liquid, or solution. It occurs when the molecules of the substance are asymmetric, so that they can exist in two different structural forms each being a mirror image of the other. The two forms are *optical isomers* also called as *enantiomers*. The existence of such forms is also known as *enantiomorphism* (the mirror images being *enantiomorphs).* One form will rotate the light in clockwise (right) direction, and the other will rotate it by an equal amount in an anticlock wise direction (left). The two possible forms are described as dextrorotatory *d* or + or laevorotatory (l or –) respectively, according to the direction of rotation, and prefixes are used to designate the isomer, as in *d*-tartaric and *l*-tartaric acids. An equimolar mixture of the two forms is not optically active. It is called a *racemic mixture dl* or ± or) *racemate* and designated by *dl-*. In addition, certain molecules can have a *meso form* in which one part of the molecule is a mirror image of the other. Such molecules are not optically active.

Molecules that show optical activity have no plane of symmetry. The commonest case of this is in organic compounds in which a carbon atom is linked to four different groups. An atom of this type is said to be a *chiral centre.* Asymmetric molecules showing optical activity can also occur in inorganic compounds. For example, an octahedral complex in which the central ion coordinates to eight different ligands would be optically active. Many naturally occurring compounds show optical isomerism and usually only one isomer occurs naturally. For instance, glucose is found in the dextrorotatory form. The other isomer, *l*-glucose, can be synthesized in the laboratory, but cannot be synthesized by living organisms.

optical glass It is the glass used in the manufacture of lenses, prisms, and other optical parts. It must be homogeneous and free from bubbles and strain. Optical *crown glass* may contain potassium or barium in place of the sodium of ordinary crown glass and has a refractive index in the range 1.51 to 1.54. *Flint glass* contains lead oxide and has refractive index between 1.58 and 1.72. Higher refractive indexes are obtained by adding lanthanoid oxides to glasses; these are now known as lanthanum crowns and flints.

optical isomerism This type of isomerism is shown by compounds containing at least one chiral (asymmetric) carbon atom.

An object which is not superimposable on its mirror image is known as *chiral*. Those objects which are super- imposable on their mirror image are called *achiral*, for example, A, O, M, W etc. A chiral carbon atom is one that is attached to four different atoms or groups. Lactic acid shows optical isomerism and its two isomers are

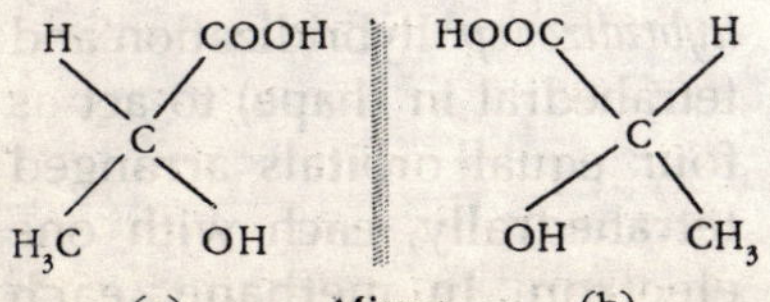

(a) and (b) are mirror images and they are known as *enantiomers*.

Number of possible stereosomers = 2^n

where n = number of chiral carbon atoms present in a molecule.

Stereoisomers which are not optical isomers are known as *diastereomers*. Stereoisomers differ only in their optical activity. One is dextro-rotatory and the other (mirror image) is laevo-rotatory.

optical rotary dispersion (ORD) The phenomenon in which the amount of rotation of plane-polarized light by an optically active substance depends on the wavelength of the light. Plots of rotation against wavelength can be used to give information about the molecular structure of optically active compounds.

optical rotation Rotation of plane-polarized light. (optical activity.)

orbit The path of an electron as it travels round the nucleus of an atom.

orbital A region around an atomic nucleus where the probability of finding electron is maximum. The modern picture of the atom according to quantum mechanics does not have electrons moving in fixed elliptical orbits. Instead, there is a finite probability that the electron will be found in any small region at all possible distances from the nucleus. In the hydrogen atom the probability is low near the nucleus, increases to a maximum, and falls off to infinity. It is useful to think of a region in space around the nucleus—in the case of hydrogen the region within a sphere—within which there is a high chance of finding the electron. Each of these, called an *atomic orbital,* corresponds to a sub-shell and can 'contain' two electrons with opposite spins. Another way of visualizing an orbital is as a cloud of electron charge (the average distribution with time).

Similarly, in molecules, the electrons move in the combined field of the nuclei and can be assigned to *molecular orbitals.* In considering bonding between atoms it is useful to treat molecular orbitals as formed by overlap of atomic orbitals.

It is possible to calculate the shapes and energies of atomic and molecular orbitals by quantum theory. The shapes of atomic orbitals depend on the orbital angular momentum (the sub-shell). For each shell there is one *s* orbital, three *p* orbitals, five *d* orbitals, etc. The *s* orbitals are spherical, the *p* orbitals each have two lobes; *d* orbitals have more complex shapes, typically with four lobes.

Molecular orbitals are formed by overlap of atomic orbitals, and again there are different types. If the orbital is completely symmetrical about an axis between the nuclei, it is a *sigma* (σ) *orbital*. This can occur, for instance, by overlap of two *s* orbitals, as in the hydrogen atom, or two *p* orbitals with their lobes along the axis. However, two *p* orbitals overlapping at right angles to the axis form a different types of molecular orbital—a *pi* (π) orbital—with regions above and below the axis. π orbitals are also formed by overlap of *d* orbitals. Each molecular orbital can contain a pair of electrons, forming a sigma bond or pi bond. A double bond, for example, the bond in ethene, is a combination of a 'σ' bond and a 'π' bond.

Hybrid orbitals are atomic orbitals formed by combinations of *s*, *p*, and *d* atomic orbitals, and are useful in describing the bonding in compounds. There are various types. In carbon, for instance, the electron configuration is $1s^2 2s^2 2p^2$. Carbon, in its outer (valence) shell, has one filled *s* orbital, two filled *p* orbitals, and one 'empty' *p* orbital. These four orbitals may *hybridize* (sp^3 hybridization and tetrahedral in shape) to act as four equal orbitals arranged tetrahedrally, each with one electron. In methane, each hybrid orbital overlaps with a hydrogen *s* orbital to form a σ bond. Alternatively, the *s* and two of the *p* orbitals may hybridize (sp^2 hybridization) and act as three orbitals in a plane at 120°. The remaining *p* orbital is at right angles to the plane, and can form pi bonds. Finally, *sp* hybridization may occur, giving two orbitals in a line (Linear). More complex types of hybridization, involving *d* orbitals, explain the geometries of inorganic complexes.

The combination of two atomic orbitals, in fact, produces two molecular orbitals. One—the *bonding orbital*—has a concentration of electron density between the nuclei, and thus tends to hold the atoms together. The other—the *antibonding orbital*—has slightly higher energy and tends to repel the atoms. If both atomic orbitals are filled, the two molecular orbitals are also filled and cancel each other out—there is no net bonding effect. If each atomic orbital has one electron, the pair occupies the lower energy bonding orbital, producing a net attraction.

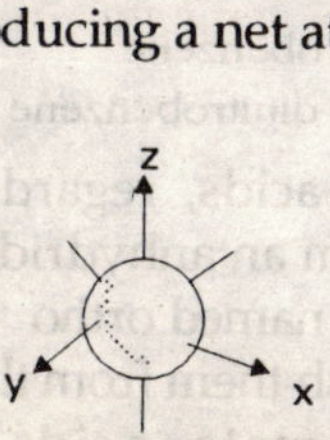

symmetrical s-orbital

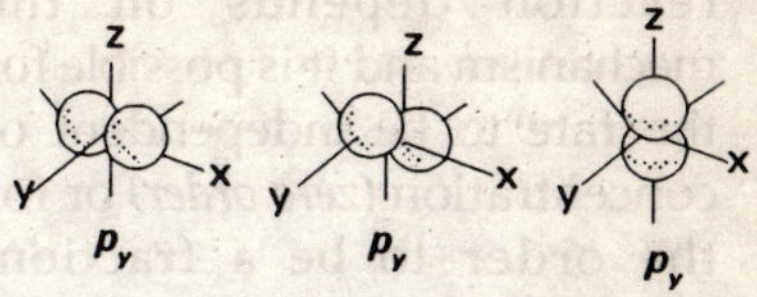

three equivalent *p*-orbitals, each having 2 lobes

Atomic orbitals

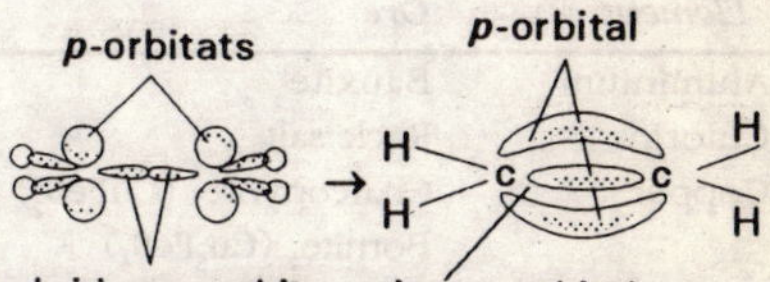

hybrid sp_3 orbitals sigma orbital

Orbitals

orbital splitting The phenomenon of the splitting up of degenerate orbitals into two or more sets of degenerate orbitals under the influence of ligand fields is called orbital splitting, for example, five degenerate d- orbitals split up to give two sets of degenerate orbitals called e_g and t_{2g}.

order The order of a chemical reaction may be defined as the sum of the powers of the concentrations is the overall order of the reaction. For instance, in a reaction

$$A + B \rightarrow C$$

the rate equation may have the form

$$R = k\,[A][B]^2$$

This reaction would be described as *first order* in A and *second order* in B. The overall order is three. The order of a reaction depends on the mechanism and it is possible for the rate to be independent of concentration (*zero order*) or for the order to be a fraction. (pseudo order).

ore A mineral source of a chemical element.

Element	*Ore*
Aluminium	Bauxite
Chlorine	Rock salt
Copper	Chalcopyrite ($CuFeS_2$)
	Bornite (Cu_5FeS_4)
Iron	Haematite (Fe_2O_3)
Lead	Magnetite (Fe_3O_4)
Zinc	Galena (PbS)
	Zinc blende (ZnS)

ores Elements and the ores extracted from them.

organic chemistry The branch of chemistry concerned with compounds of carbon. (e.g. alcohols, phenols, esters etc.)

organic compounds They are generally characterised by their non-ionic character, insolubility in polar solvents (e.g. water), inflammability and covalent linkages etc.

The main sources of organic compounds are plants and animals, coal, petroleum and oil etc.

organometallic compound A compound in which a metal atom or ion is bound to an organic group. Organometallic compounds may have single metal-carbon bonds, as in the aluminium alkyls (e.g. Al $(CH_3)_3$). In some cases, the bonding is to the π electrons of a double bond, as in complexes formed between platinum and ethene, or to the pi electrons of a ring, as in ferrocene.

ornithine (orn) An amino acid, $H_2N(CH_2)_3CH(NH_2)COOH$, do not contain this acid. It is important in living organisms as an intermediate in the reactions of the urea cycle and in arginine synthesis.

ortho (a) Designating the form of a diatomic molecule in which both nuclei have the same spin direction;e.g. orthohydrogen, orthodeuterium.

(b) Designating a benzene compound with substituents in the 1,2 positions. The position next to a substituent is the ortho position on the benzene ring. This was used in the systematic naming of benzene derivatives. For example, ortho-dinitrobenzene (or o-dinitrobenzene) is 1,2-dinitrobenzene.

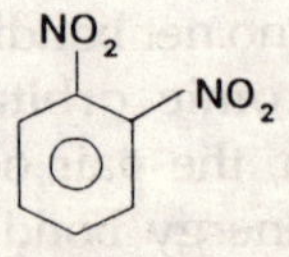

o - dinitrobenzene
or 1, 2 - dinitrobenzene

(c) Certain acids, regarded as formed from an anhydride and water, were named ortho acids to distinguish them from the less hydrated meta acids. For example, H_4SiO_4 (from SiO_2 + $2H_2O$) is orthosilicic acid; H_2SIO_3 (SiO_2 + H_2O) is metasilicic acid.

orthoboric acid, H_3BO_3 It is used as a preservative for milk and foodstuffs, for washing eyes, manufacture of enamels and heat and shock resisting glasses.

osmiridium A hard white naturally occurring alloy consisting principally of osmium (17-48%) and iridium (49%). It also contains small quantities of platinum, rhodium, and ruthenium. It is used in manufacture of small items subject to wear, e.g. electrical contacts or the tips of pen nibs.

osmium Symbol: Os; m.p. 2730°C; b.p. 4230°C; r.d. 22.6; a.n. 76; r.a.m. 190.2. A transition metal belongs to *'d'* block in periodic table and is found associated with platinum. It oxidizes readily and is used in pen nibs, pivots, and electrical contacts.

osmium(IV) oxide (also known as **osmium tetroxide**) A yellow solid, having formula OsO_4, made by heating osmium in air. It is used as an oxidizing agent in organic chemistry, as a catalyst, and as a fixative in electron microscopy.

osmosis It is the process of flow of pure solvent into a solution through a semi-permeable membrane from the region of higher concentration to that of lower concentration.

osmotic pressure The pressure that must be exerted on a solution to prevent the passage of solvent molecules into it when the solvent and solution are separated by a semi-permeable membrane. The osmotic pressure is, therefore, the pressure required to maintain equilibrium between the passage of solvent molecules through the membrane in either direction and thus prevent the process of osmosis proceeding. The osmotic pressure can be measured by placing the solution, containing a small perforated thimble covered by a semi-permeable membrane (which allows the passage of selective particles only) and fitted with a length of glass tubing, in a beaker of the pure solvent. Solvent molecules pass through the membrane, diluting the solution and thereby increasing the volume on the solution side and forcing the solution to rise up the glass tubing. The process continues until the pressure exerted by the solvent molecules on the membrane is balanced by the hydrostatic pressure of the solution in the tubing. A sample of the solution is then removed and its concentration determined. Osmosis is a colligative property, therefore, the method can be applied to the determination of relative molecular masses, particularly for large molecules, such as proteins, but it is restricted by the difficulty of preparing good semi-permeable membranes.

As the osmotic pressure is a colligative property it is directly proportional to the molar concentration of the solute if the temperature remains constant; thus π is proportional to n/V, where π is osmotic pressure and n/V, is the concentration. The osmotic pressure is also proportional to the absolute temperature. Combining these two proportionalities gives $\pi V = nCT$, which has the same form as the gas equation, $PV = nRT$, and experimental values of C are similar to those for R, the universal gas constant. This gives considerable weight to the kinetic description of colligative properties.

Ostwald's law of dilution It refers to a relationship that relates the dissociation constant (K) and the degree of dissociation (α) of a weak electrolyte solution of concentration C moles/litre. In case of a binary electrolyte we have

$$K = \frac{C\alpha^2}{(1-\alpha)}$$

overpotential It is a potential that must be applied in an electrolytic cell in addition to the theoretical potential required to liberate a given substance at an electrode. The value depends on the electrode material and on the current density. It is a kinetic effect occurring because of the significant activation energy for electron transfer at the electrodes, and is particularly important for the liberation of such gases as hydrogen and oxygen. For example, in the electrolysis of a solution of zinc ions, hydrogen (E = 0.76 V) would be expected to be liberated at the cathode in preference to zinc E = –0.76 V). In fact, the high overpotential of hydrogen on zinc (about I V under suitable conditions) means that zinc can be deposited instead.

oxalate A salt or ester of oxalic acid.

oxalic acid, $\begin{array}{c}\text{COOH}\\ |\\ \text{COOH}\end{array} .2H_2O$

(a) Gains oxygen:

$2Mg(s) + O_2(g) \rightarrow 2Mg\,O(s)$

(b) Loses hydrogen:

$CH_4(g)+Cl_2(g) \rightarrow CH_3Cl(l)+HCl(g)$

(c) Loses electrons:

$Cu(s) \rightarrow Cu^{2+}(aq) + 2e^-$

It is a colourless, crystalline solid (melting point is 189.5°C). It is poisonous in nature. It is soluble in water and is insoluble in ether. It is used in the manufacture of ink and bleaching straw.

oxidation It can be defined by three ways:

(i) A process in which loss of electrons take place.
(ii) A process of addition of oxygen take place.
(iii) A process of removal of hydrogen take place.

A process which causes a chemical change by reacting with oxygen. A substance undergoes oxidation if it:

oxidation number It is a purely formal number that is associated with an atom accepting that in a compound the bonds are formed solely by giving or acquisition of electrons. The number is preceded by +ve or –ve sign according to whether the atom has given off or acquired electrons.

oxide A *compound* formed between an *element* and *oxygen* only. Oxides can be formed by:

(a) Direct combustion of the elements;
(b) Oxidizing compounds;
(c) The action of heat on a *carbonate, a hydroxide* or some *nitrates.*

Examples of oxides are

$2Mg(s) + O_2(g) \rightarrow 2MgO(s)$
$CH_4(g) + 2O_2(g) \rightarrow CO_2(g) + 2H_2O(g)$
$CuCO_3(s) \rightarrow CuO(s) + CO_2(g)$
$Pb(OH)_2(s) \rightarrow PbO(s) + H_2O(g)$
$2Zn(NO_3)_2(s) \rightarrow 2ZnO(s) + 4NO_2(g) + O_2(g)$

Oxides can be reduced to the element with a suitable *reducing agent,* for example *hydrogen, carbon* or carbon monoxide. Oxides may be either of these types *basic oxide, acidic oxide, amphoteric oxide.*

oxidizing acid An acid that can act as strong oxidizing agent as well as an acid. Nitric acid (HNO_3) is a common example. It is able to attack metals, such as copper, that are below hydrogen in the electromotive series, by oxidizing the metal:

$$2HNO_3 + Cu \rightarrow CuO + H_2O + 2NO_2$$

This is followed by reaction between the acid and the oxide:

$$2HNO_3 + CuO \rightarrow Cu(NO_3)_2 + H_2O$$

oxidizing agent also called an (oxidant) A substance that brings about oxidation in other substances. It achieves this by being itself reduced. Oxidizing agents contain atoms with high oxidation numbers; that is the atoms have suffered electron loss. In oxidizing other substances these atoms gain electrons.

oxime Organic compounds having the functional group >C = N— OH. They are obtained by the action of hydroxylamine (NH_2OH) on an aldehyde or a ketone. e.g. :

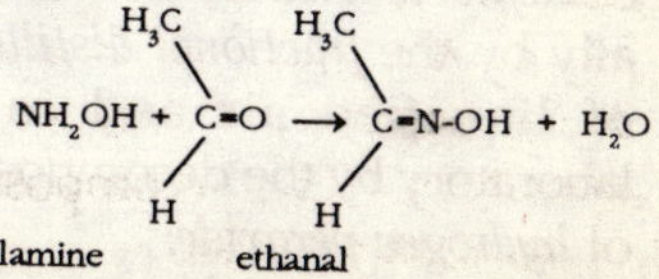

Hydroxylamine ethanal

oxonium ion An ion of the type

R_3O^+, in which R indicates hydrogen or an organic group. The hydroxonium ion, H_3O^+, is formed when acids dissociate in water.

oxyacetylene burner A welding or cutting torch that burns a mixture of oxygen and acetylene (ethyne) in a specially designed jet. The flame temperature of about 3300°C enables all ferrous metals to be welded. For cutting, the point at which the steel is to be cut is preheated with the oxy-acetylene flame and a powerful jet of oxygen is then directed onto the steel. The oxygen reacts with the hot steel to form iron oxide and the heat of this reaction melts more iron, which is blown away by the force of the jet.

oxygen Symbol: O; a.n. 8; r.a.m. 15.999; d 1.429 g dm^{-3}; m.p. –214°C; b.p. –183°C. A gaseous, non-metallic *element* in *group* VI '*p*' block element of the *periodic table*. It makes up 21% of the *atmosphere*. It is a vigorous *oxidizing agent* and is vital for the *respiration* of plants and animals.

It is a reactive gas, readily forming *oxides* with most *elements*. It is obtained industrially by the *fractional distillation* of liquefied air and in the laboratory by the decomposition of *hydrogen peroxide*:

$$2H_2O_2(aq) \rightarrow 2H_2O(l) + O_2(g)$$

A *catalyst* such as manganese (IV) oxide is usually used.

Oxygen is a colourless, odourless *diatomic* gas. It is *neutral* and is only slightly soluble in water (40 cm^3 per cubic decimetre). It is sufficiently soluble to allow fish and other aquatic life to live in water. Problems arise if the oxygen in water drops to very low level. Then, fish suffocate and die. Such a drop in the *concentration* of oxygen is usually caused by *pollution*.

The chemical test for oxygen is to plunge a glowing splint into the gas. If the gas is oxygen, the splint will relight. The gas will also make anything which is already burning in air, burn much more fiercely.

oxygen carrier It refers to a molecule that can react directly with molecular oxygen and can subsequently use oxygen in an oxidation reaction, generally of some organic substrate, for example, haemoglobin.

ozone (trioxygen) Symbol: O_3 A colourless gas soluble in cold water and in alkalis; m.p. –192.7°C; b.p. –111.9°C. Liquid ozone is dark blue in colour and is diamagnetic (dioxygen, O_2, is paramagnetic). The gas is made by passing oxygen through a silent electric discharge and is usually used in mixtures with oxygen. It is produced in the stratosphere by the action of high-energy ultraviolet radiation on oxygen and its presence there acts as a screen for ultraviolet radiation (*ozone* layer). It is a powerful oxidizing agent and is used to form ozonides by reaction with alkenes and subsequently by hydrolysis to carbonyl compounds.

ozone layer It is the part of the *Earth's atmosphere* which contains *ozone*. About one molecule in every 10,000,000 in the Earth's atmosphere is ozone. Although this doesn't sound a lot, because the atmosphere is so large, there are billions of tonnes of the gas which is concentrated in a 20 km thick region round the Earth in the stratosphere. Here it provides protection against *ultraviolet (u.v.) radiation* from the sun. The ozone (O_3) molecules stop most of the u.v. reaching the Earth where it would destroy crops and marine life and to human skin.

The u.v. breaks down the ozone into oxygen, but ozone is continuously reformed by the action of u.v. radiation on oxygen. Every day, on average, 300 million tonnes of ozone are destroyed and produced in the stratosphere.

Since 1980, the amount of ozone in the stratosphere has been reduced, particularly over the poles where the coverage can become thin during the spring. This reduction is blamed on atmospheric *pollutants* such as *CFCs*.

ozonides (a) A group of compounds formed by reaction of ozone with alkali metal hydroxides and formally containing the ion O_3-, (b) Unstable compounds formed by the addition of ozone to the C = C double bond in alkenes. (Please refer to ozonolysis).

ozonolysis The process of addition of ozone (O_3) to an unsaturated hydrocarbon resulting in the formation of an ozonide is called ozonolysis. Ozonides on hydrolysis yield hydrogen peroxide (H_2O_2) and a mixture of carbonyl compounds. It is used for determination of the structure of organic compounds.

P

Palladium Symbol: Pd; m.p. 1825K; b.p. 3413K; r.d. 12.0; a.n. 46; r.a.m 106.4. A transition metal occurring in platinum ores in Canada. It is used in electrical relays and as a catalyst in hydrogenation processes.

palmitate (hexadecanoate) A salt or ester of palmitic acid.

paper chromatography In this type of chromatography a chromatographic paper is used as absorbent. It is based on the fact that the rate of migration of different constituents is different.

para (a) It designate the form of diatomic molecule in which both nuclei have opposite spin directions; e.g. parahydrogen, paradeuterium.

(b) It designate a benzene compound with substituents in the 1,4 positions. The position on a benzene ring directly opposite a substituent is the para position. This was used in the systematic naming of benzene compounds. For example, para-dinitrobenzene (or *p*-dinitrobenzene) is 1,4-dinitrobenzene.

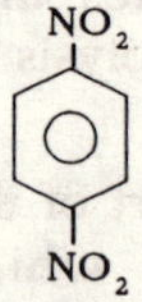

P-dinitrobenzene or 1,4-dinitrobenzene

parahydrogen Hydrogen molecules in which the spins of the two constituent nuclei are anti-parallel.

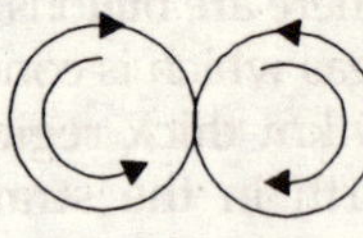

parahydrogen

Paraldehyde The trimer formed by polymerization of ethanal in dilute acid. Used as a drug for inducing sleep.

partition It refers to a substance which is in contact with two different phases then, in general, it will have a different affinity for each phase. Part of the substance will be absorbed or dissolved by one and part by the other, the relative amounts depending on the relative affinities. The substance is said to be *partitioned* between the two phases. For example, if two immiscible liquids are taken and a third compound is shaken up with them, then an equilibrium is reached in which the concentration in one solvent differs from that in the other. The ratio of the concentrations is the *partition coefficient* of the system. The *partition law* states that this ratio is a constant for given liquids.

Paschen series A series of lines in the infrared spectrum emitted by excited hydrogen atoms is called Paschen series. The lines correspond to the atomic electrons falling into the third lowest energy level and emitting energy as radiation. The wavelength (λ) of the radiation in the Paschen series is given by $1/\lambda = R\,(1/3^2 - 1/n^2)$ where n is an integer and R is the Rydberg constant.

pascal The SI unit of pressure equal to one newton per square metre.

passive Describing a solid that has reacted with another substance to form a protective layer, so that further reaction stops. The solid is said to have been 'rendered passive'. For example, aluminium reacts spontaneously with oxygen in air to form a thin layer of aluminium oxide, which prevents further oxidation. Similarly, pure iron forms a protective oxide layer with concentrated HNO_3 and is not dissolved further.

pasteurization A heat-treatment process to reduce the number of micro-organisms present in food so as to extend its shelf-life. Milk is pasteurized by being heated to 71.7°C for at least 15 seconds. Pasteurized milk can be kept in the fridge for 4-5 days without turning sour.

Pauli's exclusion principle It states, "No two electrons in an atom have the same set of four quantum numbers". It means an orbital cannot have more than 2 electrons and these 2 must have opposite spins.

p-block elements The elements of the main groups III A (B to Tl), IV A (C to Pb), VA (N to Bi), VIA (O to Po), VIIA (F to At) and O (He to Rn). They are so called because they have outer electronic configurations that have occupied *p* levels.

pearl It is a secretion consisting mainly of calcium carbonate ($CaCO_3$).

pectin A *carbohydrate polymer* which is found in many soft fruits. Pectin is useful in the formation of *gels* and is necessary in getting jams to set.

penicillin An antibiotic derived from the mould *Penicillium notatum;* specifically it is known as *penicillin G* and belongs to a class of similar substances called penicillins. They produce their effects by disrupting synthesis of the bacterial cell wall, and are used to treat a variety of bacterial infections.

pentahydrate A crystalline hydrate containing five molecules of water per molecule of compound.

pentane (C_5H_{12}) It is a straight-chain alkane obtained by distillation of crude oil.

pentanoic acid (valeric acid) A colourless liquid carboxylic acid having formula $CH_3(CH_2)_3COOH$; r.d. 0.9; m.p. –34°C; b.p. 185°C. It is used in the perfume industry.

pentavalent also known as **(quinquevalent) having a valency of five.**

pentiandite A mineral consisting of a mixed iron-nickel sulphide, $(Fe,Ni)_9S_8$ crystallizing in the cubic system. It is the chief ore of nickel. It is yellowish-bronze in colour with a metallic lustre. The chief occurrence of the mineral is at Sudbury in Ontario, Canada.

peptide It refers to an organic compound having a peptide linkage (–NHCO–).

peptones These are the products of hydrolysis of proteins, the hydrolysis is carried out by the action of *pepsin* in stomach. Peptones are soluble in water and are absorbed by the body.

period One of the horizontal rows in the conventional periodic table. Each period represents the elements arising from progressive filling of the outer shell (i.e. the addition of one extra electron for each new element), the elements being arranged in order of ascending proton number. In a strict sense hydrogen and helium represent one period but convention refers to the elements lithium to neon (8 elements) as the first *short peroid* (n = 2), and the elements sodium to argon (8 elements) as the second *short period* (n = 3). With entry to the n = 4 level there is filling of the 4*s*, then back filling of the 3*d*, before the 4*p* are filled. Thus this set contains a total of 18 electrons [potassium (z = 19) to krypton (z = 36)– and is called a *long period.* The next set, Rubidium (z = 37) to xenon (z = 54) is similarly a long period.

periodic table It is a way of presenting all the *elements* so as to show their similarities and differences.

The elements are arranged in increasing order of *atomic number (Z)* as you go from left to right across the table. For example:

Period 3

Na	Mg	Al	Si	P	S	Cl	Ar
11	12	13	14	15	16	17	18

The horizontal rows are called *periods* and the vertical rows, *groups.* A *noble gas* is found at the right hand side of each period.

Period	1	He
	2	Ne
	3	Ar
	4	Kr
	5	Xe
	6	Rn

There is a progression from *metals* (*s*-block elements) to non-metals (*p*-block elements) across each period.

Similar elements are found in a group, e.g. these elements have a similar *electronic configuration* and are found in the same group, for example:

group I	alkali metals	Li	Na	K
group VII	halogens	F	Cl	BrI

The number of *electrons* in the outer shell is the same as the number of the group, for example group I:

lithium	2.1
sodium	2.8.1
potassium	2.8.8.1

The block of elements between groups II and III are called the *transition metals*. (*d*-block elements). These are similar in many ways: they produce coloured compounds, have variable *valency* and are often used as *catalysts*. Elements 58 to 71 are known as *lanthanide* or rare earth elements. These elements are found on earth in only very small amounts.

Elements 90 to 103 are known as the *actinide* elements. They include most of the well known elements which are found in *nuclear reactions*. The elements with larger atomic numbers than 92 do not occur naturally. They have all been produced artificially by bombarding other elements with particles. *Plutonium* is formed in nuclear reactors.

In modern periodic table, IUPAC has recommended the numbering of groups in continuation from 1 to 18. (see *in Appendix* periodic table).

Elements with atomic numbers of 104 and above are not being named after famous scientists or places. They are now being named in a systematic way according to their atomic number. For example:

element 104 is *Unnilquadium*	un	=1	Symbol
	nil	=0	*Unq*
	quad	=4	

105 unnilpentium Unp
106 Unnilhexium Unh

permalloys A group of alloys of high magnetic permeability consisting of iron and nickel (usually 40-80%) often with small amounts of other elements (e.g. 3-5% (Mo, Cu, Cr or W). They are used in thin foils in electronic transformers, for magnetic shielding, and in computer memories.

permanent gas A gas, such as oxygen or nitrogen, that was formerly thought to be impossible to liquefy. A permanent gas is now regarded as one that cannot be liquefied by pressure alone at normal temperatures (i.e. a gas that has a critical temperature below room temperature).

peroxide (a) It refers to an oxide containing the ⁻O–O⁻ ion. and

(b) A compound containing the –O-O– group.

peroxosulphuric(VI) acid The term commonly refers to *peroxamonosulphuric(VI) acid*, H_2SO_5, which is also called *permonosulphuric(VI) acid* and *Carp's acid*. It is a crystalline compound made by the action of hydrogen peroxide on concentrated sulphuric acid. It decomposes in water and the crystals decompose, with melting, above 318K. The compound *peroxodisulphuric acid*, $H_2S_2O_8$, also exists (formerly called *perdisulphuric acid*). It is made by the high-current electrolysis of sulphate solutions. It decomposes at 338K (with melting) and is hydrolysed in water to give the mono acid and sulphuric acid. Both peroxo acids are very powerful oxidizing agents.

petrochemicals Organic chemicals obtained from petroleum or natural gas are known as petrochemicals.

petroleum It is a *mixture* of *hydrocarbons* which are found in the Earth's crust, e.g. *natural gas* and crude *oil*. It has been produced over millions of years from the remains of marine animals and plant organisms. It is the *raw material* for the petrochemical industry and is the source of our *petrol, diesel* fuel, heating oil, *fuel* oil and *gas* supplies. Vast reserves of petroleum are found in the Middle East, the United States, the Soviet Union, Central America and the North Sea.

Petroleum has replaced *coal* as the chief source of raw materials for the chemical industry. But the supply of petroleum will not last forever and the search is now on for the substance which will replace it in our lives.

Petroleum is converted into useful products by refining.

petroleum ether A colourless volatile flammable mixture of hydrocarbons (not an ether), mainly pentane and hexane. It boils in the range 303K-343K and is used as a solvent.

pewter An alloy of Pb and Sn. It usually contains 63% tin; pewter tankards and food containers should have less than 35% of lead so that the lead remains in solid solution with the tin in the presence of weak acids in the food and drink. Copper is sometimes added to increase ductility and antimony is added if a hard alloy is required.

pH A scale for measuring the acidity or basicity of a *solution.*

(i) pH of a solution of weak acid:

$$\frac{1}{2}\ pk_2 - \frac{1}{2}\ \log C$$

$$pKa = -\log K_a$$

c = concentration of undissociated acid.
K_a = ionisation constant of weak acid.
It (K_a) is given by $HA + H_2O \rightleftharpoons H^3O^+ + A^-$

$$K_a = \frac{[H_3O^+][A^-]}{[HA]}$$

(ii) pH of a solution of weak base:

$$pH = 14\frac{1}{2}\ pK_b + \frac{1}{2}\ \log C$$

$$pK_b = -\log K_b$$

C = concentration of undissociated base
K_b = dissociation constant of weak base. K_b is given by

$$B + H_2O \rightleftharpoons BH^+ + OH^-$$

$$K_b = \frac{[BH^+]\,[OH^-]}{[B]}$$

phase One of the physically separable parts of a chemical system. For example, a mixture of ice (solid phase) and water (liquid phase) consists of two phases. A system consisting of only one phase is said to be homogeneous. A system consisting of more than one phase is said to be heterogeneous.

phase change (or *change of state*) A change which occurs when a substance goes from one physical *state* to another

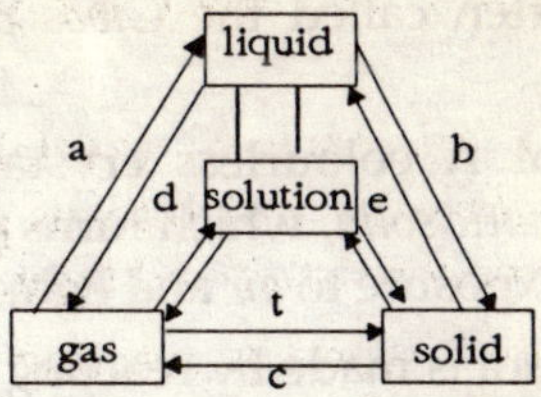

a is condensation d is vaporization
b is freezing e is melting
c is sublimation

phase change Possible phases in a chemical system.

phase diagram A graph showing the relationship between solid, liquid and gaseous phases over a range of conditions (such as temperature and pressure).

phase equilibrium A state in which the proportions of the various phases in a chemical system are fixed. When two or more phases are present at fixed temperature and pressure a dynamic condition will be established in which individual particles will leave one phase and enter another; at equilibrium this will be balanced by an equal number of particles making the reverse change, leaving the total composition unchanged.

phase rule For any system at equilibrium, the relationship $F = C - P + 2$ holds, where P is the number of distinct phases, C the number of components, and F the number of degrees of freedom of the system. The relationship which was derived by Josiah Willard Gibbs in 1876, is often called the *Gibbs phase rule.*

phenol A colourless crystalline *aromatic solid,* which turns pink on exposure to *air* and light.

Phenol is made by reacting *benzene* with *propene* ($CH_3CH = CH_2$) and then oxidizing the product. Phenol can also be prepared by hydrolysis of benzene diazonium salt e.g.

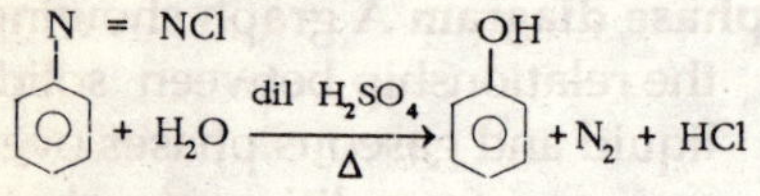

Benzene diazonium chloride   Phenol

It is a very corrosive chemical and is *poisonous.* 35% of phenol production is used in the production of *phenol/methanal* polymers and a further 27% in the production of the transparent *poly(carbonates)* materials and *epoxy resins.*

phenolphthalein An acid-base indicator that is colourless in acid solutions and becomes red if the pH rises above the transition range of 8-9.6. It is used as the indicator in titrations for which the end point lies clearly on the basic side (pH>7), e.g. oxalic acid or potassium hydrogen tartrate against caustic soda.

phenylamine (aniline; aminobenzene) A colourless oily liquid aromatic amine,

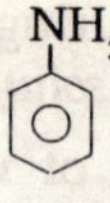

or $C_6H_5NH_2$

with an 'earthy' smell; r.d. 1.027; m.p. –6.2°C; b.p. 185°C. The compound turns brown on exposure to sunlight. It is basic, forming the *phenylammonium* (or *anilinium) ion,* $C_6H_5NH_3^+$, with strong acids. It is manufactured by the reduction of nitrobenzene or by the addition of ammonia to chlorobenzene using a copper (II) salt catalyst at 200°C and 55 atm.

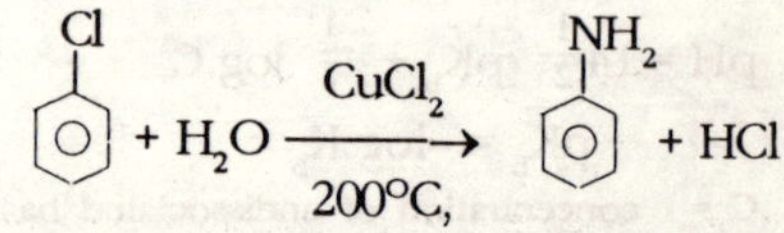

Chlorobenzene   55 atm   Aniline

The compound is used extensively in the rubber industry and in the manufacture of drugs and dyes.

phenylethene (styrene, $C_6H_5CHCH_2$) A liquid hydrocarbon used as the starting material for the production of polystyrene. The manufacture of phenylethene is by dehydrogenation of ethyl benzene:

$$C_6H_5C_2H_5 \rightarrow C_6H_5CH{:}CH_2 + H_2$$

phenylmethanol (benzyl alcohol) A liquid aromatic alcohol, $C_6H_5CH_2OH$; r.d. 1.04; m.p. –15.3°C; b.p. 205.4°C. It is used mainly as a solvent.

Phillips process A process for

making high-density polyethene by polymerizing ethene at high pressure (30 atmospheres) and 423K. The catalyst is chromium (III) oxide supported on silica and alumina.

phosphates These are the *salts* of *phosphoric*(V) *acid.* Phosphoric acid is a *tribasic* acid and, therefore, gives rise to three kinds of salts:

(a) Sodium phosphate Na_3PO_4
(b) Sodium hydrogenphosphate Na_2HPO_4
(c) Sodium dihydrogenphosphate NaH_2PO_4

Phosphates are used in *fertilizers* to replace the *phosphorus*-containing compunds in the soil. It comes in several forms.

Superphosphate is a mixture of calcium sulphate and calcium dihydrogenphosphate ($Ca(H_2PO_4)_2$). A mixture of ammonium nitrate and ammonium hydrogenphosphate $(NH_4)_2HPO_4$ is made by reacting ammonia with a mixture of *phosphoric*(V) and *nitric acids.* Calcium phosphate is the chief constituent of animal bones and phosphates are used extensively in washing powders and *detergents.*

Slag from *blast furnaces* is put directly onto the soil since it contains calcium phosphate.

phosphinic acid; Also known as **Hypophosphorous acid, H_3PO_2** A white crystalline solid, soluble in water. Its sodium, potassium and calcium salts are used as tonics.

phospholipid (phosphatide) One of a group of lipids having both a phosphate group and one or more fatty acids. *Glycerophospholipids* are based on glycerol; the three –OH groups are esterified with two fatty acids and a phosphate group, which may itself be bound to one of a variety of simple organic groups. *Sphingophospholipids* are based on the alcohol sphingosine and contain only one fatty acid linked to an amino group. With their hydrophilic polar phosphate groups and long hydrophobic hydrocarbon 'tails', phospholipids readily form membrane-like structures in water. They are a major component of cell membranes.

phosphonic acid Also called as **(phosphorous acid; orthophosphorous acid)** A colourless to pale-yellow deliquescent crystalline solid, H_3PO_3; r.d. 1.65; m.p. 73.6°C; decomposes at 473K, very soluble in water and soluble in alcohol. Phosphonic acid may be crystallized from the solution obtained by adding ice-cold water to phosphours(III) oxide or phosphours trichloride. The structure of this material is unusual in that it contains one direct P—H bond and is more correctly written $(HO)_2HPO$. The acid is dibasic, giving rise to the ions $H_3PO^-_3$ and HPO_3^{2-} (*phosphonates;* formerly *phosphites)*, and has moderate reducing properties. On heating it gives phosphine and phosphoric(V) acid.

phosphonium ion The ion PH_4^+, or the corresponding organic derivatives of the type R_3PH^+, RPH_3^+. The phospho- nium ion PH_4^+ is formally analogous to the ammonium ion NH_4^+ but PH_3 has a much lower proton affinity than NH_3 and reaction of PH_3 with acids is necessary for the production of phosphonium salts.

phosphor bronze An alloy of copper containing 4% to 10% of tin and 0.05% to 1% of phosphorus as a deoxidizing agent. It is used particularly for marine purposes and where it is exposed to heavy wear, as in gear wheels.

phosphorescence It is the property of a substance to glow in dark.

phosphoric(V) acid (orthophos phoric acid, H_3PO_4) A white solid that can be made by reacting phosphorus(V) oxide with water or by heating yellow phosphorus with HNO_3. The naturally occurring *phosphates* (orthophosphates, M_3PO_4) are salts of phosphoric(V) acid. An aqueous solution of phosphoric(V) acid has a sharp taste and has been used in the manufacture of soft drinks. At about 493K phosphoric(V) acid is converted to *pyrophosphoric acid* (H_4P_2O-). Pure pyrophosphoric acid in the form of colourless crystals is made by warming solid phosphoric(V) acid with phosphorus(III) chloride oxide. *Metaphosphoric acid* is obtained as a polymer, $(HPO_3)_n$ by heating phosphoric(V) acid to 320°C. Both meta and pyrophosphoric acids change to phosphoric(V) acid in acqueous solution; the change will take place faster at higher temperatures. Phosphoric(V) acid is tribasic, forming three series of salts with the anions $H_2PO_4^-$, HPO_4^{2-}, and PO_4^{3-}. These series of salts are acidic, neutral, and alkaline respectively. The alkali metal phosphates (except lithium phosphate) are soluble in water but other metal phosphates are insoluble. Phosphates are used for water softening and as fertilizers.

phosphorus, Symbol **P** A a.n. 15; r.a.m. 3097.38; r.d. 1.82 (white), 2.20 (red); m.p. 44-.1°C (α-White); b.p. 280°C (α-white). **P**.A non-metallic solid. It exists in two allotropic forms—white and red. White phosphorus is soluble in carbon disulphide but insoluble in water whereas red phosphorus is insoluble in water as also in carbon disulphide. Red phosphorus is used in preparation of alloys, matches and other compounds of phosphorus. White phosphorus is poisonous in nature.

phosphorus(III) bromide (phosphorus tribromide) A colourless fuming liquid, PBr_3; r.d. 2.85; m.p. –40°C; b.p. 173°C; It is prepared by passing bromine vapour over phosphorous but avoiding an excess, which would lead to the phosphorus(V) bromide. Like the other phosphorus(III) halides, PBr_3 is pyramidal in the gas phase. In the liquid phase the P—Br bonds are labile; for example, PBr_3 will react with PCl_3 to give a mixture of products in which the halogen atoms have been redistributed. Phosphorus(III) bromide is rapidly hydrolysed by water to give phosphonic acid and hydrogen bromide. It reacts readily with many organic —OH groups and is used as a reagent for introducing bromine atoms into organic molecules.

phosphorus trichloride, PCl_3 A mobile liquid used for preparation of phosphorous pentachloride (PCl_5) and in a number of organic reactions. It fumes in moist air and reacts violently with water forming phosphorus acid.

phosphorus(V) chloride (phosphorus pentachloride) A yellow-white rhombic solid, PCl_5, which fumes in air; r.d. 3.6; m.p. 148°C (under pressure); sublimes at 160-162°C. It is decomposed by water to give hydrogen chloride and phosphoric(V) acid.

$$PCl_5 + 4H_2O \xrightarrow{\text{decomposition}} H_3PO_4 + 5HCl$$

It is soluble in organic solvents. The compound may be prepared by the reaction of chlorine with phosphorus(III) chloride. Phosphorus(V) chloride is structurally interesting in that, in the gas phase it has the expected trigonal bipyramidal form but in the solid phase it consists of the ions $[PCl_4]^+[PCl_6]^-$. The same ions are detected when phosphorus(V) chloride is dissolved in polar solvents. It is used in organic chemistry as a chlorinating agent.

phosphorus(III) chloride oxide also known as (phosphorus oxychloride; phosphoryl chloride) A colourless fuming liquid, $POCl_3$; r.d.1.67; m.p. 2°C; b.p. 105.3°C. It may be prepared by the reaction of phosphorus(III) chloride with oxygen or by the reaction of phosphorus(V) oxide with phosphorus(V) chloride. Its reactions are very similar to those of phosphorus(III) chloride. Hydrolysis with water gives phosphoric(V) acid.

Phosphorus(III) chloride oxide has a distorted tetrahedral shape and can act as a donor towards metal ions, thus giving rise to a series of complexes.

phosphorus(III) oxide also called as (phosphorus trioxide, P_2O_3) A white waxy solid with a characteristic smell of garlic; it usually exists as P_4O_6 molecules. It is soluble in organic solvents, such as benzene (C_6H_6) and carbon disulphide (CS_2) and is prepared by burning phosphorus in a limited supply of air. Phosphorus(III) oxide oxidizes in air to phosphorus (V) oxide at room temperature and inflames above 70°C. It dissolves slowly in cold water or dilute alkalis to give phosphonic acid or one of its salts. Phosphorus(III) oxide reacts violently with hot water to form phosphine and phosphoric(V) acid.

phosphorus(V) oxide also called as (phosphorus pentoxide; phosphoric anhydride) A white powdery and extremely deliquescent solid, P_4O_{10}; r.d. 2.39; m.p. 853K under pressure; sublimes at 633K. It reacts violently with water to give phosphoric(V) acid. It is prepared by burning elemental phosphorus in a plentiful supply of oxygen, then purified by sublimation. The hexagonal crystalline form consists of P_4O_{10} molecular units; these have the phosphorus atoms arranged tetrahedrally, each P atom linked to three others by oxygen bridges and having in addition one terminal oxygen atom. The compound is used as a drying agent and as a dehydrating agent; for example, amides are converted into nitrites and sulphuric acid is converted to sulphur trioxide.

photochemical reactions Chemical reactions which are brought about by light. The process of photography depends on light. When silver bromide is exposed to light it decomposes:

$$2AgBr(s) \rightarrow 2Ag(s) + Br_2(g)$$

The black part of the negative of a film is a thin layer of *silver*. This is then processed to produce the final pictures.

Photosynthesis is the most important photochemical *reaction*. Our existence on this planet depends on it.

Other examples are the reaction between *hydrogen* and *chlorine* which can be started off by a bright light, for example burning magnesium:

$$H_2(g) + Cl_2(g) \rightarrow 2HCl(g)$$

In hot areas of the world, e.g. California, where there are a lot of vehicle exhaust fumes, photochemical *smog* can be produced by the reaction of the exhaust fumes. This is an acrid haze which is very unpleasant.

The *bleaching* action of the sun is also a photochemical reaction, conversion of cholesterol in the skin into *vitamin* D is another example of a photochemical reaction.

In all these reactions light provides the *energy* that makes the reactions work.

photochemistry The branch of chemistry concerned with photochemical reactions.

photoelectric effect The emission of electrons from a solid (or liquid) surface when it is irradiated with electromagnetic radiation is known as the photoelectric effect. For most materials the photoelectric effect occurs with ultraviolet radiation or radiation of shorter wavelength; some show the effect with visible radiation.

In the photoelectric effect, the number of electrons emitted depends on the intensity of the radiation and not on its frequency. The kinetic energy of the electrons that are ejected depends on the frequency of the radiation. This was explained, by Einstein, by the idea that electromagnetic radiation consists of streams of photons. The *photon energy is* $h\Upsilon$; where h is the Planck constant (value is 6.62×10^{-34} Js) and Υ the frequency of the radiation. To remove an electron from the solid a certain minimum energy must be supplied, known as the *work function*, ϕ. Thus, there is a certain minimum threshold frequency Υ_o for radiation to eject electrons: $h\Upsilon_o = \theta$. If the frequency is higher than this threshold the electrons are ejected. The maximum kinetic energy (W) of the electrons is given by *Einstein's equation:*

$$W = h\Upsilon - \phi$$

The photoelectric effect also occurs with gases.

photoelectron spectroscopy It is a technique for determining the ionization potentials of molecules. The sample is a gas or vapour irradiated with a narrow beam of ultraviolet radiation (usually from a helium source at 58.4 nm, 21.21 eV photon energy). The photoelectrons produced in accordance with Einstein's equation are passed through a slit into a vacuum region, where they are deflected by magnetic or electrostatic fields to give an energy spectrum. The photoelectron spectrum obtained has peaks corresponding to the ionization potentials of the molecule (and hence the orbital energies). The technique also gives information on the vibrational energy levels of the ions formed. *ESCA* (electron spectroscopy for chemical analysis) is a similar analytical technique in which a beam of X-rays is used. In this case, the electrons ejected are from the inner shells of the atoms. Peaks in the electron spectrum for a particular element show characteristic chemical shifts, which depend on the presence of other atoms in the molecule.

photoionization It is the ionization of an atom or molecule as a result of irradiation by electromagnetic radiation. For a photoionization to occur the incident photon of the radiation must have an energy in excess of the ionization potential of the species being irradiated. The ejected photoelectron will have an energy, *E*, given by

$$E = hf - I,$$

where *h* is the Planck constant, *f* is the frequency of the incident radiation, and *I* is the ionization potential of the irradiated species.

photolysis A chemical reaction produced by exposure to light or ultraviolet radiation. Photolytic reactions often involve free radicals, the first step being homolytic fission of a chemical bond.

photon A particle with zero rest mass consisting of a quantum of electromagnetic radiation. The photon may also be regarded as a unit of energy equal to *hf*, where *h* is the Planck constant (value is 6.62×10^{-34}Js) and *f* is the frequency of the radiation in Hz. Photons travel at the speed of light. They are required to explain the photoelectric effect and other phenomena that require light to have particle character.

photosensitive substance (a) Any substance when exposed to electromagnetic radiation produces a photoconductive, photoelectric, or photovoltaic effect.

(b) Any substance, such as the emulsion of a photographic film, in which electromagnetic radiation produces a chemical change.

photosensitization Some substances give photochemical reaction only in presence of a particular substance which is known as photosensitiser and the process is known as photosensitization, for example, chlorophyll (green pigment in plants) acts as photosensitizer in the photosynthesis of plants.

photosynthesis The chemical process by which green plants synthesize organic compounds from CO_2 and H_2O in the presence of sunlight. It occurs in the chloroplasts (most of which are in the leaves) and there are two principal series of reactions. In the *light reactions,* which require the presence of light, energy from sunlight is absorbed by photosynthetic pigments (chiefly the green pigment chlorophyll) and converted into chemical energy. In the ensuing *dark reactions,* which can take place either in light or darkness, this chemical energy is used in the production of simple organic compounds from carbon dioxide and water. Further chemical reactions convert these compounds into chemicals useful to the plant. The following reaction takes place.

$$CO_2 + 2H_2O \rightarrow [CH_2O] + H_2O + O_2$$

Since virtually all other forms of life are directly or indirectly dependent on plants for food, photosynthesis is the basis for all life on earth. Furthermore virtually all the atmospheric oxygen has originated from oxygen released during photosynthesis.

photosynthetic pigments These are the plant pigments responsible for the capture of light energy during the light reactions of photosynthesis. The green pigment chlorophyll is the principal light receptor, absorbing blue and red light. However, the carotenoids and various other pigments also absorb light energy and pass this on to the chlorophyll molecules.

physical chemistry The branch of chemistry concerned with the effect of chemical structure on physical properties. It includes chemical thermodynamics and electrochemistry.

physical adsorption also known as **physiosorption** If the adsorbate is held on a surface by weak vander Waals forces then the adsorption process is known as physiosorption.

pickling 1. The treatment of *metals* with *acid* (usually dilute) in order to remove the surface layer of *oxide* so that they can be painted or treated in some way. It is necessary to pickle *steel* if it has been allowed to cool down in the *air.* **2.** Treatment of foods with *vinegar* in order to preserve them for eating at a later date. Chutneys, sauces and pickles are examples.

pig iron The impure form of iron produced by a blast furnace, which is cast into pigs (blocks) for converting at a later date into cast iron, steel, etc. The composition depends on the ores used, the smelting procedure, and the use to which the pigs will later be put.

pigment It is a chemical which gives colour to a material. Pigments may be *organic* and be produced from *petroleum* and natural sources, or *inorganic* and be based on *metal oxides.* The white pigment, titanium oxide (TiO_2) makes up 70% of all pigments used.

pirsonnite A mineral consisting

of a hydrated mixed carbonate of sodium and calcium, $Na_2CO_3.CaCO_3.2H_2O$.

pitch A black or dark-brown residue resulting from the distillation of coal tar, wood tar, or petroleum (bitumen). The term is also sometimes used for the naturally occurring petroleum residue (asphalt). Pitch is used as a binding agent (e.g. in road tars), for waterproofing (e.g. in roofing felts), and as a fuel.

pK The logarithm to the base 10 of the reciprocal of an acid's dissociation constant:

$$\log_{10} (1/K)$$

Planck constant It is denoted by '*h*'. The fundamental constant equal to the ratio of the energy of quantum of energy to its frequency. It has the value 6.626196×10^{-34} Js. It is named after Max Planck (1858-1947).

plasma A mixture of ions and electrons, as in an electrical discharge. Sometimes, a plasma is described as a fourth state of matter.

plaster It is the material used to coat walls to produce a smooth surface which can be painted or papered. Plaster consists of a *mixture* of *lime* and *sand* which is mixed with *water* just before it is applied.

plaster of paris The hemihydrate of calcium sulphate, $2CaSO_4.H_2O$, prepared by heating the mineral gypsum. When ground to a fine powder and mixed with water, plaster of Paris sets hard, forming interlocking crystals of gypsum. The setting results in an increase in volume and so the plaster fits tightly into a mould. It is used for making pottery, as a cast for setting broken bones, and as a constituent of the plaster used in the building industry.

plastic (a) A substance which is capable of being shaped or moulded by *heat* and *pressure*.

(b) *Synthetic polymers*, e.g. *poly(ethene)*, *nylon*, etc. Over 30 different types of polymers exist and by combining them it is now possible to produce a synthetic substance with specific properties.

platinum Symbol Pt. A silvery white metallic transition element (*see also* platinum metals); a.n. 78; r.a.m. 195.09; r.d. 21.37; m.p. 1772°C; b.p. ~3800°C. It occurs in some nickel and copper ores and is also found native in some deposits. The main source is the anode sludge obtained in copper-nickel refining. The element is used in jewellery, laboratory apparatus (e.g. thermocouples, electrodes, etc.), electrical contacts, and in certain alloys (*e.g.* with iridium or rhodium). It is also used as a catalyst in hydrogenation. The element does not oxidize nor dissolve in hydrochloric acid.

Most of its compounds are platinium(II) or platinium (IV) complexes.

platinum black Black finely divided platinum metal produced by vacuum evaporation. It is used as an absorbent and a catalyst.

platinum-iridium An alloy of platinum containing up to 30% iridium. Hardness and resistance to chemical attack increase as the iridium content is increased. It is used in jewellery, electrical contacts, and hypodermic needles.

platinum metals The three members of the second and third transition series immediately proceeding silver and gold: ruthenium (Ru), rhodium (Rh), and palladium (Pd); and osmium (Os), iridium (Ir), and platinum (Pt). These elements, together with Fe, Co and Ni were formerly classed as group VIII of the periodic table. The platinum-group metals are relatively hard and resistant to corrosion and are used in jewellery and in some industrial applications (e.g. electrical contacts). They have certain chemical similarities that justify classifying them together. All are resistant to chemical attack. In solution they form a vast range of complex ions. They also form coordination compounds with carbon monoxide and other pi-bonding ligands. A number of complexes can be made in which a hydrogen atom is linked directly to the metal.

plumbane (lead(IV) hydride, PbH_4) A colourless unstable gas that can be obtained by the action of acids on a mixture of magnesium and lead pellets.

plutonium Symbol Pu. A dense silvery radioactive metallic transuranic element belonging to the actinoids *'f'* block elements; a.n. 94; mass number of most stable isotope 244 (half-life 7.6×10^7 years); r.d. 19.84; m.p. 641°C; b.p. 3232°C. Thirteen isotopes are known, by far the most important being plutonium-239 (half-life 2.44×10^4 years), which undergoes nuclear fission with slow neutrons and is, therefore, a vital power source for nuclear weapons and some nuclear reactors. About 20 tonnes of plutonium are produced annually by the world's nuclear reactors. The element was first produced by Seaborg, McMillan, Kennedy, and Wahl in 1940.

plywood It is a wooden *laminated* material. Plywood is made up of layers of wood or *veneer* glued together. The grain of adjacent layers runs at right angles to each other. Plywood is stronger than a similar *mass* of wood.

pnicogen It refers collectively to the elements of group 15 *'p'* block element i.e. nitrogen, phosphorus, arsenic, antimony and bismuth.

poison A substance which is harmful if taken into the body and which will lead to death or injury. Poisons can be breathed in, for example hydrogen cyanide (HCN), *carbon monoxide* (CO) or *lead* fumes in the air; they may be eaten or drunk, for example *arsenic*(III) oxide, strychnine, or paraquat; they may pass into the body through the skin, for example *benzene* and nerve gases.

Radiation from nuclear *isotopes* can also be considered as a poison.

polar compound A compound that is ionic; for example sodium chloride NaCl or that has molecules with a large permanent dipole moment (for example water).

polariscope also known as a **polarimeter** A device used to study optically active substances (*see* optical activity). The simplest type of instrument consists of a light source, collimator, polarizer, and analyser. The specimen is placed between polarizer and analyser, so that any rotation of the light can be assessed by turning the analyser.

polarization (a) The process of confining the vibrations of the vector constituting a transverse wave to one direction. In unpolarized radiation the vector oscillates in all directions perpendicular to the direction of propagation. (polarization of light.) (b) The formation of products of the chemical reaction in a voltaic cell in the vicinity of the electrodes resulting in increased resistance to current flow and, frequently, to a reduction in the e.m.f. of the cell. (depolarization) (c) The partial separation of electric charges in an insulator subjected to an electric field (d). The separation of charge in a polar chemical bond.

polarization of light The process of confining the vibrations of the electric vector of light waves to one direction is known as polarization of light. In unpolarized light the electric field vibrates in all directions perpendicular to the direction of propagation. After reflection or transmission through certain substances (*see*Polaroid) the electric field is confined to one direction and the radiation is said to be *plane-polarized light*. The plane of plane-polarized light can be rotated when it passes through certain substances (optical activity).

In *circularly polarized light*, the tip of the electric vector describes a circular helix about the direction of propagation with a frequency equal to the frequency of the light. The magnitude of the vector remains constant. In *elliptically polarized light,* the vector also rotates about the direction of propagation but the amplitude changes; a projection of the vector on a plane at right angles to the direction of propagation describes an ellipse. Circularly and elliptically polarized light are produced using a retardation plate.

polar molecule A molecule in which the individual polar bonds are not perfectly symmetrically arranged and are therefore not 'in balance'. Thus the charge separation in the bonds gives rise to an overall charge separation in the molecule as for example, in water. Such molecules possess a dipole moment.

polarography It is one of the methods of electrochemical analysis. It is suitable for dilute solutions of those substances which are susceptible to reduction at the mercury cathode. In it a (DME) dropping mercury electrode is used and the polarogram (current—voltage curve) for the solution is recorded. This shows step for each reducible species present in solution. This is characteristic potential and height is proportional to the concentration of the component. This method can be used to determine even trace amounts of metal. It can be used to investigate complexes in solution and also for bodies in non-aqueous solvents.

pollution It is caused by dangerous or dirty materials which are harmful to the environment or life. Pollution can occur when waste materials are not treated properly or when *toxic* materials escape from containers.

polonium Symbol Po. A rare radioactive metallic element of group VIB, '*p*' block of the periodic table; a.n. 84; r.a.m. 210; r.d. 9.32; m.p. 254°C; b.p. 962°C. The element occurs in uranium ores to an extent of about 100 micrograms per 1000 kilograms. It has 27 isotopes, more than any other element. The longest-lived isotope is polonium-209 (half-life 103 years). Polonium has attracted attention as a possible heat source for spacecraft as the energy released as it decays is 1.4×10^5 J kg^{-1} s^{-1}. It was discovered by Marie Curie in 1898 in a sample of pitchblende.

polyamides The polymers which have amide linkage

$$-\overset{\displaystyle O}{\overset{\|}{C}}-NH-$$ e.g. Nylon 6, 6 and Nylon 6

polychloroethene (PVC) A *polymer* is made from chloroethene (CH_2 = CHCL). PVC has variety of uses: vinyl floorings, food containers, fibres, guttering, bottles, windows and cables.

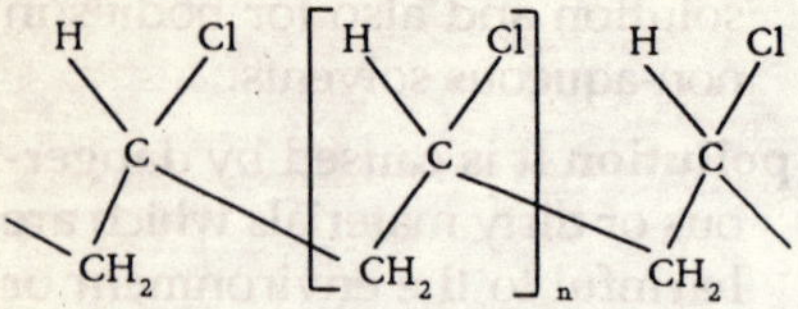

polychloroethene

polycrystalline Describing a substance composed of very many minute interlocking crystals that have solidified together.

polycyclic Denoting a compound that has two or more rings in its molecules. Polycyclic compounds may contain single rings (as in phenylbenzene, $C_6H_5.C_6H_5$) or fused rings (as in naphthalene, $C_{10}H_8$).

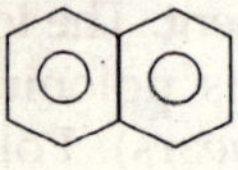

Napthalene

polysters Polymers of esters, for example terelyne which is obtained by condensation of ethylene glycol and *p*-terephthalic acid.

polyhydric alcohol An alcohol that has several –OH groups per molecule *see* also glycol, glycerol.

polymer (Repeated units) A compound in which there are very large molecules made up of repeating molecular units (monomers). Polymers do not usually have a definite relative molecular mass, as there are variations in the lengths of different chains. They may be natural substances (for example polysaccharides or proteins) or synthetic materials (for example nylon or polyethene).

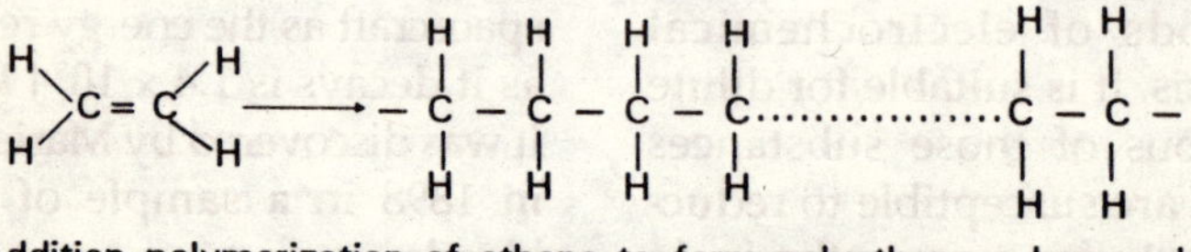

Addition polymerization of ethene to form polyethene a homopolymer

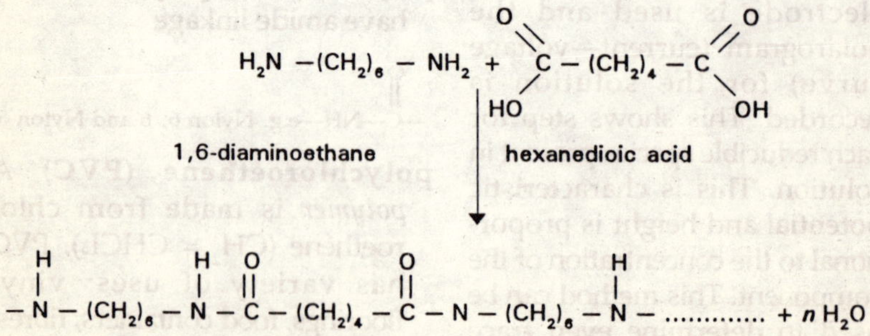

Condensation polymerization to form nylon : a heteropolymer

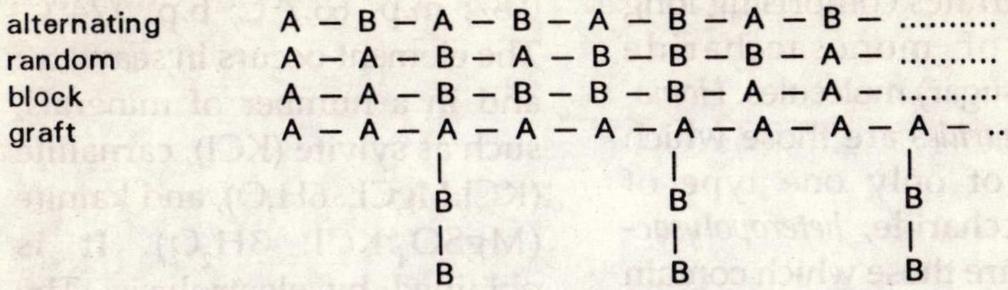

Types of copolymer depending on the arrangement of the monomers A and B

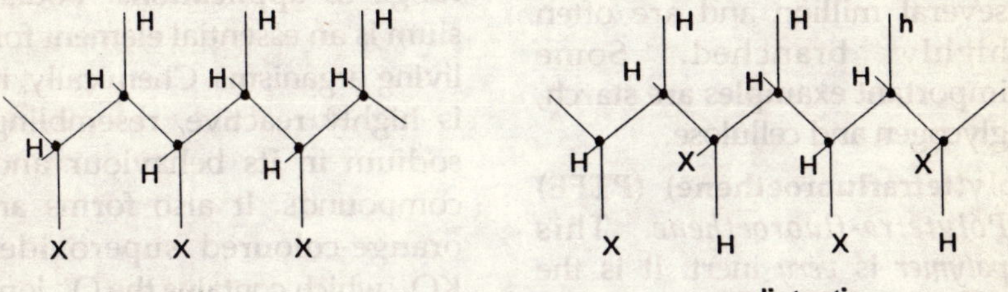

Types of stereospecific polymer
Polymers

polymerization A chemical reaction in which molecules join together to form a polymer. If the reaction is an addition reaction, the process is *addition polymerization;* condensation reactions cause *condensation polymerization,* in which a small molecule is eliminated

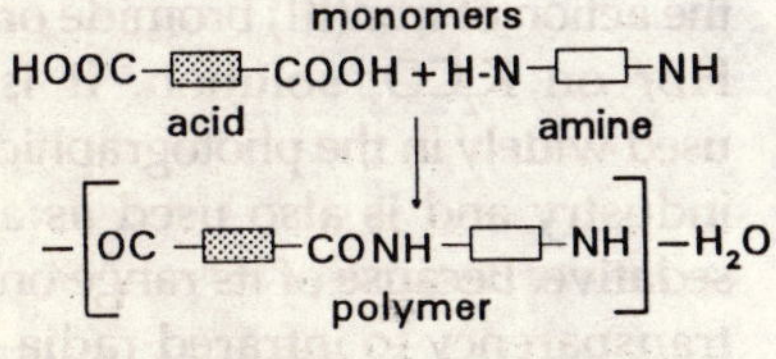

polymers Condensation polymerization.

during the reaction. Polymers consisting of a single monomer are called *homopolymers; while* those formed from two different monomers are *copolymers.*

polypropene also called as polypropylene) A synthetic polymer made from propene. It is similar in properties to polythene, but stronger and lighter. The propene is polymerized by the Ziegler process.

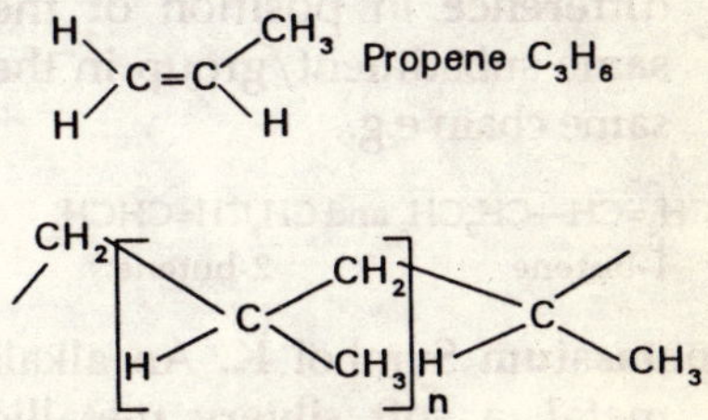

poly(propene)

poly(propene)

polysaccharide Any of a group of carbohydrates comprising long chains of monosaccharide (simple-sugar) molecules. *Homopolysaccharides* are those which consist of only one type of monosaccharide; *heteropolysaccharides* are those which contain two or more different types. Polysaccharides may have molecular weights of up to several million and are often highly branched. Some important examples are starch, glycogen and cellulose.

poly(tetrafluoroethene) (PTFE) *Polytetra-fluoroethene.* This *polymer* is *very* inert. It is the non-stick surface for saucepans, for example, *Teflon, Fluon.* It is also used for bearings and replacement joints in the body because it has low coefficient of friction.

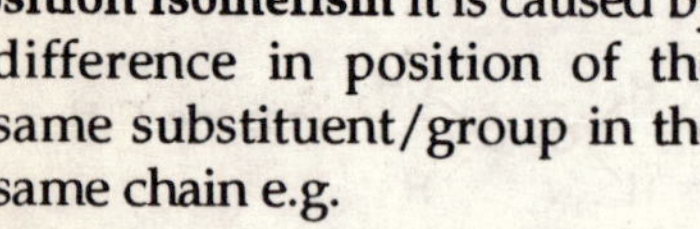

poly(tetrafluoroethene)

position isomerism It is caused by difference in position of the same substituent/group in the same chain e.g.

$CH_2=CH—CH_2CH_3$ and $CH_3CH=CHCH_3$
1-butene 2-butene

potassium Symbol **K**. An alkali metal, a soft silvery metallic element belonging to group I *'s'* block of the periodic table (alkali metals); a.n. 19; r.a.m. 39.098; r.d. 0.87; m.p. 63.7°C; b.p. 774°C. The element occurs in seawater and in a number of minerals, such as sylvite (KCl), carnallite ($KCl.MgCl_2.6H_2O$), and kainite ($MgSO_4.KCl.3H_2O$). It is obtained by electrolysis. The metal has few uses but potassium salts are used for a wide range of applications. Potassium is an essential element for living organisms. Chemically, it is highly reactive, resembling sodium in its behaviour and compounds. It also forms an orange-coloured superoxide, KO_2, which contains the O_2^- ion. Potassium was discovered by Sir Humphry Davy in 1807.

potassium bromide A white or colourless crystalline solid, KBr, slightly hygroscopic and soluble in water and very slightly soluble in ethanol; cubic; r.d. 2.73; m.p. 734°C; b.p. 1435°C. Potassium bromide may be prepared by the action of bromine on hot KOH solution or by the action of iron(III) bromide or HBr on K_2CO_3 solution. It is used widely in the photographic industry and is also used as a sedative. Because of its range on transparency to infrared radiation, KBr is used both as a matrix for solid samples and as a prism material in infrared spectroscopy.

potassium carbonate, K_2CO_3 (Pearl Ash) A white hygroscopic solid m.p. = 1173K.

potassium chlorate A colourless crystalline compound, having molecular formula $KClO_3$, which is soluble in water and moderately soluble in ethyl alcohol (CH_3CH_2OH) monoclinic; r.d. 2.33; m.p. 360°C; decomposes above 400°C giving off oxygen. The industrial route to potassium chlorate involves the fractional crystallization of a solution of potassium chloride and sodium chlorate but it may also be prepared by electrolysis of hot concentrated solutions of potassium chloride. It is a powerful oxidizing agent finding applications in weedkillers and disinfectants and, because of its ability to produce oxygen, it is used in explosives, pyrotechnics, and matches.

potassium chromate It is a bright yellow crystalline solid, having molecular formula K_2CrO_4, soluble in water and insoluble in alcohol; rhombic; r.d. 2.73; m.p. 971°C; decomposes without boiling. It is produced industrially by roasting powdered chromite ore with potash and limestone and leaching the resulting cinder with hot potassium sulphate solution. Potassium chromate is used in leather finishing, as a textile mordant, and in enamels and pigments. In the laboratory it is used as an analytical reagent and as an indicator. Like other chromium(III) compounds it is toxic when ingested or inhaled.

potassium cyanide, KCN A white solid m.p. = 926K. It is quite hygroscopic and is highly poisonous in nature. It is used in electroplating and in metallurgy of gold and silver.

potassium dichromate (potassium bichromate) An orange-red crystalline solid having molecular formula $K_2Cr_2O_7$, soluble in water and insoluble in alcohol; monoclinic or triclinic; r.d. 2.67; monoclinic changes to triclinic at 241.6°C; m.p. 396°C; decomposes above 500°C. It is prepared by acidification of crude potassium chromate solution (the addition of a base to solutions of potassium dichromate reverses this process). The compound is used industrially as an oxidizing agent in the chemical industry and in dyestuffs manufacture, in electroplating, pyrotechnics, glass manufacture, glues, tanning, photography and lithography, and in ceramic products. In laboratory, it is used as an analytical reagent and as an oxidizing agent. Potassium dichromate is toxic and considered a fire risk on account of its oxidizing properties.

potassium hydride (KH) A white ionic solid prepared by passing hydrogen over heated potassium, the metal being suspended in an inert medium. It is an excellent reducing agent.

potassium hydrogencarbonate (potassium bicarbonate) A white crystalline solid, $KHCO_3$, soluble in water and insoluble in ethyl alcohol; r.d. 2.17; decomposes about 120°C. It occurs naturally as *calcinite* and is prepared by passing carbon dioxide into saturated potassium carbonate solution. It is used in baking, soft-drinks manufacture, and in CO_2 fire extinguishers. Because of its buffering capacity, it is added to some detergents and also used as a laboratory reagent.

potassium hydroxide (KOH) Commonly known as caustic potash, a white solid manufactured by the electrolysis of potassium chloride solution in a mercury-cathode cell. It can also be prepared by heating either potassium carbonate or potassium sulphate with slaked lime. The process closely resembles the Gossage process for making sodium hydroxide. In the laboratory, it can be made by reacting potassium, potassium monoxide, or potassium superoxide with water. Potassium hydroxide resembles sodium hydroxide but is more soluble in water and alcohol. It is preferred to sodium hydroxide for the absorption of carbon dioxide and sulphur dioxide because of its greater solubility. Potassium hydroxide is used as an electrolyte in the Ni-Fe electric storage battery and in the production of soft soaps.

It forms crystalline hydrates with 1, 1½, and 2 molecules of water.

potassium iodate A white crystalline solid KIO_3, soluble in water and insoluble in ethyl alcohol (C_2H_5OH); monoclinic; r.d. 3.9; m.p. 561°C. It may be prepared by the reaction of iodine with hot concentrated potassium hydroxide or by careful electrolysis of potassium iodide solution. It is an oxidizing agent and is used as an analytical reagent. Some potassium iodate is used as a food additive.

potassium iodide A white crystalline solid KI, with a strong bitter taste, soluble in water, ethyl alcohol and acetone; cubic; r.d. 3.12; m.p. 686°C; b.p. 1330°C. It may be prepared by the reaction of iodine with hot potassium hydroxide solution followed by separation from the iodate (which is also formed) by fractional crytallization. In solution it has the interesting property of dissolving iodine to form the triiodide ion I_3^-, which is brown. Potassium iodide is widely used as an analytical reagent, in photography, and also as an additive to table salt to prevent goitre and other disorders due to iodine deficiency.

potassium manganate(VII) (potassium permanganate, $KMnO_4$) A purple solid soluble in water. It is prepared by oxidizing potassium manganate (VI) with chlorine. Potassium permanganate is used in volumetric analysis as an oxidizing agent, as a bactericide, and as a disinfectant. In aqueous solution its behaviour as an oxidizing agent depends on the pH of the solution.

potassium monoxide A grey crystalline solid, K_2O; cubic; r.d. 2.32; decomposition occurs at 350°C. It can be prepared by the oxidation of potassium metal with potassium nitrate. It reacts with ethyl alcohol to form potassium ethoxide (KOC_2H_5), and with liquid ammonia to form potassium hydroxide and potassamide (KNH_2).

potassium nitrate, KNO_3 A white needle like crystals. It is commonly known as salt petre. It is used in food preservation and also in explosives (gun powder, fire-works etc.)

potassium nitrite (KNO_2) A creamy deliquescent solid that is readily soluble in water. It reacts with cold dilute mineral acids to produce solutions of nitrous acid. Potassium nitrite is used in organic chemistry in the process of diazotization.

potassium sulphate A white crystalline powder, K_2SO_4, soluble in water and insoluble in ethyl alcohol; rhombic or hexagonal; r.d. 2.66; m.p. 1072°C. It occurs naturally as *schonite* (Strassfurt deposits) and in lake brines, from which it is separated by fractional crystallization. It has also been produced by the Hargreaves process, which involves the oxidation of potassium chloride with sulphuric acid. In the laboratory it may be obtained by the reaction of either potassium hydroxide or potassium carbonate with sulphuric acid. Potassium sulphate is used in cements, in glass manufacture, as a food additive, and as a fertilizer (source of K^+) for chloride-sensitive plants, such as tobacco and citrus.

potassium sulphide (K_2S) A yellowish-brown solid prepared by saturating an aqueous solution of potassium hydroxide with hydrogen sulphide and then adding an equal volume of potassium hydroxide.

$$\underset{(aq)}{2KOH} + H_2S \rightarrow K_2S + 2H_2O$$

Industrially it is produced by heating potassium sulphate and carbon at high temperature. The sulphide crystallizes out from aqueous solution as $K_2S.5H_2O$. Its aqueous solutions undergo hydrolysis, the solution being strongly alkaline.

potassium superoxide (potassium dioxide) A yellow paramagnetic solid, KO_2, produced by burning potassium in an excess of oxygen; it is very soluble (by reaction) in water, soluble in ethyl alcohol and slightly soluble in diethyl ether. m.p. 490°C. When treated with cold water or dilute mineral acids, hydrogen peroxide is obtained. The compound is a powerful oxidizing agent and on strong heating releases oxygen with the formation of the monoxide, K_2O.

potential barrier A region containing a maximum of potential that prevents a particle on one side of it from passing to the other side. According to classical theory a particle must possess energy in excess of the height of the potential barrier to pass it. However, in quantum theory there is a finite probability that a particle with less energy will pass through the barrier (*see* tunnel effect). A potential barrier surrounds the atomic nucleus and is important in nuclear physics; a similar but much lower barrier exists at the interface between semiconductors and metals and between differently doped semiconductors. These barriers are important in the design of electronic devices.

potentiometric titration Titration operations (acid-base, Redox, precipitation and complexation) are carried out by measuring the e.m.f. of a cell (or battery) consisting of an appropriate indicating electrode, the potential of which depends upon the activity of one of the ions concerned in the titration reaction, and by a reference electrode connected by a salt bridge.

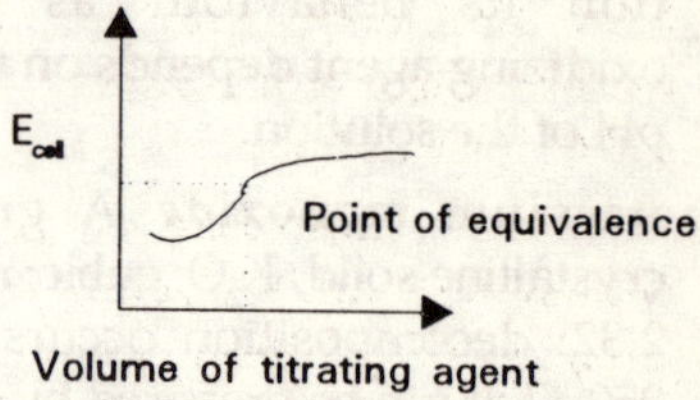

Variation in the e.m.f. of one cell during potentiometric titration, the drawing shows a generic curve of potentiometric titration.

powder metallurgy A process in which powdered metals or alloys are pressed into a variety of shapes at high temperatures. The process started with the pressing of powdered tungsten into incandescent lamp filaments in the first decade of this century and is now widely used for making self-lubricating bearings and cemented tungsten carbide cutting tools.

The powders are produced by atomization of molten metals, chemical decomposition of a compound of the metal, or crushing and grinding of the metal or alloy. The parts are pressed into moulds at pressures ranging from 140×10^6 Pa to 830 × 10^6 Pa after which they are heated in a controlled atomosphere to bond the particles together.

praseodymium Symbol Pr. A soft silvery metallic element belonging to the lanthanoids 'f 'block element, a.n. 59; r.a.m. 140.91; r.d. 6.769 (20°C); m.p. 934°C; b.p. 3512°C. It occurs in bastnasite and monazite, from which it is recovered by an ion-exchange process. The only naturally occurring isotope is praseodymium-141, which is not radioactive; however, fourteen radioisotopes have been produced. It is used in misch-metal, a rare-earth alloy containing 5% praseodymium, for use in lighter flints. Another rare-earth mixture containing 30% praseodymium is used as a catalyst in cracking crude oil. The element was discovered by C.A. von Welsbach in 1885.

precipitate A suspension of small particles of a solid in a liquid formed by a chemical reaction is known as a precipitate.

precipitation 1. All liquid and solid forms of water that are deposited from the atmosphere; it includes rain, drizzle, snow, hail, dew and hoar frost. **2.** The formation of a precipitate.

precursor A compound that leads to another compound in a series of chemical reactions.

pressure It is the measure of the force pressing onto an object's surface. The *SI unit* of pressure is the *pascal.* Other units used are *atmospheres* and mmHg.

The pressure that a *gas* exerts upon its container is caused by *molecules* striking the container's walls. The pressure of a gas is dependent on its *volume* and its temperature.

primary cell A voltaic cell in which the chemical reaction producing the e.m.f. is not satisfactorily reversible and the cell cannot, therefore, be recharged by the application of a charging current. (Daniell cell; Leclanche cell; Weston cell; mercury cell.)

principle quantum number Its symbol is 'n'. It specifies the location and energy of an electron. It can have any integral value except zero. It gives the average distance of electron from the nucleus, n = 1 is the energy level closest to the nucleus and is called 1st orbit (shell) or K-orbit. Energy of electron increases with increase in value of n.

producer gas (air gas) A mixture of CO and N_2 made by passing air over very hot carbon. Usually some steam is added to the air and mixture contains hydrogen. The gas is used as a fuel in some industrial processes.

promethium Symbol: Pm; m.p. 1168°C (approx.); b.p. 2460°C (approx.); r.d. 7.22; a.n. 61; stablest isotope ^{145}Pm (half-life 18 years). A radioactive element of the lanthanoid series '*f*' block of metals. It is not found naturally on Earth but can be produced artificially by the fission of uranium. Possible uses involve its radioactive properties.

promoter A substance added to a catalyts to increase its activity.

propanal (propionaldehyde, C_2H_5CHO) A colourless liquid aldehyde. It can be prepared by oxidation of propanol.

$$\underset{\text{Propanol}}{C_2H_5CH_2OH} + [O] \xrightarrow{K_2Cr_2O_7} \underset{\text{Propanal}}{C_2H_5CHO} + H_2O$$

propane (C_3H_8) An *alkane* which is obtained from *petroleum*. It is chiefly used as a *fuel:*

$$C_3H_8(g) + 5O_2(g) \rightarrow 3CO_2(g) + 4H_2O(g)$$

Although a *gas* at *room temperature*, it is easily liquefied and it is sold as bottled gas, e.g. *Calor Gas or Camping Gas* where it is mixed with *butane.*

C_3H_8

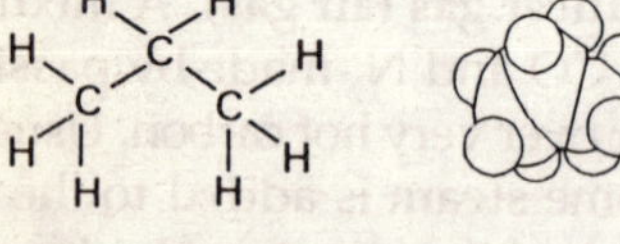

propane

propanoic acid (propionic acid) A colourless liquid carboxylic acid, CH_3CH_2COOH. It can be prepared by oxidation of propanal.

$$\underset{\text{Propanol}}{CH_3CH_2CH_2OH} \xrightarrow{[O]} \underset{\text{Propanal}}{CH_3CH_2CHO} \xrightarrow{[O]} \underset{\text{Propanoic acid}}{CH_3CH_2COOH}$$

r.d. 0.99; m.p. –20.8°C; b.p. 141°C. It is used to make calcium propanate – an additive in bread.

propanone (acetone) A colourless flammable volatile compound, CH_3COCH_3; r.d. 0.79; m.p. –95.4°C; b.p. 56.2°C. The simplest ketone, propanone is miscible with water. It is made by oxidation of propan -2-ol.

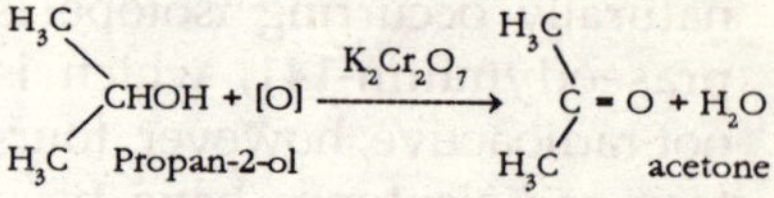

(*see* propanol) or is obtained as a by-product in the manufacture of phenol from cumene; it is used as a solvent and as a raw material for making plastics.

propene hydrocarbon gas with formula C_3H_6. Propene is an *alkene* which is the *monomer* of the important *polymer, poly (propene).*

propenoic acid also known as **(acrylic acid)** An unsaturated liquid carboxylic acid, CH_2:CHCOOH; m.p. 7°C; b.p. 141°C. It readily polymerizes and it is used in the manufacture of acrylic resins.

propenonitrile (acrylonitrile; vinyl cyanide) A colourless liquid, H_2C:CHCN; r.d. 0.81; m.p. –83.5°C. It is an unsaturated nitrile, made from propene and used to make acrylic resins.

protactinium Symbol Pa. A radioactive metallic element belonging to the actinoids; a.n. 91; r.a.m. 231.036; r.d. 15.37 (calculated); m.p. <1600°C (estimated). The most stable isotope, protactinium—231, has a half-life of 3.43×10^4 years; ten other radioisotopes are known. Protactinium—231 occurs in all uranium ores as it is a member of the uranium series. Protactinium has no practical applications; it was discovered by Lise Meitner and Otto Hahn in 1917.

proteins These are the large, organic compounds made up of *chains* of *amino* acids. The *amino acids* are joined by *peptide* links. They are widespread in animal bodies: skin, hair, nail, wool, gristle, muscle.

Proteins form a vital part of our diet. Good sources are: meat, nuts, fish, eggs, milk, cheese, beans, bread. The *enzymes* which play so important a role in living organisms are made up of protein molecules. Animals obtain the food which they need in order to make proteins in their bodies by eating other animals or plants. Plants *make* proteins from the *nitrogen*-containing compounds in the soil.

protein synthesis The process by which living cells manufacture proteins from their constituent amino acids, in accordance with the genetic information carried in the DNA of the chromosomes. This information is encoded in messenger RNA, which is transcribed from DNA in the nucleus of the cell; the sequence of amino acids in a particular protein is determined by the sequence of nucleotides in messenger RNA. At the ribosomes the information carried by messenger RNA is translated into the sequence of amino acids of the protein in the process of translation.

proton An elementary particle that is stable, bears a positive charge equal in magnitude to that of the electron, and has a mass of 1.672614×10^{-27} kg, which is 1836.12 times that of the electron. The proton is a hydrogen ion and occurs in all atomic nuclei.

proton number (atomic number) Symbol: Z The number of protons in the nucleus of an atom. The proton number determines the chemical properties of the element because the electron structure, which determines chemical bonding, depends on the electrostatic attraction to the positively charged nucleus. e.g.:

For Sodium z = 11
Oxygen z = 8

pseudoaromatic A compound that has a ring of atoms containing alternating double and single bonds, yet does not have the characteristic properties of aromatic compounds. Such compounds do not obey the Huckel rule. Cyclooctatetraene (C_8H_8), for instance, has a ring of eight carbon atoms with conjugated double bonds, but the ring is not planar and the compound acts like an alkene, undergoing addition reactions.

pseudohalogens A group of compounds, including cyanogen $(CN)_2$ and thiocyanogen $(SCN)_2$, that have some resemblance to the halogens. Thus they form hydrogen acids (HCN and HSCN) and ionic salts containing such ions as CN^- and SCN^-.

pseudo order An order of a chemical reaction that appears to be less than the true order because of the experimental conditions used. Pseudo orders occur when one reactant is present in large amount. For example, a reaction of substance A undergoing hydrolysis may appear to be proportional only to [A] because the amount of water present is so large.

ptyalin An enzyme that digests carbohydrates (amylase). It is present in mammalian saliva and is responsible for the initial stages of starch digestion.

pure Containing only one *element* or *compound*. For example, sodium chloride crystals can be obtained in a pure state, but table salt is impure because it is mixed with other substances.

purine, $C_5H_4N_4$ A white crystalline solid (m.p. = 489K). Its derivatives are of biological importance since they occur in ATP and nucleic acids. e.g. Adenine and guanine.

pyridine It is a colourless liquid with a strong unpleasant smell, C_5H_5N; r.d. 0.9; m.p. –42°C; b.p. 115°C. Pyridine is an aromatic heterocyclic compound present in coal tar. It is used in making other organic chemicals.

pyrogallol A white crystalline solid (m.p.=405K). It is a powerful reducing agent. Oxygen is rapidly absorbed by its alkaline solution. It is used in photography for developing and in gas analysis for the estimation of oxygen.

pyrometer An instrument used in the chemical industry to measure high temperature, e.g. in reactor vessels.

pyrometry The measurement of high temperatures (beyond the range of thermometers) using a *pyrometer*. Modern *narrow-band* or *spectral* pyrometers use infrared-sensitive photoelectric cells behind filters that exclude visible light. In the *optical pyrometer* (or disappearing filament pyrometer) the image of the incandescent source is focused in the plane of a tungsten filament that is heated electrically. A variable resistor is used to adjust the current through the filament until it blends into the image of the source, when viewed through a red filter and an eyepiece. The temperature is then read from a calibrated ammeter or a calibrated dial on the variable resistor. In the *total-radiation pyrometer* radiation emitted by the source is focused by a concave mirror onto a blackened foil to which a thermopile is attached. From the e.m.f. produced by the thermopile the temperature of the source can be calculated.

pyrophoric (a) Describing a compound that ignites spontaneously in air.

(b) Describing a metal or alloy that gives sparks when struck. (Lighter flints are made of pyrophoric alloy).

Q

Quadrivalent A substance having a valency of four.

quadruple point It is the point at which four phases of a system can coexist.

qualitative analysis The analysis carried out with the purpose of identifying the components of a sample. Classical methods involved simple preliminary tests followed by a carefully devised scheme of systematic tests and procedures. Modern methods include the use of such techniques such as infrared spectroscopy and emission spectography. *Compare* quantitative analysis.

quantitative analysis The analysis to find the quantities of various components present in a compound, for example H_2O contains two atoms of hydrogen and one atom of oxygen.

quantized Describing a physical quantity that can only take certain discreet values, and not a continuous range of values. Thus, in an atom or molecule the electrons around the nucleus can have certain energies, E_1, E_2, etc., and cannot have intermediate values. Similarly, in atoms and molecules, the electrons have quantized values of spin angular momentum and orbital angular momentum.

quantum The minimum amount by which certain properties, such as energy or angular momentum, of a system can change. Such properties do not, therefore, vary continuously, but in integral multiples of the relevant quantum. This concept forms the basis of the quantum theory. In waves and fields the quantum can be regarded as an excitation, giving a particle-like interpretation to the wave or field. Thus, the quantum of the electromagnetic field is the photon and the graviton is the quantum of the gravitational field. (*See* quantum mechanics)

quantum mechanics A system of mechanics which was developed from quantum theory. It is used to explain the properties of atoms and molecules. Using the energy quantum as a starting point it incorporates Heisenberg's uncertainty principle and the de Broglie wavelength to establish the wave-particle duality on which Schrodinger's equation is based. This form of quantum mechanics is called *wave mechanics.* An alternative but equivalent formalism, *matrix mechanics,* is based on mathematical operators.

quantum number An integer or half integer that specifies the value of a quantized physical quantity, for example, (energy, angular momentum, etc.).

quantum state The state of a quantized system as described by its quantum numbers. For instance, the state of a hydrogen atom is described by the four quantum numbers n, l, m, m_s. In the ground state they have values 1, 0,1, and ½ respectively.

quantum statistics A statistical description of a system of particles that obeys the rules of quantum mechanics and not that of classical mechanics. In quantum statistics, energy states are considered to be quantized. If the particles are treated as indistinguishable, *Bose-Einstein statistics* apply if any number of particles can occupy a given quantum state. Such particles are called *bosons.* All known bosons have an angular momentum nh, where n is zero or an integer and h is the Planck constant. For identical bosons the wave function is always symmetric. If only one particle may occupy each quantum state, *Fermi-Dirac statistics* apply and the particles are called *fermions.* All known fermions have a total angular momentum $(n+½)\ h/2\pi$ and any wave function that involves identical fermions is always antisymmetric.

quantum theory This was put forward by Max Planck. It states that absorption or emission of energy occurs in discrete units (quantas) and not continuously.

quartz The transparent *mineral* form of *silica* (silicon oxide SiO_2). It is used in optical instruments such as microscopes and spectroscopes More *u.v. radiation* passes through quartz than through *glass.*

quaternary ammonium compound A compound formed from an amine by addition of a proton to produce a positive ion. Quaternary compounds are salts, the simplest example being ammonium compounds formed from ammonia and an acid, for example:

$$NH_3 + HC1 \longrightarrow NH_4^+C1^-$$

Other amines can also add protons to give analogous compounds. For instance methylamine (CH_3NH_2) forms the compound.

$$[CH_3NH_3]^+X^-$$

where X^- is an acid radical.

The formation of quaternary compounds occurs because the lone pair on the nitrogen atom can form a coordinate bond with a proton. This can also occur with heterogeneous nitrogen compounds, such as adenine, cytosine, thymine, and guanine. Such compounds are known as *nitrogenous bases.*

quenching (a) (in metallurgy) The rapid cooling of a metal by immersing it in a bath of liquid in order to improve its properties. Steels are quenched to make them harder but some non-ferrous metals are quenched for other reasons (copper, for example, is made softer by quenching). (b) (in physics) The process of inhibiting a continuous discharge in a Geiger counter so that the incidence of further ionizing radiation can cause a new discharge. This is achieved by introducing a quenching vapour, such as ether or a halogen gas into the tube.

quicklime The common name of calcium oxide (CaO).

quinhydrone electrode A half-cell consisting of a platinum electrode in an equimolar solution of quinone (cyclohexadiene-1,4,-dione) and hydroquinone (benzene-1,4-diol). It depends on the redox reaction

$$C_6H_4(OH)_2 \rightleftharpoons C_6H_4O_2 + 2H^+ + 2e$$

R

Racemic mixture (racemate) A mixture of equal quantities of the dextrorotatory and laevorotatory forms of an optically active compound. Racemic mixtures are denoted by the prefix *dl (eg. dl*-lactic acid). A racemic mixture shows no optical activity. *See* optical activity.

racemization It is a chemical reaction in which an optically active compound is converted into racemic mixture (*dl*).

rad It is a unit of energy. It is used to measure (express) the energy absorbed from radiation by tissue or some other biological material.

1 rad=1×10^{-2} J/Kg of material.

radiation 1. Energy travelling in the form of electromagnetic waves or photons. 2. A stream of particles, especially alpha-or beta-particles from a radioactive source or neutrons from a nuclear reactor.

radiation units Units are the measurement which are used to express the activity of a radionuclide and the dose of ionizing radiation. The units *curie,roentgen, rad,* and *rem* are not coherent with SI units but their temporary use with SI units has been approved while the derived SI units *becquerel, gray,* and *sievert* be- come familiar.

The becquerel (Bq), the SI unit of activity, is the activity of a radionuclide decaying at a rate, on average, of one spontaneous nuclear transition per second. Thus 1 Bq=1 s^{-1} . The former unit, the curie (Ci), is equal to 3.7×10^{10} Bq. The curie was originally chosen to approximate the activity of 1 gram of radium-226.

The gray (Gy), the SI unit of absorbed dose, is the absorbed dose when the energy per unit mass imparted to matter by ionizing radiation is 1 J kg^{-1}. The former unit, the rad (rd), is equal to 10^{-2} Gy.

The sievert (Sv), the SI unit of dose equivalent, is the dose equivalent when the absorbed dose of ionizing radiation multiplied by the stipulated dimensionless factors is 1 J kg^{-1}. As different types of radiation cause different effects in biological tissue a weighted absorbed dose, called the *dose equivalent,* is used in which the absorbed dose is modified by multiplying it by dimensionless factors stipulated by the International Commission on Radiological Protection. The former unit of dose equivalent, the rem (originally an acronym for roentgen equivalent *man)*, is equal to 10^{-2} Sv.

In SI units, exposure to ionizing radiation is expressed in coulombs per kilogram, the quantity of X- or gamma-radiation that produces ion pairs carrying 1 coulomb of charge of either sign in 1 kilogram of pure dry air. The former unit, the roentgen (R) equal to 2.58×10^{-4} C kg^{-1}.

radical Organic compounds may be considered to consist of two parts, functional group and alkyl radical e.g. $C_2H_5NH_2$ consists of amino (—NH_2) group and ethyl (–C_2H_5) radical, CH_3 COOH consists of carboxylic (–COOH) group and methyl (–CH_3) radical. A radical can be defined as an atom or group of atoms, present in a series of compounds, that maintains its identity during chemical changes during which rest of the molecule undergoes changes. e.g. NH_4^+, – C_2H_5 etc.

radioactive age It is the age of an archaeological or geological specimen as determined by a process that depends on a radioactive decay. (carbon dating; fission-track dating; potassium-argon dating; rubidium-strontium dating; uranium-lead dating.)

radioactive elements Those elements which exhibit the phenomenon of radioactivity are known as radioactive elements e.g. Ra, U, Th etc.

radioactive series A series of radioactive nuclides in which each member of the series is formed by the decay of the nuclide before it. The series ends with a stable nuclide. Three radioactive series occur naturally, those headed by thorium-232 *(thorium series)*, uranium-235 *(actinium series)*, and uranium-238 *(uranium series)*. All three series end with an isotope of lead. The *neptunium series* starts with the artificial isotope plutonium-241, which decays to neptunium-237, and ends with bismuth-209.

radioactivity The spontaneous disintegration of the *nucleus* of an *atom* accompanied by the emission of electromagnetic radiation *(gamma rays)* or particles *(alpha* or *beta particles)* is known as radioactivity.

All *elements* do not have radioactive *isotopes*, though many can now be created artificially. Some radioactivity occurs naturally, e.g. isotopes found within rocks. *Granite* usually has quite a large concentration. Living things contain radioactive *carbon* and this can be used for finding the age of their remains.

radiochemistry It is the branch of chemistry that is concerned with the study and application of chemical techniques of purification of radioactive materials and the formation of compounds containing radioactive elements.

radiolysis A chemical reaction produced by high-energy radiation for example (X-rays, gamma rays, or particles).

radium Symbol Ra. A radioactive metallic element belonging to group II *'s'* block of the periodic table; atomic number 88; r.a.m. 226.0254; r.d. ~5; m.p. 700°C; b.p. 1140°C. It occurs in uranium ores (e.g. pitchblende). The most stable isotope is radium-226 (half-life 1602 years), which decays to radon. It is used as a radioactive source in research and, to some extent, in radiotherapy. The element was isolated from pitchblende in 1898 by Marie and Pierre Curie.

radon Symbol Rn. a.n. 86; r.a.m. 222; d. 9.73 g dm^{-3}; m.p. –71°C; b.p. –61.8°C. A colourless radioactive gaseous element belonging to group 0 *'p'* block element of the periodic table (the noble gases). At least 20 isotopes are known, the most stable being radon-222 (half-life 3.8 days). It is formed by decay of radium-226 and undergoes alpha decay. It is used in radiotherapy. As a noble gas, radon is practically inert, although radon fluoride can be made. It was first isolated by Ramsey and Gray in 1908.

raney nickel A type of nickel which is spongy and is used as a catalyst especially in hydrogenation of oils. It is obtained by dissolving aluminium in nickel-aluminium alloy with some sodium hydroxide (NaOH).

ranksite A mineral consisting of a mixed sodium carbonate, sodium sulphate, and potassium chloride, $2Na_2CO_3.9Na_2SO_4.KCl$.

Raoult's law It gives the relationship between the pressure exerted by the vapour of a solution and the presence of a solute. It states that the partial vapour pressure of a solvent above a solution (p) is proportional to the mole fraction of the solvent in the solution (X) and that the proportionality constant is the vapour pressure of pure solvent, (p_0), at the given temperature: i.e. $p = p_0X$. Solutions that obey Raoult's law are said to be *ideal* solutions and which do not obey Raoult's law are called non-ideal solutions. There are some binary solutions for which Raoult's law holds over all values of X for either component. Such solutions are said to be *perfect* and this behaviour occurs when the intermolecular attraction between molecules within one component is almost identical to the attraction of molecules of one component for molecules of the other (for example chlorobenzene/bromobenzene). Because of solvation forces this behaviour is rare and in general Raoult's law holds only for dilute solutions.

For solutions that are ideal but not perfect the solute behaviour is similar in that the partial pressure of the solute, P_s, is proportional to the mole fraction of the solute, X_s, but in this case the proportionality constant, P', is not the vapour pressure of the pure solute but must be determined experimentally for each system. This solute equivalent of Raoult's law has the form $P_s = P'X_s$, and is called Henry's law. Because of intermolecular attractions P' is usually less than P_0.

rasch parameter It refers to the parameter used to express quantitatively the inter-electronic repulsion between various energy levels of an atom.

raschig process An industrial process for making chlorobenzene (and phenol) by a gas-phase reaction between benzene vapour, hydrogen chloride, and oxygen (air) at 230°C

$$2C_6H_6 + 2HCl + O_2 \rightarrow 2H_2O + 2C_6H_5Cl$$

The catalyst is copper(II) chloride. The chlorobenzene is mainly used for making phenol by the reaction

$$C_6H_5Cl + H_2O \rightarrow HCl + C_6H_5OH$$

This reaction proceeds at 763K with a silicon catalyst.

rate constant (velocity constant) It is denoted by 'k'. The constant in an expression for the rate of a chemical reaction in terms of concentrations (or activities). For instance, in a simple unimolecular reaction

$$A \rightarrow B$$

the rate is proportional to the concentration of A, i.e.

$$\text{rate} = k[A]$$

where k is the rate constant, which depends on the temperature. The equation is the *rate equation* of the reaction, and its form depends on the reaction mechanism.

rate equation It is a mathematical expression that gives the relationship between the rate of a reaction and concentration of reactants. For a general reaction

$$A + B \rightarrow C + D$$

$$\text{Rate} = -\frac{d[A]}{dt} = -\frac{d[B]}{dt} = +\frac{d[C]}{dt} = +\frac{d[C]}{dt}$$

This is called rate equation.

rate-determining step It is the slowest step in a chemical reaction that involves a number of steps. In such reactions, there is often a single step that is appreciably slower than the other steps, and the rate of this determines the overall rate of the reaction.

rate of radioactive decay It is given by

$$N_1 = N_0 e^{-\lambda t}$$

or $$\log = \frac{N_0}{N_1} = \frac{\lambda . t}{2.303}$$

or $$\lambda = \frac{2.303}{t} \log \frac{N_0}{N_1}$$

where N_0 = number of radioactive nuclei present initially.

N_1 = number of radioactive nuclei after time t.

λ = disintegration constant.

rate of reaction A measure of the amount of reactant used in a chemical reaction in unit time is called the rate of reaction. It is thus a measure of the number of effective collisions between reactant molecules per unit time. The rate at which a reaction proceeds can be measured by the rate the reactants disappear or by the rate at which the products are formed. The principal factors affecting the rate of reaction are temperature, pressure, concentration of reactants, light, and the action of a catalyst. The units usually used to measure the rate of a reaction are mol dm^{-3} s^{-1}.

rationalized units It is a system of units in which the defining equations have been made to conform to the geometry of the system in a logical way. Thus, equations that involve circular symmetry contain the factor 2π, while those involving spherical symmetry contain the factor 4π. SI units are rationalized; c.g.s. units are unrationalized.

raw materials Materials used as the starting point in the production of chemicals or manufactured goods. The major raw materials used in the UK chemical industry are:

(a) *Hydrocarbons;*

(b) *Air;*

(c) *Metallic ores;*

(d) *Minerals;*

(e) *Water.*

For example, the raw material in the production of chlorine is *rock salt* which is then dissolved in water and electrolysed. In the production of *ammonia,* the raw materials used in the UK are *natural gas* and *air.*

rayon A textile made from cellulose. There are two types, viscose rayon and acetate rayon, both made from wood pulp. In the viscose process, the pulp is dissolved in carbon disulphide and sodium hydroxide to give a thick brown liquid containing cellulose xanthate. The liquid is then forced through fine nozzles into acid, where the xanthate is decomposed and a cellulose filament is produced. The product is *viscose rayon.* In the acetate process cellulose acetate is made and dissolved in a solvent. The solution is forced through nozzles into air, where the solvent quickly evaporates leaving a filament of *acetate rayon.*

reactant These are the compounds taking part in a chemical reaction.

reagent It is the substance that is used to produce a chemical reaction with a certain chemical. For example, $AgNO_3$ is a reagent that is used to test the presence of halides in a solution. It reacts with halides and forms a ppt. of silver halides.

rearrangement A type of chemical reaction in which the atoms in a molecule rearrange to form a new molecule.

rectification The process of purifying a liquid by distillation.

rectified spirit A constant-boiling mixture of ethyl alcohol (C_2H_5OH) (95.6°) and water; it is obtained by distillation.

redox indicator Any compound which undergoes a definite colour change during its reversible oxidation or reduction can be used as a redox indicator. Some of the redox indicator are given in table.

Name	*colour (ox)*	*colour (red)*	E^0_{trans} *(in volts) at pH=O*
Diphenyl benzidine	Violet	Colour -less	0.76
4, 7-dimethyl ferroine (in HCl)	Green	Orange	0.88
Ferrone	Blue	Red	1.06
Nitroferrine	Blue	Red violet	1.31

reducing agent also known as **(reductant)** A substance that brings about reduction in other substances and gets itself oxidised. Reducing agents contain atoms with low oxidation numbers; that is the atoms have gained electrons. In reducing other substances, these atoms lose electrons.

reduction It is a process which involves the gain of electrons by an atom or group of atoms.

$$Fe^{3+} + e^- \rightarrow Fe^{2+}$$
$$MnO_4^- \rightarrow MnO_4^{2-}$$

Reduction results in a decrease in positive charge or an increase in negative charge.

Reduction involves addition of hydrogen or removal of oxygen.

$$Cl_2 + H_2 \rightarrow 2HCl$$
$$ZnO + C \rightarrow Zn + CO$$

Reduction can be summerised as follows:

(i) Process of gain of electrons;

(ii) Removal of oxygen;
(iii) Addition of hydrogen.

refining A process for either the removal of impurities from a substance or the removal of components from a mixture is called refining.

(i) **Metals.** When a metal has been extracted from its ores it is often not in a pure state. For some uses this might be acceptable, e.g. pig iron contain impurities. Other uses demand a purer product and then the metal is refined until the right purity is achieved.

(ii) **Petroleum.** A complex *mixture* of *hydrocarbons.* To make it more useful it is first of all split up into separate parts. These parts are known as *fractions* and the separation is done by fractional distillation. The fractions are also mixtures but are not so complicated. They contain compounds whose *boiling points* are within a certain range.

Conditions vary from refinery to refinery and depend on what products are required. The major product might be *petrol* or it might be petrochemical feedstock which is then turned into *alkenes,* etc. for the production of polymers.

refluxing It is a laboratory technique in which a liquid is boiled in a container attached to a condenser *(reflex condenser),* so that the liquid continuously flows back into the container. It is used for carrying out reactions over long periods in organic synthesis.

reforming The cyclization of straight-chain hydrocarbons from crude oil by heating under pressure with a catalyst, usually Pt on alumina. For example, the manufacture of methylbenzene from heptane:

$$\underset{\text{Heptane}}{C_7H_{16}} \rightarrow \underset{\text{methylcyclohexane}}{C_6H_{11}CH_3}$$

This first step is the production of methyl cyclohexane, which then loses six hydrogen atoms to give methylbenzene or toluene.

$$C_6H_{11}CH_3 \rightarrow \underset{\text{Toluene}}{C_6H_5CH_3} + 3H_2$$

refrigeration It is a method of transferring energy from a cool box to the warmer outside air. This is the opposite direction to normal net energy transfer and is achieved by a pump powered by a motor. The pump circulates a special fluid around a closed loop. When the pump raises the fluids' pressure it becomes a liquid and gives off latent heat. At this stage the liquid goes through the black radiator coil outside so that heat can be transferred to air. Further around the loop the liquid is forced through the valve to low pressure side of loop. The lower pressure causes the liquid to evaporate, absorbing latent heat from the surroundings. At this stage the substance is within the cool box. Such methods which transfer heat from one place to another are often called *heat pumps.*

Regnault's method A method used for the determination of the density of gases. A bulb of known volume is evacuated and weighed then the gas is admitted at a known pressure (from a vacuum line) and the bulb weighed again. The temperature is also noted and the data corrected to STP. The method is readily applicable to the obtaining of approximate molecular weights of gaseous samples.

relative atomic mass (atomic weight; r.a.m.) It is denoted by 'A_r'. The ratio of the average mass per atom of the naturally occurring form of an element to 1/12 of the mass of a carbon-12 atom.

relative density (r.d.) The ratio of the density of a substance to the density of some reference substance. For liquids or solids it is the ratio of the density (usually at 293K) to the density of water (at its maximum density). This quantity was formerly called *specific gravity.* Sometimes relative densities of gases are used; for example, relative to dry air, both gases being at S.T.P.

relative lowering of vapour pressure Relative lowering of vapour pressure of a solution is the ratio of lowering of vapour pressure to the vapour pressure of the pure solvent, thus

$$\text{Relative lowering of Vapour pressure} = \frac{P^o - P_s}{P^o}$$

where $P^o - P_s$ is the lowering in vapour pressure and P^o is the vapour pressure of pure solvent.

relative molecular mass Its symbol is 'M_Y'. The ratio of the average mass per molecule of the naturally occurring form of an element or compound to 1/12 of the mass of an atom of nuclide ^{12}C. This was formerly called *molecular weight.* It does not have to be used only for compounds that have discrete molecules; for ionic compounds (e.g. NaCl) and giant-molecular structures (e.g. BN) the formula unit is used.

rennin An enzyme secreted by cells lining the stomach in mammals which is responsible for clotting milk. It acts on a soluble milk protein *(caseinogen),* which it converts to the insoluble form casein. This ensures that milk remains in the stomach long enough to be acted on by protein-digesting enzymes.

residue The waste product remaining after any chemical process is complete is called a residue.

resin It is a synthetic or naturally occurring polymer. Synthetic resins are used in making plastics. Natural resins are acidic chemicals secreted by many trees (especially conifers) into ducts or canals. They are found either as brittle glassy substances or dissolved in essential oils. Their functions are probably similar to those of gums and mucilages.

resistance denoted by **(R)** Resistance of any conductor is the obstruction offered to the flow of current.

$$R \propto l$$

$$R \propto \frac{1}{a}$$

$$\text{or } R = \rho \frac{l}{a}$$

where ρ is the proportionality constant and is known as *specific resistance or resistivity.*

$$\rho = R. \frac{a}{l}$$

units of R - ohms.

where *'l'* is the length of conductor and *'a'* is the area of cross-section.

resolution (of racemates) The process of the separation of a racemate into the two optical isomers. This cannot be done by normal methods, such as crystallization or distillation, because the isomers have identical physical properties. The main methods are:

(a) *Mechanical separation.* Certain optically active compounds form crystals with distinct left and right-handed shapes. The crystals can be sorted out by hand.

(b) *Chemical separation.* The mixture is reacted with an optical isomer. The products are then not optical isomer of each other, and can be separated by physical means. For instance, a mixture of D- and L-forms of an acid, acting with a pure L-base, produces two salts that can be separated by fractional crystallization and then reconverted into the acids.

(c) *Biochemical separation.* Certain organic compounds can be separated by using bacteria that feed on one form only, leaving the other.

resorcinol *See* 1, 3-dihydroxybentene

resonance The representation of the structure of a molecule by two or more conventional formulae. For example, the formula of formaldehyde (HCHO) can be represented by a covalent structure $H_2C = O$, in which there is a double bond in the carbonyl group. It is known that in such compounds the oxygen has some negative charge and the carbon some positive charge. The true bonding in the molecule is somewhere between $H_2C = O$ and the ionic compound $H_2C^+O^-$. It is said to be a *resonance hybrid* of the two, indicated by

$$H_2C = O \leftrightarrow H_2C^+O^-$$

The two possible structures are called *canonical forms,* and they need not contribute equally to the actual form. Note that the double-headed arrow does not imply that the two forms are in equilibrium *See* also bentene.

retort 1. A laboratory apparatus consisting of a glass bulb with a long neck. 2. A vessel used for reaction or distillation in industrial chemical processes.

reverberatory furnace It is a furnace having a low roof above the hearth which helps to direct the heat, from the fire, to the reactants on the hearth. This type of hearth is used for smelting ores.

reverse osmosis A method of obtaining pure water from water containing a salt, as in desalination. Pure water and the salt water are separated by a semipermeable membrane and the pressure of the salt water is raised above the osmotic pressure, causing water from the brine to pass through the membrane into the pure water. This process requires a pressure of some 25 atmospheres, which makes it difficult to apply on a large scale.

reversible reactions The reactions that can go in both directions, that is forward as well as backward, depending on the conditions that exist. For example:

$$Fe_2O_3(s) + 3H_2(g) \Leftrightarrow 2Fe(s) + 3H_2O(g)$$

Steam can react with hot *iron* or *hydrogen* can reduce iron(III) oxide. In both cases, an *equilibrium* will exist with all four substances present unless the products are removed.

rhe A unit of fluidity equal to the reciprocal of the poise.

rhenium Symbol Re. A silvery-white metallic transition element; a.n. 75; r.a.m. 186.2;' r.d. 21.0; m.p. 3180°C; b.p. 5620°C. The element is obtained as a by-product in refining molybdenum, and is used in certain alloys (e.g. rhenium-molybdenum alloys are superconducting). The element forms a number of complexes with oxidation states in the range 1-7.

rhodium Symbol Rh. A silvery-white metallic transition element; (*d*-block element) having atomic number 45; r.a.m. 102.9; r.d. 12.4; m.p. 1966°C; b.p. 3727°C. It occurs with platinum and is used in certain platinum alloys (e.g. for thermocouples) and in plating jewellery and optical reflectors. Chemically, it is not attacked by acids (dissolves only slowly in aqua regia) and reacts with non-metals (e.g. oxygen and chlorine) at red heat. Its main oxidation state is + 3 although it also forms complexes in the + 4 state. The element was discovered in 1803 by W.H. Wollaston.

ribose ($C_5H_{10}O_5$) A monosaccharide; a component of RNA.

ring A closed chain of atoms in a molecule. In compounds, such as naphthalene,

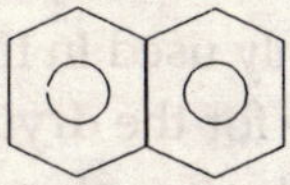

in which two rings share a common side, the rings are *fused rings. Ring closures* are chemical reactions in which one part of a chain reacts with another to form a ring, as in the formation of lactones.

ring closure A reaction in which one part of an open chain in a molecule reacts with another part so that a ring of atoms is formed.

RNA (ribonucleic acid) A complex organic compound (a nucleic acid) in living cells that is concerned with protein synthesis. In some viruses, RNA is also the hereditary material. (Transfer of characters from parents to offsprings) Most RNA is synthesized in the nucleus and then distributed to various parts of the cytoplasm. An RNA molecule consists of a long chain of nucleotides in which the sugar is ribose and the

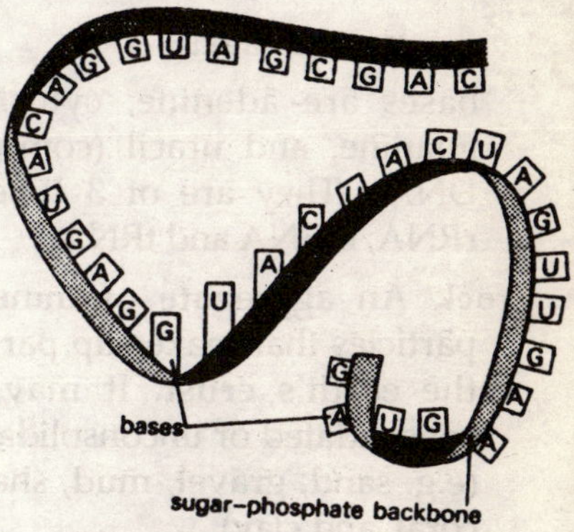

Single-stranded structure of RNA

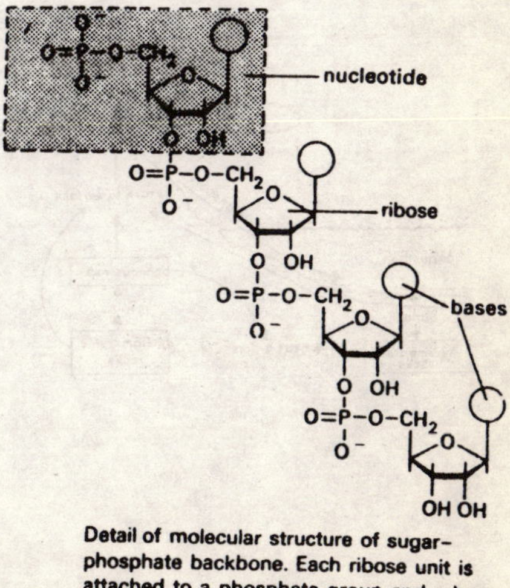

Detail of molecular structure of sugar-phosphate backbone. Each ribose unit is attached to a phosphate group and a base, forming a nucleotide

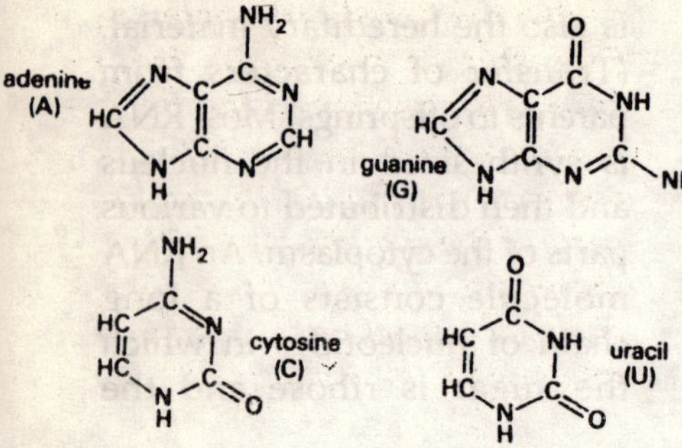

The four bases of RNA

Molecular structure of RNA

bases are adenine, cytosine, guanine, and uracil (compare DNA). They are of 3 types : rRNA, mRNA and tRNA.

rock An aggregate of mineral particles that makes up part of the earth's crust. It may be consolidated or unconsolidated (e.g. sand, gravel, mud, shells, coral, and clay).

rock cycle The change over long periods of time (millions of years) as rocks on Earth change from one kind to another. This is also known as the *geochemical cycle.* See *sedimentary* rock, *igneous* rock, *metamorphic* rock, *Earth* structure.

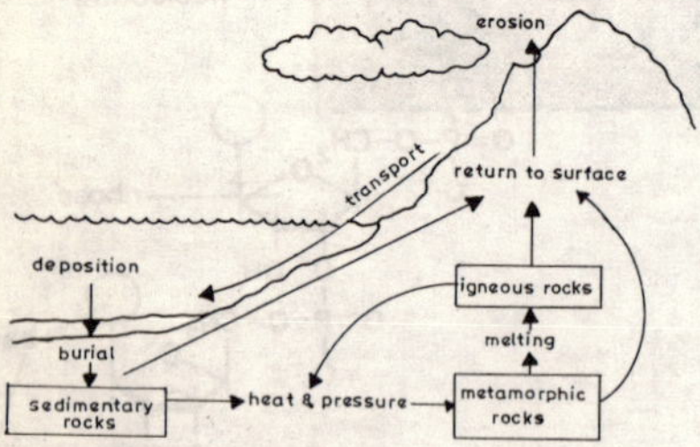

roentgen It is the former unit of dose equivalent (*see* radiation units). It is named after the discoverer of X-rays, W.K. Roentgen (1845-1923).

rose's metal An alloy of low melting point (about 373K) consisting of 50% bismuth, 25-28% lead, and 22-25% tin.

rotary dryers These are the devices commonly used in the chemical industry for the drying, mixing, and sintering of solids. They consist essentially of a rotating inclined cylinder, which is longer in length than in diameter. Gases flow through the cylinder in either a countercurrent or cocurrent direction to regulate the flow of solids, which are fed into the end of the cylinder. Rotary dryers can be applied to both batch and continuous processes.

rubber A natural *polymer*. It is a *hydrocarbon* and its structure is shown below:

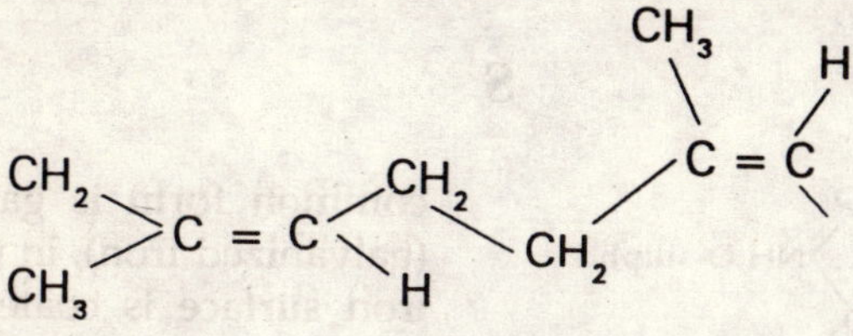

Natural ruber

Today most 'rubber' is made from butadiene:

$(CH_2 = CH - CH = CH_2)$

by *polymerization*. Rubber is elastic and a good *insulator*. Its uses are widespread from tyres and gloves to waterproofing.

rubidium Symbol 'Rb' having m.p. 38.89°C; b.p. 688°C; r.d. 1.53 (solid), 1.47 (liquid); a.n. 37; r.a.m. 85.47. A soft silvery highly reactive element of the alkali-metal group 's' block element. Naturally occurring rubidium comprises two isotopes, one of which, rubidium-87, is radioactive (half-life 5×10^{10} years). It is found in small amounts in several complex silicate minerals, including lepidolite. Rubidium is used in vacuum tubes, photocells, and in making special glass.

rust The reddish-brown product of corrosion (unwanted decay) of *iron* which has been exposed to *air* and *water*. It is hydrated iron(III) oxide ($Fe_2O_3.xH_2O$).

Rusting is of great economic importance. It is most commonly prevented by coating the iron with *paint, plastic* or another *metal*. *(electroplating, galvanizing.)*

ruthenium Symbol **Ru**. A hard white metallic transition element; a.n. 44; r.a.m. 101.07; r.d. 12.41; m.p. 2310°C; b.p. 3900°C. It is found associated with platinum alloys. Chemically, it dissolves in fused alkalis but is not attacked by acids. It reacts with oxygen and halogens at high temperatures. It also forms complexes with a range of oxidation states. The element was isolated by K.K. Klaus in 1844.

Rydberg constant It is a constant that relates to those atomic spectra which are similar to the hydrogen spectra. In case of hydrogen the value of Rydberg constant (R) is $1.09677 \times 10^7\ m^{-1}$.

S

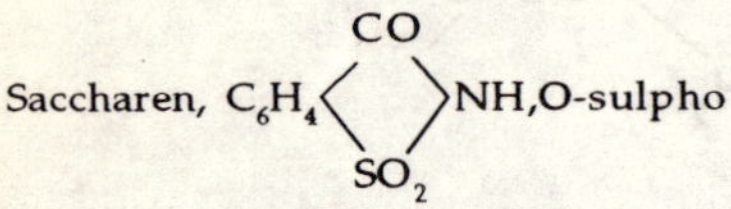

benzoic Amide

It is a crystalline solid which is 550 times as sweet as sugar. It is used as sweetening agent in cheap drinks. It is also used by diabetic patients and fatty persons.

Sachse reaction A process for the manufacture of ethyne from natural gas (methane). Part of the methane is burned in two stages to raise the furnace temperature to about 1723K. Under these conditions, the rest of the methane is converted to ethyne and hydrogen:

$$\underset{\text{Methane}}{2CH_4} \rightarrow \underset{\text{Ethene}}{C_2H_2} + 3H_2$$

The process is important since it provides a source of ethyne from readily available natural gas, thus avoiding the expensive 'carbide process'.

sacrificial protection It is a method of protection from corrosion **(cathodic protection)** The protection of iron or steel against corrosion (rusting) by using a more reactive metal. A common form is galvanizing (galvanized iron), in which the iron surface is coated with a layer of zinc. Even if the zinc layer is scratched, the iron does not rust because zinc ions are formed in solution in preference to iron ions. Similarly pieces of magnesium alloy are used in protecting pipelines, etc.

salicylic acid (2-hydroxybenzoic acid) A naturally occurring carboxylic acid found in certain plants, HOC_6H_4COOH;

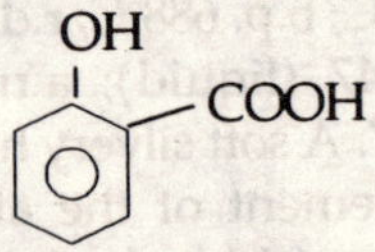

Salicylic acid

Salicylic acid r.d. 1.4; m.p. 157°C. It is used in making aspirin and in the foodstuffs and dyestuffs industries.

saline Containing a salt, especially an alkali-metal halide such as sodium chloride.

salinity It gives the idea of salt content of sea water or brine. Salinity is equal to the weight in grams of dissolved salt present in 1 kg of sea water or brine.

salinometer It is an instrument for

measuring the salinity of a solution. There are two main types: one is a type of hydrometer to measure density; the other is an apparatus for measuring the electrical conductivity of the solution.

salt A compound with an acidic and a basic radical, or a compound formed by total or partial replacement of the hydrogen in an acid by a metal. In general terms it is a material that has identifiable cationic and anionic components.

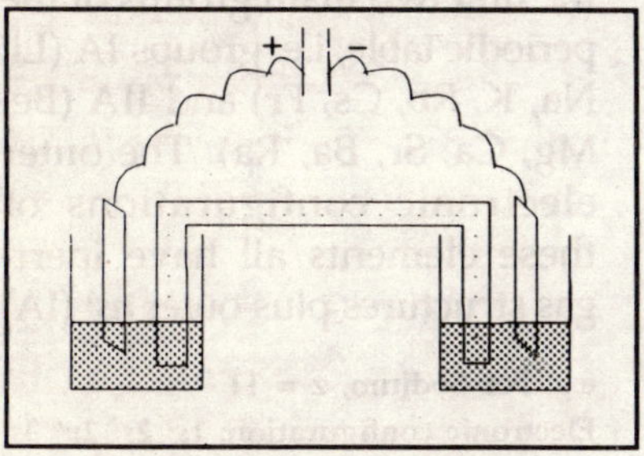

Salt bridge

salt bridge An electrical connection made between two half cells. It usually consists of a glass U-tube filled with agar jelly containing a salt, such as KCl/KNO_3. A strip of filter paper soaked in the salt solution can also be used.

salt cake Industrial sodium sulphate.

samarium Symbol Sm. A soft silvery metallic element belonging to the lanthanoids *'f'* block element; a.n. 62; r.a.m. 150.35; r.d. 7.52 (20°C); m.p. 1073°C; b.p. 1791°C. It occurs in monazite and bastnatite. There are seven naturally occurring isotopes, all of which are stable except samarium-147, which is weakly radioactive (half-life 2.5×10^{11} years). The metal is used in special alloys for making nuclear-reactor parts as it is a neutron absorber. Samarium oxide (Sm_2O_3) is used in small quantities in special optical glasses. The largest use of the element is in the ferromagnetic alloy $SmCo_5$, which produces permanent magnets five times stronger than any other material. The element was discovered by Francois Lecoq de Boisbaudran in 1879.

Sand Meyer's reaction It refers to the reaction in which benzene diazonium chloride is converted into corresponding phenyl halide/cyanide when heated with cuprous chloride/cuprous bromide/cuprous cyanide. e.g.

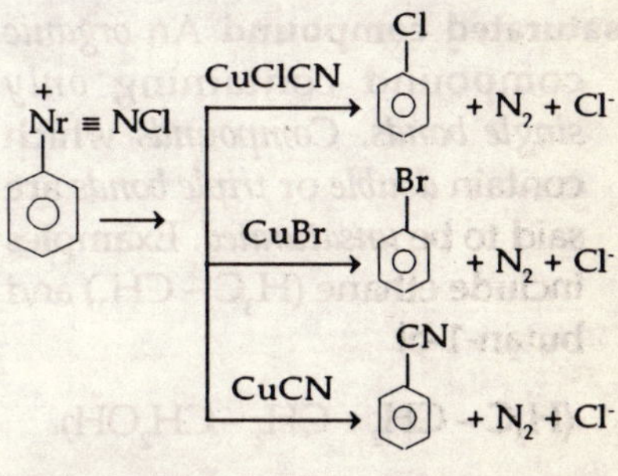

saponification The process of the *hydrolysis* of an *ester* when *alkaline* conditions are used. The breakdown of natural fats to produce soap is an example of saponification. Here sodium hydroxide *solution* is used to produce an *alcohol* and the *sodium salt* of the *carboxylic acid (soap).*

saponification number It is the number of milligrams of KOH required for the complete saponification of one gram of a fat or an oil.

sapphire Any of the gem varieties of corundum except ruby, especially the blue variety, but other colours of sapphire include yellow, brown, green, pink, orange, and purple. Sapphires are obtained from igneous and metamorphic rocks and from alluvial deposits. The chief sources are Sri Lanka, Kashmir, Burma, Thailand, East Africa, the USA, and Australia. Sapphires are used as gemstones and record-player styluses. They are synthesized by the Verneuil flame-fusion process.

saturated compound An *organic* compound containing *only single bonds. Compounds* which contain *double* or *triple bonds* are said to be *unsaturated*. Examples include ethane ($H_3C - CH_3$) and butan-1-ol

$$(H_3C - CH_2 - CH_2 - CH_2OH).$$

saturated vapour A vapour that is in equilibrium with the solid or liquid is known as saturated vapour. A saturated vapour is at the maximum pressure (the saturated vapour pressure) at a given temperature. If the temperature of a saturated vapour is lowered, the vapour condenses. Under certain circumstances, the substance may stay temporarily in the vapour phase; i.e. the vapour contains *more* than the equilibrium concentration of the substance. The vapour is then said to be *super-saturated*.

***s*-block elements** The elements of the first two main groups of the periodic table; i.e. groups IA (Li, Na, K, Rb, Cs, Fr) and IIA (Be, Mg, Ca, Sr, Ba, Ra). The outer electronic configurations of these elements all have inert-gas structures plus outer ns^1 (IA)

e.g. For Sodium, z = 11

Electronic configuration: $1s^2\ 2s^2\ 2p^6\ 3s^1$

or ns^2 (IIA) For Magnesium, z = 12

Electronic configuration: $1s^2\ 2s^2\ 2p^6\ 3s^2$

electrons. The term thus excludes elements with incomplete inner *d*-levels (transition metals) or with incomplete inner *f*-levels (lanthanoids and actinoids) even though these often have outer ns^2 or occasionally ns^1 configurations. Typically, the *s*-block elements are reactive metals forming stable ionic compounds containing M^+ or M^{2+} ions.

scandium A light-weight silvery element belonging to the first transition series '*d*' block element. It is found in minute amounts in over 800 minerals, often associated with lanthanoids. Scandium is used in high-intensity lights. It is designated by symbol Sc having a.n. 21; m.p. 1541°C; b.p. 2831°C; r.d. 2.99; r.a.m. 44.96.

scheelite A mineral form of calcium tungstate, $CaWO_4$, used as an ore of tungsten. It occurs in contact metamorphosed deposits and vein deposits as colourless or white tetragonal crystals.

Schiff's base It is a compound formed by a condensation reaction between an aromatic amine and an aldehyde or ketone, for example

$$RNH_2 + R'CHO \rightarrow RN{:}CHR' + H_2O$$

The compounds are often crystalline and are used in organic chemistry for characterizing aromatic amines (by preparing the Schiff's base and measuring the melting point). They are named after the German chemist Hugo Schiff (1834-1915).

Schiff's reagent It is an aqueous solution of magenta dye decolorized by reduction with sulphur(IV) oxide. It is a test for aldehydes and ketones. Aliphatic aldehydes restore the colour quickly; aliphatic ketones and aromatic aldehydes slowly; aromatic ketones give no reaction.

schönite A mineral form of potassium sulphate, K_2SO_4.

Schotten-Baumann reaction A method for the preparation of *N*-phenyl-benzamide (benzanilide) in which a mixture of phenylamine (aniline) and sodium hydroxide is stirred while benzoyl chloride is added slowly. The *N*-phenyl-benzamide precipitates and can be recrystallized from hot ethyl alcohol (CH_3CH_2OH)

$$C_6H_5NH_2 + C_6H_5COCl \rightarrow C_6H_5NH.COC_6H_5 + HCl$$

Schottky defect *See* defect.

secondary cell (rechargeable cell) A voltaic cell in which the chemical reaction producing the e.m.f. is reversible and the cell can therefore be charged by passing a current through it.

second-order reaction A reaction in which the rate of reaction is proportional to the product of the concentrations of two of the reactants or to the square of the concentration of one of the reactants; i.e.

$$\text{rate} = k\,[A][B]$$

or

$$\text{rate} = k\,[A]^2$$

For example, the hydrolysis by dilute alkali of an ester is a second-order reaction:

$$\text{rate} = k\,[\text{ester}][\text{alkali}]$$

The rate constant for a second-order reaction has the units mol dm^{-3} S^{-1}. Unlike a first-order reaction, the time for a definite fraction of the reactants to be consumed is dependent on the original concentrations.

sedative It is a drug that is used for reducing nervousness and excitement.

sedimentary rock This is the *rock* formed from *sediments*—solid materials—which have been laid down in the sea over millions of years. As the layers of materials build up, the pressure increases and the particles are compressed to form a new rock. Most of the Earth's crust is covered by a thin layer of sedimentary rocks.

sedimentation The process of the settling of the solid particles through a liquid either to produce a concentrated slurry from a dilute suspension or to clarify a liquid containing solid particles is called sedimentation. Usually this relies on the force of gravity, but if the particles are too small or the difference in density between the solid and liquid phases is too small, a centrifuge may be used. In the simplest case the rate of sedimentation is determined by Stokes's law, but in practice the predicted rate is rarely reached. Measurement of the rate of sedimentation in an ultracentrifuge can be used to estimate the size of macromolecules.

seed A crystal used to induce other crystals to form from a gas, liquid, or solution.

selenium Symbol: **Se**, a.n. 34; r.a.m. 78.96; r.d. 4.79 (grey); m.p. 217°C (grey); b.p. 684.9°C A metalloid present in '*p*' block of periodic table exists in a number of allotropic forms (at least four forms are known). It is used in glass industry as a decolouriser and as a catalyst.

selenium cell Either of two types of photoelectric cell; one type relies on the photoconductive effect, the other on the photovoltaic effect (*see* photoelectric effect). In the photoconductive selenium cell an external e.m.f. must be applied; as the selenium changes its resistance on exposure to light, the current produced is a measure of the light energy falling on the selenium. In the photovoltaic selenium cell, the e.m.f. is generated within the cell. In this type of cell, a thin film of vitreous or metallic selenium is applied to a metal surface, a transparent film of another metal, usually gold or platinum, being placed over the selenium. Both types of cell are used as light meters in photography.

semi-conductor In this type of conductors the presence of impurities increases the conductance. Elements, compounds or metalloids can act as semiconductors.

semipermeable membrane It is a membrane that is permeable to molecules of the solvent but not the solute in osmosis. Semipermeable membranes can be made by supporting a film of material (e.g. cellulose) on a wire gauze or porous pot.

Separation factor It is denoted by α' .In chromatography,

$$\alpha = K_A/K_B$$

where K_A and K_B are constant of division of the two components A and B respectively.

serpentine Any of a group of hydrous magnesium silicate minerals with the general composition $Mg_3Si_2O_5(OH)_4$. Serpentine is monoclinic and occurs in two main forms: *chrysotile,* which is fibrous and the chief source of asbestos; and *antigorite,* which occurs as platy masses. It is generally green or white with a mottled appearance, sometimes resembling a snakeskin—hence the name. It is formed through the metamorphic alteration of ultra-basic rocks rich in olivine, pyroxene, and amphibole. *Serpentine;* is a rock consisting mainly of serpentine; it is used as an ornamental stone.

sesame oil It is a yellow oil obtained from sesame seeds. It is used in the manufacture of margarine and cosmetics.

sherardizing The process of coating iron or steel with a zinc corrosion-resistant layer by heating the iron or steel in contact with zinc dust to a temperature slightly below the melting point of zinc. At a temperature of about 644K the two metals amalgamate to form internal layers of zinc-iron alloys and an external layer of pure zinc. The process was invented by Sherard Cowper-Coles (d. 1935).

SI units It is an international system of *units* based on the metric system of measurement.

Quantity	*Unit*	*Symbol*
Length	metre	m
Mass	kilogramme	kg
Time	second	s
Current	ampere	A
Temperature	kelvin	K
Amount of substance	mole	mol
Luminous intensity	candela	cd

side chain It refers to an aliphatic radical or group that is attached to a straight chain of carbon atoms or to a benzene ring or to some other cyclic group in the organic compound, e.g. In case of toluene, , $-CH_3$ is side chain.

In case of Aniline, 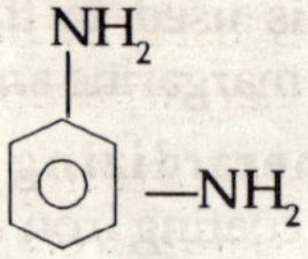 is the side chain.

side reaction It is a chemical reaction that occurs at the same time as a main reaction but to a lesser extent, thus leading to other products mixed with the main products.

siemens Denoted by symbol *'S'*. The SI unit of electrical conductance equal to the conductance of a circuit or element that has a resistance of 1 ohm. 1 S = 10^{-1} Ω. The unit was formerly called the mho or reciprocal ohm. It is named after Ernst Werner von Siemens (1816-92).

sigma bond (σ-bond) This type of bond is formed by the axial overlap of atomic orbitals. A single bond is always a sigma bond. e.g. H—H (H_2 molecule) σ-bond is stronger than that of a π-bond and its strength depends upon degree of overlapping.

s–s >s—p > p–p overlapping.

silane (silicane) (a) It is a colourless gas, SiH_4, which is insoluble in water; d. 1.44 g dm^{-3}; r.d. 0.68 (liquid); m.p. –185°C; b.p. –112°C. Silane is produced by reduction of silicon tetrachloride using lithium tetrahydrido (III). It is also formed by the reaction of magnesium silicide (Mg_2Si) with acids, although other silicon hydrides are also produced at the same time. Silane itself is stable in the absence of air but is spontaneously flammable, even at low temperatures. It is used for controlled silicon doping of semiconductors in the electronics industry. It is also a reducing agent and has been used for the removal of corrosion in inaccessible plants (e.g. pipes in nuclear reactors). (b) (or *silicon hydride*) Any of a class of compounds of silicon and hydrogen. They have the general formula Si_nH_{2n+2}. The first three in the series are silane itself (SiH_4), *disilane* (Si_2H_6), and *trisilane* (Si_3H_8). The compounds are analogous to the alkanes but are much less stable and only the lower members of the series can be prepared in any quantity (up to Si_6H_{14}). No silicon hydrides containing double or triple bonds exist (i.e. there are no analogues of the alkenes and alkynes).

silica A widely found *mineral* form of silicon oxide (SiO_2) which is used as an *ore* of *silicon*. Some silica is found as coloured crystals, for example amethyst (containing the Fe^{3+} *ion*); other forms of silica include *flint*, which is an *amorphous* form.

silicide A compound of silicon with a more electropositive element. The silicides are structurally similar to the interstitial carbides but the range encountered is more diverse. They react with mineral acids to form a range of silicanes.

silicon, Symbol Si; A metalloid of *'p'* block of the periodic table. an. 14; r.a.m. 28.08; r.d. = 2.33; m.p. 1410°; b.p. 2355°; Its electronic configuration is $1s^2\ 2s^2\ 2p^6\ 3s^2\ 3p^2$. It is a semi-conductor. It is used in the form of silicon chips in micro electronic engineering. It is used for making magnets, transformer cores, anti-corrosion steel and as deoxidiser. Silicon bronze (an alloy) is used for telegraph and telephone wires.

silicon carbide (SiC) Also known as carborundum. A black very hard crystalline solid made by heating silicon(IV) oxide (sand) with carbon (coke) in an electronic furnace. It is used as an abrasive.

silicon(IV) oxide It exists in two crystalline forms crystalline and amorphous (Quartz). It has no action with water and other mineral acids. It reacts with HF (Hydrofluoric acid) as under

$$SiO_2 + HF \rightarrow SiF_4 + 2H_2O$$

silicones These are the polymeric compounds containing chains of silicon atoms alternating with oxygen atoms, with the silicon atoms linked to organic groups. A variety of silicone materials exist, including oils, waxes, and rubbers. They tend to be more resistant to temperature and chemical attack than their carbon analogues.

siloxanes They are the group of compounds containing silicon atoms bound to oxygen atoms, with organic groups linked to the silicon atoms, e.g. $R_3SiOSiR_3$, where R is an organic group. Silicones are polymers of siloxanes.

silver Symbol: Ag; a.n. 47; r.a.m. 107; 87; r.d. 10.5; m.p. 961. 93°C; b.p. 2212°C. A *transition metal.* It is used for jewellery and decorative purposes and has been used for coinage. It is often alloyed with *copper* to give strength. It is an excellent *conductor* of electricity and heat. When exposed to the *air* it slowly becomes covered in a black film of silver sulphide.

Silver is low in the *reactivity series.* Its *oxide* is unstable:

$$Ag_2O(s) \xrightarrow{\Delta} 2Ag(s) + O_2(g)$$

Its *halides* are also unstable. This property is used in photography.

silver(I) bromide A yellowish solid compound, AgBr; r.d. 6.5; m.p. 705K. It can be precipitated from silver(I) nitrate solution by adding a solution containing bromide ions. It dissolves in concentrated ammonia solutions (but, unlike the chloride, does not dissolve in dilute ammonia). The compound is used in photographic emulsions.

silver(I) chloride ($AgCl$) A compound prepared as a curdy white precipitate by the addition of a soluble chloride solution to a solution of silver(I) nitrate.

$$AgNO_3 + NaCl \rightarrow AgCl + NaNO_3.$$

It occurs in nature as the mineral 'horn silver'. Silver(I) chloride is insoluble in water but dissolves in concentrated hydrochloric acid and concentrated ammonia solution. It is rather unreactive but is affected by sunlight, being used extensively in photography. Silver(I) chloride crystallizes in the sodium chloride lattice pattern. It absorbs ammonia gas forming amines, e.g. $AgCl.2NH_3$ and $AgCl.3NH_3$.

silver(I) iodide A yellow solid compound, AgI; r.d. 6.01; m.p. 556°C; b.p. 1506°C. It can be precipitated from silver(I) nitrate solutions by adding a solution of iodide ions.

$$AgNO_3 + KI \rightarrow AgI + KNO_3.$$

Unlike the chloride and bromide, it does not dissolve in ammonia solutions.

silver-mirror test A test for the aldehyde (–CHO) group. A few drops of the sample are warmed with Tollen's reagent. An aldehyde reduces Ag^+ to silver metal, causing a brilliant silver mirror to coat the inside wall of the tube.

silver nitrate, $AgNO_3$ It is used in silvering of glass, laundry marking inks, hair dyes. It is also used in photography and as a laboratory reagent in qualitative analysis and in volumetric analysis.

silver(I) oxide A brown slightly water-soluble amorphous powder, Ag_2O; r.d. 7.14. It can be made by adding sodium hydroxide solution to silver(I) nitrate solution. Silver (I) oxide is strongly basic and is also an oxidizing agent. It is used in certain reactions in preparative organic chemistry; for example, moist silver(I) oxide converts haloalkanes into alcohols; dry silver oxide converts alkyl halides into ethers. The compound decomposes to the elements at 160°C and can be reduced by hydrogen to silver. With ozone it gives the oxide AgO (which is diamagnetic and probably $Ag^IAg^{III}O_2$).

single bond A covalent bond between two elements that involves one pair of electrons only. Often referred to as a sigma bond, (σ bond), it is represented by a single line, for example, H—Br.

The sigma bond is formed by the overlap of sigma-atomic orbitals from each atom (i.e. orbitals that are on the internuclear axis). Another example of single bond is in alkanes. $H_3C—CH_3$.

sintering The process of heating and compacting a powdered material at a temperature below its m.p. in order to weld the particles together into a single rigid shape. Materials commonly sintered include metals and alloys, glass, and ceramic oxides. Sintered magnetic materials, cooled in a magnetic field, make especially retentive permanent magnets.

slag It is the material produced during the smelting or refining of metals by reaction of the flux with impurities (e.g. calcium silicate formed by reaction of calcium oxide flux with silicon dioxide impurities). The liquid slag can be separated from the liquid metal because it floats on the surface.

smelting An industrial process for extracting metals from their ores at high temperatures. Generally the ore is reduced with carbon (for zinc and tin) or CO (for iron). Copper and lead are obtained by reduction of the oxide with the sulphide; for example:

$$2Cu_2O + Cu_2S \rightarrow 6Cu + SO_2$$

A flux is also used to combine with impurities and form a slag on top of the molten metal.

soap A cleaning agent which is made by the action of an *alkali,* for example NaOH solution, on naturally occurring esters. (*saponification.)*

e.g. $C_{17}H_{35}COO^-Na^+$

The *hydrocarbon* end of the *molecule* is *hydrophobic.* The carboxylate end of the molecule is *hydrophilic.*

Soap is made from a mixture of animal *fat,* and vegetable *oils* such as coconut oil. An *antioxidant* is usually added to prevent the soap from producing 'off' smells. Soap is *biodegradable.*

soda Any of a number of sodium compounds, such as caustic soda (NaOH) or, especially, washing soda ($Na_2CO_3.10H_2O$) hydrated sodium carbonate.

soda lime It is a mixed hydroxide of sodium and calcium made by slaking lime with caustic soda solution (to give NaOH + $Ca(OH)_2$) and recovering greyish white granules by evaporation. The material is produced largely for industrial absorption of carbon dioxide and water, but also finds some applications in pollution and effluent control. It is also used as a laboratory drying agent.

sodamide, $NaNH_2$ A white solid (m.p. = 483K). It is used in explosive industry. It is also used in castner process. It can be obtained by passing ammonia (NH_3) gas over heated sodium.

$$2\ Na \rightarrow NH_3 \rightarrow 2\ NaNH_2 + H_2$$

sodium Symbol Na. A soft silvery reactive element belonging to group I 's' block element of the periodic table (*see* alkali metals); a.n. 11; Electronic configuration is $1s^2\ 2s^2\ 2p^6\ 3s^1$ r.a.m. 22.9898; r.d. 0.97; m.p. 97.5°C; b.p. 892°C. Sodium occurs as the chloride in sea water and in the mineral halite. It is extracted by electrolysis in a Downs cell. The metal is used as a reducing agent in certain reactions and liquid sodium is also a coolant in nuclear reactors. Chemically, it is highly reactive, oxidizing in air and reacting violently with water (it is kept under oil). It dissolves in liquid ammonia to form blue solutions containing solvated electrons. Sodium is a major element required by living organisms. The element was first isolated by Humphry Davy in 1807.

sodium compounds

Sodium carbonate Na_2CO_3	Compound made in the *Solvay process* and an important chemical. One of its many uses is in the manufacture of *glass*. Unlike most carbonates, it is *soluble* in water. It is not decomposed by heat, its aqueous *solution* is *alkaline*.
Sodium chloride NaCl	Known as *common salt*. Obtained from *rock salt* and is used to make *sodium hydroxide, sodium metal* and *chloride*. It is used for flavouring and preserving foods.
Sodium hydrogen carbonate $NaHCO_3$	Used in *baking powder*. It is decomposed by the action of heat or *acids*. Also used in fire extinguishers and in anti-indigestion powders.
Sodium hydroxide NaOH	Produced by the *electrolysis* of *brine* and has wide uses in industry. e.g. making *soap*, fibres such as *rayon* and *paper*. It is a *caustic alkali*. Solutions have pH > 10.

sodium nitrate, $NaNO_3$ It is commonly called chile salt petre. It is deliquescent in nature. In nature it also exists as *caliche*. Chile salt petre is pure form (90-95%) whereas caliche is impure form (20-25%). It is used as a fertilizer and in preservation of meat.

sodium nitrite A yellow hygroscopic crystalline compound,

$NaNO_2$, soluble in water, slightly soluble in ether and in ethyl alcohol; rhombohedral; r.d. 2.17; m.p. 271°C; decomposes above 320°C. It is formed by the thermal decomposition of sodium nitrate and is used in the preparation of nitrous acid (reaction with cold dilute hydrochloric acid). Sodium nitrite is used in organic diazotization and as a corrosion inhibitor.

sodium sesquicarbonate A white crystalline hydrated double salt, Na_2CO_3. $NaHCO_3.2H_2O$, soluble in water but less alkaline than sodium carbonate; r.d. 2.12; decomposes on heating. It may be prepared by crystallizing equimolar quantities of the constituent materials; it also occurs naturally as *trona* and in Searles Lake brines. It is widely used as a detergent and soap builder and, because of its mild alkaline properties, it is used as a water-softening agent and bath-salt base. *See also* sodium carbonate.

sodium sulphate, Na_2SO_4 A white solid which is used in manufacture of glass and paper. The hydrated form of sodium sulphate salt (Na_2SO_4. 10 H_2O) is known as *Glauber's salt.*

sodium superoxide (sodium dioxide) A whitish-yellow solid, NaO_2, formed by the reaction of sodium peroxide with excess oxygen at elevated temperatures and pressures. It reacts with water to form hydrogen peroxide and oxygen.

sodium tetraborate, $Na_2B_4O_7$. $10H_2O$ It is commonly known as borax. It occurs in nature as *tincal.* When heated it forms transparent solid (borax bead test). It is used as an antiseptic, in fire proofing, as a flux, in the manufacture of glass and ceramics.

sodium thiosulphate (sodium hyposulphate) A colourless efflorescent solid, $Na_2S_2O_3$, soluble in water but insoluble in ethanol, commonly encountered as the pentahydrate (monoclinic; r.d. 1.73; m.p. 315K), which loses water at 100°C to give the anhydrous form (r.d. 1.66). It is prepared by the reaction of sulphur dioxide with a suspension of sulphur in boiling sodium hydroxide solution. Aqueous solutions of sodium thiosulphate are readily oxidized in the presence of air to sodium tetrathionate and sodium sulphate. The reaction with dilute acids gives sulphur and sulphur dioxide. It is used in the photographic industry and in analytical chemistry.

sol A colloid consisting of solid particles distributed in a liquid medium. A wide variety of sols are known; the colours often depend markedly on the particle size. The term *aerosol* is used for solid or liquid phases dispersed in a gaseous medium.

solder An alloy used to join metal surfaces. A *soft solder* melts at a temperature in the range 473-573 K and consists of a tin-lead alloy. The tin content varies between 80% for the lower end of the melting range and 31% for the higher end. *Hard solders* contain substantial quantities of silver in the alloy. *Brazing solders* are usually alloys of copper and zinc, which melt at over 1073K.

solid A state of matter in which there is a three-dimensional regularity of structure, resulting from the proximity of the component atoms, ions, or molecules and the strength of the forces between them. True solids are crystalline (*also* amorphous). If a crystalline solid is heated, the kinetic energy of the components increases. At a specific temperature, called the *melting point* (m.p.), the forces between the components become unable to contain them within the crystal structure. At this temperature, the lattice breaks down and the solid becomes a liquid. Atoms in solids are compactly arranged.

solid solution It is a solid composed of two or more substances mixed together at the molecular level. Atoms, ions, or molecules of one component in the crystal are at lattice positions normally occupied by the other component. Certain alloys are solid solutions of one metal in another. Isomorphic salts can also sometimes form solid solutions, as in the case of crystalline alums.

soluble Describes a substance which can be *dissolved* in a *solvent*. The extent to which any *solute* dissolves depends on the solvent and the *temperature*. At any given temperature there is a maximum amount of solute which can dissolve in a fixed *volume* of solvent. This produces a *saturated solution*. See solubility.

solubility The quantity of solute that dissolves in a given quantity of solvent to form a saturated solution is known as solubility. Solubility is measured in kilograms per metre cubed, moles per kilogram of solvent, etc. The solubility of a substance in a given solvent depends on the temperature. Generally, for a solid in a liquid, solubility increases with temperature; for a gas, solubility decreases.

solubility product It is denoted by K_{sp}. The product of concentration of ions in a saturated solution of an electrolyte at a given temperature is constant and is called solubility product. In case of silver chloride (Ag Cl) we have

$$AgCl(s) \Leftrightarrow Ag^+(aq) + Cl^-(aq)$$

Equilibrium constant

$$K = \frac{[Ag^+][Cl^-]}{[AgCl]}$$

Since concentration of undissolved substance is constant say (k) at a particular temperature

$$\text{Thus, } K = \frac{[Ag^+][Cl^-]}{k}$$

or $K.\ k = [Ag^+][Cl^-]\ K_{sp}$

where K_{sp} is a called solubility product.

solute A material that is dissolved in a solvent to form a solution is called solute.

solution It is homogeneous mixture of two or more substances whose composition can be varied within certain limits, for example solution of common salt in water. Solution of ammonia in water.

solvation The attraction of an ion in solution for molecules of solvent. In water, for example, a positive ion will be surrounded by water molecules, which tend to associate around the ion because of attraction between the positive charge of the ion, and the negative part of the polar water molecule. The energy of this solution (hydration in the case of water) is the 'force' overcoming the attraction between anions and cations when an ionic solid dissolves. The attraction of the dissolved ion for solvent molecules may extend for several layers. In the case of transition metal elements, ions may also form complexes by coordination to the nearest layer of molecules.

Solvay process (ammonia-soda process) An industrial method of making sodium carbonate from calcium carbonate and sodium chloride. The calcium carbonate is first heated to give calcium oxide and carbon dioxide, which is bubbled into a solution of sodium chloride in ammonia. Sodium bicarbonate ($NaHCO_3$) is precipitated:

$$H_2O + CO_2(g) + NaCl(aq) + NH_3\ (aq) \rightarrow NaHCO_3(s) + NH_4Cl(aq)$$

The sodium bicarbonate is heated to give sodium carbonate and carbon dioxide. The ammonium chloride is heated with calcium oxide (from the first stage) to regenerate the ammonia. The process was patented in 1861 by the Belgian chemist Ernest Solvay (1838-1922).

solvent (Generally, solvent is one which is present in large quantity in solution) It is a *liquid* in which a *solute dissolves* to form a *solution*. *Water* is the most common solvent. Solvents may be polar, for example water, or non-polar, e.g. *ether*. Polar solvents dissolve in ionic or polar solutes, for example *salts*. Non-polar solvents dissolve *covalent* molecules, for example *hydrocarbons*.

solvent extraction It is the process of separating one constituent from a mixture by dissolving it in a solvent in which it is soluble but in which the other constituents of the mixture are not. The process is usually carried out in the liquid phase, in which case it is also known as *liquid-liquid extraction*. In liquid-liquid extraction, the solution containing the desired constituent must be immiscible with the rest of the mixture. The process as widely used in extracting oil from oil-bearing materials.

spatula It is a tool shaped like a spoon and having a flat surface. It is used for removing small quantities of solids.

species A chemical entity, such as a particular atom, ion, or molecule.

specific Denoting a physical quantity per unit mass. For example, volume (V) per unit mass (m) is called specific volume:

$$V = V_m$$

In certain physical quantities the term does not have this meaning: for example, *specific gravity* is more properly called relative density.

specific reaction rate constant (K) For a reaction it is, "the rate of reaction, when the concentration of the reactant is unity". The value of specific reaction constant (K) depends upon: (i) temperature (ii) order of reaction.

specific rotatory power Symbol: α_m The rotation of plane-polarized light in degrees produced by a 10 cm length of solution containing 1 g of a given substance per millilitre of stated solvent. The specific rotatory power is a measure of the optical activity of substances in solution. It is measured at 293K using the D-line of sodium.

spectator ions These are the *ions* which play no part in a *reaction*. They are only *spectators*. In the example shown below the spectator ions are underlined.

$$\underline{Na^+(aq)}+Cl^-(aq)+Ag^+(aq)+\underline{NO_3^-(aq)} \rightarrow \underline{Na^+(aq)+NO_3^-(aq)}+AgCl(s)$$

spectral series A group of related lines in the absorption or emission spectrum of a substance. The lines in a spectral series occur when the transitions all occur between one particular energy level and a set of different levels.

spectrometer Any of various instruments for producing a spectrum and measuring the wavelengths, energies, etc., involved are called spectrometers. A simple type, for visible radiation, is a spectroscope equipped with a calibrated scale allowing wavelengths to be read off or calculated. In the X-ray to infrared region of the electromagnetic spectrum, the spectrum is produced by dispersing the radiation with a prism or diffraction grating (or crystal, in the case of hard X-rays). Some form of photoelectric detector is used, and the spectrum can be obtained as a graphical plot, which shows how the intensity of the radiation varies with wavelength. Such instruments are also called *spectrophoto meters*. Spectrometers also exist for investigating the gamma-ray region and the microwave and radio-wave regions of the spectrum (*see* electron spin resonance; nuclear magnetic resonance). Instruments for obtaining spectra of particle beams are also called spectrometers.

spectroscope An instrument used to examine various wave lengths present in electromagnetic radiation is called a spectroscope.

spectroscopy It is the study of methods of producing and analysing spectra using spectroscopes, spectrometers, spectrographs, and spectrophotometers. The interpretations of the spectra so produced can be used for chemical analysis, examining atomic and molecular energy levels and molecular structures, and for determining the composition and motions of celestial bodies.

sphalerite (also known as: **zinc blende**) A mineral form of zinc sulphide, ZnS, crystallizing in the cubic system; the principal ore of zinc. It is usually yellow-brown to brownish-black in colour and occurs, often with galena, in metasomatic deposits and also in hydrothermal veins and replacement deposits. Sphalerite is mined on every continent, the chief sources including the USA, Canada, Mexico, the USSR, Australia, Peru, and Poland.

spin It is the property of certain elementary particles whereby the particle acts as if it were spinning on an exis; i.e. it has an angular momentum. Such particles also have a magnetic moment. In a magnetic field the spins line up at an angle to the field direction and precess around this direction. Certain definite orientations to the field direction occur such that $m_s h/2\pi$ is the component of angular momentum along this direction. m_s is the spin quantum number. For an electron it has values +1/2 and –1/2. Spin can be clockwise or anti- clockwise.

spinel A group of oxide minerals with the general formula $F^{2+}R_2^{3+}O_4$, where F^{2+} = Mg, Fe, Zn, Mn or Ni and R^{3+} = Al, Fe, or Cr, crystallizing in the cubic system. The spinels are divided into three series: spinel ($MgAl_2O_4$), magnetic, and chromite. They occur in high-temperature igneous or metamorphic rocks.

spin quantum number quantum number denoted by symbol 's'. It gives an idea about the spin of an electron in an atom. An electron can spin in two possible ways (clockwise and anticlockwise) accordingly spin quantum number can have two values +½ or –½.

spirits of salt Hydrogen chloride, so-called because it can be made by adding sulphuric acid to common salt (sodium chloride).

spontaneous combustion The combustion in which a substance produces sufficient heat within itself, usually by a show oxidation process, for ignition to take place without the need for an external high-temperature energy source.

spontaneous reaction It is a reaction that occurs of its own without any outside help e.g. formation of white precipitate of silver chloride when silver nitrate reacts with sodium chloride.

$$\underset{(aq)}{AgNO_3} + \underset{(aq)}{NaCl} \rightarrow AgCl + NaNO_3$$

sputtering The process by which some of the atoms of an electrode (usually a cathode) are ejected as a result of bombardment by heavy positive ions. Although the process is generally unwanted, it can be used to produce a clean surface or to deposit a uniform film of a metal on an object in an evacuated enclosure.

stability constant of complex ion:

$$K = \frac{ML_n^{b+}}{[M^+]\,[L^{x-}]^n};\ m^a + nL^{x-} \rightarrow [M\,L_n]^{b+}$$

The magnitude of stability constant gives an indication of the stability of complex in solution.

stabilization energy The amount by which the energy of a delocalized chemical structure is less than the theoretical energy of a structure with localized bonds. It is obtained by subtracting the experimental heat of formation of the compound (in kJ mol^{-1}) from that calculated on the basis of a classical structure with localized bonds.

stabilizer A substance added to prevent chemical change. It is also called as a negative catalyst.

stalactites, stalagmites *Mineral* growths found in caves. When *water* containing *calcium salts* falls into the cave there is a gradual build up of *calcium carbonate* from the roof (forming stalactites) and onto the floor (forming stalagmites) as the *solution* containing the calcium salts decomposes.

$$\underset{\text{Calcium bicarbonate}}{Ca(HCO_3)_2(aq)} \rightarrow \underset{\text{Calcium carbonate}}{CaCO_3(s)} + H_2O(l) + CO_2(g)$$

standard cell A voltaic cell whose e.m.f. is used as a standard.

standard electrode An electrode (a half cell) used in measuring electrode potential).

standard solution Any solution whose strength or normality is known is called as standard solution.

standard state A state of a system used as a reference value in thermodynamic measurements. Standard states involve a reference value of pressure (usually 1 atmosphere, 101.325 kPa) or concentration (usually 1 M). Thermodynamic functions are designated as 'standard' when they refer to changes in which reactants and products are all in their standard and their normal physical state. For example, the standard molar enthalpy of formation of water at 25°C is the enthalpy change for the reaction

$$H_2(g) + \tfrac{1}{2}O_2(g) \xrightarrow{\text{Electric spark}} H_2O(l)$$

$\Delta H_{298} = -285.83$ kJ mol^{-1}. Note the superscript is used to denote standard state and the temperature should be indicated.

standard temperature An internationally agreed value for which many measurements are quoted. It is the melting temperature of water, 0°C (273.15 K).

stannate A compound formed by reaction of tin oxides (or hydroxides) with alkali. Tin oxides are amphoteric (weakly acidic) and react to give stannate ions. Tin(IV) oxide with molten alkali gives the stannate(IV) ion

$$SnO_2 + 2OH^- \rightarrow SnO_3^{2-} + H_2O$$

In fact, there are various ions present in which the tin is bound to –OH groups, the main one being the hexahydroxostannate (IV) ion, $Sn(OH)_6^{2-}$. This is the negative ion present in crystalline 'trihydrates' of the type $K_2Sn_2O_3.3H_2O$.

Tin(II) oxide gives the trihydroxostannate(II) ion in alkaline solutions

$$SnO(s) + OH^-(aq) + H_2O(l) \rightarrow Sn(OH)_3^-(aq)$$

Stannate(IV) compounds were formerly referred to as *orthostannates* (SnO_4^{4-}) or *metastannates* (SnO_3^{2-}). Stannate (II) compounds were called *stannites.*

stannane (tin(IV) hydride, SnH_4) A colourless poisonous gas prepared by the action of lithium aluminium hydride on tin(II) chloride. It is unstable, decomposing immediately at

423K. Stannane acts as a reducing agent.

stannic compounds Compounds of tin in its higher (+4) oxidation state; e.g. stannic chloride is tin(IV) chloride.

stannous compounds Compounds of tin(II).

starch It is a polysaccharide consisting of various proportions of two glucose polymers, amylose and amylopectin. It occurs widely in plants, especially in roots, tubers, seeds, and fruits, as a carbohydrate energy store. Starch is therefore a major energy source for animals. When digested it ultimately yields glucose. Starch granules are insoluble in cold water but disrupt if heated to form a gelatinous solution. This gives an intense blue colour with iodine solutions and starch is used as an indicator in certain titrations.

state of matter There are three physical states in which matter can exist, i.e. solid, liquid, or gas. Plasma is sometimes regarded as the fourth state of matter.

stationary state A state of a system when it has an energy level permitted by quantum mechanics. A transition from one stationary state to another can only occur by the emission or absorption of an appropriate quantum of energy in the form of photons.

statistical mechanics The branch of physics in which statistical methods are applied to the microscopic constituents of a system in order to predict its macroscopic properties. The earliest application of this method was Boltzmann's attempt to explain the thermodynamic properties of gases on the basis of the statistical properties of large assemblies of molecules.

In classical statistical mechanics, each particle is regarded as occupying a point in *phase space,* that is to have an exact position and momentum at any particular instant. The probability that this point will occupy any small volume of the phase space is taken to be proportional to the volume. The Maxwell-Boltzmann law gives the most probable distribution of the particles in phase space.

With the advent of quantum theory, the exactness of these premises was disturbed (by the Heisenberg uncertainty principle). In the quantum statistics that evolved as a result, the phase space is divided into cells, each having a volume hf, where h is the Planck constant (value is 6.624 $\times 10^{-34}$ Js) and f is the number of degrees of freedom of the particles. This new concept led to Bose-Einstein statistics, and for particles obeying the Pauli exclusion principle, to Fermi-Dirac statistics.

steam distillation A method of isolating or purifying substances by exploiting Dalton's law of partial pressures to lower the boiling point of the mixture. When two immiscible (which do not mix) liquids are distilled, the b.p. will be lower than that of the more volatile component and consequently will be below 373K if one component is water. The method is particularly useful for recovering materials from tarry mixtures.

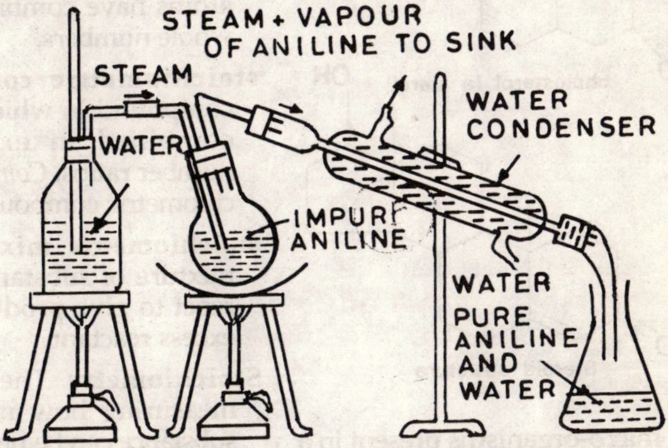

step A single stage in a chemical reaction. For example, the addition of hydrogen chloride to ethene involves three steps:

$$HCl \rightarrow H^+ + Cl^-$$
$$H^+ + C_2H_4 \rightarrow CH_3CH_2^+$$
$$CH_3CH_2^+ + Cl^- \rightarrow CH_3CH_2Cl$$

stereochemistry It is the branch of chemistry which is concerned with the spatial arrangement of atoms or groups in a molecule.

stereoisomerism It is the type of isomerism in which isomers differs with respect to the arrangement of atoms or groups in space. The two common types of stereoisomerism are (i) optical isomerism (ii) geometrical isomerism.

steel It is an alloy of iron containing 1-1.5% carbon and small quantities of some other metals.

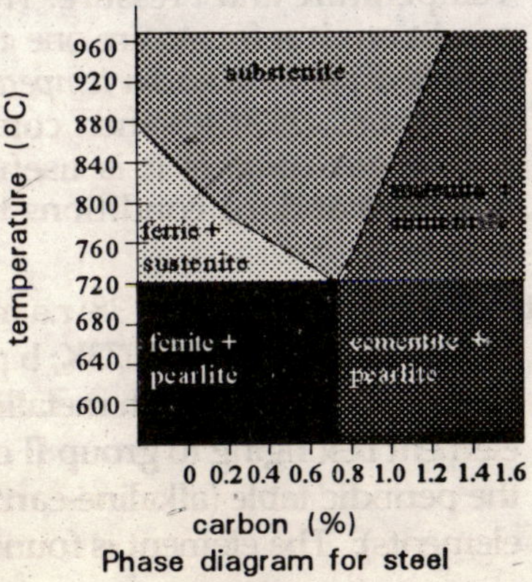

Phase diagram for steel

steric effect An effect in which the rate or path of a chemical reaction depends on the size or arrangement of groups in a molecule.

sterilization It is a process of heat treatment to reduce the number

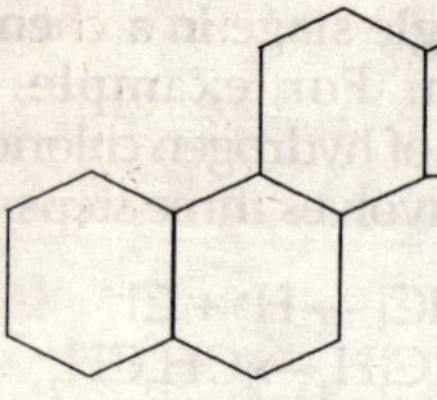

steroid nucleus

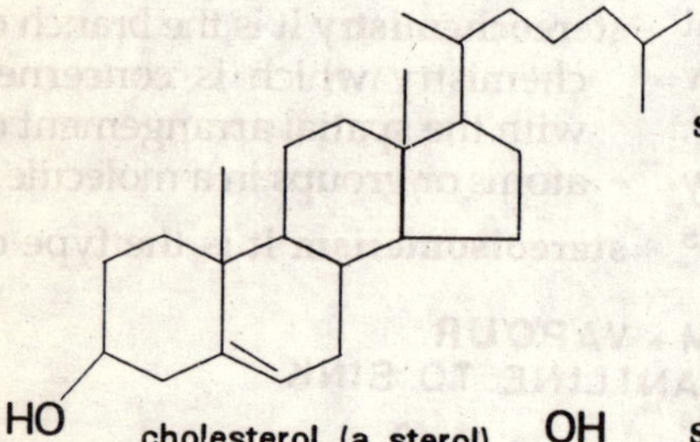

cholesterol (a sterol)

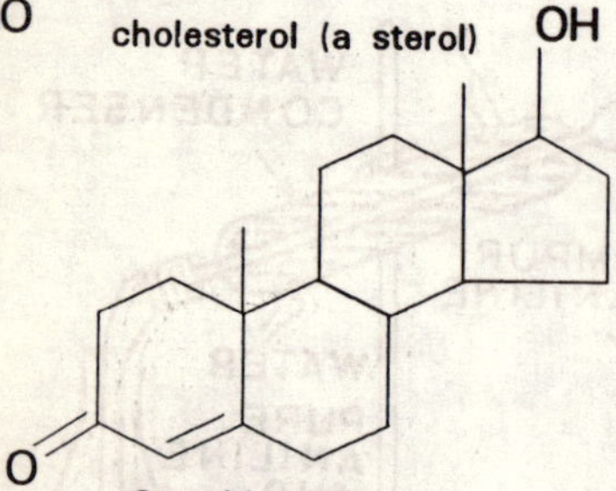

Steroid structure

of micro-organisms present in a substance. This extends the shelf-life of food such as milk which is sterilized in the bottle by being heated to between 388K and 403K for between 10 and 20 minutes. Sterilized milk can be kept without refrigeration for upto 5 months.

steroid Any of a group of lipids derived from a saturated compound called cyclopentano perhydrophenanthrene, which has a nucleus of four rings. Some of the most important steroid derivatives are the steroid alcohols, or sterols. Other steroids include the bile acids, which aid digestion of fats in the intestine; the sex hormones (androgens and oestrogens); and the corticosteroid hormones, produced by the adrenal cortex. Vitamin D is also based on the steroid structure.

stoichiometry The proportions in which elements form compounds. A *stoichiometric compound* is one in which the atoms have combined in small whole numbers.

stoichiometric compound A compound in which atoms are combined in exact whole-number ratios. *Compare* nonstoichiometric compound.

stoichiometric mixture It is a mixture of substances that can react to give products with no excess reactant.

Stoichiometry The science of measuring how much of one substance can be produced from given quantities of others.

STP Its full form is Standard Temperature and Pressure. The conditions it refers to are one *atmosphere pressure* and a *temperature* of 0°C (273K). When comparing gas *volumes* it is useful to have standard conditions to refer to.

strontium Symbol Sr. a.n. 38; r.a.m. 87.62; r.d. 2.54; m.p. 1073K; b.p. 1573K. A soft yellowish metallic element belonging to group II of the periodic table (alkaline-earth elements); The element is found in the minerals strontianite ($SrCO_3$) and celestine ($SrSO_4$). It can be obtained by roasting the ore to give the oxide, followed by reduction with aluminium (i.e. the Goldschmidt process). The element, which is highly reactive, is used in certain alloys and as a vacuum getter. The isotope strontium-90 is present in radioactive fall out (half-life 28 years), and can be metabolized with calcium so that it collects in bone. Strontium was discovered by Klaproth and Hope in 1798 and isolated by Humphry Davy in 1808.

strontium carbonate A white solid, having molecular formula $SrCO_3$; orthorhombic; r.d. 3.7; decomposes at 2043 K. It occurs naturally as the mineral *strontianite* and is prepared industrially by boiling celestine (strontium sulphate) with ammonium carbonate. It can also be prepared by passing carbon dioxide over strontium oxide or hydroxide or by passing the gas through a solution of strontium salt. It is a phosphor, used to coat the glass of cathode-ray screens, and is also used in the refining of sugar, as a slagging agent in certain metal furnaces, and to provide a red flame in fireworks.

strontium chloride Molecular formula ($SrCl_2$) A white solid obtained directly from strontium and chlorine or by passing chlorine over heated strontium oxide. It is used in fireworks to give a red flame. The hexahydrate ($SrCl_2.6H_2O$) is prepared by the neutralization of hydrochloric acid by strontium hydroxide or carbonate.

$$3Sr(OH)_2 + 6HCl \rightarrow 3SrCl_2.6H_2O$$

strontium hydrogencarbonate also called as **(strontium bicarbonate)** A compound, $Sr(HCO_3)_2$, which is stable only in solution. It is formed by the action of carbon dioxide on a suspension of strontium carbonate in water. On heating, this process is reversed.

strontium hydroxide It is a solid having molecular formula $Sr(OH)_2$ that normally occurs as the octahydrate ($Sr(OH)_2.8H_2O$), which is prepared by crystallizing an aqueous solution of strontium oxide. Strontium hydroxide is readily soluble in water and aqueous solutions are strongly basic. It is used in the purification of sugar.

strontium nitrate, $Sr(NO_3)_2$ Tetrahedral crystals (*sp^3* hybridised) soluble in water. When ignited with carbon or sulphur gives 'red fire'. It is used in fireworks and signal shells.

strontium sulphate It is a white salt having molecular formula $SrSO_4$ which is sparingly soluble and that occurs naturally as the mineral celestine. It can be prepared by dissolving strontium oxide, hydroxide, or carbonate in sulphuric acid. It is used as a substitute for barium sulphate in paints.

structural formula The formula of a substance which shows the bonds between its atoms and their positions relative to each other e.g.

(i) ethane (C_2H_6)

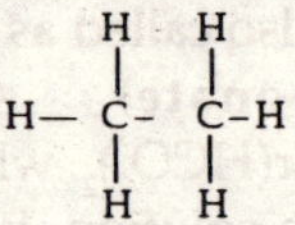

(ii) ethanol (CH_3CH_2OH)

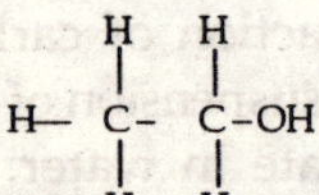

(iii) ethanal (CH_3CHO)

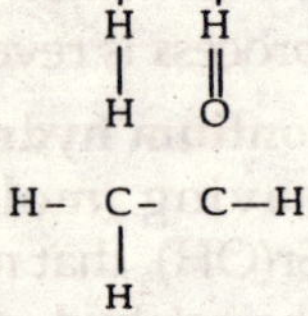

Structural formula gives more information than the molecular formula. Compounds having same molecular formula but different structural formula are called structural isomers.

Styrene *See* Phenylethene.

sublimate A solid formed by sublimation.

sublimation It refers to the process in which a solid changes directly to gaseous state without going through the liquid state. [Solid → gas]. The substance which shows this behaviour is known as *sublime substance* e.g. Ammonium chloride (NH_4Cl), Benzoic acid (C_6H_5COOH), Iodine etc.

substituent It refers to an atom or group substituted for another in a compound. Often the term is used for groups that have replaced hydrogen; for example, in benzene derivatives.

substitution reaction (displacement reaction) A reaction in which one atom or molecule is replaced by another atom or molecule. *See* electrophilic substitution; nucleophilic substitution.

sucrose It is *a disaccharide* having molecular formula $C_{12}H_{22}O_{11}$ which is made up of a *fructose* unit and a *glucose* unit. It is the white crystalline *sugar* that is used in the home. It is obtained from sugar beet and cane sugar.

sugar (saccharide) Any of a group of water-soluble carbohydrates of relatively low molecular weight and typically having a sweet taste. The simple sugars are called monosaccharides. More complex sugars comprise between two and ten monosaccharides linked together: disaccharides contain two, trisaccharides three, and so on. The name is often used to refer specifically to sucrose (table sugar).

sulphates These are the *compounds* containing the SO_4^{--} *ion* (*valency* = 2). They are widespread in nature, e.g. *gypsum* ($CaSO_4$).

They can be produced in the laboratory by the action of *sulphuric acid* on *metals* or *oxides* and *hydroxides*.

The test for a sulphate is to add a *solution* to an acidified (HCl) solution of barium chloride. If a sulphate is present a white *precipitate* is formed which is insoluble in dilute acid.

$$\underset{\text{acidified}}{SO_4^{-}{}^{-} + BaCl_2} \longrightarrow \underset{\text{white ppt.}}{BaSO_4} + Cl^-$$

sulphide 1. A compound of sulphur with a more electropositive element. Simple sulphides contain the ion S^{2-}. *Polysulphides* can also be formed containing ions with chains of sulphur atoms (S_x^{2-}).

sulphonation A type of chemical reaction in which a sulphonic ($-SO_3H$) group which is substituted on a benzene ring to form a sulphonic acid. The reaction is carried out by refluxing with concentrated sulphuric(VI) acid for a long period. It can also occur with cold disulphuric(VI) acid, olcum ($H_2S_2O_7$). Sulphonation is an example of electrophilic substitution in which the electrophile is a sulphur trioxide molecule, SO_3.

sulphonium compounds The compounds containing the ion R_3S^+ (sulphonium ion), where R is any organic group. Sulphonium compounds can be formed by reaction of organic sulphides with halogen compounds. For example, diethyl sulphide, $C_2H_5SC_2H_5$, reacts with chloromethane, CH_3Cl, to give diethylmethyl- sulphonium chloride, $(C_2H_5)_2.CH_3S^+Cl^-$.

sulphur Symbol S. A yellow nonmetallic element belonging to group VI '*p*' block element of the periodic table; a.n. 16; r.a.m. 32.06; r.d. 2.07 (rhombic); m.p. 112.8°C; b.p. 444.674°C. The element occurs in many sulphide and sulphate minerals and native sulphur is also found in Sicily and the USA (obtained by the Frasch process). It is an essential element for living organisms.

sulphur dichloride dioxide also known as (sulphuryl chloride, having molecular formula, SO_2Cl_2). A colourless fuming liquid formed by the reaction of chlorine with sulphur(IV) oxide in sunlight. It is used as a chlorinating agent.

sulphur dichloride oxide (thionyl chloride) A colourless fuming liquid, $SOCl_2$; m.p. –99.5°C; b.p. 75.7°C. It hydrolyses rapidly in water but is soluble in benzene. It may be prepared by the direct action of sulphur on chlorine monoxide or, more commonly, by the reaction of phosphorus (V) chloride with sulphur dioxide. $2PCl_5 + SO_2 \rightarrow SOCl_2 +$ Some additional product. It is used as a chlorinating agent in synthetic organic chemistry (replacing –OH groups with Cl).

sulphur dioxide Its formula is SO_2. A colourless gas with pungent smell. It is used as a bleaching agent, fumigant and also as a refrigerant. Its shape is V-Shape.

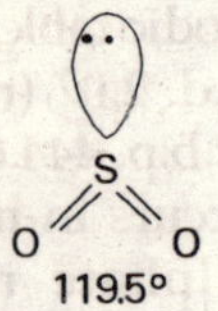

Lone pair of electrons

sulphuric acid (H_2SO_4) One of the most important chemicals produced. It is a colourless, oily *liquid* which is a *strong acid* and a vigorous *oxidizing agent*. It is made in the *contact process* and the annual production in the UK is about 2.5 million *tonnes*. The chart shows the main uses of the acid and the approximate amounts of the acid which are used.

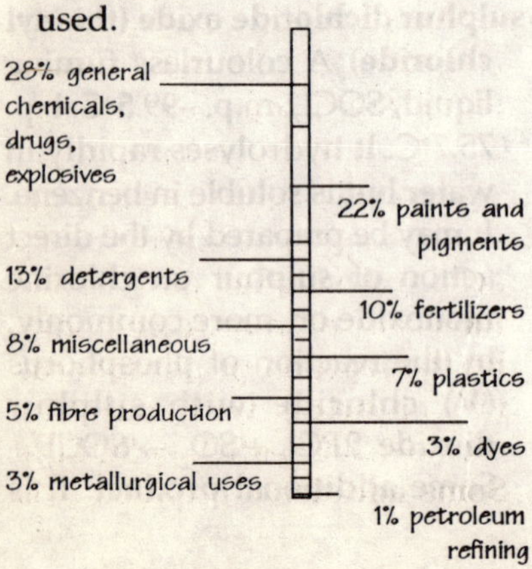

sulphurous acid (sulphuric(IV) acid) A weak diabasic acid, H_2SO_3, known in the form of its salts: the sulphites and hydrogensulphites. It is considered to be formed (along with sulphuric acid) when SO_2 is dissolved in water. It is probable, however, that the molecule H_2SO_3 is not present and that the solution contains hydrated SO_2. It is a reducing agent. The systematic name is *trioxosulphuric(IV) acid.*

super conductivity The property of certain material to have almost zero electrical resistance at absolute zero. Super conductivity is shown by most metals between 2-5°C but certain substances can exhibit this property of super conductivity even at higher temperatures e.g.

$Y\ Ba_2\ Cu_3\ O_7$ shows super conductivity at 90K.

$Tl_2\ Ca_2\ Ba_2\ Cu_3\ O_{10}$ shows super conductivity at 120 K. Such materials are known as super conductors. Super conductors are quite important in electronics engineering.

superoxides A group of inorganic compounds that contain the O_2^- ion. They are formed in significant quantities only for sodium, potassium, rubidium, and caesium. They are very powerful oxidizing agents and react vigorously with water to give oxygen gas and hydroxyl ions.

The superoxide ion has an unpaired electron and is paramagnetic and coloured (orange).

superphosphate It is a *fertilizer* which is a valuable source of *phosphorus*. Superphosphate is formed by heating (insoluble) *calcium phosphate* and *sulphuric acid* under *pressure*. It is a mixture of calcium dihydrogen-phosphate (which is *soluble*), *calcium sulphate* and other *compounds*.

superplasticity It is the ability of some metals and alloys to stretch uniformly by several thousand per cent at high temperatures, unlike normal alloys, which fail after being stretched 100% or less. Since 1962, when this property was discovered in an alloy of zinc and aluminium (22%), many alloys and ceramics have been shown to possess this property. For superplasticity to occur, the metal grain must be small and rounded and the alloy must have a slow rate of deformation.

supersaturated solution A *solution* which contains a higher *concentration* of *solute* than a *saturated solution*. It is usually produced by cooling the saturated solution. If the solution is disturbed, e.g. by a mechanical shock, by dust falling into it or by a crystal of the solute being added to it, the excess solute will usually crystallize out.

supersaturation (a) The state of the atmosphere in which the relative humidity is over 100%. This occurs in pure air where no condensation nuclei are available. Supersaturation is usually prevented in the atmosphere by the abundance of condensation nuclei (for example smoke and dust). (b) The state of any vapour whose pressure exceeds that at which condensation usually occurs (at the prevailing temperature).

surface tension It is denoted by symbol 'γ' and it may be defined as the property of a liquid that makes it behave as if its surface is enclosed in an elastic skin. The property results from intermolecular forces: a molecule in the interior of a liquid experiences a force of attraction from other molecules equally from all sides, whereas a molecule at the surface is only attracted by molecules below it in the liquid. The surface tension is defined as the force acting over the surface per unit length of surface perpendicular to the force. It is measured in newtons per metre. It can equally be defined as the energy required to increase the surface area by one square metre, that is, it can be measured in joules per metre square (which is equivalent to Nm^{-1}).

The property of surface tension is responsible for the formation of liquid drops, soap bubbles, and meniscuses, as well as the rise of liquids in a capillary tube *(capillarity)*, the absorption of liquids by porous substances, and the ability of liquids to wet a surface.

suspension When a *solid* is added to a *liquid* and the solid neither *dissolves* in the liquid nor sinks to the bottom of the vessel, the *mixture* is referred to as a suspension because the solid is *suspended* in the liquid.

synthesis The preparation of chemical compounds from simpler compounds is called synthesis.

synthesis gas A *mixture* of *carbon monoxide* and *hydrogen* gas produced by the *steam reforming* of *natural gas* or *naphtha* using nickel oxide as the catalyst. There are two steps in the process:

Step I $CH_4(g)+H_2O(g) \rightarrow 3H_2(g)+CO(g)$

Step II $CO(g)+H_2O(g) \rightarrow H_2(g)+CO_2(g)$

As the name implies, synthesis gas is used to produce other chemicals. It is an important feedstock for the chemical industry.

synthetic Describing a substance that has been made artificially; i.e. one that does not come from a natural source.

T

Talc, 3 MgO. 4 SiO_2. H_2O It is naturally occurring hydrated magnesium silicate. It is used in talcum powder and also as a lubricant.

tannic acid A yellowish complex organic compound present in certain plants. It is used as a mordant in dyeing.

tannin One of a group of complex organic chemicals. It is commonly found in leaves, unripe fruits, and the bark of trees. Their function is uncertain though the unpleasant taste may discourage grazing animals. Some tannins have commercial uses, especially in the production of leather and ink.

tantalum Symbol: **Ta**; m.p. 3000°C; b.p. 5400°C; r.d. 16.6; a.n. 73; r.a.m. 180.95. A transition element. (*d*-block element). It is strong, highly resistant to corrosion, and is easily worked. Tantalum is used in turbine blades and in surgical and dental work.

tartaric acid COOH
|
CHOH
|
CHOH
|
COOH

It is α, α' dihydroxy succinic acid Tartaric acid is optically active. Its potassium salt is used in dyeing and in the manufacture of baking powder.

tautomerism A type of isomerism in which the two isomers (*tautomers*) are in equilibrium. (*See* ketoenol tautomenism).

technetium Symbol Te. A radioactive metallic transition element; a.n. 43; m.p. 2171°C; b.p. 4876°C. The element can be detected in certain stars and is present in the fission products of uranium. It was first made by Perrier and Segre by bombarding molybdenum with deuterons to give technetium—97. The most stable isotope is technetium—99 (half-life 2.12 × 10^5 years); this is used to some extent in labelling for medical diagnosis. There are sixteen known isotopes. Chemically, the metal has properties intermediate between manganese and rhenium.

tellurium Symbol **Te**. A silvery metalloid element belonging to group VI of the periodic table; a.n. 52; r.a.m. 127.60; r.d. 6.24 (crystalline); m.p. 451°C; b.p. 1390 ± 3°C. It occurs mainly as tellurides in ores of gold, silver, copper and nickel and it is obtained as a by-product in copper refining. There are eight natural isotopes and nine radioactive isotopes. The element is used in semiconductors and small amounts are added to certain steels. Tellurium is also added in small quantities to lead. Its chemistry is similar to that of sulphur. It was discovered by Franz Muller in 1782.

TEL (Tetraethyl lead), $(C_2H_5)_4Pb$ It is the best known antiknock agent. Gasoline containing TEL is known as ethyl gasoline or leaded gasoline.

temperature It is the measure of the *kinetic energy* of a substance. The temperature scale used in everyday life is the Celsius (or centigrade) scale. In scientific work, the *Kelvin* scale is usually used.

temperature scale A practical scale for measuring temperature. A temperature scale is determined by fixed temperatures which are reproducible systems assigned an agreed temperature. On the Celsius scale the two fixed points are the temperature of pure melting ice (the *ice temperature)* and the temperature of pure boiling water (the *steam temperature).* The difference between the fixed points is the *fundamental interval* of the scale, which is further divided into temperature units. The International Temperature Scale has 11 fixed points covering the range 13.81 kelvin to 1337.58 kelvin.

tempering The process of increasing the toughness of an alloy, such as steel, by heating it to a predetermined temperature for a predeter- mined time, and cooling it to room temperature at a predetermined rate is called tempering. In steel, the purpose of the process is to heat the alloy to a temperature that will enable the excess carbide to precipitate out of the supersaturated solid solution of martensite and then to cool the saturated solution fast enough to prevent further precipitation or grain growth. For this reason steel is quenched rapidly by dipping into cold water.

temporary hardness A type of water hardness caused by the presence of dissolved calcium, iron and magnesium hydrogencarbonates is called temporary hardness. This form of hardness can be removed by boiling the water. Temporary hardness arises because rainwater combines with carbon dioxide from the atmosphere to form weak carbonic acid. This reacts with carbonate rocks, such as limestone, to produce calcium hydrogencarbonate $Ca(HCO_3)_2$ which then goes into solution. When this solution is heated, the complete reaction sequence is reversed so that calcium carbonate ($CaCO_3$) is precipitated. If this is not removed, it will accumulate in boilers and hot water pipes and reduce their efficiency. *Compare* permanent hardness.

terpenes A group of unsaturated hydrocarbons present in plants (essential oil). Terpenes consist of isoprene units, CH_2:C(CH_3)CH:CH_2. Monoterpenes have two units, $C_{10}H_{16}$, sesquiterpenes three units, $C_{15}H_{24}$, diterpenes four units, $C_{20}H_{32}$, etc.

tetrahedral compound A *compound* in which four atoms are arranged as if at the corners of a tetrahedron and linked to an atom at the centre of it by *covalent* or *coordinate bonds.* In a *carbon compound* such as *methane,* where there are four

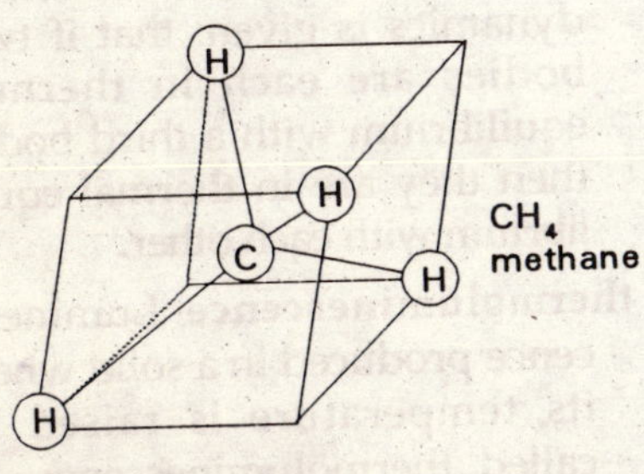

Tetrahedral The bonds in a carbon atom.

single bonds leading to four *atoms,* the atoms are arranged tetrahedrally around the carbon atom. The bonds point to the corners of the imaginary cube that the carbon atom is in the centre of. In this way, the atoms are as far away from each other as possible. The angle between the bonds is 109° 28' -*tetrahedral angle.*

terbium Symbol Tb. A silvery metallic element belonging to the lanthanoids; a.n. 65; r.a.m. 158.92; r.d. 8.23 (20°C); m.p. 1365°C.; b.p. 3230°C. It occurs in apatite and xenotime, from which it is obtained by an ion-exchange process. There is only one natural isotope, terbium—159, which is stable. Seventeen artificial isotopes have been identified. There are virtually no uses for this element although its potentialities are still being explored. It was discovered by C. G. Mosander in 1843.

tetrahydrate r.a.m. 204.39; r.d. 11-85 (20°C); m.p. 303.3°C; b.p. 1460°C. A crystalline hydrate containing four molecules of water per molecule of compound.

thallium, Symbol **Tl** a.n. 81, an element of group IIIB, '*p*' block element. It is used in manufacture of highly refractive optical glass. Its compounds are used as anti-knock agents, in photocells and in infra-red detectors.

thermite It consists of three parts of Fe_2O_3 and one part of aluminium powder. It can be ignited using a magnesium ribbon. On ignition Fe_2O_3 is reduced by aluminium. Fe_2O_3+

$2Al \rightarrow Al_2O_3 + 2Fe$. This process is used for welding and is known as *thermite process.*

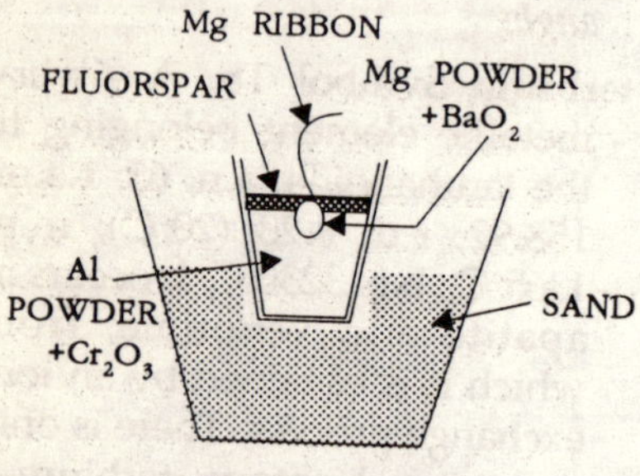

Thermite Process.

thermochemistry It may be defined as the branch of physical chemistry concerned with heats of chemical reaction, heats of formation of chemical compounds, etc.

thermodynamics It refers to the study of heat and other forms of energy and the various related changes in physical quantities such as temperature, pressure, density, etc.

(i) The *first law of thermodynamics* states that the total energy in a closed system is conserved (constant). In all processes energy is simply converted from one form to another, or transferred from one system to another. (Also refered as the law of conservation of energy).

A mathematical statement of the first law is:

$$\delta Q = \delta U + \delta W$$

Here, δQ is the heat transferred to the system, δU the change in internal energy (resulting in a rise or fall of temperature), and δW is the external work done by the system.

(ii) The *second law of thermodynamics* can be stated in a number of ways, all of which are equivalent. It deals with the entropy concept. One way is that heat cannot pass from a cooler to a hotter body without some other process occurring. Another is the statement that heat cannot be totally converted into mechanical work - i.e. a heat engine cannot be 100% efficient.

(iii) The *third law of thermodynamics* states that the entropy of a perfect crystalline substance is zero at 0° absolute of temperature.

(iv) Often a zeroth law of thermodynamics is given: that if two bodies are each in thermal equilibrium with a third body, then they are in thermal equilibrium with each other.

thermoluminescence Luminescence produced in a solid when its temperature is raised is called thermoluminescence. It arises when free electrons and holes, trapped in a solid as a result of exposure to ionizing radiation, unite and emit photons of light. The process is made use of in *thermoluminescent dating,* which assumes that the number of electrons and holes trapped in a sample of pottery is related to the length of time that has elapsed since the pottery was fired. By comparing the luminescence produced by heating a piece of pottery of unknown age with the luminescence produced by heating similar materials of known age, a fairly accurate estimate of the age of an object can be made.

thermometer It is an instrument used for measuring the temperature of a substance. A number of techniques and forms are used in thermometers, depending on such factors as the degree of accuracy required and the range of temperatures to be measured, but they all measure temperature by making use of some property of a substance that varies with temperature. For example, *liquid-in-glass thermometers* depend on the expansion of a liquid usually mercury or alcohol coloured with dye. These consist of a liquid-filled glass bulb attached to a partially filled capillary tube. In the *bimetallic thermometer* the unequal expansion of two dissimilar metals that have been bonded together into a narrow strip and coiled is used to move a pointer round a dial. The *gas thermometer*, which is more accurate than the liquid-in-glass thermometer, measures the variation in the pressure of a gas kept at constant volume. The *resistance thermometer* is based on the change in resistance of conductors or semiconductors with temperature change. Platinum nickel, and copper are the metals most commonly used in resistance thermometers.

thermonuclear reactions Those chemical reactions which involves the changes in the nucleus of the reactants. They may be fission or fusion reactions. They evolve enormous amounts of heat energy (i.e. the reactions are exothermic) of the order of Mev.

thermostat A device that controls the heating or cooling of a substance in order to maintain it at a constant temperature. It consists of a temperature-sensing instrument connected to a switching device. When the temperature reaches a predetermined level the sensor switches the heating or cooling source on or off according to a predetermined program. The sensing thermometer is often a bimetallic strip that triggers a simple electrical switch. Thermostats are used for space-heating controls, in water heaters and refrigerators, and to maintain the environment of a scientific experiment at a constant temperature.

thin-layer chromatography It is a technique for the analysis of liquid mixtures using chromatography. (It is one of the techniques which is used for separation). The stationary phase is a thin layer of an absorbing solid (for example alumina) prepared by spreading a slurry of the solid on a plate (usually glass) and drying it in an oven. A spot of the mixture to be analysed is placed near one edge and the plate is stood upright in a solvent. The solvent rises through the layer by capillary action carrying the components up the plate at different rates (depending on the extent to which they are absorbed by the solid). After a given time, the plate is dried and the location of spots noted. It is possible to identify constituents of the mixture by the distance moved in a given time. The technique needs careful control of the thickness of the layer and of the temperature.

third order reaction It is that reaction whose rate is found to be directly proportional to three times of the concentration of a single reactant or equal to the square of concentration of one reactant and concentration of another reactant.

rate = k $[A]^3$
rate = k $[A]^2$ [B]
rate = k [A] $[B]^2$
rate = k [A] [B] [C]
unit of K = L^2 mol^{-2} S^{-1}

thorium Symbol Th. A grey radioactive metallic element belonging to the actinoids; a.n. 90; r.a.m. 232.038; r.d. 11.5-11.9 (17°C); m.p. 1740-1760°C; b.p. 4780-4800°C. It occurs in monazite sand in Brazil, India, and USA. The isotopes of thorium have mass numbers from 223 to 234 inclusive; the most stable isotope, thorium-232, has a half-life of 1.39×10^{10} years. It has an oxidation state of (+4) and its chemistry resembles that of the other actinoids. It can be used as a nuclear fuel for breeder reactors as thorium-232. Captures slow neutrons to bread uranium—233. Thorium dioxide (*thoria*, ThO_2) is used on gas mantles and in special refractories. The element was discovered by J.J. Berzelius in 1829.

thulium Symbol **Tm**. A soft gray metallic element belonging to the lanthanoids; a.n. 69; r.a.m. 168.934; r.d. 9.321 (20°C); m.p. 1545°C; b.p. 1950°C. It occurs in apatite and xenotime. There is one natural isotope, thulium-169, and seventeen artificial isotopes have been producted. There are no uses for the element, which was discovered by P.T. Cleve in 1879.

tin Symbol: Sn; a.n. 50; r.a.m. 118.6; r.d. 7.29; m.p. 231.9°C; b.p. 2270°C. A *metal* which is in group IV 'P' block element of the *periodic table*. It occurs as *allotropes,* the most common being grey tin and white tin. The grey form is stable at low temperatures and the data given in the diagram refers to the white form. White tin is a shiny metal which shows normal metallic reactions. It is found naturally as the *oxide,* SnO_2.

Tin is used to make *tinplate, bronze, solder* and *alloys* for bearings. It is also used in the production of *glass.* Glass is floated onto the surface of molten tin. In this way large areas of glass without defects are formed.

tin(II) chloride ($SnCl_2$) A transparent solid with a fatty lustre. It is made by dissolving tin in hydrochloric acid. Tin(II) chloride is a reducing agent, it combines with NH_3, and forms hydrates with water. It is used as a mordant.

tin(IV) chloride, $SnCl_4$ It is highly reactive and catches fire with turpentine oil. $SnCl_4.5H_2O$ is used as a mordant in dyeing and also to prepare fire proof cotton.

tin(IV) hydride (stannane) A highly reactive and volatile gas (b.p. –53°), SnH_4, which decomposes on moderate heating (150°C). It is prepared by the reduction of tin chlorides using lithium tetrahydridoaluminate (III). It is used in the synthesis of some organo-tin compounds. The compound has reducing properties.

tin(II) oxide (SnO) A dark green or black solid. It can also be obtained in an unstable red form, which turns black on exposure to air. Tin(II) oxide can be made by precipitating the hydrated oxide from a solution containing tin(II) ions and dehydrating the product at 373K.

tin(IV) oxide (tin dioxide) It is a white solid, having formula SnO_2, insoluble in water; tetrahedral; r.d. 6.95; m.p. 1127°C; sublimes at about 1850°C. Tin(IV) oxide is trimorphic: the common form, which occurs naturally as the ore cassiterite, has a rutile lattice but hexagonal and rhombic forms are also known. There are also two so-called dihydrates, $SnO_2.2H_2O$, known as α- and β-stannic acid. These are essentially tin hydroxides. Tin(IV) oxide is amphoteric, dissolving in molten alkalis to form stannates; in the presence of sulphur, thiostannates are produced.

tin(II) sulphide A grey-black cubic or monoclinic solid, SnS, virtually insoluble in water; r.d. 5.22; m.p. 882°C; b.p. 1230°C. It has a layer structure similar to that of black phosphorus. Its heat of formation is low and it can be made by heating the elements together. Above 538K it slowly decomposes (disproportionates) to tin(IV) sulphide and tin metal. The compound reacts with hydrochloric acid to give tin(II) chloride and hydrogen sulphide.

tin(IV) sulphide, SnS_2 It is a yellowish solid soluble in yellow ammonium sulphide because of formation of $(NH_4)_2SnS_3$, ammonium thiocyanate.

$$SnS_2 + (NH_4)_5S \rightarrow (NH_4)_2SnS_3$$

It is used as a pigment for bronzing wood articles.

titanium Symbol: Ti, a.n. 22; r.a.m. 47.9; r.d. 4.507; m.p. 1660°C; b.p. 3280°C. A transition metal that occurs in various ores as titanium(IV) oxide and also in combination with iron and oxygen. It is extracted by conversion of titanium(IV) oxide to the chloride, which is reduced to the metal by heating with sodium. Titanium is reactive at high temperatures. It is used in the aerospace industry as it is strong, resistant to corrosion, and has a low density. It forms compounds with oxidation states + 4, + 3, and + 2, the + 4 state being the most stable.

titanium (IV) oxide, TiO_2 A white powder which dissolves in fused alkalies to form titannates (TiO_3^{2-}). It is used as a pigment.

titration The reaction of two *solutions* used in *analysis* to discover the *concentration* of one of the solutions. An accurately measured volume of one solution is normally placed in a conical *flask* and the other in a *burette.* The solution from the burette is added slowly until the other solution has been completely used up. This is shown by the use of an *indicator* or by means of a *pH* meter or a conductivity meter. The technique is most commonly used for *acid-base reactions,* for example

HCl vs NaOH,

Strong	Strong
acid	base

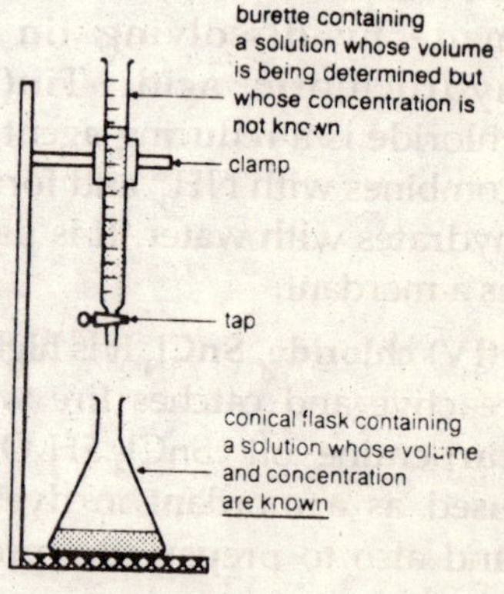

Titration Discovering the concentration of a solution.

Tollen's reagent A reagent used for testing the presence of aldehydes. It is made by adding sodium hydroxide to silver nitrate to give silver(I) oxide, which is dissolved in aqueous ammonia (giving the complex ion $[Ag(NH_3)_2]^+$). The sample is warmed with the reagent in a test tube. Aldehydes reduce the complex Ag^+ ion to metallic silver, forming a bright silver mirror on the inside of the tube (hence the name *silver-mirror test*). Ketones give a negative result.

topaz It is a variably coloured aluminium silicate mineral, $Al_2(SiO_4)(OH,F)_2$, that forms orthorhombic crystals. It occurs chiefly in acid igneous rocks, such as granites and pegmatites. Topaz is valued as a gemstone because of its transparency, variety of colours (the wine-yellow variety being most highly prized), and great hardness (8 on the Mohs' scale). When heated, yellow or brownish topaz often becomes a rose-pink colour. The main sources of topaz are Brazil, the USSR, and the USA.

torr It is a unit of pressure, used in high-vacuum technology, defined as 1 mmHg. 1 torr is equal to 133.322 pascals. The unit is named after Evangelista Torricelli (1609-47).

tourmaline A group of minerals composed of complex cyclosilicates containing boron with the general formula $NaR_3^{2+}Al_6B_3Si_6O_{27}(H,F)_4$, where R = Fe^{2+}, Mg, or (Al + Li). The crystals are trigonal, elongated, and variably coloured, the two ends of the crystals often having different colours. Tourmaline is used as a gemstone and because of its double refraction and piezoelectric properties is also used in polarizers and some pressure gauges.

tans designating an isomer with the groups on opposite sides. *See* geometrical isomerism.

trans effect It refers to an effect in the substitution of inorganic square-planar complexes, in which certain ligands in the original complex are able to direct the incoming ligand into the trans position. The order of ligands in decreasing trans-directing power is:

$$CN^- > NO_2^- > I^- > Br^- > Cl^- > NH_3 > H_2O.$$

transition state (activated complex or intermediate unstable stage) symbol;≠ A short-lived high-energy molecule, radical, or ion formed during a reaction between molecules possessing the necessary activation energy. The transition state decomposes at a definite rate to yield either the reactants again or the final products. The transition state can be considered to be at the top of the energy profile.

For the reaction,

$$AA + BC = A...B...C^{\neq} \rightarrow AB + C$$

the sequence of events is as follows. A approaches BC and

when it is close enough the electrons are rearranged producing a weakening of the bond between B and C. A partial bond is now formed between A and B producing the transition state. Depending on the experimental conditions, the transition state either breaks down to form the products or reverts back to the reactants.

trans mutation The change of one element into another (by a nuclear reaction).

transport number Symbol *t*. The fraction of the total charge carried by a particular type of ion in the conduction of electricity through electrolytes.

transuranic elements Elements with an atomic number greater than 92, i.e. elements above uranium in the periodic table. e.g. Np (z = 93), Pu (n = 94), Am (n = 95) etc.

triatomic Denoting a molecule, radical, or ion consisting of three atoms. For example, O_3 and H_2O are triatomic molecules.

triboluminescence Luminescence caused by friction; for example, some crystalline substances emit light when they are crushed as a result of static electric charges generated by the friction.

trichloroethanal Commonly known as (chloral, CCl_3CHO) A colourless liquid aldehyde made by chlorinating ethanal. It was used to make the insecticide DDT. It can be hydrolysed to 2,2,2-*trichloroethanediol* (chloral hydrate, $CCl_3CH(OH)_2$). Normally, compounds with two hydroxyl groups on the same carbon atom are unstable. However, in this case the effect of the three chlorine atoms stabilizes the compound. It is used as a sedative and give test with Tollen's reagent.

trichloromethane (chloro- form) A colourless volatile sweet-smelling liquid haloform, $CHCl_3$; r.d. 1.48; m.p. –63.5°C; b.p. 61°C. It can be made by chlorination of methane

$$\underset{\text{Methane}}{CH_4} \xrightarrow[\text{u.v. light}]{Cl_2} CH_3Cl \xrightarrow{Cl_2} CH_2Cl_2 \xrightarrow{Cl_2} \underset{\text{Chloroform}}{CHCl_3}$$

$-HCl \qquad -HCl \qquad +HCl$

(followed by separation of the mixture of products) or by the haloform reaction. It is an effective anaesthetic but can cause liver damage and it has now been replaced by other halogenated hydrocarbons. Chloroform is used as a solvent and raw material for making other compounds.

triglyceride also known as (**tri-acylglycerol)** An ester of glycerol (propane-1,2,3-triol) in which all three hydroxyl groups are esterified with a fatty acid. Triglycerides are the major constituent of fats and oils and provide a concentrated food energy store in living organisms as well as cooking fats and oils, margarines, soaps, etc. Their physical and chemical properties depend on the nature of their constituent fatty acids. In *simple triglycerides* all three fatty acids are identical; in *mixed triglycerides* two or three different fatty acids are present.

trioxane It is a solid polymer of formaldehyde (methanal; HCHO).

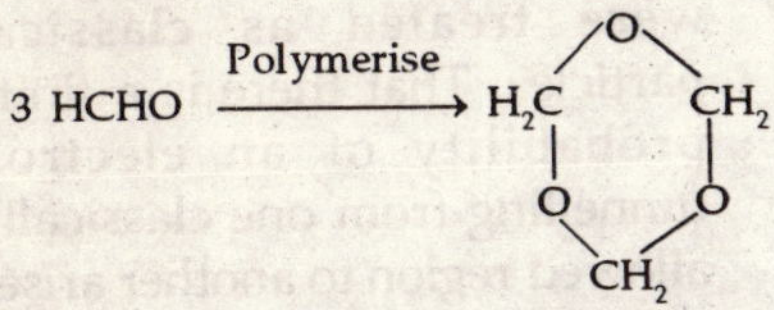

triple bond A bond which contains three shared pairs of *electrons* and is found in *alkynes* and *nitrogen*-containing *compounds*. Examples:

ethyne $H-C\equiv C-H$ nitrogen $N\equiv N$

triple point The temperature and pressure at which the vapour, liquid, and solid phases of a substance are in equilibrium. For water the triple point occurs at 273.16 K and 611.2 Pa. This value forms the basis of the definition of the kelvin and the thermodynamic temperature scale.

trisodium phosphate(V) (sodium orthophosphate) A colourless crystalline compound, Na_3PO_4, soluble in water and insoluble in ethyl alcohol C_2H_5OH. It is known both as the decahydrate (octagonal; r.d. 2.54) and the dodecahydrate (trigonal; r.d. 1.62). The dodecahydrate loses water at about 76°C and the decahydrate melts at 100°C. Trisodium phosphate may be prepared by boiling sodium carbonate with the stoichiometric amount of phosphoric acid and subsequently adding sodium hydroxide to the disodium salt thus formed. It is useful as an additive for high-pressure boiler feed water (for removal of calcium and magnesium as phosphates), in emulsifiers, as a water-softening agent, and as a component in detergents and cleaning agents. Sodium phosphate labelled with the radioactive isotope ^{32}P is used in the study of the role of phosphate in biological processes and is also used (intravenously) in the treatment of polycythaemia.

tritium, ^3_1H or ^3_1T It is the rarest isotope of hydrogen (one part is 10^{13} parts of hydrogen). Its nucleus consists of 1 proton and 2 neutrons.

trypsin An enzyme that digests proteins (protease). It is secreted in an inactive form *(trypsinogen)* by the pancreas into the duodenum. There, trypsinogen is acted on by an enzyme *(enterokinase)* produced in the duodenum to yield trypsin. The active enzyme plays an important role in the digestion of proteins in the anterior portion of the small intestine.

tungsten Symbol W. a.n. 74; r.a.m. 183.85; r.d. 19.3; m.p. 3410°C; b.p. 5660°C. It is a white or grey metallic transition element (d-block element) (formerly called *wolfram*); It is found in a number of ores, including the oxides wolframite, (Fe,Mn)-WO_4; and scheelite, $CaWO_4$. The ore is heated with concentrated sodium hydroxide solution to form a soluble *tungstate*. The oxide WO_3 is precipitated from this by adding acid, and is reduced to the metal using hydrogen. It is used in various alloys, especially high-speed steels (for cutting tools) and in lamp filaments. Tungsten forms a protective oxide in air and can be oxidized at high temperature. It does not dissolve in dilute acids. It forms compounds in which the oxidation state ranges from +2 to +6. The metal was first isolated by J. J. and F. *d'*Elhuyer in 1783.

tunnel effect An effect in which electrons are able to tunnel through a narrow potential barrier that would constitute a forbidden region if the electrons were treated as classical particles. That there is a finite probability of an electron tunnelling from one classically allowed region to another arises as a consequence of quantum mechanics. The effect is used in the tunnel diode.

tyrosine A white solid amino acid present in most proteins.

U

Ulmann's reaction It refers to the condensation of Iodobenzene to produce diphenyl molecule. The condensation takes place in presence of copper powder.

$$C_6H_5I + 2Cu + IH_5C_6 \rightarrow H_5C_6 - C_6H_5 + 2CuI$$

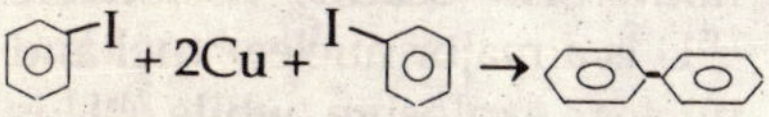

Iodobenzene Diphenyl

ultracentrifuge A high-speed centrifuge used for separating out very small particles. The sedimentation rate depends on the particle size, and the ultracentrifuge can be used to measure the mass of colloidal particles and large molecules (e.g. proteins).

ultramicroscope A form of microscope that uses the Tyndall effect to reveal the presence of particles that cannot be seen with a normal optical microscope. Colloidal particles, smoke particles, etc., are suspended in a liquid or gas in a cell with a black background and illuminated by an intense cone of light that enters the cell from the side and has its apex in the field of view. The particles then produce diffraction-ring systems, and appear as bright specks on the dark background.

ultraviolet (UV) It is a form of electromagnetic radiation, shorter in wavelength than visible light. Ultraviolet wavelengths range between about 1 nm and 400 nm. Ordinary glasses are not transparent to these waves; quartz is a much more effective material for making lenses and prisms for use with ultraviolet. Like light, ultraviolet radiation is produced by electronic transitions between the outer energy levels of atoms. However, having a higher frequency, ultraviolet photons carry more energy than those of light and can induce photolysis of compounds.

ultraviolet radiations (U.V) Electromagnetic radiations with wave length 1-400 nm.

uniaxial crystal A double-refracting crystal (*See* double refraction) having only one optic axis.

unimolecular reaction A chemical reaction or step involving only one molecule. An example is the decomposition of dinitrogen tetroxide to give nitrogen dioxide:

$$N_2O_4 \rightarrow 2NO_2$$

Molecules colliding with other molecules acquire sufficient activation energy to react, and the activated complex only involves the atoms of a single molecule.

unit A reference value of a quantity used to express other values of the same quantity.

unit cell It is the smallest unit of lattice which when translated along the axis of the lattice produces the crystal lattice.

universal indicator It is the mixture of indicators. Because it is a *mixture* it changes colour several times as the pH of the *solution* changes. It is possible to tell the approximate pH of a solution by adding a few drops of universal indicator to it and reading the p^H off the chart such as the one shown below. Universal indicator paper strips are also available.

Colour←	red	orange	yellow	green	blue	purple →

pH 0 1 2 3 4 5 6 7 8 9 10 11 12 13 14

unsaturated 1. (of a compound) Having double or triple bonds in its molecules. Unsaturated compounds can undergo addition as well as substitution reactions.

uracil A pyrimidine derivative and one of the major component bases of nucleotides and the Ribose nucleic acid RNA.

uranium Symbol: **U**; m.p. 1132°C; b.p. 3818°C; r.d. 18.95; a.n. 92; r.a.m. 238.03. A toxic radioactive silvery element of the actinoid series '*f*' block element of metals. Its three naturally occurring radioisotopes, uranium-238 (99.283% in abundance), uranium-235 (0.711%), and uranium-234 (0.005%), are found in numerous minerals including the uranium oxides, pitchblende, uraninite, and carnotite. The readily fissionable ^{235}U is a major nuclear fuel and nuclear explosive, while ^{238}U is a source of fissionable plutonium-239.

uranium hexafluoride (UF_6) It is a deliquescent, crystalline compound. It fumes in moist air. It is used to separate uranium isotopes.

uranium(IV) oxide A black solid, UO_2; r.d. 10.9; m.p. 3273K. It occurs naturally as uraninite and is used in nuclear reactors.

urea A colourless substance found in the urine of all mammals, but also produced commercially by the reaction of *carbon dioxide* and *ammonia* at 473K and 400 atmospheres pressure.

$$CO_2(g)+2NH_3(g) \rightarrow NH_2CONH_2(g) + H_2O(g)$$

Urea is used as a *fertilizer*, in the production of *adhesives* and pharmaceuticals and in the production of *urea/formaldehyde (HCHO) resins.*

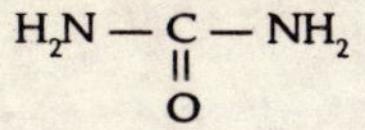

urea

urea-formaldehyde resins These are the synthetic resins made by copolymerizing urea with formaldehyde (methanal). They are used as adhesives or thermosetting plastics.

urethanes These are the esters of carbamic acid, H_2NCOOH.

uric acid The end product of purine breakdown in most primates, birds, terrestrial reptiles, and insects and also (except in primates) the major form in which metabolic nitrogen is excreted. Being fairly insoluble, uric acid can be expelled in solid form, which conserves valuable water in arid environments. The accumulation of uric acid in the synovial fluid of joints causes gout.

urotropine It is hexamethylene tetramine. It is obtained by reacting methanal (HCHO) with ammonia.

V

Vacuum The space that contains no atoms/molecules etc. It is not possible to get perfect vacuum but only partial vacuum is obtained at low pressure.

vacuum distillation The distillation of liquids under a reduced pressure, so that the b.p. is lowered. Vacuum distillation is a common laboratory technique for purifying or separating unstable compounds (i.e. ones that would decompose at their 'normal' b.p.)

vacuum pump A pump used to reduce the gas pressure in a container. The normal laboratory rotary oil-seal pump can maintain a pressure of 10^{-1} Pa. For pressures down to 10^{-7} Pa a diffusion pump is required. Ion pumps can achieve a pressure of 10^{-9} Pa and a cryogenic pump combined with a diffusion pump can reach 10^{-13} Pa.

valency (valence) The combining power of an atom or radical, equal to the number of hydrogen atoms that the atom could combine with or displace in a chemical compound (hydrogen has a valency of 1). It is equal to the ionic charge in ionic compounds; for example, in Na_2S, sodium has a valency of 1 (Na^+) and sulphur a valency of 2 (S^{2-}) in KCl, both potassium and chlorine have valencies of 1. In covalent compounds it is equal to the number of bonds formed; in CO_2 oxygen has a valency of 2 and carbon has a valency of 4.

valence electron An outer electron in an atom that can participate in forming chemical bonds is called as the valence electron.

valency defect Such a defect arises in a crystal when an atom is missing from its lattice site. An anion vacancy creates an excess of positive charge and so an electron can migrate to this site replacing the absent atom. This defect is called F-centre. F is Farbe means colour.

vanadium Symbol: V, a.n. 23. r.a.m. 50.94; r.d. 6.1; m.p. 1890°C; b.p. 3380°C. A *transition metal.* Its chief use is in the production of vanadium-steel *alloys* which are valuable because of their high tensile strength and hardness, that is, their ability to withstand stress. They often include *chromium* or *manganese* in addition to vanadium.

Vanadium(V) oxide V_2O_5 is the *catalyst* used in the *contact process.*

vanadium(V) oxide (vanadium pentoxide) A crystalline compound, V_2O_5, used extensively as a catalyst in industrial gas-phase oxidation processes.

van der Waals equation It is an equation of state for real gases. For one mole of gas the equation is

$$(p + a/V_m^2)(V_m - b) = RT$$

where p is the pressure, V_m the molar volume, and T the thermodynamic temperature, a and b are constants for a given substance and R is the gas constant. The equation gives a better description of the behaviour of real gases than the perfect gas equation ($pV_m = RT$).

The equation contains two corrections: b is a correction for the non-negligible size of the molecules; a/V_m^2 corrects for the fact that there are attractive forces between the molecules, thus slightly reducing the pressure from that of an ideal gas.

van der Waals' force An attractive force between atoms or molecules. It is named after J.D. van der Waals (1837-1923). The force accounts for the term a/V^2 in the van der Waals equation (*See* equation of state). These forces are much weaker than those arising from valence bonds and are inversely proportional to the seventh power of the distance between the atoms or molecules. They are the forces responsible for non-ideal behaviour of gases and for the lattice energy of molecular crystals. There are three factors causing such forces: (a) dipole-dipole interaction, i.e. electrostatic attractions between two molecules with permanent dipole moments; (b) dipole-induced dipole interactions, in which the dipole of one molecule polarizes a neighbouring molecule; (c) dispersion forces arising because of small instantaneous dipoles in atoms.

Vant Hoff factor; denoted by (i) It is defined as the ratio of normal molecular mass to the observed molecular mass.

$$i = \frac{\text{normal molecular mass}}{\text{observed molecular mass}}$$

This factor is introduced in the equations for colligative properties if the solution shows some abnormal behaviour due to association/dissociation of solute molecules in solution or due to reaction between solute and solvent molecules. The modified equation then used are:

Elevation of boiling point,

$$\Delta T_b = i.\ k_b.\ m.$$

Depression of freezing point,
$\Delta T_f = i.k_f\ m.$
Osmotic pressure, $\pi V = i.\ nRT.$

vapour *Atoms* or *molecules* in the gaseous state *but* below their *critical temperature,* i.e. the *temperature* above which *liquid* cannot exist.

For example, when water evaporates from a saucer when it is left in the house, H_2O (v) is formed and not *steam.*

vapour density The density of a gas or vapour relative to hydrogen, oxygen, or air. Taking hydrogen as the reference substance, the vapour density is the ratio of the mass of a particular volume of a gas to the mass of an equal volume of hydrogen under identical conditions of pressure and temperature. Taking the density of hydrogen as 1, this ratio is equal to half the relative molecular mass of the gas.

vapour pressure of liquid The pressure exerted by the vapour in equilibrium with the liquid form of the same substance is known as the vapour pressure of the liquid.

Vapour phase ⇌ Liquid phase

veneer A very thin sheet of wood, cut from a log. Veneers from attractive woods such as mahogany, walnut, oak and yew are used for covering cheaper materials to give them an improved appearance.

verdigiris It is the green deposit that is formed on copper vessels and it consists of basic copper carbonate or sulphate. It has variable composition.

Victor Meyer's method It is a method of measuring vapour density, devised by Victor Meyer (1848-97). A weighed sample in a small tube is dropped into a heated bulb with a long neck. The sample vaporizes and displaces air, which is collected over water and the volume measured. The vapour density can then be calculated.

vinegar A *solution* which is made by the action of bacteria on wine or cider. It contains about 4% *ethanoic acid* (C_3COOH). It is used widely in the food industry for preserving foods.

vinyl chloride *See* chloroethene

virial equation A gas law that attempts to account for the behaviour of real gases, as opposed to an ideal gas. It takes the form

$$pV = RT + B_p + C_p^2 + D_p^3 + \ldots,$$

where *B, C,* and *D* are known as *virial coefficients.*

viscosity It is the resistance to flow offered by a liquid.

vitamin One of a number of organic compounds required by living organisms in relatively small amounts to maintain normal health. There are some 14 generally recognized major vitamins: the water-soluble vitamin B complex (containing 9) and vitamin C and the fat-soluble vitamin A, vitamin D, vitamin E, and vitamin K. Most B vitamins and vitamin C occur in plants, animals, and microorganisms; they function typically as coenzymes. Vitamins A, D, E, and K occur only in animals, especially vertebrates, and perform a variety of metabolic roles. Animals are unable to manufacture many vitamins themselves and must have adequate amounts in the diet. Foods may contain vitamin precursors (called *provitamins*) that are chemically changed to the actual vitamin on entering the body. Many vitamins are destroyed by light and heat, e.g. during cooking.

voltaic cell It is a simple device of producing electrical energy by chemical reactions e.g. Daniell cell. Such a cell is also known as *Galvanic cell* or *Electro-chemical cell.*

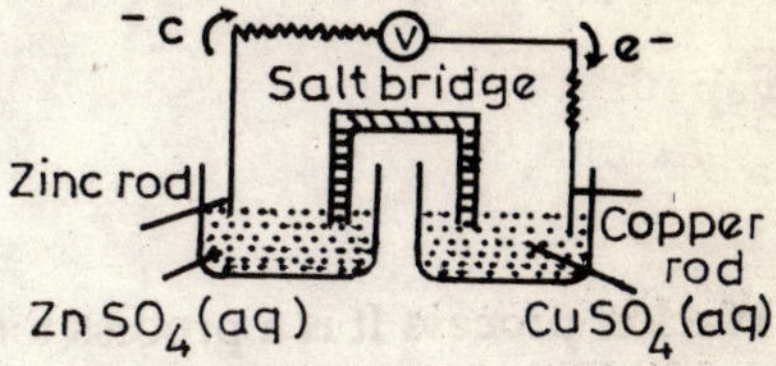

Electro chemical cell

voltameter (also known as coulombmeter) A device for determining electric charge or electric current using electrolysis. The mass m of material released is measured and this can be used to calculate the charge (Q) and the current (I) from the electro-chemical equivalent of the element, using $Q = m/z$ or $I = m/zt$.

volumetric analysis It is a method of *quantitative analysis* which uses accurately measured volumes of *solutions*.

vulcanite (ebonite) A hard black insulating material made by the vulcanization of rubber with a high proportion of sulphur (up to 30%).

vulcanization The process of adding *sulphur* to *rubber* to make it harder.

W

Wacker process It is a process for the manufacture of ethanal by the air oxidation of ethene. A mixture of air and ethene is bubbled through a solution containing palla- dium(II) chloride and copper(II) chloride. The Pd^{2+} ions form a complex with the ethene in which the ion is bound to the pi electrons in the C = C bond. This decreases the electron density in the bond, making it susceptible to nucleophilic attack by water molecules. The complex formed breaks down to ethanal and palladium metal. The Cu^{2+} ions oxidize the palladium back to Pd^{2+}, being reduced to Cu^{+} ions in the process. The air present oxidizes Cu^{+} back to Cu^{2+}. Thus the copper(II) and palladium(II) ions effectively act as catalysts in the process, which is now the main source of ethanal and, by further oxidation, ethanoic acid. It can also be applied to other alkenes.

Walden inversion A reaction in which an optically active compound reacts to give an optically active product in which the configuration has been inverted. This happens in the S_N2 mechanism.

warfarin $C_{19}H_{16}O_4$ A white solid (m.p. 434K) used as a rat poison.

washing soda Hydrated sodium carbonate ($Na_2CO_3.10H_2O$). The name comes from the use of the salt to soften water which was to be used for washing. See *hardness of water.*

water It is a colourless liquid, having formula H_2O; r.d. 1.000 (4°C); m.p. 0.000°C; b.p. 100.000°C. In the gas phase water consists of single H_2O molecules in which the H-O-H angle is 105°. The structure of liquid water is still controversial; hydrogen bonding of the type $H_2O...H-O-H$ imposes a high degree of structure and current models supported by X-ray scattering studies have short-range ordered regions, which are constantly disintegrating and re-forming. This ordering of the liquid state is sufficient to make the density of water at about 0°C higher than that of the relatively open-structured ice; the maximum density occurs at 3.98°C. This accounts for the well-known phenomenon of ice floating on water and the contraction of water below ice, a fact of enormous biological significance for all aquatic organisms.

Ice has nine distinct structural modifications of which ordinary ice, or ice I, has an open structure built of puckered six-membered rings in which each H_2O unit is tetrahedrally surrounded by four other H_2O units.

water cycle The continual movement of *water* around the Earth, both in the oceans and in the *air*. Water falls to Earth as rain, snow, hail, sleet, and freezes out of the air as frost and *ice*. It falls onto the oceans and these act as a vast source of water. It falls on land and here it enters the Earth and eventually flows into lakes and rivers and then flows into the oceans. From these large areas of water, *evaporation* occurs and water re-enters the *atmosphere*. In this way the cycle continues. Plants and animals take water out of the ground for their own use and it can re-enter the atmosphere (transpiration, excretion and *respiration*) or the Earth. Large quantities of water are stored as glaciers and the polar ice caps.

water gas A mixture of carbon monoxide and hydrogen produced by passing steam over hot carbon (coke):

$$H_2O(g) + C(s) \rightarrow CO(g) + H_2(g)$$

The reaction is strongly endothermic (i.e. ΔH is +ve) but the reaction can be used in conjunction with that for producer gas for making fuel gas. The main use of water gas before World War II was in producing hydrogen for the Haber process. Here the above reaction was combined with the *water-gas shift reaction* to increase the amount of hydrogen:

$$CO + H_2O \rightleftharpoons CO_2 + H_2$$

Most hydrogen for the Haber process is now made from natural gas by steam reforming.

water glass A viscous colloidal solution of sodium silicates in water. It is used to make silica gel and as a size and preservative.

water of crystallisation It refers to water molecules present in a molecule as water of crystallisation e.g. $CuSO_4 . 5H_2O$, $FeSO_4 . 7H_2O$, $Na_2CO_3 . 10H_2O$ etc.

watt Symbol: W. The SI unit of power, defined as a power of one joule per second. $1\ W = 1\ J\ s^{-1}$.

wave function It is a function $\psi\ (x,\ y,\ z)$ appearing in Schrödinger's equation in wave mechanics. The wave function is a mathematical expression involving the coordinates of a particle in space. If the Schrödinger equation can be solved for a particle in a given system (e.g. an electron in an atom) then, depending on the boundary conditions, the solution is a set of allowed wave functions (*eigen functions*) of the particle, each corresponding to an allowed energy level (*eigen value*). The physical significance of the wave function is that the square of its absolute value, $|\psi|^2$, at a point is proportional to the probability of finding the particle in a small element of volume, *dx dy dz*, at that point. For an electron in an atom, this gives rise to the idea of atomic and molecular orbitals.

wave length (λ) It is the distance covered during one complete cycle by a wave. It is related to speed (C) and frequency (υ) as C = υ.λ.

wave number Symbol: σ The reciprocal of the wavelength of a wave. It is the number of wave cycles in unit distance, and is often used in spectroscopy. The unit is the metre^{-1} (m^{-1}). The circular wave number (Symbol: *k*) is given by:

$$k = 2\pi\sigma$$

wax Any of various solid or semi-solid substances is known as wax. There are two main types. Mineral waxes are mixtures of hydrocarbons with high molecular weights. Paraffin wax, obtained from petroleum, is an example. Waxes secreted by plants or animals are mainly esters of fatty acids and usually have a protective function.

weak acid It refers to an acid having a low value of degree of ionisation (α=10-15%), for example

COOH (oxalic acid), acetic acid (CH_3COOH)
|
COOH

weak electrolytes Substances like organic acids, organic bases (weak bases), water etc. which are poor conductors in solution are known as weak electrolytes. Such substances are only weakly ionised in solution. e.g. oxalic acid, acetic acid (They donot dissociate completely into ions).

weber Symbol Wb. The SI unit of magnetic flux equal to the flux that, linking a circuit of one turn, produces in it an e.m.f. of one volt as it is reduced to zero at a uniform rate in one second.

Weston cadmium cell A standard cell that produces a constant e.m.f. of 1.0186 volts at 293K. It consists of an H-shaped glass vessel containing a negative cadmium-mercury amalgam electrode in one leg and a positive mercury electrode in the other. The electrolyte—saturated cadmium sulphate solution—fills the horizontal bar of the vessel to connect the two electrodes. The e.m.f. of the cell varies very little with temperature, being given by the equation

$E=1.0186—0.000—037(T—293)$,

where T is the thermodynamic temperature.

wet corrosion It involves flow of electric current from one point to another through some perceptible distance in the presence of liquid or moisture in air.

Williamson's synthesis A method for the preparation of mixed ethers by nucleophilic substitution. An alkyl halide is refluxed with an alcoholic solution of sodium alkoxide (from sodium dissolved in alcohol):

$R'Cl + RO^-Na^+ \rightarrow R'OR + NaCl$

e.g.

$CH_3Cl + CH_3ONa \rightarrow CH_3OCH_3 + NaCl$

methyl chloride	sodium methoxide	dimethyl ester (simple ether)

The product ether is termed 'mixed' if the alkyl groups R and R′ are different. This synthesis can produce both simple and mixed ethers.

witherite A mineral form of barium carbonate, $BaCO_3$.

Wöhler's synthesis A synthesis of urea performed by the German chemist Friedrich Wöhler (1800-82) in 1828. He discovered that urea ($CO(NH_2)_2$) was formed when a solution of ammonium isocyanate (NH_4NCO) was evaporated. At the time it was believed that organic substances such as urea could be made only by living organisms, and its production from an inorganic compound was a notable discovery. It is sometimes (erroneously) cited as ending the belief in vitalism.

wolframite (iron manganese tungsten) A mineral consisting of a mixed iron-manganese tungstate, $(FeMn)WO_4$, crystallizing in the monoclinic system; the principal ore of tungsten. It commonly occurs as blackish or brownish tabular crystal groups. It is found chiefly in quartz veins associated with granitic rocks. China is the major producer of wolframite.

wood's metal A low-melting (m.p. 71°C) alloy of bismuth (50%), lead (25%), tin (12.5%), and cadmium (12.5%). It is used for fusible links in automatic sprinkler systems. The m.p. can be changed by varying the composition.

wood sugar It is xylose, $C_5H_{10}O_5$, a pentose.

wool A *natural fibre* which comes from sheep, goats and similar animals. Wool is a *protein* fibre which has a crinkled and scaly structure. Because of this, the fibres are elastic and can trap air. Clothes made from wool tend to be warm.

work hardening An increase in the hardness of metals as a result of working them cold. It causes a permanent distortion of the crystal structure and is particularly apparent with iron, copper, aluminium, etc., whereas with lead and zinc it does not occur as these metals are capable of recrystallizing at room temperature.

Woulf bottle A two necked glass bottle, used to pass gases through a liquid.

Wolf-Kischner reduction It is the process of reduction of carbonyl compounds to hydrocarbons using H_2N-NH_2/KOH as reducing agent. The > C = O gets reduced to > CH_2 group.

$$C_6H_5CHO \xrightarrow{455\text{-}475K} C_6H_5CH_3$$

$$CH_3CHO \xrightarrow{455\text{-}475K} CH_3CH_3$$

wrought iron A low-carbon steel obtained by refining the iron produced in a blast furnace. Wrought iron is processed by heating and hammering to reduce the slag content and to ensure its even distribution. It was used to make the girders for the Eiffel tower, and is now used to make chains and fences.

Wurtz reaction A reaction to prepare alkanes by reacting an alkyl halide with sodium:

$$2RX + 2Na \rightarrow 2NaX + RR$$

The haloalkane is refluxed with sodium in dry ether. The method is named after the French chemist Charles-Adolphe Wurtz (1817-84). The analogous reaction using an alkyl halide and a haloarene, for example:

$$C_6H_5Cl + CH_3Cl + 2Na \rightarrow 2NaCl + C_6H_5CH_3$$

is called the *fitting reaction* after the German chemist Rudolph Fittig (1835-1910).

Wurtz Fitting Reaction If an haloalkane react with an aryhalide in presence of sodium to produce alkylderivative of aryl, the reaction is called wurtz-fitting reaction e.g.

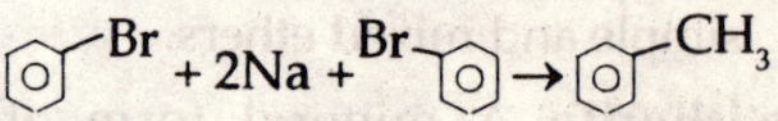

X

Xanthates Salts or esters containing the group –SCS(OR), where R is an organic group. Cellulose xanthate is an intermediate in the manufacture of rayon by the viscose process.

xenon Symbol: Xe; m.p. –111.9°C; b.p. –107.1°C; d. 5.89 kg m^{-3}; a.n. 54; r.a.m. 131.3. A colourless, odourless monatomic element of the noble gas group, *'p'* block element now known to form compounds. It occurs in trace amounts in air. Xenon is used in electron tubes and strobe lighting.

X-rays Electromagnetic radiation which has high *energy*. It is produced by firing *electrons* at *metals*. It is a very penetrating radiation and will easily pass through flesh but is stopped by bone and other dense substances such as metals.

X-ray crystallography The use of X-ray diffraction to determine the structure of crystals or molecules is known as X-ray crystallography. The technique involves directing a beam of X-rays at a crystalline sample and recording the diffracted X-rays on a photographic plate. The diffraction pattern consists of a pattern of spots on the plate, and the crystal structure can be worked out from the positions and intensities of the diffraction spots. X-rays are diffracted by the electrons in the molecules and if molecular crystals of a compound are used, the electron density distribution in the molecule can be determined.

X-ray diffraction The diffraction of X-rays by a crystal. The wavelengths of X-rays are comparable in size to the distances between atoms in most crystals, and the repeated pattern of the crystal lattice acts like a diffraction grating for X-rays. Thus, a crystal of suitable type can be used to disperse X-rays in a spectrometer. X-ray diffraction is also the basis of X-ray crystallography.

X-ray fluorescence The emission of X-rays from excited atoms produced by the impact of high-energy electrons, other particles, or a primary beam of other X-rays. The wavelengths of the fluorescent X-rays can be measured by an X-ray spectrometer as a means of chemical analysis X-ray fluorescence is used in such techniques as electron-probe micro analysis.

xylan It is a complex polysaccharide. It occurs in plants in close association with cellulose.

Xylene Or xylol,

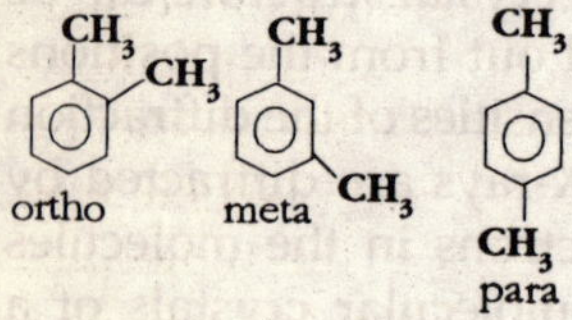

It occurs in coal tar; used in manufacture of dyes.

Xylidine, dimethylaniline It is used in the manufacture of dyes.

Xylol It is another name for xylene.

Xylose wood sugar, $C_5H_{10}O_5$ A white solid (m.p. 417K). It is a pentose found in xylan.

Y

Yeasts It is a microscopic organism, quite useful to mankind. They are used in fermentation (in brewing, baking etc.) e.g.

$$C_6H_{12}O_6 \xrightarrow{\text{Yeast}} 2C_2H_5OH + 2CO_2$$

It is used to manufacture beer and wine. Yeast contains *enzyme* which acts on sugar.

yetterbium, Symbol **Yb** a.n. 70; r.a.m. 173.04; r.d. 6.966 (20°C); m.p. 819°C; b.p. 1196°C. It is one of the members of the lanthanide series (z = 70). It is added to steel to improve the properties of steel.

yield of a reaction Many chemical reactions do not produce as much product as would be expected from looking at the chemical equations. It is useful to express the amount of product as a percentage of what it is theoretically possible to produce:

$$\text{Yield of reaction} = \frac{\text{amount of product produced}}{\text{maximum amount of product that it is possible to produce}}$$

For example,

$CuO(s)$	$+ H_2(g)$	$\rightarrow Cu(s)$	$+ H_2O$
copper(II) oxide	hydrogen	copper	water
80 g		$\rightarrow$64 g (maximum yield)	

If 80 g of oxide actually produce 56 g of copper metal the percentage yield of the reaction is $(^{56}/_{64} \times 100)\% = 87.5\%$.

yttrium Symbol Y. A silvery-grey metallic element belonging to group IIIB '*d*' block element of the periodic table; atomic number 39; r.a.m. 88.905; r.d. 4.469 (20°C); m.p. 1522°C; b.p. 3338°C. It occurs in uranium ores and in lanthanoid ores, from which it can be extracted by an ion exchange process. The natural isotope is yttrium-89, and there are 14 known artificial isotopes. The metal is used in superconducting alloys and in alloys for strong permanent magnets (in both cases, with cobalt). The oxide (Y_2O_3) is used in colour-television phosphors, neodymium-doped lasers, and microwave components. Chemically it resembles the lanthanoids, forming ionic compounds containing Y^{3+} ions. The metal is stable in air below 673K. It was discovered in 1828 by Friedrich Wöhler.

Z

Z The symbol which is given to represent the *atomic number* of an *element*, i.e. the number of *protons* in the *atom*. e.g. For Li, z = 3.

Zeeman effect The splitting of the lines in a spectrum when the source of the spectrum is exposed to a magnetic field. It was discovered in 1896 by P. Zeeman (1865-1943). In the *normal Zeeman effect* a single line is split into three if the field is perpendicular to the light path or two lines if the field is parallel to the light path. This effect can be explained by classical electromagnetic principles.

zeolite A member of a group of hydrated aluminosilicate minerals, which occur in nature and are also manufactured for their ion-exchange properties. They are used for water softening and for sugar refining. The zeolites have an open crystal structure and can be used as molecular sieves.

zero order Describing a chemical reaction in which the rate of reaction does not depend on the concentration of a reactant; i.e.

$$\text{rate} = k\,[X]^0$$

The concentration of the reactant remains constant for a period of time although other reactants are being consumed. The hydrolysis of 2-bromo-2-methyl propane using aqueous alkali has a rate expression,

$$\text{rate} = k\ [\text{2-bromo-2-methyl propane}]$$

i.e. the reaction is zero order with respect to the concentration of the alkali. The rate constant for a zero reaction has the units mol $dm^{-3}\ s^{-1}$.

zero point energy The energy possessed by the atoms and molecules of a substance at absolute zero (0 K).

Ziegler catalyst It has the capability of initiating the polymerisation of ethene and propene at N.T.P. It consists of a mixture of tetra triadkyl.

Ziegler-Natta polymerisation Stereospecitic polymerisation of olefins using a ziegler catalyst. Ziegler catalysts are prepared by interaction between an organometallic derivative and a transition metal derivative e.g. $TiCl_4$ and $ACBu_3$.

Ziesel reaction A method of determining the number of

methoxy ($-OCH_3$) groups in an organic compound. The compound is heated with excess hydriodic acid, forming an alcohol and iodomethane

$$R—O—CH_3 + HI \rightarrow ROH + CH_3I$$

The methyl iodide is distilled off and led into an alcoholic solution of silver nitrate, where it precipitates silver iodide. This is filtered and weighed, and the number of iodine atoms and hence methoxy groups can be calculated. The method was developed by S. Ziesel in 1886.

zinc Symbol Zn. A blue-white metallic element; a.n. 30; r.a.m. 65.38; r.d. 7.1; m.p. 419.57°C; b.p. 907°C. It is a transition element belongs to *d*-block. It occurs in sphalerite (or zinc blende, ZnS), which is found associated with the lead sulphide, and in smith sonite ($ZnCO_3$). Ores are roasted to give the oxide and this is reduced with carbon (coke) at high temperature, the zinc vapour being condensed. Alternatively, the oxide is dissolved in sulphuric acid and the zinc obtained by electrolysis. There are five stable isotopes (mass numbers 64, 66, 67, 68, and 70) and six radioactive isotopes are known. The metal is used in galvanizing and in a number of alloys (brass, bronze, etc.). Chemically it is a reactive metal, combining with oxygen and other non-metals and reacting with dilute acids to release hydrogen. It also dissolves in alkalis to give zincates. Most of its compounds contain the Zn^{2+} ion.

zincate A salt formed in solution by dissolving zinc or zinc oxide in alkali. The formula is often written ZnO_2^{2-} although in aqueous solution the ions present are probably complex ions in which the Zn^{2-} is coordinated to OH-ions. ZnO_2^{2-} ions may exist in molten sodium zincate, but most solid 'zincates' are mixed oxides.

zinc blende A mineral form of zinc sulphide, ZnS, the principal ore of zinc (*See* sphalerite). The *zinc-blende structure* is the crystal structure of this compound (and of other compounds). It has zinc atoms surrounded by four sulphur atoms at the corners of a tetrahedron. Each sulphur is similarly surrounded by four zinc atoms. The crystals belong to the cubic system.

zinc chloride ($ZnCl_2$) A white crystalline solid prepared by the action of dry hydrogen chloride or chlorine on heated zinc.

$$Zn + HCl \xrightarrow{\Delta} ZnCl_2 + [H]$$

The anhydrous product undergoes sublimation. The hydrated salt may be prepared by the addition of excess zinc to dilute hydrochloric acid and crystallization of the solution. Hydrates with 4, 3, 5/2, 3/2, and 1 molecule of water exist. Zinc chloride is extremely deliquescent and dissolves easily in water. It is used in dentistry, Leclanché cells, as a flux, and as a dehydrating agent in organic reactions.

zinc chromate, Zn CrO_4 A yellow pigment used in rust inhibiting paints.

zinc group The group of elements in the periodic table consisting of zinc (Zn), cadmium (Cd), and mercury (Hg). (Group II elements).

zinc sulphide A yellow-white water-soluble solid, ZnS. It occurs naturally as sphalerite (*see also* zinc blende) and wurtzite. The compound sublimes at 1453K. It is used as a pigment and phosphor.

zirconium Symbol Zr. A grey-white metallic transition element; belongs to *'d'* block element; a.n. 40; r.a.m. 91.22; r.d. 6.44; m.p. 1853°C; b.p. 4376°C. It is found in zircon ($ZrSiO_4$; the main source) and in baddeleyite (ZnO_2). Extraction is by chlorination to give $ZrCl_4$ which is purified by solvent extraction and reduced with magnesium (Kroll process). There are five natural isotopes.

zinc-copper couple It consists of metallic zinc having a thin film of copper. It can be prepared by dipping a zinc.

zone refining This is a method of purification of metals in metallurgy. It is used when a metal of very high purity (100%) is required e.g. For use as semiconductors we need very pure silicon and germanium. It is based on the fact that impurities show difference in solubility in liquid and solid states of the metal.

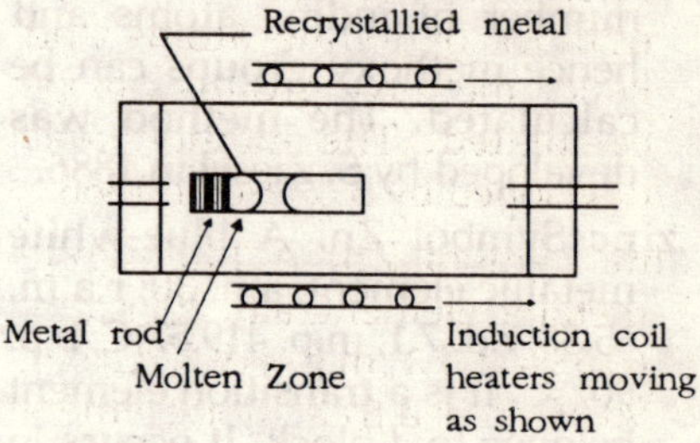

zwitter ion It is a dipolar ion e.g.

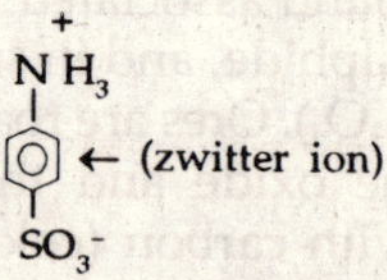

It is obtained because of transfer of proton (H^+) from sulphonic ($-SO_3H$) group to amino ($-NH_2$) group in sulphanilic acid.

zymase An enzyme present in yeast which helps to convert sugar into ethanol.

$$\underset{\text{Glucose}}{C_6H_{12}O_6} \xrightarrow{\text{Zymase}} \underset{\text{ethanol}}{2C_2H_5OH} + 2CO_2$$

The Chemical Elements

'Relative atomic mass' in brackets is nucleon number of most stable isotope

Element	*Symbol*	*Proton No.*	*Relative atomic mass*
actinium	Ac	89	[227]
aluminium	Al	13	26.9815
americium	Am	95	[243]
antimony	Sb	51	121.75
argon	Ar	18	39.948
arsenic	As	33	74.9216
astatine	At	85	[210]
barium	Ba	56	137.34
berkelium	Bk	97	[247]
beryllium	Be	4	9.0122
bismuth	Bi	83	208.98
boron	B	5	10.81
bromine	Br	35	79.904
cadmium	Cd	48	112.40
caesium	Cs	55	132.905
calcium	Ca	20	40.08
californium	Cf	98	[251]
carbon	C	6	12.011
cerium	Ce	58	140.12
chlorine	Cl	17	35.453
chromium	Cr	24	51.996
cobalt	Co	27	58.9332
copper	Cu	29	63.546
curium	Cm	96	[247]
dysprosium	Dy	66	162.50
einsteinium	Es	99	[254]
erbium	Er	68	167.26
europium	Eu	63	151.96
fermium	Fm	100	[257]
fluorine	F	9	18.9984
francium	Fr	87	[223]
gadolinium	Gd	64	157.25
gallium	Ga	31	69.72

Element	*Symbol*	*Proton No.*	*Relative atomic mass*
germanium	Ge	32	72.59
gold	Au	79	196.967
hafnium	Hf	72	178.49
helium	He	2	4.0026
holmium	Ho	67	164.930
hydrogen	H	1	1.00797
indium	In	49	114.82
iodine	I	53	126.9044
iridium	Ir	77	192.2
iron	Fe	26	55.847
krypton	Kr	36	83.80
lanthanum	La	57	138.91
lawrencium	Lr	103	[257]
lead	Pb	82	207.19
lithium	Li	3	6.939
lutetium	Lu	71	174.97
magnesium	Mg	12	24.305
manganese	Mn	25	54.938
mendelevium	Md	101	[258]
mercury	Hg	80	200.59
molybdenum	Mo	42	95.94
neodymium	Nd	60	144.24
neon	Ne	10	20.179
neptunium	Np	93	[237]
nickel	Ni	28	58.71
niobium	Nb	41	92.906
nitrogen	N	7	14.0067
nobelium	No	102	[255]
osmium	Os	76	190.2
oxygen	O	8	15.9994
palladium	Pd	46	106.4
phosphorus	P	15	30.9738
platinum	Pt	78	195.09
plutonium	Pu	94	[244]
polonium	Po	84	[209]
potassium	K	19	39.102
praseodymium	Pr	59	140.907
promethium	Pm	61	[145]
protactinium	Pa	91	[231]

Element	*Symbol*	*Proton No.*	*Relative atomic mass*
radium	Ra	88	[226]
radon	Rn	86	[222]
rhenium	Re	75	186.20
rhodium	Rh	45	102.905
rubidium	Rb	37	85.47
ruthenium	Ru	44	101.07
samarium	Sm	62	150.35
scandium	Sc	21	44.956
selenium	Se	34	78.96
silicon	Si	14	28.086
silver	Ag	47	107.868
sodium	Na	11	22.9898
strontium	Sr	38	87.62
sulphur	S	16	32.064
tantalum	Ta	73	180.948
technetium	Tc	43	[97]
tellurium	Te	52	127.60
terbium	Tb	65	158.924
thallium	Tl	81	204.37
thorium	Th	90	232.038
thulium	Tm	69	168.934
tin	Sn	50	118.69
titanium	Ti	22	47.90
tungsten	W	74	183.85
uranium	U	92	238.03
vanadium	V	23	50.942
wolfram (tungsten)	W	74	183.85
xenon	Xe	54	131.30
ytterbium	Yb	70	173.04
yttrium	Y	39	88.905
zinc	Zn	30	65.37
zirconium	Zr	40	91.22

Physical Constants

Quantity	*Magnitude*	*Unit*
speed of light	$2.997\ 925 \times 10^{8}$	ms^{-1}
Planck constant	$6.626\ 196 \times 10^{-34}$	Js
Boltzmann constant	$1.380\ 622 \times 10^{-23}$	JK^{-1}
Avogadro constant	$6.022\ 169 \times 10^{23}$	mol^{-1}
mass of proton	$1.672\ 614 \times 10^{-27}$	kg
mass of neutron	$1.674\ 920 \times 10^{-27}$	kg
mass of electron	$9.109\ 558 \times 10^{-31}$	kg
charge of proton or electron	$\pm 1.602\ 191\ 7 \times 10^{-19}$	C
specific charge of electron	$-1.758\ 796 \times 10^{11}$	$C\ kg^{-1}$
molar volume at s.t.p.	$2.241\ 36 \times 10^{-2}$	$m^{3}\ mol^{-1}$
Faraday constant	$9.648\ 670 \times 10^{4}$	$C\ mol^{-1}$
triple point of water	273.15	K
absolute zero	–273.15	°C
permittivity of vacuum	$8.854\ 185\ 3 \times 10^{-12}$	Fm^{-1}
permeability of vacuum	$4\pi \times 10^{-7}$	Hm^{-1}
Stefan constant	5.66961×10^{-8}	$Wm^{-2}\ K^{-4}$
molar gas constant	8.31434	$J\ mol^{-1}\ K^{-1}$
gravitational constant	6.6732×10^{-11}	$Nm^{2}\ kg^{-2}$

Elementary Particles

Particle	*Symbol*	*Charge*	*Mass*	*Spin*
leptons				
electron	e^{-}	–1	0.511	1/2
neutrino	ν	0	0	1/2
	$\nu\mu$	0	0	1/2
muon	μ^{-}	–1	105.66	1/2
baryons				
proton	p	+1	938.26	1/2
neutron	n	0	939.55	1/2
xi particle	Ξ^{o}	0	1314.9	1/2
	Ξ^{-}	–1	1321.3	1/2
sigma particle	Σ^{+}	+1	1189.5	1/2
	Σ^{o}	0	1192.5	1/2
	Σ^{-}	–1	1197.4	1/2

Particle	*Symbol*	*Charge*	*Mass*	*Spin*
lambda particle	Λ	0	1115.5	1/2
omega particle	Ω^-	–1	1672.5	3/4
mesons				
kaon	k^-	–1	493.8	0
	k^+	+1	493.8	0
pion	Π^+	+1	139.6	0
	Π^o	0	135	0
	Π^-	–1	139.6	0
phi particle	ϕ	0	1020	1
psi particle	Ψ	0	3095	1
eta particle	η^o	0	548.8	0

Note: It is common to measure the mass of particles in units energy/c^2, where c^2 is the speed of light. The values above are in units of MeV/c^2. 1 MeV/c^2=178 × 10^{30} kg.

The Greek Alphabet

Letters		*Name*
Α	α	alpha
Β	β	beta
Γ	γ	gamma
Δ	δ	delta
Ε	ε	epsilon
Ζ	ζ	zeta
Η	η	eta
Θ	θ	theta
Ι	ι	iota
Κ	κ	kappa
Λ	λ	lambda
Μ	μ	mu
Ν	ν	nu
Ξ	ξ	xi
Ο	ο	omicron
Π	π	pi
Ρ	ρ	rho
Σ	σ	sigma
Τ	τ	tau
Υ	υ	upsilon

Letters		Name
Φ	φ	phi
Χ	χ	chi
Ψ	ψ	psi
Ω	ω	omega

Appendix 1. SI units

Table 1.1 Base and supplementary SI units

Physical quantity	Name	Symbol
length	metre	m
mass	kilogram	kg
time	second	s
electric current	ampere	A
thermodynamic temperature	kelvin	K
luminous intensity	candela	cd
amount of substance	mole	mol
*plane angle	radian	rad
*solid angle	steradian	sr

*supplementary units

Table 1.2 Derived SI units with special names

Physical quantity	Name of SI unit	Symbol of SI unit
frequency	hertz	Hz
energy	joule	J
force	newton	N
power	watt	W
pressure	pascal	Pa
electric charge	coulomb	C
electric potential difference	volt	V
electric resistance	ohm	Ω
electric conductance	siemens	S
electric capacitance	farad	F
magnetic flux	weber	Wb
inductance	henry	H

Physical quantity	*Name of SI unit*	*Symbol of SI unit*
magnetic flux density (magnetic induction)	tesla	T
luminous flux	lumen	lm
illuminance	lux	lx
absorbed dose	gray	Gy
activity	becquerel	Bq
dose equivalent	sievert	Sv

Table 1.3 Decimal multiples and submultiples to be used with SI units

Submultiple	*Prefix*	*Symbol*	*Multiple*	*Prefix*	*Symbol*
10^{-1}	deci	d	10	deca	da
10^{-2}	centi	c	10^2	hecto	h
10^{-3}	milli	m	10^3	kilo	k
10^{-6}	micro	μ	10^6	mega	M
10^{-9}	nano	n	10^9	giga	G
10^{-12}	pico	p	10^{12}	tera	T
10^{-15}	femto	f	10^{15}	peta	P
10^{-18}	atto	a	10^{18}	exa	E

Table 1.4 Conversion of units to SI units

From	*To*	*Multiply by*
in	m	2.54×10^{-2}
ft	m	0.3048
sq. in	m^2	6.4516×10^{-4}
sq. ft	m^2	9.2903×10^{-2}
cu. in	m^3	1.63871×10^{-5}
cu. ft	m^3	2.83168×10^{-2}
l (itre)	m^3	10^{-3}
gal(lon)	m^3	$4.546\ 09 \times 10^{-3}$
gal(lon)	l(itre)	4.546 09
miles/hr	ms^{-1}	0.477 04

From	*To*	*Multiply by*
km/hr	ms^{-1}	0.277 78
lb	kg	0.453 592
g cm^{-3}	kg m^{-3}	10^3
lb/in^{-3}	kg m^{-3}	$2.767\ 99 \times 10^4$
dyne	N	10^{-5}
kgf	N	9.806 65
poundal	N	0.138 255
lbf	N	4.448 22
mm Hg	Pa	133.322
atmosphere	Pa	$1.013\ 25 \times 10^5$
pH	W	745.7
erg	J	10^{-7}
eV	J	$1.602\ 10 \times 10^{-19}$
kWh	J	3.6×10^6
cal	J	4.1868

Appendix 2. Fundamental Constants

Constant	*Symbol*	*Value in SI units*
acceleration of free fall	g	$9.806\ 65$ m s^{-2}
Avogadro constant	L, N_A	$6.022\ 52 \times 10^{23}$ mol^{-1}
Boltzmann constant	$k=R/N_A$	$1.380\ 622 \times 10^{-23}$ JK^{-1}
electric constant	ε_0	8.854×10^{-12} F m^{-1}
electronic charge	e	$1.602\ 192 \times 10^{-19}$ C
electronic rest mass	m_e	$9.109\ 558 \times 10^{-31}$ kg
Faraday constant	F	$9.648\ 670 \times 10^4$ C mol^{-1}
gas constant	R	8.314 34 JK^{-1} mol^{-1}
gravitational constant	G	6.664×10^{-11} Nm^2 kg^{-2}
Loschmidt's constant	N_L	$2.687\ 19 \times 10^{25}$ m^{-3}
magnetic constant	μ_0	$4\pi \times 10^{-7}$ H m^{-1}
neutron rest mass	m_n	$1.674\ 92 \times 10^{-27}$ kg
Planck constant	h	$6.626\ 196 \times 10^{-34}$ Js
proton rest mass	m_p	$1.672\ 614 \times 10^{-27}$ kg
speed of light	c	$2.997\ 924\ 58 \times 10^8$ m s^{-1}
Stefan-Boltzmann constant	σ	5.6697×10^{-8} W m^{-2} K^{-4}

Appendix 3. The solar system

Planet	*Equatorial diameter (km)*	*Mean distance from sun (10^6 km)*	*Sidereal period*
Mercury	4878	57.91	87.969 days
Venus	12 100	108	224.7 days
Earth	12 756	149.60	365.256 days
Mars	6762	227.94	686.980 days

PERIODIC TABLE

Group Numbers																		
Classical	IA	IIA	IIIB	IVB	VB	VIB	VIIB		VIII		IB	IIB	IIIA	IVA	VA	VIA	VIIA	0
Amended	IA	IIA	IIIA	IVA	VA	VIA	VIIA		VIII		IB	IIB	IIIB	IVB	VB	VIB	VIIB	0
Modern	**1**	**2**	**3**	**4**	**5**	**6**	**7**	**8**	**9**	**10**	**11**	**12**	**13**	**14**	**15**	**16**	**17**	**18**
	1 H																	2 He
	3 Li	4 Be											5 B	6 C	7 N	8 O	9 F	10 Ne
	11 Na	12 Mg											13 Al	14 Si	15 P	16 S	17 Cl	18 Ar
	19 K	20 Ca	21 Sc	22 Ti	23 V	24 Cr	25 Mn	26 Fe	27 Co	28 Ni	29 Cu	30 Zn	31 Ga	32 Ge	33 As	34 Se	35 Br	36 Kr
	37 Rb	38 Sr	39 Y	40 Zr	41 Nb	42 Mo	43 Tc	44 Ru	45 Rh	46 Pd	47 Ag	48 Cd	49 In	50 Sn	51 Sb	52 Te	53 I	54 Xe
	55 Cs	56 Ba	57* La	72 Hf	73 Ta	74 W	75 Re	76 Os	77 Ir	78 Pt	79 Au	80 Hg	81 Tl	82 Pb	83 Bi	84 Po	85 At	86 Rn
	87 Fr	88 Ra	89† Ac	104 Unq	105 Unp	106 Unh												
			*	58 Ce	59 Pr	60 Nd	61 Pm	62 Sm	63 Eu	64 Gd	65 Tb	66 Dy	67 Ho	68 Er	69 Tm	70 Yb	71 Lu	
			†	90 Th	91 Pa	92 U	93 Np	94 Pu	95 Am	96 Cm	97 Bk	98 Cf	99 Es	100 Fm	101 Md	102 No	103 Lr	